Saul Lieberman

the Man and His Work

Saul Lieberman

The Man and His Work

Elijah J. Schochet

and

Solomon Spiro

The Jewish Theological Seminary of America
New York 2005

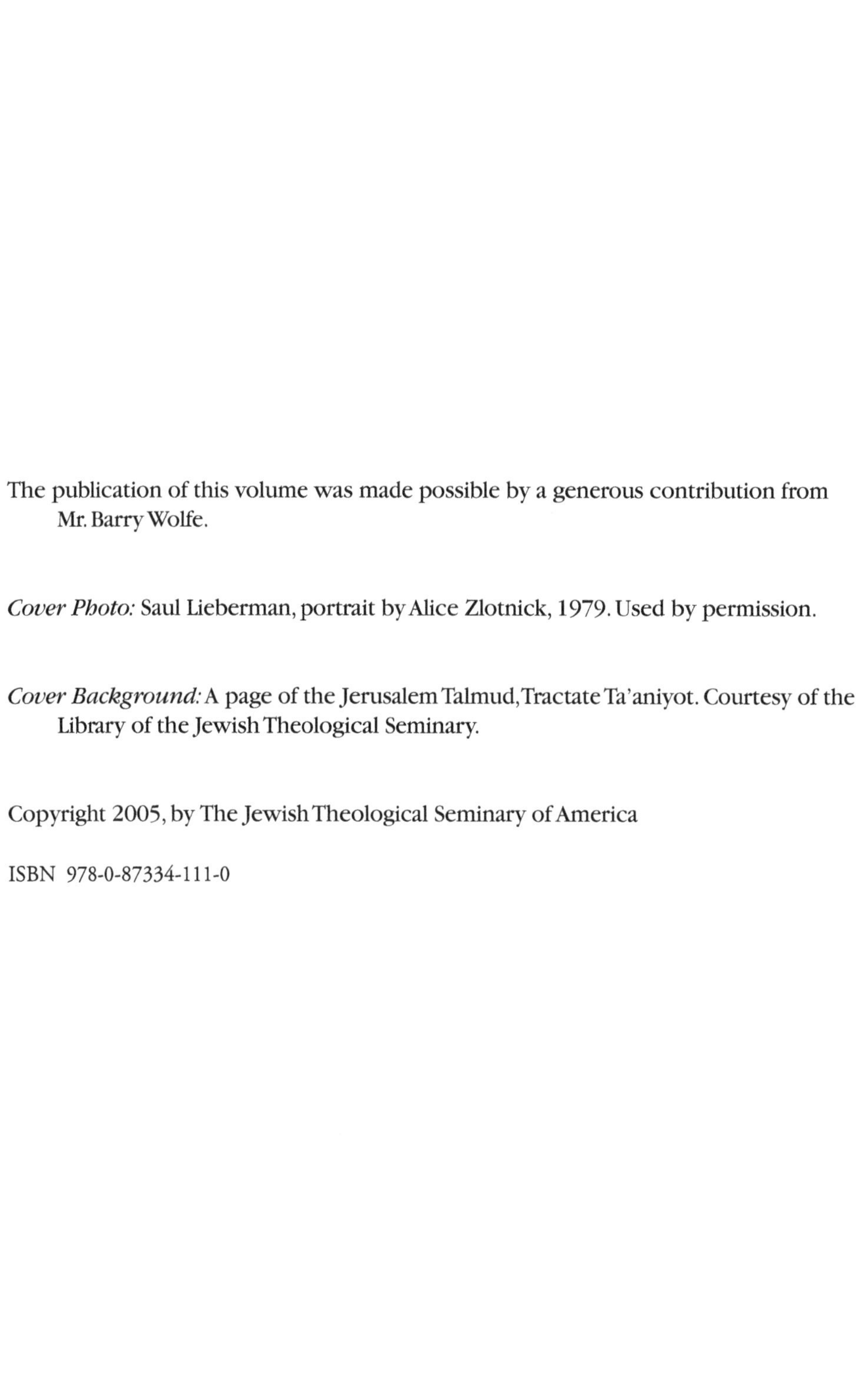

The publication of this volume was made possible by a generous contribution from Mr. Barry Wolfe.

Cover Photo: Saul Lieberman, portrait by Alice Zlotnick, 1979. Used by permission.

Cover Background: A page of the Jerusalem Talmud, Tractate Ta'aniyot. Courtesy of the Library of the Jewish Theological Seminary.

ISBN 978-0-87334-111-0

CONTENTS

PHOTOS *arranged by Alice Zlotnick*

PART II

APPENDICES

PREFACE

The Jewish Theological Seminary in Breslau, the spiritual forerunner of the Jewish Theological Seminary in New York, was founded in 1854. No tribute could be more fitting than to mark the occasion of its 150th anniversary with the publication of this expansive and intimate biography of Saul Lieberman. At the helm of Breslau stood Zacharias Frankel, the unrivaled pioneer in the modern critical study of rabbinic literature. His ethos of positive, historical Judaism aimed to perpetuate the centrality of Talmud in the education of the modern rabbi but to infuse it with historical perspective. The combination kept Breslau at the forefront of talmudic research in the persona of scholars such as Frankel, Graetz, Israel Lewy, and Michael Guttmann until it was closed by the Nazis in 1938.

The Seminary in New York proved to be a worthy embodiment of the Breslau ethos. Throughout, it has been home to an unbroken line of world-class students of rabbinic literature from Alexander Kohut and Solomon Schechter to Louis Ginzberg and Saul Lieberman to David Weiss Halivni and Shamma Friedman in our own day. In 1936, at its tercentenary, Harvard University expressed its high regard for Jewish scholarship by awarding an honorary doctorate to Ginzberg; in 1966, it did so again by conferring one on Lieberman. Our Department of Talmud and Rabbinics continues to be the largest department at JTS and the equal of any in the world.

It is this record of Seminary commitment to the critical study of rabbinic Judaism and its permutations that created the culture that enabled the genius of Lieberman to realize its full potential. His talent could not have found a more hospitable playing field. As this biography shows in spades, the Seminary provided Lieberman for over four decades with the students and colleagues, the compatibility and circumstances to revolutionize the field of rabbinics.

Metaphor may be the only way to limn the contours of greatness. Once when Lieberman was called upon to introduce Gershom Scholem, he took recourse to the world of manuscripts in which both men lived. In the early nineteenth century, said Lieberman, when a scholar needed to see a manuscript located in a far-off library, he would hire a scribe to copy it. The scholarship that resulted rested heavily on the accuracy of the copyist. Later, with the invention of photography, manuscripts could be reproduced mechanically. But the film often failed to capture the margins of the manuscript, again impairing the scholar's work. Not until the introduction of infrared rays could a scholar receive a copy that was every bit as good as the original—indeed, even revealing features of the manuscript invisible to the naked eye.

What an unforgettable image of the difference between the pedant and the genius. The former does not lack for expertise, methodology, and diligence. It is the depth vision that is missing, the ability to penetrate beneath the surface. Great scholarship is always three-dimensional. Scholem and Lieberman were both richly endowed with powers of radiation that could restore the ruins of ancient heirlooms. For all the divergence in their origins and lifestyle, both achieved, largely on their own, extraordinary feats of scholarly virtuosity. And both left their respective fields of study transformed. In tandem and tension, they brought to the fore one of the fundamental polarities that imbue Judaism with its never-ending vibrancy.

The achievement of Elijah J. Schochet and Solomon Spiro, who both studied with Lieberman and over many years gained an impressive mastery of his legacy, is to put a human face on an austere scholar. Aside from assiduously collecting the anecdotes about the man, they make extensive use of his unpublished correspondence, which is often of a personal nature. The result is a relief that projects beyond the life of the mind. Behind his chiseled prose loomed a poetic disposition.

At the funeral of his beloved wife, Judith Berlin, who died in 1978, Lieberman barely mustered the self-control to speak. He told how he would approach her bedside during her illness, only to be reprimanded: when Judith caught sight of him, she would order him back to his study; his scholarship was not to be disrupted by her ordeal. Reluctantly, he did her bidding, except that in his agitated state all he could do was to copy the manuscript on which he was working. His tears wet the paper as he transcribed. Concluding the story, Lieberman, by then quite overwrought, declared that the world would never know, once the manuscript appeared in print, which words he had watered with his tears. Judith died as she had lived: in service to his scholarship.

This biography is as much about Lieberman the poet as the scholar, about his tears of joy and torment, about the self-control and self-denial that gave birth to a superhuman effort. His achievement is an epitaph that time will not efface.

ISMAR SCHORSCH
CHANCELLOR, JEWISH THEOLOGICAL SEMINARY
OF AMERICA

Introduction

Over twenty years have passed since Professor Saul Lieberman died on his way to Israel. Yet despite his prodigious intellectual attainments and seminal scholarly publications, no full-scale biography of Lieberman has appeared. For many, his life story is simply described by noting his early education in Lithuania's traditional yeshivot, his introduction to the tools of modern scholarship in Palestine, where he commenced some of his most influential work, and the flourishing of his scholarship in America, where he taught for over forty years.

In this volume, we have sought to present a broader and deeper portrait of Lieberman the academic as well as Lieberman the man—a book that we hope will prove to be of interest to the scholar and layperson alike.

Ours has not been an easy task. While Lieberman's academic contributions stand brilliantly revealed, his personal life remains obscured to a substantial degree, owing to his own reticence. It interested him less to discuss his personal history, experiences, and emotions than to revel in the true meaning of what others had considered an unintelligible rabbinical text. Although Lieberman loved playing the role of raconteur, only infrequently would he let down his guard by sharing personal anecdotes and recollections. We therefore enlisted the assistance of those who knew him best—relatives, friends, colleagues, and students—to share with us their memories of more intimate conversations.

We encountered another difficulty in researching and writing this volume. Not only were we Lieberman's students; we were the beneficiaries of his friendship and kindness outside the classroom. Our responsibility, therefore, was to try to present as objective and dispassionate a portrait of this man as possible, notwithstanding our warm personal feelings for him. Indeed, Lieberman would never have condoned a gilded or embellished portrayal of his life and work.

It was our good fortune to have been able to read a great deal of Lieberman's extensive personal correspondence. He clearly enjoyed exchanging thoughts with other scholars. He would send copies of his new publications to colleagues whom he respected, responding to their letters and comments late at night or in the early hours of the morning. If the scholar was a close friend, the letters would touch on personal as well as academic matters. All in all, this correspondence provided valuable insights into Lieberman's character.

We express our deepest thanks to those without whose assistance this book could not have been completed. We are delighted that the Jewish Theological Seminary has published this volume. It is indeed fitting that the institution in which Professor Lieberman conveyed his wisdom and insights to several generations of rabbis and scholars has chosen to perpetuate his memory in this way. Dr. Ismar Schorsch, chancellor of the Jewish Theological Seminary, has been enormously supportive from the outset and has graciously added his own personal reflections on a revered teacher and mentor. We are deeply indebted to Dr. Alan Cooper, chairman of the Seminary's publication committee, for his tremendous effort and energy in guiding this project to fruition. Professor Dov Zlotnick of the Jewish Theological Seminary provided extraordinary assistance throughout. He and his wife, Alice, always made themselves available to us. They were particularly helpful in arranging for Israeli friends and colleagues of Professor Lieberman to meet with Solomon Spiro when he visited Israel in the summer of 1999. The inclusion of numerous photographs in this volume is largely due to Alice, who shared her collection with us. Along with Professor Zlotnick, Professor Edward M. Gershfield of the Jewish Theological Seminary read the manuscript and contributed enormously helpful comments.

We acknowledge the contribution of Dr. Marc Shapiro of the University of Scranton, who directed us to an important source of correspondence by Professor Lieberman. Dr. Haym Soloveitchik of the Bernard Revel Graduate School of Yeshiva University was very generous in providing us with important background information. We are immensely grateful to our teacher Dr. Haim Zalman Dimitrovsky for his encouragement and guidance.

A debt of gratitude is also extended to the libraries and librarians who opened their archives to us. We benefited from the assistance of Rafael Weiser, director of the Department of Manuscripts and Archives of the Jewish National and University Library in Jerusalem; and Etty Alagem, university archivist of the Central Archives of the Hebrew University of Jerusalem. We are grateful for the assistance of the staff of the Jewish Theological Seminary library in general and the staff of the manuscript room in particular. Rabbi Clifford B. Miller of the catalog department and Yisrael Dubitsky, the public service librarian, were especially helpful. Dr. Jack Wertheimer, provost, and Julie Miller of the Joseph and Miriam Ratner Center for the Study of Conservative Judaism at the Jewish Theological Seminary were also extraordinarily generous with their time. We also thank the staff of the Robarts Library at the University of Toronto and Dr. David Novak, J. Richard and Dorothy Shiff Chair in Jewish Studies, for making available to us the immense resources of the University of Toronto library system. We could not have completed the book without having at our disposal the correspondence provided by Chedva Rochel, director of Genazim, the National Institute of the Association of Hebrew Writers of Israel.

Our copyeditor, Janice Meyerson, also deserves our gratitude. Her attention to detail is exceeded only by her grasp of the big picture. Her good humor and gentle prodding invariably resulted in significant improvements to the text.

Many others, too numerous to be mentioned by name, assisted us in significant ways by providing facts critical to this book. Their contributions, acknowledged in the endnotes, have earned our sincerest gratitude.

It is unfortunate that Professor Lieberman's books have not enjoyed the wide distribution they deserve. It is our hope that this modest biography will encourage readers to seek out his works and will, at the very least, enhance the degree of recognition of his remarkable contributions to Jewish scholarship.

As for us, this project was truly a labor of love, rekindling our appreciation and our gratitude for the privilege of having studied at our master's feet over forty years ago. The passage of time notwithstanding, we shall always remain his students.

ELIJAH J. SCHOCHET
SOLOMON SPIRO
November 2003

PART I

LIFE

Except for a brief autobiographical essay entitled "Bimhitzat Rabbanim," Saul Lieberman never wrote of his youth in Lithuania, and even that essay provides only sparse, fragmentary episodes during his years of wandering with the Slobodka yeshiva and his sojourn in Minsk.[1] Otherwise, he left no autobiographical memoirs. Moreover, virtually all of his colleagues and intimates whom we interviewed spoke of a reticence on his part in sharing information about his younger years. He was often private, if not secretive, on the subject.

Lieberman delighted in recounting that the major-league baseball pitcher Dizzy Dean provided a dozen reporters who wanted to know his authentic life story with a dozen biographies, each significantly different from the other. With a twinkle in his eye, Lieberman concluded, "But all of them were authentic."[2] So much for any pretense on our part at composing an "authentic" biographical sketch of Saul Lieberman!

To be sure, many accounts are in circulation that depict the Lithuania and Jerusalem periods of Lieberman's life. However, it is difficult, if not impossible, to authenticate some of them, so they have not been included in this volume. Furthermore, even where there may be general agreement about a certain episode in his life, there is often disagreement as to significant details. It is almost as if there are, indeed, several "authentic" versions of Saul Lieberman's life.

We therefore confess to our inadequacy in accurately and comprehensively portraying the first several decades of Lieberman's life. In truth, he has joined the ranks of numerous great rabbinic scholars of generations past whose personal biographies are hardly known to us and who, for the most part, are more familiar to us by the titles of their books than by their personal names. In rabbinic scholarship, this is perhaps meant to be: the books of the man, not the life of the man, are what ultimately matter. Saul Lieberman would surely have agreed.

Lithuanian Origins

Family

Saul Lieberman was born in the small village of Motol, more popularly known to its Jewish population as the Yiddishized "Motele," near Pinsk, in Lithuania–White Russia, on May 23, 1898.[3] Best known as the birthplace of Chaim Weizmann,[4] Motol is described by Weizmann:

> In the spring and autumn the area was a sea of mud, in the winter a world of snow and ice; in the summer it was covered with a haze of dust. . . .
>
> A very tiny and isolated metropolis [Motol] was, with some four or five hundred families of White Russians and fewer than two hundred Jewish families. Communication with the outside world was precarious and intermittent. No railway, no metaled road, passed within twenty miles of us. There was no post office. Mail was brought in by anyone from the townlet who happened to pass by the nearest railway station on his own business. Sometimes these chance messengers would hold on to the mail for days, or for weeks, distributing it when the spirit moved them. But letters played no very important part in our lives; there were few in the outside world who had reason to communicate with us. . . . Motol was situated in one of the darkest and most forlorn corners of the Pale of Settlement, that prison house created by czarist Russia for the largest part of its Jewish population.[5]

Meir Lieberman, Saul's younger brother by nine years, said of Motol that it was "*a klayn shtetl ober a grobenke*" (a small town, but a great one).[6] Motol also produced several Jewish scholars and prominent personalities, all of whom have made significant contributions to Jewish life and learning. Azriel

Shohat, a historian who wrote about Jewish life in Eastern Europe, served as a professor of modern Jewish history at Haifa University.[7] Dov Yarden, a scholar of medieval Hebrew literature, demonstrated his talent as a philologist with his contribution to the *Even Shoshan Dictionary,* and published poetry of Shlomo Ibn Gabirol and Yehudah Halevi.[8] Other prominent figures from Motol include Zvulun Ravid, an expert in Hebrew literature. Ravid was an educator in Israel who came to the United States to serve as a professor of Hebrew literature at Columbia University and the Jewish Theological Seminary (JTS). David Bartov served as a judge in Israel. These distinguished people, born in Motol, also have in common their dedication to the State of Israel and the advancement of Hebrew language and culture.[9]

Lieberman's family was of distinguished rabbinical lineage, and he bore the name of his maternal grandfather, R. Saul Katzenellenbogen (*av beit din* of Kosov, and later of Kobrin), whose father was R. Meir Halevi Epstein, *av beit din* of Vilna (1770–1851).[10] R. Saul Katzenellenbogen was a descendant of R. Aryeh Leib, the chief rabbi of Koenigsberg, who was popularly known as the Pardes. Lieberman's mother, Liba, had a sister, Rashka Leah, who married R. Shmaryahu Yosef Karelitz. Their son, R. Avraham Yeshayahu, achieved great renown in rabbinic circles and was known as the Hazon Ish.

Paternally, Lieberman was a descendant of R. Isaac ben Aaron of Karlin (b. Minsk, 1788–1852), the author of *Keren Orah,* a collection of novellae on the Talmud. R. Isaac's brother, Jacob, was the author of *Mishkenot Yaakov* and *Kehillat Yaakov,* and his grandfather R. Baruch Shklov, known as R. Borukh "Doctor," studied in the yeshiva of Volozhin and received his rabbinic ordination from R. Avraham Katzenellenbogen of Brisk.[11] An uncle of Lieberman's father, R. Moshe Lieberman, was the noted scholar R. Malkiel Zvi Halevi Tenenbaum, author of a collection of responsa in five volumes titled *Divrei Malkiel.*[12] Lieberman was also related to R. Zadok Hakohen of Lublin (1823–1900), the noted Lithuanian-trained talmudist who later became a hasidic rebbe.[13] Lieberman was related by marriage to R. Baruch Halevi Epstein, author of *Torah Temima,* whose uncle was R. Naftali Zevi Yehudah Berlin (the Netziv), the distinguished *rosh yeshiva* of Volozhin, and to R. Joseph Baer Soloveitchik (known as the Rav), whose grandfather married into the Netziv's family.[14]

Schooling

It would appear that Lieberman's family was financially comfortable. His father owned the yeast monopoly in Motol, a profitable enterprise supplying the Jews as well as the non-Jews of the community with the means for baking bread and producing vodka. Lieberman recalled his having been a "spoiled child" by virtue of the fact that he would invariably walk about with coins in his pocket.[15]

Lieberman's father sent him to the village of Malch at the age of twelve to study under R. David Tevel Dinovsky.[16] Although Malch was only twenty kilometers from Motol, the journey required several days, as there was no train stop in Malch. In the nearby town of Kosov, Lieberman celebrated his bar mitzvah, presided over by his uncle, R. Shmaryahu Karelitz.[17] Shortly thereafter, Lieberman left Malch to study at the renowned Knesset Yisrael yeshiva of Slobodka, under R. Moshe Mordechai Epstein and R. Natan Zevi Finkel, the "Alter" of Slobodka.[18] His study companions at Slobodka included Gedalyahu Alon, later professor at the Hebrew University in Jerusalem; and Moshe Gevirtzman, later the vice mayor of Jerusalem.[19] Another study partner of Lieberman's was Moshe Silberg, later to become deputy president of the Supreme Court of the State of Israel. Students Silberg and Lieberman would test each other's mental acumen by memorizing road signs. Silberg, being of extremely short stature and therefore exempt from military conscription, once risked certain death by posing as Lieberman in order to free the latter from military service in the czar's army.[20]

Although Lieberman's stay at Slobodka was of relatively short duration—approximately three years—he always took great pride in referring to himself as a "Slobodker."[21] When unstable social and military conditions resulted in the uprooting of the yeshiva from Slobodka in 1915, Lieberman's own life became uprooted. He and classmate Shraga Abramson are described as having wandered from yeshiva to yeshiva in Lithuania.[22]

Both of Lieberman's parents died in 1916, of unknown causes, three months apart. Lieberman did not learn of their deaths until three years later, for at the time he lived in Kiev under Russian rule while the German army occupied Motol, and there was no communication between the two locales. Ironically, Lieberman was informed of his parents' demise while he was preparing to embark on a train to visit them.[23] It was during the turmoil of those years of civil war following the Russian Revolution that Lieberman barely escaped death at the hands of the White Army.[24] After spending a brief period in Kiev with relatives, Lieberman relocated to Minsk to rejoin the Slobodka yeshiva in exile.[25] He also studied under R. Yosef Yosel Hurwitz in the yeshiva of Novogrudok (Novaredok) and in 1917 studied in the yeshivas in Kremenchug and Yelizavetgrad, where his study companions and close friends were R. Simcha Soloveitchik and R. Mikhael Rashkes (Rosenberg).[26] Lieberman received his rabbinic ordination in 1916, at the age of eighteen.[27] However, Lieberman's interest later turned to secular studies, and by 1919 he had completed eight divisions in the Kiev gymnasium, where he was admitted by virtue of his proficiency in self-taught secular studies.[28]

Subsequently, Lieberman returned to Minsk, where in 1922 he married into a prestigious rabbinical family, taking for his wife Rachel, daughter of R. Eliezer Rabinowitz of Minsk, the son-in-law of the renowned R. Yerucham Yehuda Leib Perelmann, a Lithuanian talmudist known as "The Great One of Minsk" (1835–96).[29] For several months, Lieberman resided in the Rabinowitz home in Minsk. Lieberman later relocated to Kiev in pursuit of a livelihood. For a brief period, he worked in the carbon-paper business, and he later entered into business with two of his uncles who were engaged in the exchange of newly minted gold coins for old gold coins.[30] However, Lieberman feared involving himself in such "dangerous" financial transactions. His brother, Meir, recalls that Lieberman once declined to report a stolen watch lest he be associated with a location in which money-changing transpired.[31] Indeed, in 1925, his uncle's business collapsed when the Bolsheviks terminated the NEP (New Economic Policy). Without a means of livelihood in Russia, Lieberman chose to emigrate to Palestine. After great difficulty in procuring passports for himself and his wife, Lieberman set sail for Palestine from Odessa in 1927.[32]

Palestinian Developments

Education

In 1927, not long after his arrival in Palestine, Lieberman was again drawn to secular studies and decided to go to Paris to study medicine at the Sorbonne. While still in Russia, Lieberman had shown an affinity for medicine; during World War I, he had enrolled in a correspondence course in medical studies from the University of Yekaterinoslav while studying under R. Shlomo Polachek in Yelizavetgrad.[33] An interesting vignette depicts Lieberman and the educator Noah Pines of Tel Aviv's Bet Hatalmud visiting the Alter of Slobodka in Hebron. When informed of Lieberman's plans to study medicine abroad, the Alter responded, "I am puzzled. Why are you wasting your time? In the end, you will return to your yeshiva studies."[34] The Alter was partially correct. A year later, in 1928, Lieberman did return to Palestine, purportedly because the Sorbonne refused to issue him credits for the courses he took in Kiev;[35] however, Lieberman did not resume his yeshiva studies in Hebron. He instead enrolled at the Hebrew University of Jerusalem.

His decision to study at the Hebrew University did not come easily. Lieberman was an established member of the Orthodox yeshiva community of Jerusalem and studied regularly with the chief rabbi of Palestine, R. Abraham Isaac Hakohen Kook. Indeed, Lieberman initially resisted suggestions that he attend the Hebrew University and be exposed to secular-style Germanic-type scholarship; however, he was eventually persuaded by Michel Rabinowitz, an old acquaintance from Minsk, to enroll at the Hebrew University.[36]

At first, Lieberman felt out of place at the Hebrew University. He was unfamiliar with many of the well-known names of Western European Jewish academicians, including that of Zacharias Frankel,[37] and he resisted the methodological approach to rabbinic studies espoused by Professor Jacob Nahum Epstein. Lieberman admitted that it took him a full year to understand Epstein's approach and methodology.[38] However, Lieberman came to appreciate Epstein; and under Professor Moshe Schwabe, he mastered Greek, a language with which he was familiar from his student years in Lithuania. On many occasions, Lieberman later expressed his appreciation to these scholars in his writings.

In 1932, Lieberman graduated from the Hebrew University with a final rating of excellent, acquiring his master of arts degree with a specialization in talmudic studies and a subspecialty in Palestinology—Greco-Roman languages and culture and ancient history.[39]

Educator

Lieberman's early employment opportunities in Palestine appear to have been less than impressive. He served as a clerk in the Tel Aviv Chamber of

Commerce and as a teacher in Herzeliah.[40] In 1931, while attending the Hebrew University, Lieberman served as a part-time lecturer in Talmud at the Mizrachi Teachers Institute in Jerusalem, which was established by R. Eliezer Meir Lifshutz, whom Lieberman had met on several occasions in Michel Rabinowitz's Jerusalem bookstore, a gathering place for Jerusalem's literary intelligentsia.[41] In desperate need of money, Lieberman also worked as a secretary at the Yeshivat Shaar Hashamayim under R. Chaim Leib Auerbach.[42] However, he now found himself under consideration for a teaching position at the Hebrew University. In August 1930, Judah Magnes had requested a Hebrew University student to teach gratis a preparatory course in Talmud, and Professor Klein of the Hebrew University had proposed that Lieberman teach the course, conditional on his completing his own studies at the Hebrew University.

In November 1931, Magnes praised Lieberman as one of the two most brilliant students in the university's graduating class and requested a scholarship of $1,800 to establish a Talmud preparatory course with Lieberman to function as a research department member in Talmud. Magnes also referred to a treatise on the Jerusalem Talmud that had been authored by Lieberman.[43] On February 18, 1932, an official letter from the Hebrew University detailed Saul Lieberman's teaching terms. He was to teach the Talmud preparatory course from February through October for four hours a week at a salary of ten lirot a month. Lieberman rejoiced in his good fortune in a May 18, 1932, letter to Professor Louis Ginzberg of the Jewish Theological Seminary of America, informing him that his economic situation was comfortable because he was able to draw a salary from both the Mizrachi Teachers Institute and the Hebrew University.

Five years later, the board of the Hebrew University recommended discontinuing the course taught by Lieberman.[44] A more elementary Talmud class, taught by Lieberman's colleague Gedalyahu Alon, had a larger enrollment. Lieberman's "advanced" Talmud preparatory course had decreased from six students in 1934 to only two students in 1937, and was therefore to be dropped. The university rector claimed that he reflected the majority of the members of the board of the Hebrew University in stating that there were worthier projects for the Hebrew University to pursue with its limited funds than funding Lieberman's class. On March 17, 1937, S. Ginsberg, the

Hebrew University administrator, informed Lieberman that his services would no longer be needed as of the end of the academic year. Why was Lieberman's position terminated? The official reason for the nonrenewal of his contract was fiscal; the Hebrew University simply could not afford to underwrite a class for only two students. However, other reasons have been suggested.

Although it was not the policy of the Hebrew University to award doctorates at the time, Lieberman apparently sought one; but he seemed to have encountered problems in gaining approval for his doctoral dissertation.[45] J. N. Epstein purportedly rejected Lieberman's *Tosefet Rishonim* as a doctoral thesis on the grounds that it was not the analytical type of work appropriate for a Ph.D. and that it was lacking a broad historical approach.[46] Alon's work, on the other hand, was more acceptable to Epstein. We shall attempt to demonstrate later that Lieberman's work was indeed more commentary than historical analysis, and more reflective of Eastern European–style scholarship than of Western European *Wissenschaft.* According to Yitzhak Raphael, former minister of religion of the State of Israel, who studied under Lieberman in his Hebrew University Talmud preparatory course, it was because Lieberman lacked an advanced academic degree at that time that "people with strong elbows blocked the road to his advancement."[47]

Lieberman evinced great bitterness over his dismissal from the Hebrew University faculty. In a letter to Gershom Scholem on February 3, 1958—almost a quarter century later—he relates that a full year after his termination he still had not received his severance pay from the university, and that it was only by accident that he discovered that indeed a check had been made out to him; however, it remained undelivered. He described his dismissal as having been carried out in a style akin to firing a worker "who is guilty of stealing." On frequent occasions many years later, Lieberman was reputed to have carried on his person his dismissal letter from the Hebrew University as a painful reminder of the insensitivity shown him.[48]

Lieberman's economic straits in Palestine were now dire. He served for approximately five years as dean of the Harry Fischel Institute for Research in Talmud, a Jerusalem institution founded in 1932 with the enthusiastic support of Chief Rabbi Kook.[49] Lieberman's friend R. Isaac Herzog was president, and R. Dov Kook, a brother of R. Abraham Isaac Hakohen Kook, was principal.[50] However, the remuneration was not generous, and the institute was not respected in Hebrew University circles. It was perceived as more of a yeshiva than a university—more of a religious institution than an academic center. But since Lieberman lacked a Ph.D., his potential for advancement at the Hebrew University was limited even if he could overcome the opposition of those who may have feared they would be overshadowed by his intellect.

Limitations of a different nature confronted Lieberman at the Harry Fischel Institute. One need only look at the membership of the institute's advisory board (R. Herzog [later, chief rabbi], R. Isser Zalman Meltzer [*rosh yeshiva* of Etz Chaim], R. Yaakov Moshe Charlap [rabbi of Mercaz Harav], and R. Meir Berlin) to realize that the institute would not serve as an adequate vehicle for Lieberman's advanced and expansive approach to talmudic research and scholarship. For example, the Harry Fischel Institute's publications during Lieberman's tenure dealt with relating the talmudic text to halakhah. Indeed, that was the purpose of R. Kook's commentary, *Halakhah Berurah,* in the edition of the tractate *Betzah,* that was published by the institute.[51] Lieberman's interests lay elsewhere, and nowhere did the advisory board seem to express interest in or enthusiasm for Lieberman's emphasis on "an adequate acquaintance with outside non-Jewish literary and historical sources that have a bearing upon the matter embodied in the talmudic sources," or Lieberman's concern for "a sound and extensive knowledge of contemporary life and culture, history and archaeology of the Jewish people and of the outside non-Jewish world."[52]

One could also theorize that Lieberman was troubled for a number of reasons by the institute's plans to embark upon the publication of a scientific edition of the Mishnah. He thought the student body inadequate for this sort of scholarship, he was concerned that Epstein might view such a work as "an infringement upon his territory,"[53] and he probably sensed discomfort on the part of the institute's advisory board with the publication of a scientific Mishnah.

It became clear to Lieberman in the late 1930s that his position at the institute was becoming untenable. Since the Hebrew University remained closed to him, he would be forced to relocate in order to seek appropriate employment.

In 1938–39, Lieberman briefly returned to Lithuania to visit the graves of his parents and relatives in Motol and Pinsk and to see his younger brother, Meir, in Bialystok. He also traveled to Vilna to meet with Vilna's chief rabbi, Hayyim Ozer Grodzinski. Lieberman was later able to help his brother, along with his brother's wife and four-year-old daughter, to obtain visas from the British consulate in Vilna to emigrate to Palestine in January 1941.[54] Lieberman's sister, four years his junior, remained in Europe and survived World War II.[55]

Lieberman left Palestine in 1940 and, for the first time in his life, traveled to the United States, where he joined the faculty of the Jewish Theological Seminary of America (JTS) in New York. His wife, Rachel, had died in 1930 and was buried on the Mount of Olives in Jerusalem. According to one report, she died of kidney disease,[56] although others ascribed her death to a difficult childbirth.[57] J. N. Epstein, in a letter to Louis Ginzberg, described this tragedy as yet another grievous addition to Lieberman's "serious plight."[58] In 1932, Lieberman remarried, taking for his wife Judith Berlin (b. Moseiki, Lithuania, August 18, 1904; d. New York, December 21, 1978), whose father, R. Meir Berlin (Bar-Ilan; 1880–1949), was president of the World Mizrachi Center, and whose grandfather, R. Naftali Zevi Yehudah Berlin, had served as dean of the yeshiva of Volozhin. Judith, an eminent educator in her own right, taught at the same Mizrachi school where Lieberman had taught in Jerusalem.[59]

In 1940, Judith and Saul Lieberman arrived in New York. Later that year, Judith became the Hebrew studies principal of Shulamith, a girls' day school in the Orthodox community of Borough Park in Brooklyn. She also taught the senior class in her first years as principal. Many parents enrolled their daughters in Shulamith because they wanted them to be exposed to at least some Jewish education. Judith's objective, however, was to provide the students with an intensive Jewish education by giving them an understanding of the basic concepts of the Torah, proficiency in Hebrew, and the ability to read and understand the sacred texts. She instituted homework, in the face of considerable opposition from parents who wondered whether they had sent their daughters to a school that was training them as rebbetzins (rabbis' wives)![60] Francine Klagsbrun, a noted writer on Jewish topics and a graduate of Shulamith, gives her teachers at the school credit for providing a strong foundation for her later Judaic studies: "My passion for Jewish texts stems in large part from Nehama Cohen . . . and Judith Lieberman, our Hebrew school principal. . . . If you wanted to learn, these women taught Torah with unmatched scholarship."[61] There is little doubt that Lieberman was proud of his wife's achievements at Shulamith and believed it was essential for girls to have a comprehensive Jewish education. In Lieberman's view, it was important for women to have a deep knowledge of the sources of Jewish religion and culture and to study Talmud. To that end, following Judith's death, Lieberman endowed the Judith Lieberman Institute for Women, one of three branches of Ramot Shapira Educational Center, at Moshav Beit Meir (in the Judean hills, west of Jerusalem).[62]

Lieberman also endowed the "Judith Lieberman Prize," which he awarded to Nehama Leibowitz in 1980–81. Lieberman had to persuade Leibowitz, a humble scholar and educator, to accept the award.[63] In thanking Leibowitz for agreeing to be the recipient, Lieberman, not noted for hyperbole, said, "There is not, in our generation, even a single individual, whether male or female, whose contribution to Jewish education equals yours." He expressed his pleasure that the name of his Judith would be linked with the name of Nehama Leibowitz. In a letter to Leibowitz following the award ceremony, Lieberman acknowledged that pursuit of honor is deplorable. However, he asserted, if others insist upon bestowing honors, give them the pleasure, particularly if goodwill comes of it either for the community or an individual. He concluded the letter with the hope that he would share her destiny in the dissemination and teaching of Torah in Israel.

Lieberman's speech at the award ceremony praised Nehama Leibowitz's character and achievements. He described her as a woman of integrity who studied the Bible intensively, and revolutionized the method of interpreting it. She gleaned the inner meaning of the text as she sought the true explanation. Her name became synonymous with the *parshat hashavua* (weekly Torah portion). She taught her students to analyze the words of the great interpreters Rashi, Ibn Ezra, Ramban, and Abravanel and encouraged them to find meaning and insight for themselves in the text. Lieberman delivered his speech of praise of Leibowitz two years before his own death. He had instructed those close to him that he did not wish to be eulogized. However, the words he spoke about Nehama Leibowitz would have been appropriate for himself. His speech reflected the values, characteristics, and achievements that he most likely would have wished to be associated with himself in connection with the study of Talmud.[64]

After Judith Lieberman's death in 1978, the Shulamith school commissioned her portrait. It was presented to Saul Lieberman at the school's annual dinner in January 1979 and was then hung in the principal's office. Rabbi Moshe Zwick, executive director of Shulamith, assured Lieberman that the portrait would remain there for as long as Rabbi Zwick remained with the school.[65]

American Fulfillments

JTS Affiliation

In accepting an academic appointment at the Jewish Theological Seminary, Lieberman had now associated himself with the fountainhead institute of Conservative Judaism. Why had he made this choice? Persistent, but unsubstantiated, rumors describe him as also negotiating for a teaching position at Rabbi Isaac Elhanan Theological Seminary (RIETS).[66] He is also purported to have received an offer from his Slobodka colleague R. Yitzhak Hutner, to teach at Hutner's Mesivta Chaim Berlin in Brooklyn.[67] Why did Lieberman choose to assume an academic position at JTS, the training institution for Conservative rabbis?

Livelihood Pressures. Since his student days in Lithuania and Russia, Lieberman, to all appearances, had been unsuccessful in earning an adequate living. Indeed, he suffered from great poverty at various times. As he testified, "I learned to live like a dog during the years of hunger under the Bolsheviks."[68] He knew firsthand of the famine and deprivation gripping Russia.

To earn money for food, Lieberman sometimes participated in chess tournaments and swimming contests. Slobodka students were known to be able swimmers, as it was their practice during the summer to swim in a nearby river for the seventy minutes between Mincha and Ma'ariv (afternoon and evening) religious services. Lieberman's brother, Meir, reports that Lieberman would make it a practice during those years to visit people during mealtime hours in the hope that he would be able to partake in at least one decent meal a day. Later, under more comfortable circumstances, in 1920–23, Lieberman played a prominent role in helping his father-in-law, the rabbi of Minsk, distribute food packages to starving Russian Jews, thereby saving the lives of hundreds of families.[69]

In describing Lieberman's impecunious state in Palestine in 1927, Meir suggested that Lieberman's wife Rachel died because her husband lacked the means to take her to Vienna for a needed surgery.[70] Florence Bar-Ilan, Lieberman's sister-in-law, claimed that the true reason for Lieberman's suspending his medical studies in Paris was lack of funds,[71] although Lieberman tried valiantly to sustain himself there as a wallpaper salesman.[72]

After his dismissal from the Hebrew University, Lieberman had no viable financial options open to him in Palestine. Indeed, his father-in-law, R. Meir Bar-Ilan, testified that there was simply no way for Lieberman to support himself while pursuing his scholarship.[73] Judah Avida lamented that "Jerusalem sinned" in failing to provide Lieberman with a source of livelihood, thus "causing him to go into exile to the Alexandria across the sea."[74] In his own final commentary on his dire financial straits at that time, Lieberman muses, in a letter written over forty years later, on how at that time life on the kibbutz would have seemed an attractive option to him, for only there would he be free of financial concern.[75] Now JTS was offering him a handsome salary as well as the opportunity to pursue his talmudic research. It was an offer that Lieberman could not refuse.

Research Opportunities. In contrast to the Reform movement's Hebrew Union College in Cincinnati, JTS was an institution emphasizing the primacy of textual research, with Solomon Schechter (1847–1917), the first president of JTS, renowned first and foremost as a textual scholar (although popularly known as a theologian).[76] In addition to providing him with a comfortable salary, the Jewish Theological Seminary of America also afforded Lieberman ideal conditions under which to pursue his studies and research.

In a letter to Gershom Scholem, written only a few months after his arrival in the United States, Lieberman related in amazement that his teaching schedule was extremely undemanding on his time. His classroom duties entailed only four to five hours of instruction per week, and JTS faculty meetings took place infrequently—sometimes only once every two months.[77]

Therefore, Lieberman confessed that his *yetser harah* (evil inclination) was trying to persuade him to extend his stay at the Seminary. Where else could he possibly find so much leisure time with which to pursue his scholarship? Indeed, Lieberman informed Scholem that he was more than willing to renew his contract with the Seminary for an additional year, adding that the Seminary had suggested to him that he stay on permanently. Likewise, Judith Lieberman informed Scholem that her husband's workload was an exceedingly easy one, for he taught only four hours a week and gave one bimonthly seminar. She reported that he already felt like a "retired professor."[78]

When interviewed by the *Jerusalem Post* almost thirty years later, Lieberman recalled his light teaching schedule at the Seminary: "I teach four hours a week and the rest of my time is my own. . . . Over the years, I have published a great deal; this would not have been possible anywhere else."[79] In addition to having many free hours for research at his disposal, Lieberman was provided with "a luxurious setting" in which to study: an office consisting of two giant rooms, and unlimited access to the rich collection of rare manuscripts and books housed in the Seminary library.[80]

To say that Lieberman was given preferential treatment in the use of Seminary manuscripts would be an understatement. Seminary librarian Nahum Sarna advised Menahem Schmelzer, his successor, to make himself available to open the rare-manuscript room at the Seminary library *any* time Lieberman needed to consult the thirteenth-century manuscript of Maimonides' *Mishne Torah,* which was placed on a table there especially for his use.[81] In referring to Lieberman's privileged status, Seminary administrator Bernard Mandelbaum put it simply: "[JTS chancellor Louis] Finkelstein gave Lieberman whatever he needed."[82] Indeed, in the preface to his *Hilkhot Hayerushalmi l'Harambam,* Lieberman profusely thanks Finkelstein for "always having concerned himself with providing me, in every possible way, with all the amenities necessary for and conducive toward the study of Torah."

Traditional Ambiance. What made the Jewish Theological Seminary such an attractive place for Lieberman was not only the accommodations and conveniences it provided to him for his scholarly pursuits but also the institution's traditional religious ambiance. Although the Seminary was officially described as the fountainhead of Conservative Judaism, its religious character was quite different from that of most Conservative congregations. An Orthodox Jew could feel quite comfortable there. Indeed, around the same time that Lieberman was being offered a position at JTS, R. Moses Soloveitchik had approached the Seminary's professor of Talmud, Louis Ginzberg, inquiring whether an academic position might be available at the Seminary for his son, the renowned R. Joseph Baer Soloveitchik, a recent immigrant from Lithuania.[83]

There were several factors accounting for the Seminary's traditional religious posture and its relative "independence" from the other arms of the Conservative movement. To begin with, the Seminary came into existence long before there was a "Conservative movement" in the United States. It functioned for a quarter century as a rabbinical seminary and an academic center unconnected to a movement or denomination.[84] From its inception, the Seminary as an institution represented "non-Reform Judaism," that is, "Orthodox-Conservative Judaism," rather than Conservative Judaism per se. Solomon Schechter perceived his institution as confronting Reform Judaism, not so much Orthodox Judaism. Not surprisingly, it could be said that "for Schechter and his generation the words Conservative and Orthodox are used interchangeably."[85]

Cyrus Adler, president of the Jewish Theological Seminary from 1915 to 1940, was opposed to the institution being identified as the center of a new movement in Judaism; he preferred the broader name "Agudat Yeshurun" (Union of Israel) to that of "Conservative" in describing the United Synagogue. He wanted the Seminary to stand above factionalism and to be identified as part of traditional Judaism rather than as a distinct ideological institution.[86]

Indeed, the historian Jeffrey Gurock designates the Seminary of that era as a modern Orthodox rather than a Conservative institution.[87] On several occasions during Adler's presidency, discussions were held concerning a possible merger between the Jewish Theological Seminary of America and the Rabbi Isaac Elhanan Theological Seminary.[88] As Adler wrote in a letter to the philanthropist Jacob Schiff, the Jewish Theological Seminary of America was "a religious institution with a definite aim in view to preserve the Jewish tradition and make it livable in modern surroundings. You once called this reasonable Orthodoxy. Some people call it Conservative Judaism. I prefer the name of Traditional Judaism or Historical Judaism."[89]

During the 1920s, many Jews "did not understand wherein . . . Yeshiva differed from the Jewish Theological Seminary of America. . . . [M]any persons active in the administration and faculty of the Jewish Theological Seminary during this period were Orthodox or close to Orthodox in their theology and practice."[90] Not surprisingly, the Seminary's early faculty numbered among its ranks several prominent Orthodox rabbis, such as Bernard Drachman, Moses Hyamson, and Alexander Marx (the son-in-law of R. David Zvi Hoffman, rector of the Berlin Orthodox Rabbinical Seminary). The Seminary was a place in which many an Orthodox Jew could feel comfortable.

It is also significant that Lieberman's earliest contacts and communications with the Jewish Theological Seminary were not at all with the professional Conservative leadership of the United States, that is, members of the Rabbinical Assembly, but rather with Professor Louis Ginzberg, his renowned fellow talmudist and fellow Litvak.[91] It was not the Rabbinical Assembly or the Conservative movement that brought Lieberman to the Seminary, but rather Louis Ginzberg. Indeed, Louis Finkelstein praised Ginzberg for his indefatigable efforts in persuading Lieberman to come to the Seminary: "It is not every academician who, as he grows older, is motivated to bring to his institution someone thirty years younger, who is his equal in learning and in insight."[92]

What Louis Ginzberg saw in Saul Lieberman was readily apparent. It was Ginzberg's conviction that a thorough knowledge of the rabbinic sources was indispensable for anyone who wanted to labor in the vineyard of classical Jewish scholarship, and he deemed a number of Western Jewish scholars deficient in this prerequisite:

> Their neglect of the study of the halakhah greatly impaired the quality of many of the historical investigations undertaken by the German scholars. Few among them seem to have realized that sound generalizations can follow only after the determination of precise facts. . . . Great as the achievements of the *Wissenschaft des Judentums* are in all other branches of Jewish learning, it failed in

> the field of the Talmud—I am using the name in a broad sense . . . because its study was superficial and limited to generalities. . . .
>
> How much more would the study of both Talmuds have profited by a combination of the thorough talmudic learning of the Eastern talmudist and the philologic-historical approach of the student of the *Wissenschaft des Judentums*.[93]

Ginzberg's reputed ideal for a scholar of Judaica was for one "to have studied at a Lithuanian yeshiva and to have worked under Noeldeke (at Strassburg)."[94] In Saul Lieberman, Ginzberg discovered his ideal, albeit in a "Lithuanian yeshiva–J. N. Epstein Hebrew University" synthesis.

The Lieberman-Ginzberg relationship goes back to the winter of 1929, when Ginzberg was a guest lecturer at the Hebrew University. Ginzberg, obviously impressed with Lieberman's qualifications, asked him to prepare for publication Ginzberg's lecture "The Significance of the Halakhah for Jewish History."[95] Their relationship continued via correspondence. On June 1, 1930, Lieberman wrote to Ginzberg, detailing his theory regarding the composition of the Talmud of Caesarea and asking for suggestions as to possible dissertation topics for himself. Intimacy and honesty characterize their correspondence. Lieberman commiserated with Ginzberg over a most inadequate review of the latter's *Ginze Schechter*. Lieberman informed him that he had been asked by Dr. Levin to read Levin's review of Ginzberg's book for the *Jewish Quarterly Review*. Ginzberg later requested that Lieberman write a review of Ginzberg's *Legends of the Jews*.[96]

Finkelstein's tribute to Ginzberg for bringing to the Seminary "someone thirty years younger, who is his equal in learning and in insight" is reflected in the Lieberman-Ginzberg correspondence. At one point, Lieberman states bluntly that there is no longer anything for him to learn at the Hebrew University—and this was written on July 20, 1930! In the same year, Lieberman confidently stated his reasons for disagreeing with a number of Ginzberg's views. Their correspondence, notwithstanding Lieberman's use of deferential titles vis-à-vis Ginzberg, reads as a correspondence between equals "in learning and in insight."

It is conceivable that discussions between the two concerning the possibility of Lieberman's coming to JTS were already taking place during this time. On November 14, 1931, Lieberman wrote to Ginzberg that he was interested in visiting the United States, since his teaching responsibilities at the Hebrew University and the Mizrachi Teachers Institute were not due to commence for a while. Such a trip apparently never materialized. It was not until nine years later, at the end of Passover, 1940, that Lieberman expressed his appreciation to Ginzberg for having issued the invitation to him to teach at JTS. He then prepared for his trip to America.

Lieberman's acceptance of this offer was not an easy matter for him. In a letter of April 30, 1940, he explained to Ginzberg the dilemma confronting him. Although there was no written contract that obligated him to remain at the Harry Fischel Institute, Lieberman felt a personal obligation to Fischel. He was also concerned that JTS not be embarrassed by the possibility of public reports that he "refused their offer," should Fischel decline to grant him a year's leave of absence. On the other hand, should a leave of absence be extended to him to teach in New York, and should the Seminary want to renew his contract at a later date, then ethical dilemmas would surely confront all parties in the matter. Lieberman concluded his letter by reiterating that he would love to come to JTS, and he implored Ginzberg to attempt to amicably and fairly facilitate the matter with Fischel. We have no details as to the facilitation process, but clearly Ginzberg and Louis Finkelstein were the initiators responsible for bringing Lieberman to the Seminary, not the Conservative movement (the leaders of the Rabbinical Assembly and of the United Synagogue) itself.

On June 12, 1940, Lieberman tersely cabled Finkelstein, "Accepting terms, Lieberman." The Liebermans left Palestine on August 20, and after a stopover at the British oil wells of Bahrain, they went to Bombay, where they spent several weeks (because of the war, this was not an uncommon route to the U.S.). On September 12, Lieberman cabled Finkelstein even more tersely, "Leaving, Lieberman."[97] He arrived in the United States on October 22, 1940.

On June 24, 1940, Finkelstein sent a formal letter to the United States Department of State in Washington, D.C., requesting a visa for Lieberman;[98] on July 1, 1940, he requested the same from the U.S. consulate in Jerusalem. Although it was the policy of the board of directors of JTS, when inviting foreign professors, to extend an initial call for a period of one year only, Finkelstein said that "it is the expressed intention of the board that [Lieberman's] appointment become permanent." Lieberman "was to become visiting professor of Talmud at the Seminary for the academic year 1940–41 at a salary of $4,500, including his traveling expenses."

It should be emphasized that neither the Rabbinical Assembly nor the United Synagogue had any voice when it came to faculty appointments at JTS. Indeed, it is even questionable if the Seminary board of directors had much say in the matter. Thus, when Finkelstein wrote to Lieberman on March 31, 1940, regarding his appointment as a faculty member of JTS (officially, he was to lecture in Talmud in Finkelstein's place) and urged Lieberman to accept Ginzberg's offer, Finkelstein told him that the matter *then* (our emphasis) would be brought to the JTS board of directors for its approval. The tone of the letter seems to indicate that the appointment was a *fait accompli,* with board approval a mere formality.

Rabbinical Assembly approval or disapproval was also irrelevant. Indeed, one prominent Rabbinical Assembly leader, Solomon Goldman, was openly critical of several of Finkelstein's faculty appointments, including that of Lieberman.[99] But such opposition was to no avail. Lieberman came to JTS as an academician, a talmudic scholar, not a proponent or practitioner of Conservative Judaism, and he was hired by an academic institution to function as an academician.

The religious ideology and traditional halakhic approach of Louis Finkelstein, chancellor of JTS, would surely have been consistent with Lieberman's religious sensitivities. Like his predecessor Adler, Finkelstein preferred not using the label "Conservative" in designating the Seminary or the movement spearheaded by his institution. As Finkelstein stated:

> If someone calls us traditional, orthodox, or conservative, it is he who makes a division in Judaism, not us. However, the necessities of organized Jewish life do require some term to describe our general point of view. I think that the members of the faculty generally prefer the term "traditional Judaism." It is a correct description of us because even those congregations of ours which have introduced slight deviations from the norm have done so because, in their opinion, these deviations are themselves essential

> for the preservation of traditional Judaism. There may be some disagreement regarding this judgment, but there can be no disagreement regarding their sincerity or their purpose. Summarizing the whole situation, I should say that I believe the term "traditional Judaism" accurately describes the Movement of which all of us are a part.[100]

Finkelstein preferred viewing JTS as an umbrella institution for all traditional Jews, which he hoped would attract to it Orthodox Jews, rather than one reflecting a specific denominational ideology. Indeed, Finkelstein made no secret of the fact that he hoped that Orthodoxy would eventually find a home at the Seminary. He would therefore counsel his associates, "Let's not be too Conservative; let's not prevent [Orthodox Jews] from coming."[101]

Finkelstein distanced himself from a number of Rabbinical Assembly practices and policies of a less traditional nature, explaining bluntly, "I do not feel any responsibility for the views of the Rabbinical Assembly; on the other hand, they take no responsibility for my own views."[102] Clearly, Finkelstein saw JTS as an autonomous academic institution, not a rabbinical training school reflecting a specific movement's ideology.

Not surprisingly, Lieberman found JTS to have a decidedly traditional religious flavor. Its synagogue employed an Orthodox prayer book and was characterized by a physical separation between male and female worshipers. Louis Ginzberg was the official "Rabbi" of the Seminary synagogue (a position that Lieberman would later occupy) and the sole halakhic decisor for its practices. The great majority of the student body in 1940 were from Orthodox backgrounds and were educated at yeshivot.[103] Finkelstein was deeply concerned with issues of halakhic fidelity and competence, and would later discuss with Lieberman the necessity of reassigning a member of the rabbinics faculty from pure talmudic research to handling practical issues of Jewish law confronting the Conservative movement. Otherwise, feared Finkelstein, a "*beit din* [court of law] of unqualified men" would develop.[104] Finally (as Professor David Weiss Halivni points out),[105] Lieberman did not feel uncomfortable at JTS because he was not a theologian by nature, and concerned himself little with the theological positions elaborated within the Conservative movement. JTS was the school where he taught and studied Torah, not an institution representing a movement whose religious ideology and policies he necessarily espoused.

Lieberman-Finkelstein Relationship. Although Lieberman's impetus for coming to JTS was not the warm and intimate relationship with Finkelstein, it undoubtedly was the most significant factor for his choosing to remain there for his entire life, as well as for his personal, active involvement in Seminary activities and projects, far beyond the range of his classroom duties.

The relationship between the two men was truly intimate, both professionally and personally. The claim that Lieberman exerted a "Svengali-like" influence over Finkelstein is an exaggeration, but there is no question that Lieberman was Finkelstein's mentor and confidante, and influenced him profoundly.[106] It is not difficult to surmise that this would be the case. Lieberman's presence probably helped to authenticate JTS in Finkelstein's own eyes, for Lieberman represented the authentic Lithuanian *talmid hakham* (scholar) par excellence, as a living exemplar of Rabbi Elijah, the Gaon of Vilna, and as a disciple of the disciples of Finkelstein's revered role model, Rabbi Yisrael Salanter.

Lieberman's impeccable scholarly credentials and his high personal standards of religious observance—fully, if at times grudgingly, acknowledged by the Orthodox world—bestowed a measure of legitimacy to Finkelstein's seminary. Furthermore, Lieberman's presence undoubtedly alleviated some of the anxiety felt by traditionalists on the non-Orthodox institution's faculty, and served to attract prominent Orthodox scholars to JTS. One could state, without exaggeration, that Lieberman functioned in a three-role capacity toward Finkelstein. He was Finkelstein's rabbi, rebbe, and dear personal familial friend.

The Rabbi Relationship. According to David Kogen, a prominent Seminary administrator, "Louis Finkelstein looked upon Saul Lieberman as his one and only rabbi."[107] From the very beginning of their relationship, Finkelstein treated Lieberman deferentially. On November 17, 1940, the day of his installation as Seminary president, Finkelstein chose to place Lieberman in the limelight rather than himself, by organizing a late-afternoon reception in honor of "Professor and Mrs. Saul Lieberman," and referring to himself in the formal invitation merely as Mr. Louis Finkelstein.[108]

Finkelstein had enormous respect for Lieberman's erudition and capabilities, declaring that Lieberman and RCA (Radio Corporation of America) chairman of the board David Sarnoff were the two most able people he had ever met, and that they would have succeeded extraordinarily in whatever fields they would have entered.[109] It was Finkelstein's practice to speak of Lieberman in hyperbolic terms: he referred to Lieberman's arrival in the United States as "an historic one in the development of American Judaism."[110] Six years later, Finkelstein praised Lieberman for having brought to the Seminary "a new spirit of Torah and of life that will impact positively and powerfully on Jewish life in America." A few years later, Finkelstein wrote to Lieberman: "So far as the study of rabbinic Judaism is concerned, I have a strong feeling that we are at the beginning of a Lieberman era, which will be as different from what went before it as the Zunz era was from what went before him." On the occasion of Lieberman's presenting him with the vellum copy of his *Tosefta Kifshutah* on *Zera'im,* Finkelstein expressed his gratitude in the strongest possible terms: "Even if the Seminary, across the years, had done nothing else than lay the foundations for such a work, the institution would have justified itself." Nor was Finkelstein reticent in articulating his own personal gratitude to Lieberman. He wrote as a student does to his rabbi: "I do not have to tell you, that with your coming to the Seminary a new era has been opened in my own research studies, for it is from you that I learned not only a great deal of content, but even more of method and care in reaching conclusions and in formulating them. That I have been able to do anything at all is due to your inspiration, your help, and your great kindness."[111]

In fact, Lieberman may well have exerted a powerful influence on Finkelstein's own scholarship—notably, his work on the Pharisees. Finkelstein's studies on the Pharisees predated Lieberman's arrival in New York; his essay "The Pharisees: Their Origin and Their Philosophy," was written in 1929, and his book *The Pharisees* was published in 1938.[112] Both the article and the book reflect a sociological approach to religion with quasi-Marxist emphases, following the approach of Finkelstein's teacher Louis Ginzberg.[113] Similar thinking characterizes Finkelstein's *Akiba,* a book that, as we shall see, Lieberman criticized because of its unfavorable depiction of Rabbi Simeon ben Gamliel I as an arrogant upper-class patrician.

The Pharisees was more than just a work of dispassionate scholarship. Finkelstein sought to defend the Pharisees against their polemical detractors both in Christian and in secular circles, to demonstrate that the Pharisees were the true spiritual disciples of the prophets, and that Pharisaism embodied the highest ideals of the moral vision and ethical values of the United States.[114] The book was reprinted two years later, in 1940, essentially unchanged. In 1962, a new edition appeared, radically different and thoroughly revised. In the latest edition of *The Pharisees,* Finkelstein retracted his earlier position on the nature of the socioeconomic conflicts between the Pharisees and the Sadducees. Indeed, Finkelstein admits as much, concluding a supplementary chapter on "the uniqueness of Pharisaism" with this comment:

> To demonstrate, once again, the main thesis of this book as I now understand it, I shall first undertake a reappraisal of the recorded controversies between Sadducees and Pharisees, indicating the underlying issues, supplementing those in the text of the book, and sometimes suggesting a new approach, based on more recent, perhaps more mature, investigation.[115]

Finkelstein now avers that the conflict has more to do with biblical exegesis than with economics. It is interesting to speculate on the role that Lieberman might have played in Finkelstein's revision of his thinking on this subject. In the new edition, Finkelstein noted that Lieberman's *Tosefta Kifshutah* on *Mo'ed* appeared in print while his own book was in press. This allowed him to make a number of corrections in his text, with the regret that restriction of time and space precluded more extensive revisions.[116] Finkelstein states:

> During the past twenty years, I have had the rare opportunity of a second education, through communion with Professor Saul Lieberman, rightly considered "the leader among those who speak in the field of Jewish knowledge" in this generation, and through the study of his great works, which open a new era in talmudic studies.[117]

This "second education" that Lieberman afforded Finkelstein, consisting no doubt in part of what the latter referred to as "method and care in reaching conclusions and in formulating them" may well have been an important factor in Finkelstein's revised thinking on the Pharisees.[118]

The extravagance of Finkelstein's praise for Lieberman at times seemed to be beyond belief. He declared that the *raison d'être* for the Seminary's existence was so that Professor Lieberman should have a place to study and write: "Professor Lieberman does not exist for the Seminary; the Seminary exists for Professor Lieberman."[119] As a faculty member, Judah Goldin once expressed the matter: "Finkelstein believed in God and worshiped Lieberman."[120] It is not difficult to envision the ego satisfaction that Lieberman must have derived from Finkelstein's effusive praise. After his lack of success at the Hebrew University and his financial struggles in Jerusalem, he now found himself comfortably situated in New York City. Even if Finkelstein's hyperbolic commendations sounded a bit overdone to his ear, they were, no doubt, deeply gratifying to his soul.

Several years prior to Lieberman's arrival at the Seminary, Finkelstein, then Seminary provost, had engaged in scholarly correspondence with him, eliciting both his approbation and his critiques. The first correspondence extant between the two is a 1933 letter sent to Lieberman from Finkelstein, in which the latter responded appreciatively to a letter that he had just received from Lieberman. Over a year earlier, Finkelstein had published an article entitled "Emendations of the Sifrei,"[121] to which Lieberman had responded in the *Tarbiz* periodical without identifying himself as the author, with several criticisms and suggestions.[122] Not long thereafter, Lieberman corresponded directly with Finkelstein, apparently revealing his identity as the author of the critical analysis. Finkelstein, in a letter of March 2, 1933, expressed his gratitude to Lieberman for having shared his insights, promising to include several of them in his own forthcoming work on the *Sifrei* and confessing to Lieberman that "the critique in *Tarbiz* could only have emanated from a fit scholar as yourself."

In a letter of July 7, 1937, Finkelstein thanked Lieberman for agreeing to review his newly published edition of the *Sifrei*. On October 4, 1938, he sent him a copy of his recently published book, *Akiba*. The latter volume provoked a spirited correspondence between the two, in part because of Finkelstein's largely negative depiction of Rabbi Simeon ben Gamliel I. "Social position meant everything to Simeon ben Gamliel I. . . . [V]ain, pompous and egotistical . . . with unparalleled effrontery he asserted. . . ."[123] In a lengthy letter, Lieberman praised Finkelstein's *Akiba* for so vividly bringing the period and its personalities to life, but he then proceeded to vigorously dispute Finkelstein's highly critical portrayal of the distinguished Rabbi on the grounds that it lacked scholarly justification and that there was simply no evidence to support such an assessment. Lieberman defended Rabbi Simeon ben Gamliel I against Finkelstein's indictments point by point—gently, affectionately, but firmly—and told him that it would be preferable had he deleted from his book the entire chapter on Rabbi Simeon ben Gamliel I.[124] It is interesting to speculate as to whether Finkelstein would have deleted this chapter had the volume still remained unpublished at the time of their correspondence. In all subsequent editions of *Akiba,* the text remained intact. Finkelstein made no changes and did not revise the chapter to which Lieberman objected. Indeed, in all subsequent editions of *Akiba* (1962, 1970, and 1990), the text itself remained intact. However, in a preface to the 1990 edition, Finkelstein, more than a half century after Lieberman's passionate defense of Rabbi Simeon ben Gamliel I, seven years after Lieberman's death, and approximately two years before his own death, apologized for writing of the ancient Rabbi "with less than proper respect."[125] It was as though Finkelstein wished to rectify his relationship with Lieberman before he died, by removing the one unresolved matter that stood between them. Finkelstein did not mention Lieberman by name in the section of the preface that deals with Rabbi Simeon ben Gamliel I, presumably because Lieberman's criticism was conveyed privately. However, he did call the reader's attention to "Professor Saul Lieberman's brilliant essay on the Hadrianic persecutions," which depicts the martyrdom of Rabbi Akiba.[126]

It is noteworthy that Lieberman's work on the Hadrianic persecutions was itself a response to Finkelstein's invitation, in 1942, for him to deliver a lecture, "The Jewish Attitude toward the Christian Martyrs of Caesarea," at the JTS Institute of Post-Biblical Studies. Lieberman's work in this subject was refined and revised over the years, resulting, in its final form, in the aforementioned essay that Finkelstein cited. It appears that Finkelstein's involvement and relationship to Lieberman's work in this area had come full circle, with Finkelstein citing, in a preface written during the last years of his life, Lieberman's insight on R. Akiba's martyrdom.[127] In referring to his harsh criticism of Rabbi Simeon ben Gamliel I for the marriages that the Rabbi arranged for his daughters, Finkelstein writes contritely, "In my youthful naïveté I considered these marriages as motivated by personal ambition on Rabban Simeon ben Gamliel's part. I am glad and grateful that the opportunity has come for me to make this correction, as for many years I have regretted writing of him with less than proper respect."[128]

As regards Finkelstein's request that Lieberman compose a review of his edition of the *Sifrei,* it appears that Lieberman at first declined. However, once he learned that another scholar was preparing to write a negative review, he agreed to write his own review to be published in *Kiryat Sefer* as a special favor to Finkelstein.[129] The other scholar was Lieberman's mentor, J. N. Epstein. Lieberman later sent Finkelstein a letter (November 11, 1938) in which he advised him not to respond to Epstein's critique of his *Sifrei,* which appeared in *Tarbiz,* lest Epstein take personal offense, which would lead to an unpleasant situation. Not long after his arrival in the United States, Lieberman appeared to have displaced Ginzberg as Finkelstein's principal academic mentor and halakhic authority.[130]

The Rebbe Relationship. Lieberman was not only Finkelstein's rabbi-teacher; he was also Finkelstein's rebbe-adviser, and it was in this capacity that Lieberman became involved in many JTS programs and projects far removed from pure education. The conventional portrait, depicting Lieberman as devoting all of his spare hours to scholarship and being assiduously protected from all administrative intrusions by Finkelstein, is simply not accurate. Not only did Lieberman perform several administrative functions; he was also Finkelstein's confidante and adviser in virtually all aspects of Seminary policy.

On April 5, 1949, Lieberman was appointed dean of the postgraduate department of the JTS rabbinical school; ten years later, he was invited by Finkelstein to become the institution's rector. True, he was assured that Finkelstein would excuse him from conducting faculty meetings and would function as dean to allow Lieberman more time for his scholarship. Nevertheless, Lieberman's duties as rector were formidable. He was to supervise all faculty appointments, assist in faculty recruitment, and "guide the general religious policy of the institution," with the authority to veto any proposals.

Clearly, Lieberman's role had gone far beyond that of educator. He had powerful input vis-à-vis Seminary policy at a handsome 1959 salary of minimum $18,000 a year. In 1971, Lieberman received the official title of Distinguished (Service) Research Professor of Talmud and was notified by the chairman of the board of directors, Stanley Fuld, of the unanimous vote to elect him "Rector of the Seminary for Life."[131]

The intimacy of the Lieberman-Finkelstein relationship was apparent early in Lieberman's tenure at JTS. He, more than any other faculty member, had become Finkelstein's adviser and confidante. On July 24, 1942, Finkelstein wrote Lieberman about the establishment of the Institute of Post-Biblical Studies, concluding, "I haven't yet written to Professor Ginzberg about it."

It seems that Finkelstein frequently turned to Lieberman for personal favors of a delicate nature. Thus, on July 28, 1942, he wrote to Lieberman at his vacation home on Lake Waramaug in New Preston, Connecticut, begging him to try to explain to Rabbi Menahem Kasher that Finkelstein's busy schedule precluded his meeting with him, especially since such meetings frequently took the form of fund-raising enterprises. Lieberman replied on July 31, assuring Finkelstein that he would speak to Kasher about the matter at the earliest opportunity.

On another occasion, Finkelstein asked Lieberman's assistance in "gently" influencing H. L. Ginzberg to write his article on biblical history for a proposed volume to be entitled *Judaism and the Jews* "from an extremely conservative point of view" so as to "avoid various pitfalls of higher criticism."[132]

JTS records as well as Lieberman's personal correspondence testify to his involvement in many extracurricular Seminary activities on Finkelstein's behalf. For example, he and President Van Dusen of Union Theological Seminary arranged joint faculty meetings and a joint luncheon at which time a discussion of Reinhold Niebuhr's writings would take place.[133] Lieberman's involvement in internal matters of the Conservative movement was reflected in his participation in a conference that involved JTS administration members and faculty, as well as the leadership of the Rabbinical Assembly, designed to achieve mutual cooperation in handling issues of Jewish law.[134] This was a matter of great concern to Finkelstein, who made mention, in his correspondence (July 28, 1942) with Lieberman, of "vast dangers" that he perceived in deliberations taking place at Seminary alumni conferences, and how vital it was for him and Lieberman to address these issues. We find Lieberman sending a letter to the Philadelphia region of the Rabbinical Assembly, complimenting the rabbis for insisting on high standards of Sabbath observance for kosher caterers vis-à-vis restrictions on photography and music.[135]

In 1946, six years after Lieberman's arrival at JTS, Finkelstein entrusted him with a serious mission: Lieberman was to return to Jerusalem to recruit young scholars "who may have attained some real mastery of rabbinic studies . . . and persuade them to come [to JTS] to be trained in Western methods of scholarship."[136] These young scholars were to form the nucleus of JTS's Institute of Advanced Studies, to be directed by Lieberman. Lieberman was also asked to recruit young scholars to serve on the Seminary faculty—Ephraim E. Urbach and Solomon Pines were proposed—and to arrange for faculty exchanges between JTS and the Hebrew University as part of a visiting professorship program. This was part of a broader program designed to establish closer ties between JTS and the Hebrew University, and Lieberman was to be the key facilitator. Likewise, he was to investigate the possibility of JTS establishing a research program in rabbinics in Palestine.

Lieberman embarked on this project on behalf of the Seminary in July 1946. His return to New York for the fall semester was delayed when he was forced to go to Cairo because of a steamship strike. A memorandum (dated December 26, 1946) of a JTS meeting attended by Lieberman, Alexander Marx, and Mordecai Kaplan discusses Lieberman's Palestinian recruitment mission. The names Shraga Abramson, Ezra Melamed, Gershom Scholem, J. N. Epstein, Moshe Schwabe, and Martin Buber appear as possible guest lecturers and visiting professors at JTS, with Abraham Joshua Heschel lecturing at the Hebrew University on behalf of the Seminary. Some, but not all, of Lieberman's groundwork in this area did come to fruition.

A few years later, Lieberman took upon himself another faculty procurement assignment in Jerusalem. He urged Finkelstein to extend an offer to teach at JTS to Abramson, and he informed him, regretfully, that Urbach had no interest in coming to the United States. After Lieberman had met with him, another potential prospect, Abraham Shalit, immediately was offered a position by the Hebrew University.[137] However, history testifies to

Lieberman's remarkable success in faculty recruitment. He brought to JTS three renowned talmudists, Haim Zalman Dimitrovsky, Eliezer Shimshon Rosenthal, and Shraga Abramson, thereby helping to establish the Seminary as arguably the foremost institution for talmudic research in the world.[138]

The Finkelstein-Lieberman correspondence reflects Finkelstein's sharing with Lieberman some of his most intimate thoughts and programs for the future of JTS and the Conservative movement. For example, on August 9, 1946, Finkelstein wrote to Lieberman from Los Angeles, concerning his plans for the establishment of an institution of Jewish learning there (later to be known as the University of Judaism), and emphasized how eager he was to consult with Lieberman on the matter. It is quite amusing to read Finkelstein's impressions of Los Angeles Jewry at that time. He declared that they were so estranged from traditional Judaism that the establishment of an institution of traditional Jewish study there would constitute a greater achievement than was the establishment of JTS in New York City.

A year later, while visiting Los Angeles, Finkelstein again shared his perceptions with Lieberman in a letter that affords us a glimpse of both the personal and professional intimacy of his relationship with Lieberman:

> I thank you from the bottom of my heart for your friendship and the kindnesses you have bestowed upon my family and myself. . . . I have thought a great deal about the matters we have dealt with these past months, and my hope is, that with God's help, the two of us will succeed in solving the serious problems of our institution in spite of all the difficulties and stumbling blocks. In the final analysis, nothing stands in the way of human resolve, especially as regards matters such as these pertaining to the survival of our religion and our Torah.[139]

Finkelstein consulted with Lieberman on several occasions regarding what was possibly the uppermost project in his mind: the study and the implementation of the ethical values of the Talmud, that is, how to engage in a systematic study of talmudic ethics and make available these insights to the public, and how to deal with contemporary moral issues in such a way that the decision-making processes are exemplified for others to follow.

In a personally typed letter, Finkelstein informed Lieberman that JTS received funding for this project from the trustees of the Jacob R. Schiff Fund, and that he had available the services of such capable scholars as Shraga Abramson and Haim Zalman Dimitrovsky. However, declared Finkelstein, "the whole project will fail if you have no part in it whatever. First of all, you can bring to it a combination of learning and maturity of judgment not otherwise available; secondly, I think that you have been doing this work in your own way so long, that it comes very natural to you (as in the invention of the new Ketuba)."[140]

Lieberman may well have been Finkelstein's central resource in the development of his cherished project: the Herbert Lehman Institute of Ethics, which included a special program for JTS students who concentrated on the study of rabbinics.

According to Seminary insiders, it was common practice for Finkelstein to consult beforehand with Lieberman on all matters of importance that were to be discussed at JTS faculty meetings, and most Seminary policy matters were determined by private Finkelstein-Lieberman conferences prior to public meetings.[141] For example, during the period of student protests in the late 1960s at Columbia University, JTS felt obliged to likewise institute changes in its curriculum and class hours. The strategy employed in gaining the endorsement of the Seminary faculty was simply to mention that the new proposals had the approval of Lieberman.[142]

Lieberman also played a powerful role vis-à-vis the JTS lay board of directors. In a congratulatory letter (May 22, 1958) sent to Lieberman on the occasion of his sixtieth birthday, Alan M. Stroock, chairman of the board of JTS, referred to "the personal relationships that have been developed between you and the members of the Board." Indeed, such prominent board members as David Sarnoff and Alan Stroock almost invariably endorsed any of Lieberman's proposals. In the words of a Seminary administrator, "The lay board of JTS had enormous respect for Lieberman. Without his approval, nothing would happen."[143]

The Personal–Familial Relationship. An interesting critique has been leveled against the painting of Lieberman and Finkelstein that hangs in the

JTS library, entitled *Portrait of a Friendship*. The two men are portrayed looking away from each other in different directions. W. Kahn, who painted it in 1966, has been accused of failing to correctly portray the deep intimacy that characterized their relationship.[144]

Theirs was an intimacy predating Lieberman's actual arrival at the Seminary. For example, the tone of their correspondence during the late 1930s, while Lieberman was in Jerusalem, displays far more warmth and affection than does the Lieberman-Ginzberg correspondence of the same period. They address each other with the salutation "To my friend and beloved one," and conclude with expressions such as "With complete friendship and love" or "With total love and deep affection."[145]

Their United States correspondence of later years likewise reflects considerable warmth, notwithstanding the stilted formality of their "Dear Professor Finkelstein" and "Dear Professor Lieberman" salutations. For example, in a letter of May 26, 1970, Finkelstein, deeply regretting that Lieberman would not be spending Shavuot with him that year, wrote, "I will feel your absence from here keenly. I do not have to tell you what you know so well, how much you have helped me in every way during the years of our association at the Seminary. . . . [M]y debt to you is enormous." A year later (May 24, 1971), under similar circumstances, Finkelstein wrote to Lieberman with unabashed affection:

> I will miss you, particularly on the second night of Shavuot, for your visit on your birthday is always an occasion of immense delight to me. It is a day when all of us ought to be filled with gratitude for you have rendered and are rendering immense service not only to the Jewish community as a whole and to Jewish scholarship in an orphaned generation, but you have been a source of happiness and strength to all my children and to me, and, I am sure, to many others in all the years we have had the pleasure of knowing you. . . .
>
> Let us put it simply, any time I feel down in the mouth because I happen to live in these somewhat dismal times, I find comfort in the fact that I live in the same generation that you do.

In a letter to Lieberman from London (August 1, 1967), Finkelstein stated, "Your friendship, I need not tell you again because you know it so well, is one of the great joys of my life and has brightened my years in many ways." Theirs would seem to have been a constant friendship, except possibly for a brief period of "coolness" during which Lieberman was considering leaving JTS for Harvard University—an offer that some claim Lieberman declined because of his devotion to Finkelstein.[146]

Even their exchange of gifts had a unique personal quality. When Lieberman sent Finkelstein a pair of tefillin from Israel, Finkelstein responded appreciatively. Finkelstein declared that he now prayed with greater devotion than ever, thanks to Lieberman's tefillin.[147] On another occasion, we find Lieberman warmly thanking Finkelstein for presenting him with a new tallit after his own mysteriously disappeared from the Seminary synagogue.[148]

The Lieberman-Finkelstein correspondence also testified to a deep friendship between the Liebermans and Finkelstein's three children. As Finkelstein declared in a letter to the Liebermans on January 4, 1951, "As you know, all my children have a deep and abiding affection for both of you." This affection was no doubt the outgrowth of frequent visits on the part of Finkelstein's children to the Lieberman vacation homes during the years that they were in Finkelstein's care following his separation from his wife. In noting "how Lieberman was always a part of our family life," Ezra Finkelstein points to the simple fact that "Lieberman had a wife and no children while my father had children and no wife."[149] Finkelstein's indebtedness to the Liebermans was a constant refrain in his correspondence with them, and he credited them with contributing greatly to his children's spiritual and educational growth:

> Muni [Emunah, Finkelstein's daughter] has come back more enthusiastic than I have ever known her to be for a number of years, in fact, I think more enthusiastic than I have ever seen her in her life. We took several walks and she could repeat by heart large pieces of Torah which she learned, and this gave her a great deal of pleasure, as well as me.

> Muni's staying with you this year did her even more good than in the preceding years. The friendship you and Mrs. Lieberman show her stirs me very greatly as you know, and puts me under the greatest debt of gratitude to you.[150]

Lieberman supplied enthusiastic corroboration: "Muni came with the desire to learn Talmud, which she did every day and again surprises us with her grasp of the subject matter and keen understanding of the rabbinic mind. . . . It goes without saying that we enjoy the company of Muni very much. She joined Mrs. Lieberman in her daily lesson of mishnayot and it seems that she too enjoys the country here."[151] Finkelstein also thanked the Liebermans for their hospitality toward his daughter Hadassah, commenting that she benefited not only physically but spiritually from her stay with them: "This morning when I came into her room, I found there an open Bible beside her which she had read late last night when she came in."[152]

Regarding his son, Finkelstein stated to the Liebermans, "Your influence on [Ezra], as on my other children, is enormous and is almost tangible."[153] Indeed, it was Lieberman who, at Finkelstein's suggestion, proposed to Ezra that he enroll at JTS. Finkelstein correctly surmised that while his son would have rejected such a suggestion from his own father, he would give it serious consideration if it came from Lieberman.[154]

One has the impression that the Finkelstein children enjoyed their stays with the Liebermans much as grandchildren delight in the company of loving grandparents, who are usually more permissive and accepting of them than their own parents. On occasion, Finkelstein seemed to admit as much to Judith: "[T]hank you for your great kindness to Ezra, and through him to me, while I was away. My Sabbath would have been an extremely trying one if I did not know that Ezra was under such blessed influence as that of you and Professor Lieberman. I think that under the circumstances he even enjoyed my absence very much."[155] Judith Lieberman occasionally functioned as an advocate for Finkelstein's children, taking their part against their father. For example, in a letter to Finkelstein, she wrote: "I am hurrying to write to you because of some remarks you made concerning Ezra. We like Ezra—and all your children—as they are."[156] It is interesting to find

Lieberman urging Finkelstein, in Judith's name, not to be so stringent in forbidding his children from swimming during the first eight days of the month of Av, since the summer heat was so intense. He urged Finkelstein to permit them to arrive earlier at Lieberman's country home so that they might enjoy a lengthier refreshing stay.[157]

Not surprisingly, Lieberman's warm relationship with Finkelstein's children extended to Finkelstein's grandchildren in ensuing years. Thus Lieberman wrote to Finkelstein on April 18, 1963: "It was worthwhile coming to Israel only to be *sandek* at Muni's [Emunah Katzenstein's] first son's *brit*." We also find Finkelstein thanking Lieberman in a letter of October 15, 1969, for the "stirring words" he spoke at the bar mitzvah of Ernie Davis (Hadassah's son), adding, "I am sure it will turn out that you have deeply influenced his life, as well as that of so many others."

There is no question that Lieberman, like Finkelstein, derived great practical benefit from the special relationship between the two men. Although Finkelstein credits Louis Ginzberg with "having brought Lieberman to the Seminary," the case could probably be made for Finkelstein himself having played a significant role in its facilitation. Finkelstein may have given Ginzberg all the credit, but as JTS provost and assistant to President Cyrus Adler, Finkelstein may have had the final (if not the initial) word on the matter.

For example, in a letter of October 4, 1938, while Lieberman was still in Palestine, two years prior to procuring his post at JTS, Finkelstein suggested that he send President Adler several volumes of his works, so that he would "become acquainted with you through your books, and who can tell what may emerge from this?" Lieberman expressed his concern to Finkelstein that two years had elapsed since the publication of his *Hayerushalmi Kifshuto,* so his sending these books to Adler at this late date might be negatively construed as "dust [i.e., a semblance] of flattery."[158]

During his four decades at the Seminary, Lieberman was the privileged recipient of preferential treatment at Finkelstein's hands. Finkelstein zealously protected Lieberman's privacy and precious study hours. Telephone calls to the Seminary switchboard were not to be transferred to him until after the receptionist had screened them. He was rarely called upon to appear at ceremonial functions or to deliver public lectures. Lieberman thoroughly appreciated these considerations; witness his note to Finkelstein following a rare speaking engagement on his part: "I want to thank you . . . for what you have done all the time for me, and, of course, forgive you for the torture of the luncheon, for I realize that there is no sacrifice without a victim."[159] Presumably, Lieberman rarely played the role of victim at Seminary gatherings.

Instructive is the letter of December 1, 1959, sent to Lieberman from Finkelstein, in which Lieberman was informed that he was to become rector of JTS. As noted earlier, his responsibilities sounded formidable: "to supervise all faculty appointments, in the Teachers Institute as the Rabbinical school, helping in the recruitment . . . guiding the general religious policy of the institution." However, Finkelstein also mentions that Lieberman would have "the authority to veto any proposal" and added:

> It seems obvious to me that with your increasing preoccupation with the *Tosefta Kifshutah* (which certainly deserves every minute you can give it, and will turn out to be probably the most significant single accomplishment of the Seminary), you ought not be expected to carry out the functions of a Dean, and that I should take these over again. That would enable me to handle the students directly, as part of my office, without any questions in their mind as to whether I am interfering or not. It will also enable me to work out the Faculty seminar, which I think is absolutely vital to our survival, and from which as Rector you could justly absent yourself. I would of course also go back to running the Faculty meetings. In fact, I will be doing for you what you did for me, when you agreed to take over the Deanship.

In other words, Lieberman would be endowed with full administrative powers, without the commensurate administrative responsibilities.

In a remarkably creative manifestation of public relations, Finkelstein sought to publicize and honor Lieberman's newly published *Tosefta Kifshutah,* elevating it from the domain of relative scholarly obscurity to one of global significance. We shall cite a letter sent by Finkelstein to Edward B. Lawson, the American ambassador to Israel:

Dear Mr. Ambassador:

I am writing on behalf of the Faculty and Board of Directors of this Seminary to request your assistance in the following matter.

We are going to celebrate early in August a most important event in the history of American Judaism and indeed, in the history of world Judaism. This event will be the publication in a definitive edition of a great work of talmudic scholarship, perhaps one of the foremost of such works produced in the last century.

The book involved is called "The Tosefta." This is second to the Mishnah, the foremost and most ancient code of rabbinic law. In some respects it is even more interesting than the Mishnah because it includes informal arguments of the ancient Rabbis, which led to the formulation of the norms contained in the Mishnah. Until now there has been no edition of this work that included all the valuable information relating even to its text. Therefore, those of us who studied it and quoted it could never be quite sure that what we were quoting were words of the ancient Rabbis and not mistakes of the early printers. Because of this uncertainty, there has been immense confusion in the interpretations of this great work.

Professor Saul Lieberman, who is Professor of Talmud at the Seminary and one of the most learned men in the world, has now undertaken to prepare a scientific edition of this work, bringing together the readings of all the manuscripts, some of which go back to the seventh century, and even the quotations of this work in the ancient Hebrew literature of scholars who had access to manuscripts no longer available. He is supplementing this edition with a remarkable commentary of his own, placing the work in the context of the world cultures, out of which it emerged and bringing to bear upon it not only the learning of the Rabbis, but also such works as those of Pliny, the famous scientist of the second century, and similar works. The first three volumes of this great work will appear in August and they will be the first of a series, which I believe will run to no less than eighteen volumes.

It is difficult to indicate to the world at large the delight of a student of the Talmud in the appearance of so magnificent a study of a code which, because of its intricate difficulty, has been neglected by earlier scholars and which we are now privileged to produce in this fine volume at the Seminary.

I am writing to you now because it has occurred to us that this work being a product of the scholarship of ancient Israel, indeed one of its

> main products, the first copy to come off the press should be presented to the President of the State of Israel at an appropriate ceremony.
>
> The plans seem to my colleagues and myself to have the beginnings of a Spiritual Four Point program, by which America may contribute to older civilizations new insights into their own cultural products.
>
> I am writing to ask whether you will be willing to represent the Seminary as the Ambassador of our country in making this presentation to Doctor Ben-Zvi at a time satisfactory to both you and him. We would like this to happen sometime before September 11, 1955, when we are holding a convocation here marking the opening of our next academic year and when "The Tosefta," in its new edition and with a new commentary will be presented to the American Public.[160]

It is not surprising that on several occasions, Lieberman expressed his gratitude in letters to Finkelstein for favoring him in so many ways, that is, "one link more to the long chain of kindness you have bestowed upon me ever since I have known you" (March 7, 1941); "I want to thank you for your latest efforts on my behalf. I well know that it is only a small link in a long chain of kindness you have all the time shown to me" (May 31, 1944).

The kindness shown to Lieberman by Finkelstein was of a financial nature as well; witness the fact that Finkelstein persuaded the Seminary's board of directors to purchase a luxurious apartment in Jerusalem for Lieberman's use.[161] As the beneficiary of the many links in this "chain of kindness," Lieberman, in turn, involved himself in activities and enterprises at Finkelstein's seminary far beyond the purview of teaching Talmud.

JTS Participation

Education. Lieberman's academic title upon coming to JTS was a somewhat awkward one. He was designated as the Professor of Palestinian Literature and Institutions, a compromise title obviously designed to differentiate his post from that of Louis Ginzberg, the Talmud professor of JTS. Finkelstein's original proposal to Ginzberg was to give Lieberman the title of Visiting Professor in Rabbinics, but, added Finkelstein in a letter of August 9, 1940, "If you think this would not do, we might describe him more accurately as 'Visiting Professor in Early Rabbinic Literature.' I shall be guided by your opinion in the matter."

Ginzberg replied to Finkelstein on August 13, 1940, that he was pleased that Lieberman had made arrangements to come to the Seminary (clearly, the direct negotiations were conducted between Finkelstein and Lieberman), and added: "As to the title to be given to him, I doubt whether 'Rabbinics' is descriptive enough. What would you say to 'Palestinian Literature and Institutions,' or do you think it too long?" Actually, it was Eli Ginzberg who conceived of that title in order to draw a demarcation between his father's and Lieberman's academic positions.[162]

On June 12, 1941, less than a year after his arrival, Lieberman was appointed a permanent member of the JTS faculty. On June 13, he wrote to Finkelstein in grateful response:

> It goes without saying that I consider it to be a great privilege to be able to spread the Thora in this great House of Learning under the present favorable circumstances, particularly when the head of the school happens to be a great scholar in the same branch of learning to which I have devoted my life.

Saul Lieberman was to spend forty-three years at JTS, from 1940 to 1983, except for one year in the late 1970s, when he taught at the Institute for Advanced Jewish Studies at the Hebrew University in Jerusalem.

At the time of Lieberman's arrival in the United States, the United States in general and the Jewish Theological Seminary in particular were already established as the world center for Judaic studies. At the turn of the century, Solomon Schechter, Louis Ginzberg, and Alexander Marx had emigrated to America, followed several decades later by Shalom Spiegel and Salo Baron; then a third wave of scholars, including Lieberman, arrived.

Lieberman's duties called for him to teach all senior students at JTS as well as those non-seniors who were well prepared for textual study. He taught six talmudic tractates in rotation: *Avodah Zarah, Sanhedrin, Ketubot, Gittin, Bava Metzia,* and *Nedarim,* and he occasionally gave seminars on the Palestinian Talmud and Tosefta for advanced students. He also taught a Codes course in Hebrew in the 1940s. Lieberman's teaching style was straightforward, emphasizing the simple comprehension and clarification of the text with the commentaries of Rashi and some Tosafot, along with selected rishonim (early legal authorities) such as the Tosefot Rid. Lieberman would frequently elucidate texts by means of his own studies of the realia of the Greco-Roman world and would occasionally call attention to the observations of critical scholars such as Pines and Kraus. Only rarely did he focus on textual variants and emendations. He consistently followed the traditional practice of consecutive, page-by-page study, rather than presenting materials thematically and conceptually.

Administration and Outreach. Lieberman perceived his primary function at JTS as that of educator, and he stressed that he was not among the leaders of the Conservative movement. He said his task was to teach Torah to the children of Israel. He went on to say that he didn't understand very much about politics, and therefore didn't involve himself in it.[163] However, as has been noted, no doubt because of his close association with Finkelstein, Lieberman involved himself in matters quite independent of his weekly teaching schedule. His involvement in issues pertaining to the Conservative movement was notable in several outreach programs on behalf of JTS toward the United States and Israeli Orthodox leadership.

On December 6, 1963, Lieberman wrote to the Ashkenazi chief rabbi of Israel, Yehudah Unterman, concerning the *get* (writ of divorce) crises (see below, "The *Ketubah* Clause") in the U.S., advocating for the acceptance of Conservative *gittin* in Israel. He stressed the fact that in this area, JTS had given special training to a number of Conservative rabbis, and their competence in the matter was on a par with many of their Orthodox colleagues. Lieberman wryly pointed out that a maverick Orthodox rabbinical group that was also involved in executing writs of divorce had been involved in a recent scandal concerning the kashrut certification granted to a nonkosher kitchen on an Israeli ship. On January 17, 1963, Lieberman wrote also to Israeli minister of religious affairs Zerah Warhaftig his defense of the Conservative movement's standards vis-à-vis executing writs of divorce.

Later, Lieberman unsuccessfully involved himself with Prime Minister Golda Meir and Ashkenazi chief rabbi Shlomo Goren in advocating for the acceptance of conversion ceremonies performed by Conservative rabbis in the United States (Lieberman pointed out that the reliability of a number of Orthodox rabbis in such areas might well be questioned), although he was successful in his efforts to have certain Conservative rabbis certified to perform wedding ceremonies in Israel.[164]

There is no doubt that Lieberman's role as a "defender" of the Conservative movement proved to be exceedingly unpleasant for him at times. For example, the religious Zionist leader R. Yehuda Leib Hakohen Maimon called to Lieberman's attention the rumors that Lieberman had approved the Rabbinical Assembly ruling permitting travel by automobile on the Sabbath in order to attend religious services.[165] Lieberman, like Finkelstein, vigorously disagreed with, and strongly disassociated himself from, a number of rabbinical policies. Yet because he was identified with the Conservative movement, Lieberman found himself linked to these policies, although he would have wished otherwise. Lieberman did, however, choose to play an active role on behalf of the Conservative movement in two areas of pivotal importance vis-à-vis the Orthodox community: the formulation of a clause in the *ketubah* (Jewish marriage contract); and the formation of a joint *beit din* (rabbinic ecclesiastical courts).

The* Ketubah *Clause. On March 25, 1952, Louis Finkelstein addressed a letter to Lieberman, expressing his great concern over certain developments within the Rabbinical Assembly:

> I was able to persuade the Rabbinical Assembly [henceforth, RA] Committee on Law and Standards to agree to a joint conference sponsored by the Faculty of the Seminary and the RA to consider the problem of the agunah and the whole question of a Beth Din. This is our last chance to deal with the problem of Jewish law effectively in this country. If we cannot find someone within our Faculty group, or if we cannot discover someone who will make the application of Jewish Law his life's interest, nothing that I or anyone else can say or do will prevent incompetent people from undertaking this responsibility. . . . The RA will be confirmed in its view that nobody is interested in the subject but itself. This may in fact be true; it may also be true that a number of us see the issue raised by the RA as secondary to other vital matters such as the future orientation of Jews in America and the building up of

> Torah generally. However, the rabbis who are in congregations cannot take this view and will certainly resent it in the future as they have resented it in the past.
>
> I do not know whether you feel that the diversion of the activities of such a scholar as Doctor Abramson from purely talmudic research to the issues of Jewish Law is or is not worth the prevention of the development of a Beth Din of unqualified men. This is the issue which you and I must decide: whether to prevent the emergence of a Beth Din of unqualified men or to find a qualified one, and we do not have much time.[166]

Lieberman responded to Finkelstein's request and directed his attention toward the problem of the *agunah* (lit., "chained one"; a wife who is separated from her husband but cannot obtain a bill of divorce or provide evidence of his death and is thus prevented from remarrying). According to traditional Jewish law, the husband is the active partner in executing the *get*. Thus, a recalcitrant husband may refuse to issue a divorce to his wife or may withhold issuing one until the wife meets his conditions of extortion or blackmail. In seeking to protect the rights of such a woman, characterized as an *agunah,* Lieberman composed a *takkanah* (positive enactment) in the form of a special clause to be inserted into the text of the *ketubah*. The clause stipulated that, in the event of marital difficulties, the couple would recognize the authority of the *beit din* of the Rabbinical Assembly or the Jewish Theological Seminary of America to "counsel them in the light of Jewish tradition" and to "summon either party at the request of the other." Furthermore, the *beit din* was authorized to impose such terms of compensation as it saw fit, in the event that the summons were ignored. The motion to accept the *takkanah* was put to a vote and carried unanimously.[167]

In such a manner, Lieberman sought to confront the halakhic impediment to judicially compel a party to give or to receive a *get*. The party would be merely submitting to the jurisdiction of a freely chosen rabbinic tribunal. Thus, any sanctions imposed in order to force a spouse to appear before the *beit din* would not, technically speaking, constitute a true act of "compulsion," and so the *get* would not be invalidated.

The test of the legal enforceability of Lieberman's prenuptial agreement clause came in the case of *Avitzur v. Avitzur.* Boaz and Susan Avitzur married in a religious ceremony employing the Lieberman *ketubah.* When their marriage later ended in a civil divorce, Susan sought to compel Boaz to appear before a rabbinic tribunal and initiate the granting of a *get.* Boaz refused, arguing that the "enforcement of such an agreement constitutes an impermissible and excessive entanglement in religion and violated his own free exercise rights."[168] The trial court denied the motion, but the appellate division upheld it. However, the court of appeals reversed the appellate division in ruling that the Lieberman clause was indeed enforceable. In characterizing the Lieberman clause as closely analogous to a typical arbitration agreement, the court concluded that the religious context in which the *ketubah* was executed should not deprive it of the same dignity and deference accorded to any other civil contract, as long as its enforcement violated neither the law nor public policy of the state. While the establishment clause precluded judicial resolution of questions pertaining to religious law, this type of clause may be enforced "solely upon the application of neutral principles of contract law" without need to be entangled in doctrinal or liturgical questions.[169]

It is well beyond the scope of our study to trace subsequent developments regarding the legal enforceability of the Lieberman clause; however, it is important for our purposes to focus on the reaction of the Orthodox rabbinate to Lieberman's proposal. As expected, there was immediate and intense opposition from the Orthodox leadership. The Rabbinical Alliance convened a press conference on December 3, 1954, to condemn the *ketubah* and to prohibit any Orthodox rabbi from participating in a marriage ceremony in which it would be employed. What were the reasons for this negative response?

First, the Orthodox leadership deemed the RA *beit din* to be an invalid court. Second, it perceived the clause's stipulation of an indeterminate monetary penalty to be a violation of the legal principle of *asmakhta* (lit., "surety," the act of taking upon oneself an obligation that one does not expect to have to fulfill). There is evidence, however, that the latter issue was resolvable. Rabbi J. B. Soloveitchik of Rabbi Isaac Elhanan Theological Seminary purportedly worked out a solution with Lieberman whereby the financial stipulation would not be so indefinite;[170] furthermore, it was reported that the Lieberman clause was examined by the Ashkenazi chief rabbi of Israel, Isaac Herzog, and deemed to be proper.[171] It was the former issue of "recognition," however, that was of paramount significance. Recognition of the RA *beit din* on the part of Orthodox rabbis would have meant extending some degree of *de jure* recognition to the RA and to the Conservative movement. This was a step that the Orthodox rabbinate was unwilling to take, and it had a negative impact not only on Lieberman's *ketubah takkanah* but on the broader issue of the establishment of a joint court of law, consisting of Orthodox and Conservative rabbis. Lieberman was to play the pivotal role here, too, on behalf of JTS.

***The Joint* Beit Din.** It is generally agreed that the impetus for holding talks on the formation of a joint *beit din* was the Lieberman *ketubah* clause.[172] Indeed, following the approval of the Lieberman clause, the RA Steering Committee was instructed "to enter into negotiations with representatives of other organized Jewish religious bodies (Orthodox and Reform) in our community, to persuade them to cooperate with the Joint Law Conference in setting up a *beit din*."[173] However, it was reported at the November 28, 1953, meeting of the Steering Committee that Rabbi Abrams, head of the Orthodox Rabbinical Council of America (RC), "felt that cooperation between the RA and the RC on matters of Jewish law was well nigh impossible."[174] Shortly thereafter, the RA Joint Law Conference proceeded with the creation of a *beit din* of its own, although invitations for cooperation continued to be extended to both the Orthodox RC and the Reform Central Conference of American Rabbis.

It appears that such invitations elicited serious interest on the part of the RC. Rabbi Abraham Kelman, an Orthodox rabbi who was the brother of Rabbi Wolfe Kelman, executive vice president of the RA, was the conduit for early negotiations between the two groups. Indeed, plans for the joint *beit din* had the approval of Soloveitchik ("[H]e is quite impressed with the plan and ready to support it") and the less enthusiastic endorsement of Rabbi Aaron Kotler, titular head of the "Yeshiva world."[175] Needless to say, both Finkelstein and Lieberman wanted the plan to become a reality, and

Lieberman met with Soloveitchik in June 1955 for the first in a series of several conferences that were to take place between the two scholars.

As a result of their meetings, as well as sessions involving the rabbinic leadership of the RC and the RA, an ambitious plan of action emerged, providing for the establishment of a national *beit din* that would be recognized as the official *beit din* of both the RC and the RA. Both rabbinical groups would delegate to the *beit din* exclusive authority to rule on all matters of Jewish family law, and neither group would make any decision with regard to family law that was not approved by the *beit din*. The *beit din* members would be selected by Lieberman and Soloveitchik; the judges would then provide for their successors in self-perpetuation. As for the controversial Lieberman *ketubah,* Lieberman and Soloveitchik would revise it in such a manner that it would be acceptable to all parties. On the day of the establishment of the *beit din,* each rabbinic group would convene a national convention and simultaneously extend recognition to the *beit din* as its exclusive authority in matters of Jewish law.[176]

This joint proposal never came to fruition. The halakhic commission of the RC, on January 18, 1956, voted 11–6 against the establishment of such a national *beit din*.[177] Why this rejection on the part of the Orthodox body? One of the official reasons given was the reluctance of the RA to commit itself to discipline any of its members who would act in a manner that the *beit din* would deem objectionable. Indeed, Lieberman had pleaded with Soloveitchik not to insist on this point, having argued that once the agreement was in effect, eventually it would be possible for the RA to implement such discipline within its ranks.[178] Lieberman was depicted to have spontaneously rejected such an imposition of sanctions on the grounds that "Conservative Jews do not like inquisitions."[179] Here, as in the case of the Lieberman *ketubah,* "recognition" was probably the crucial factor. Establishing a joint *beit din* would bestow recognition upon the Conservative movement, which the Orthodox leadership was unwilling to do. Moreover, wide publicity was given precisely at this time to the ban, pronounced by a prominent group of heads of yeshivot, against the participation of the RC and its lay affiliate, the Union of Orthodox Jewish Congregations of America, in any federation with non-Orthodox rabbinic or lay groups.[180] Soloveitchik's refusal to sign this ban won him much criticism and isolation from some of his Orthodox colleagues. The establishment of a joint *beit din* would surely accentuate the problems he faced.

A prominent Orthodox rabbi, Emanuel Rackman, summarized the cause of failure: "Politics, rather than faith and goodwill, prevailed."[181] Indeed, the reality was "the political fact that a modicum of *de jure* recognition would be given to a non-Orthodox group of Rabbis."[182] This was something that the Orthodox establishment could not bring itself to do, the presence of Saul Lieberman within the Conservative camp notwithstanding.

Frequently, as was noted earlier, Lieberman emphasized that his role at JTS was that of an educator, not a spokesperson for the Conservative movement. Though at times, his association with the Conservative movement embarrassed him, he nevertheless praised the movement and the people whom it comprised.[183] For example, he proudly pointed out that several of his students were excellent talmudists—equal, if not superior, to many students in the Orthodox yeshivot.[184] In responding to Alexander Marx's tribute to him,[185] Lieberman focused on a moving moment he experienced at JTS:

> I should like to conclude with a personal incident that recently happened at the Jewish Theological Seminary. About ten days ago, on a Saturday night, I was walking to the Seminary. It was a lovely night. People were flocking to the movies and theaters. At the Seminary, I found many lights shining from the dormitory windows. I came to the fifth floor, and there was not a living soul there. You know, there are offices on the fifth floor. I was seated in my study working, and I knew that at that time I would not disturb anybody if I studied in a loud voice. Late, at about midnight, when I stopped to ponder over a passage which I did not understand, I could hear the voice of someone studying in the dormitory. It was such a sweet voice that I immediately realized that it was not that of a student preparing for his examinations. It was something different. It was a real "voice of Torah." I could not refrain from going down to one of the floors of the dormitory and listening. The voice attracted me, and I must have stood there for a long time, because my cigar had already begun to burn my fingers. I stood there meditating until the voice stopped. I thought

> that what happened to me happened to him. He probably doesn't understand something, and so he too has stopped. I knocked on the door of the student, and he was startled—as a matter of fact, frightened.
>
> "Professor," he said, "I have probably disturbed you by studying in a loud voice."
>
> "No," I said, "you didn't disturb me. I merely thought that you came across a difficult passage and that I might help you."
>
> "No," he said, "I am simply tired."
>
> Finally the student observed, "I am sorry, but from now on you'll know when I am not studying."
>
> I must tell you that this kind of study, this voice of Torah that had the genuine longing of our ancestors for the Torah, brought back to me the voice of the yeshivot of the old country. It was gratifying to see that this boy was American-born, a son of one of our graduates. I could not help but reflect that as long as this goes on at the Seminary, as long as these mysterious ties between the ivory tower of the fifth floor and the floors of the dormitory continue, *od lo avdah tikvateinu* [our hope is not yet lost].[186]

It is true that Lieberman was frequently guilty of denigrating Conservative pulpit rabbis and questioning their erudition. However, this is probably best understood within the broader context of the denigration of the career pulpit rabbi of any denomination by the rabbinic academician. There is historical precedent for this negative attitude. In the Middle Ages, the communal rabbi was frequently perceived as being less than an esteemed scholar. In Lieberman's native Lithuania, in particular, the most brilliant scholars were pure talmudists, not students of legal codes. Nonutilitarian study was extolled above all else. As one of Lieberman's classmates from Slobodka, Gedalyahu Alon, recalls:

> Slobodka students used to say: If you see a student devoting himself to the study of *Yoreh De'ah,* or to the chapter of the talmudic tractate *Hullin,* beginning with the words, "These are considered *trefah,*" or to *Eben Ha'ezer,* and he prepares himself for ordination

> from the very start, you can be certain that he is neither gifted nor knowledgeable in Torah.[187]

Eli Ginzberg records a similar observation on Lieberman's part:

> Professor Lieberman informed me that twenty-one was a typical age for a young man in Lithuania or Poland to obtain *semikhah,* while in Hungary, where the study of Codes was the central part of the curriculum, students acquired it at a much younger age—at around sixteen or so. In Lithuania, where the weight of rabbinic study was on the basic texts, not on rules and regulations governing religious observance, a student would not normally master the field of Codes without a special effort. He did so only when he wanted to acquire professional standing. There was little in Codes to attract the serious student.[188]

For Lieberman, true scholarship in rabbinical literature necessitated a broad and deep comprehension of the rabbinic texts. Lieberman would frequently say that it was not enough to be a "concordance scholar." One has to master all the texts by virtue of systematic study. This is a recurrent theme in Lieberman's thought, expressed notably in his emphasis on a yeshiva-style education as an essential requisite for anyone who wanted to pursue the scientific study of rabbinic texts. In Lieberman's words: "Without yeshivot, there cannot be any *Hokhmat Yisrael* worthy of its name.[189] Lieberman stated:

> True Jewish scholarship will be sustained only by students and scholars who, after acquiring their religious knowledge, will also become accomplished in the sciences and scientific method. Without the yeshivot, there will hardly be any Jewish learning. The yeshivot could survive without Jewish learning, but the latter could not go on without diligent students to whom the Torah is an inextricable part of existence. The methods of teaching and study in the yeshivot are necessary for these youngsters; these methods include minute analysis, followed by synthesis. When one, in addition, acquires proficient knowledge of Western mathematical

> concepts and Western logic, he is able to achieve proper perspective. Actually, there is no contradiction between the two methods. Even though the methods used in the yeshivot are not scientific, they nevertheless sharpen the mind and provide a basis for later scientific analysis of texts and problems. It may well be that all this is exaggerated, however. If one should turn to study scientific methods, one will find his previous studies at the yeshiva very helpful. In conclusion: scientific methodology can be acquired in two to three years of study, whereas the Torah has to be studied for at least ten or fifteen years. Scientific methods can be studied in maturity; the Torah has to be studied from tender childhood.[190]

In his November 28, 1943, JTS address, "The Role of Professor Louis Ginzberg in Jewish Scholarship," Lieberman also spoke to this point:

> There is an accepted opinion current, that talmudic students can be divided into two categories: talmudists and talmudic scholars. The representatives of the old school, who engage in the study of rabbinic literature only, without the knowledge of, or interest in, the related fields, are styled talmudists, whereas the students who, acquainted with general culture and equipped with modern methods, apply them to rabbinic literature, are termed talmudic scholars.
>
> This division is not entirely correct. A man cannot be a talmudic scholar without being first a talmudist. Talmudic literature, which consists of the Mishnah and Tosefta, of the Palestinian and the Babylonian talmudim, of halakhic and *haggadic* midrashim, is on the one hand homogeneous, and on the other hand diversified. Although all of them are permeated with the same general rabbinic spirit, every individual unit has its own peculiarities in principles, style, terminology, and methods of reasoning. Only one who has been fortunate enough to master all those branches separately, and then coordinate them into one entity, only one who has been able to investigate the details of those independent parties, and thus grasp their general principles and spirit, only

> such a one is in a position to know the rabbinic truth, and rightly deserving of the names of talmudist *and* talmudic scholar. . . .
>
> Only after he has transferred himself into the world of the ancient Rabbis and has penetrated into their spirit and mind, only then can he begin to work with modern comparative methods.

Lieberman insisted on studying the entire Palestinian Talmud before he would commence writing about it; similarly, he expected his students to comprehensively master texts before dabbling in scholarship, as well as to know the original languages. Likewise, Salo Baron did not permit any of his students to compromise in their dissertations, and he insisted on their knowing all the applicable languages in the original.[191] Lieberman's perception of the average Conservative pulpit rabbi was refracted through the lenses of academic purism and pure Lithuanian Talmudism, and so could not help but be negatively tinged. He was, however, not alone in this perception. Decades earlier, Solomon Schechter was criticized because he used to "wither the souls of the students with his ill-timed jests about rabbis and their calling. It was he who made it fashionable for all scholars and near scholars in and about the Seminary to turn up their noses at the term 'rabbi.'"[192] Whether or not Schechter deserves "credit" for this, the fact is that many Seminary faculty members shared his attitude: Ginzberg, Marx, Friedlander, and even the "activist" Abraham Joshua Heschel.[193] Their perception of the pulpit rabbi was probably akin to a theoretical physicist's perception of an engineer. Several generations of Seminary students had been exposed to such denigration. In the words of a 1932 JTS graduate, "Our own leaders at times laugh at us, look at us as ignoramuses, as *am aratzim,* that we have been graduated as social workers and not as rabbis for humanity."[194] Lieberman was surely guilty of this offense, and in acerbic tones, but that is hardly surprising. He was not alone, and he was following established precedent. More significant were the occasions on which he spoke with obvious pride of the achievements of the Conservative pulpit rabbi standing in the breach and defending and promoting Jewish tradition for an alienated population. For the ability to make the sacred texts relevant to others may constitute a greater achievement than mastering them for oneself.

Orthodox Relationships

Commendations and Condemnations. During his early years in Lithuania, and later in Palestine, Saul Lieberman was accepted and respected in the highest Orthodox circles, despite his several forays to universities to partake of the forbidden fruit of secular studies.

His distinguished lineage, his studies at prominent yeshivot, and his impressive erudition authenticated him, although his stay at Slobodka—in its original locale in Kovne and later in Minsk—was not without some controversy. R. Natan Zevi Finkel, the Alter of Slobodka, forbade a then-fellow student, Yaakov Ruderman, to continue sharing a room with Lieberman, putting him up instead in his own home for several months. This was done presumably out of fear that Lieberman would be a bad influence upon him because of his interest in secular studies.[195] According to one report, Lieberman tried to persuade Ruderman to accompany him to the cinema, which at the time was featuring *The Great Train Robbery*. Indeed, R. Ruderman purportedly avoided any contact with Lieberman during all his years in the United States.[196] Nevertheless, Lieberman was esteemed in prestigious Orthodox circles. He was "chosen" by R. Eliezer Rabinowitz of Minsk to be his son-in-law, upon the recommendation of the Slobodka *rosh yeshiva*.[197] In Palestine in the mid-1930s, Lieberman met daily with Chief Rabbi Abraham Hakohen Kook for a one-hour (6–7 P.M.) study session. They learned together the text of the *Arba'a Turim* (R. Jacob B. Asher's fourteenth-century code of law) along with the commentary of the *Beit Yosef* by R. Joseph Karo. By mutual agreement, both parties would attend these sessions without benefit of any preparation.[198] They adhered so faithfully to their study schedule that once, when Lieberman was ill, R. Kook summoned a taxi to bring him to the session. On another occasion, on Purim day, Lieberman interrupted R. Kook's Purim feast by insisting that they go into seclusion to study and not miss a single day of learning together.[199] The intimacy of their relationship is evident from the inscription penned by R. Kook in a book that he presented to Lieberman, "given in true love to my heart's chosen one, the Gaon, Rabbi Saul Lieberman";[200] and by the publication of Lieberman's *Tosefet Rishonim,* part 1, *Zera'im* and *Mo'ed,* in the memorial volume *Azkarah,* a collection of scholarly Torah essays published as a testament to R. Kook.[201]

Lieberman once related to Rabbi Moshe Zevi Neriah an incident involving R. Kook that transpired while Lieberman was living in a small apartment in Jerusalem adjacent to the apartment of the younger brother of the head of the Gur hasidic dynasty. Rabbi Kook was invited to attend a *sheva berakhot* celebration at the rebbe's brother's apartment; however, in the corridor, when he noticed Lieberman sitting and learning in his room, R. Kook promptly detoured to engage Lieberman in a spirited discussion pertaining to his studies. Much to the surprise of the rebbe's entourage, Kook chose to remain with Lieberman for a considerable length of time, not departing until several Gur Hasidim came and personally escorted him to the proper apartment. Lieberman was certain that Kook had done this on purpose, to show his hosts that respect should be tendered to a Torah scholar, even a clean-shaven one "who does not look anything like a Gur Hasid."[202] Lieberman frequently associated with the esteemed R. Isser Zalman Meltzer[203] and was a regular guest on Friday evenings in the home of Chief Rabbi Isaac Halevi Herzog, whose daughter-in-law Penina was related to Judith Lieberman.[204] Indeed, Chaim Herzog claimed that Lieberman was his parents' "closest friend,"[205] and when Lieberman's book on Maimonides was published, Chief Rabbi Herzog cabled Lieberman from Jerusalem to request that a copy be airmailed to him immediately.[206] Lieberman was a frequent guest in Sephardi chief rabbi Yitzhak Nissin's home, where at a Passover seder the chief rabbi deferred to Lieberman concerning a question of kashrut, declaring, "If you will eat it, I will eat it."[207] He also enjoyed a close personal relationship with another Sephardi chief rabbi, Ovadiah Yosef, who was known to visit Lieberman frequently at JTS on his trips to New York, although on condition of anonymity.[208] Lieberman enjoyed the respect of R. Yosef Shalom Eliashiv, the *av beit din* of Jerusalem.[209] Even in the Me'ah She'arim district of Jerusalem, Lieberman was respectfully addressed as "Reb Shaul."[210] Little correspondence is extant between Lieberman and other rabbinic scholars (apart from Finkelstein and Ginzberg) during the period prior to his coming to the United States, but Professor Immanuel Loew's letter to Lieberman, written in 1938 (reproduced in appendix V to this volume), extolling him and his work, is probably representative of the veneration in which he was held by rabbinic colleagues and scholars.

However, when Lieberman elected to affiliate himself with JTS, a schism of sorts developed in the Orthodox world toward him. On the one hand, many distinguished Orthodox rabbis continued to relate to him warmly and respectfully, as is attested to in the correspondence he received from Chief Rabbis Yitzhak Nissin, Yehudah Unterman, and Shlomo Goren, as well as Rabbis Chaim Walkin, Raphael Kook, Yehoshua Hutner, Naftali Zevi Yehuda Riff, Abraham Aaron Price, Chaim Zimmerman, Samuel Belkin,[211] Joseph Lookstein,[212] Emanuel Rackman,[213] and Yehiel Yaakov Weinberg, former rector of the Berlin Orthodox Rabbinical Seminary in Berlin and a fellow alumnus of Lieberman's at Slobodka.[214] R. Yaakov Yisrael Kanievski, the Steipler Gaon, is reputed to have read every word Lieberman wrote. R. Moshe Feinstein urged an Agudat Yisrael conference to disallow any personal invective against Lieberman for his *ketubah* clause: "He is such a scholar, let him be."[215] Pinhas Hirschprung, chief rabbi of Montreal, who used the term "gaon" most sparingly, described Lieberman as a "true gaon" and kept his copy of Lieberman's *Tosefta Kifshutah* prominently displayed on an open shelf.[216] Rabbi J. B. Soloveitchik had "the utmost respect for Dr. Lieberman and shared a personal and scholarly relationship with him," although their interests and emphases in scholarship were quite different.[217] Yitzhak Raphael, chairman of Mosad Harav Kook and Yad Harav Maimon, stated, "I profess the greatest respect, veneration, and love toward him." Rabbi Yehuda Leib Hakohen Maimon, religious Zionist leader and minister of religion of the State of Israel, wrote to him on December 6, 1959, with great affection and admiration, and, according to Raphael, "Whenever Rabbi Maimon happened to arrive in New York, his first telephone call, sometimes even from the airport, was to Professor Lieberman to ask about his welfare and the well-being of his wife, Judith, and about how his studies were progressing."[218]

The Lubavitcher rebbe, Menachem Mendel Schneerson, held Lieberman in very high regard. Before Haim Zalman Dimitrovsky joined the faculty of JTS in 1951 (at the invitation of Lieberman), he regarded it as a strictly academic institution. Dimitrovsky said:

> I imagined [JTS] was something like a university where people study and do research. When I came to New York, I saw it was not just a scholarly institution, although I was overjoyed with the

> beautiful library, which is unique in the world. I saw that the institution is involved in many other things—theological things, religious things. I had some hesitation if I should stay because the Seminary was Conservative and I am Orthodox.

When Dimitrovsky's student Dov Zlotnick invited him to a *farbrengen* (festive religious gathering) with the rebbe, Dimitrovsky took the opportunity to ask the rebbe whether he should remain at JTS. The rebbe's advice was, "As long as Professor Lieberman is in the Seminary, you can stay there. If you resign, it won't make a good impression. If [Lieberman] decides to leave, then you leave as well."[219]

Lieberman continued to enjoy an intimate relationship with his father-in-law, R. Meir Bar-Ilan, who, in the words of a family member, "had respect for him and was indeed fond of him."[220]

However, bitter antagonism toward Lieberman erupted in certain Orthodox circles when it became known that he had joined the faculty of JTS. R. Jacob Levinson of the Agudas Harabbanim of New York convened an emergency meeting to discuss the issue. R. Meir Bar-Ilan explained to the assembly that his son-in-law was forced to make this move out of dire financial straits, citing the talmudic passage "Alas for the generation of which you are the leader, seeing that you know nothing of the troubles of the scholars, their struggles to support and sustain themselves."[221]

Several years later, an open letter in the Orthodox journal *Hapardes* bitterly attacked Lieberman for aligning himself with JTS, for he was thereby teaching alongside Mordecai Kaplan, the founder of the Reconstructionist movement. The author, whose name was not given, questioned how Lieberman could ever have chosen to associate himself with a deviant, heretical movement such as Conservative Judaism and, in particular, with Kaplan, whose newly published prayer book had been thoroughly denounced in traditional Jewish circles. The letter concluded on a somewhat conciliatory note: "We treasure and honor the sparkling personality of Rabbi Lieberman, his broad knowledge of halakhah, and his great intellectual gifts. It is for this reason that we have come forward with this open letter. We are concerned for his own honor, which is the honor of the Torah."[222]

A subsequent edition of *Hapardes*[223] reported that Lieberman, in response, wrote to R. Simha Ellberg, editor of *Hapardes,* defending his decision to teach at JTS. The letter concluded with the request that it not be published. The editor of *Hapardes* honored Lieberman's request, and the letter was not published until recently.[224] Lieberman, in his typical direct manner, said that he was very hurt by the open letter addressed to him. He made the following points:

1. The issues raised in the letter should not be discussed in public. He took this position because he was concerned that the accusations leveled in the open letter would bring rabbis and Torah scholars into disrepute.[225]
2. In a playful dare, he suggested that if the Agudas Harabbanim considered his teaching at JTS as clearly prohibited, why did they not summon him to a *din torah* (hearing before a tribunal composed of learned rabbis)? Lieberman asked, "Do they suspect that I would refuse to appear before a tribunal of *gedolei torah* [prominent Orthodox Torah scholars]?"
3. He then revealed that before deciding to leave Palestine and take the position at JTS, he sought the opinion of three *gedolei Yerushalayim* (leading scholars of Jerusalem). He would disclose their names only if necessary. Lieberman received a majority decision from a panel of three *gedolei Torah.* The first would not say whether his teaching at JTS was permitted or prohibited. The second said that there was no prohibition that would preclude Lieberman from taking a teaching position at JTS. The third said that Lieberman was the right person to teach at JTS, wished him success, but cautioned that he should not consider his position at JTS permanent. We have not been able to identify the three leading scholars of Jerusalem whom Lieberman consulted in 1940 regarding his offer of a teaching post at JTS. Dov Zlotnick speculates that the three may have been the chief rabbi, Isaac Herzog; the chief rabbi of Jerusalem, Zevi Pesah Frank; and Lieberman's father-in-law, R. Meir Berlin.
4. Lieberman was grateful that no one could tell him what and how to teach. "At JTS, I was given the freedom to teach whatever I wished to teach, and however I wished to teach."
5. JTS was a very important institution whose students were ready to respond to teachers who believe in the sanctity of the Torah. With the addition of another two or three committed teachers, JTS would become an exemplary

institution. Lieberman's invitation to R. Pinhas Hirschprung[226] to join the JTS faculty was part of his effort in this regard. A number of subsequent faculty appointments clearly advanced this objective.

6. JTS officially recognized the authority of the *Shulhan Arukh* (code of Jewish law). As long as that remained the official position of JTS, there was hope.
7. Lieberman's presence at JTS, he believed, had prevented the outbreak of considerable dissension that would have led to *hilul hashem* (desecration of the name of God). His hope was that he would act as a unifier, minimizing the potential for contention between Orthodox and Conservative Jews.

Lieberman believed that the "open letter" to him should not have been published, as he opposed the public discussion of sensitive matters such as his relationship with JTS and the Orthodox perception of the Conservative school. Such discussions inevitably result in argument and controversy, to the detriment of Conservative as well as Orthodox leaders. This is precisely the *hilul hashem* that Lieberman feared. Although a published response to the "open letter" would have been perfectly in order, Lieberman demonstrated his fundamental integrity by specifically asking that his response not be published.

Lieberman's Seminary files contain an unsigned letter that he received, bitterly indicting him for associating himself with the Seminary. It is interesting that Lieberman would have chosen to save such a letter:

> Dear Sir:
>
> For the sake of financial remuneration and glory you have sold yourself to the "other side" (i.e., "the devil"). Do you not know that you are lending prestige to Mordecai Kaplan (may his name be erased) and to the other heretics at the Seminary, as well as to the graduates? The United States has many Rabbinical schools where young men are studying Torah and developing into scholars. Is your presence at the Seminary necessary for the spreading of the Torah? Or is the glamour of being a professor among ignoramuses with a comfortable salary so powerful that even Saul Lieberman is not man enough to withstand it? Do not deceive yourself that you will change the Seminary. You will be influenced by them, and you will be separated from the society of scholars who have not sold themselves to financial gain. "Woe to the wicked and woe to his neighbor." Better be a poor rabbi in a little

synagogue than a professor who produces rabbis who are "sinners and lead others to sin." There is yet time to repent.

Yours truly,

A Friend[227]

The chorus of condemnation of Saul Lieberman comprised diverse voices. Yaakov Gil's letter to the Israeli newspaper *Ma'ariv* indicts Lieberman, "the heir apparent of J. N. Epstein," for having forsaken Jerusalem and "gone down" to teach "ignoramuses" at JTS.[228] Soon after Lieberman's death, Yedidiah Cohen speculated on the probable reasons for Lieberman's aligning himself with the Seminary: "Was it the 'honor,' or the financial compensation? Possibly, it may have been the rich and glorious Seminary library that lured him there with its magnetic pull? Or, perhaps, it was the hope beating in his heart to be able to restore wandering souls to the bosom of truth."[229]

On several occasions, Lieberman justified his presence at JTS on the grounds that he was performing a sacred mission there in seeking to exert a positive influence upon his students and "draw them near to Torah and Judaism." It is interesting that R. Moshe Hayyim Shapira, minister of religion of the State of Israel, looked approvingly upon Lieberman's departure to JTS, for he would thereby "help spread the study of Torah in the Diaspora."[230]

However, it would seem that most of Lieberman's critics attributed his move to monetary motives, although some saw him tainted by the nonkosher brush of "critical scholarship" and "secular studies." Indeed, one preposterous rumor claims that his first wife, Rachel, had divorced him on the insistence of her father because Lieberman began studying Greek and Latin literature.[231] Undoubtedly, Lieberman's scientific method of inquiry was regarded with suspicion, if not denigration, in certain Orthodox circles, and resulted in his ostracism. Lieberman speculated that the reason that R. Yehezkel Abramsky (a fellow classmate at Slobodka) failed to write to him in acknowledgment of receipt of Lieberman's *Mo'ed* of *Tosefta Kifshutah* was that "it is not pleasant for him to correspond with a Reformer."[232] Regarding Lieberman's *Tosefta Kifshutah* and its acceptance within the Orthodox community, Lieberman informed Finkelstein in a letter from Israel, "There is a black market in my *Tosefta Kifshutah*. Last week a copy was sold for 75 pounds, which is simply an outrage."[233] The claim was made that while Lieberman's work was frequently consulted in Orthodox circles, the title was often "doctored" so as to hide its Seminary identification. "Not infrequently it is carefully hidden from sight in many yeshiva libraries, and consulted secretly by a chosen few."[234] In the words of Michael Shashar, "The Orthodox use his books, but they don't mention his name."[235]

Samuel Dresner explains, "Even at the 'moderate' Yeshiva University, one must search long and hard to find mention of such classic works of scholarship as the monumental fourteen-volume edition of and commentary to the Tosephta by Rabbi Saul Lieberman or the seminal works of Abraham Heschel, because they were associated with a Conservative and not an Orthodox seminary."[236] Orthodox scholars would occasionally be observed going to Lieberman's JTS study at very late hours and under conditions of anonymity. They obviously felt it prudent to keep such visits private, and Lieberman would oblige by arranging for them to be met at the JTS entrance by a student and privately escorted to Lieberman's study.[237]

In what must have been an exceedingly embarrassing episode, Lieberman declined to accept the prestigious Kook Prize—which had been awarded him in 1957—because of opposition in Orthodox circles. Meshullam Roth, another prizewinner, announced that he would refuse to accept the award together with Lieberman, whom he designated as being "a rabbi of the Reform movement." Numerous Orthodox leaders rose to Lieberman's defense, claiming that he was not at all "reform" in religious outlook and practice, and R. Yehiel Yaakov Weinberg lamented "the great fanaticism that has increased in strength in the Orthodox camp."[238] Lieberman put an end to the furor by writing a formal letter to the committee, officially declining the prize so as to cause no further embarrassment to the committee and to put a halt to the desecration of the name of the saintly Rabbi Kook.[239]

Lieberman preferred viewing the Orthodox opposition to him as a matter of religious principle rather than personal malice. In an interview with the Israeli newspaper *Ha'aretz,* Lieberman stated:

> The dispute between myself and the [Orthodox] Rabbis is a longstanding affair; yet there has never been personal slander. I understand them. I know that all their activities are in the name of God. They think that my action will harm Orthodox Jewry, and they are

> therefore justified in considering me a person harmful to their cause. For myself, I am convinced of the opposite. They go their way and I go mine, but when we meet we always discuss matters calmly. This is an example of fair controversy. I always think to myself, "If I were in their place, perhaps, I would be even more extreme in my convictions; but I have an advantage over them, for I possess knowledge of certain facts unknown to them." It is, unfortunately, true that in the United States the controversy between Igud Harabbanim and the Rabbinical Assembly sometimes stoops to personal defamation. On the other hand, the controversy between the Rabbis and me is unsullied; it is a controversy for the sake of God.[240]

This may have been wishful thinking on Lieberman's part. It is noteworthy that the *Jewish Press,* the most prestigious of all Orthodox weeklies in the United States, chose to ignore Lieberman's death. In a letter to that newspaper, Professor Gary Rendsburg of Canisius College stated: "The absence of an obituary in your paper is inexcusable. . . .

Certainly the death of Saul Lieberman, the doyen of contemporary talmudic studies, deserves some mention in your newspaper."[241] The newspaper's editor clearly felt otherwise.

During the hours after the fire of April 1966 at the JTS library, several volunteers from the New York area came to help rescue the damaged sacred texts. Two Yeshiva University students, Hillel Goldberg and Irv Twersky, helped organize a large contingent of volunteers from their institution; however, questions were raised as to the propriety of Orthodox students assisting a Conservative institution in this manner. As R. Soloveitchik was out of town and thus unable to render a decision in the manner, the YU president, Samuel Belkin, was consulted. Belkin responded, "If you will bring me a letter from Shaul Lieberman stating that our students are *hayyavim* [halakhically obligated] to help, I will indicate to them to do so." Upon receipt of such a statement from Lieberman, Belkin authorized YU students to render assistance.[242] Lieberman's own words on religious extremism are instructive: "Extremism is a great rival and a cheap replacement for Torah. Torah study entails years of preparation, but extremism can be acquired in one night."[243]

Personal Religious Behavior. "He was scrupulous in the observance of all mitzvot, minor as well as major ones."[244] "No Orthodox rabbi could ever deny that Saul Lieberman was . . . personally an observant Jew."[245] "Professor Saul Lieberman . . . a Jew whose Orthodoxy was beyond question."[246]

These citations from prominent Orthodox rabbis reflect the common perception that Saul Lieberman was indeed "Orthodox" in his religious practices. The only time Lieberman seems to have referred to himself as a "Conservative Jew" was during the highly charged polemical debate over the joint *beit din,* when he stated, "Conservative Jews do not like inquisitions."[247] Otherwise, he never seems to have objected to his portrayal as an Orthodox Jew teaching in a Conservative seminary.

Indeed, anyone acquainted with Lieberman could not question his firm adherence to halakhic practice and accepted custom. His not writing on the intermediate days of a festival,[248] his refusal to permit himself the leniency of observing one day of a festival while in Israel unless he spent all three festivals there,[249] his refusal to fly from Israel to the United States on Fridays,[250] his stringency vis-à-vis the dietary laws,[251] his insistence on reciting prayers at their proper time, his erection of a mini-sukkah on the outside window ledge of his JTS office,[252] his recitation of only one Kaddish at each morning service during the year following Judith's death so as to permit the worshipers to respond "amen" to those with an obligation to recite the Kaddish,[253] his conducting a daily *siyum* (completion of the study of a rabbinic text) in order to be permitted to consume meat during the first eight days of the month of Av,[254] his effusive praise for a sermon on family purity delivered at the Seminary synagogue[255]—this is a random selection of illustrations.

When questioned about specific lenient halakhic rulings issued by the Rabbinical Assembly, Lieberman stated that "the marriage of a *kohen* [priest] and a divorcée cannot become legalized by halakhah," and that "no allowance can be made for traveling on the Sabbath. . . . If a man were to ask me whether he should pray at home, or even not pray at all, rather than travel on the Sabbath to pray in a synagogue, I would, of course, reply that traveling is forbidden."[256]

Lieberman objected to attempts of liberal elements in the Rabbinical Assembly to abolish the second day of festivals, exclaiming, "Who do these rabbis think they are? Whom do they think they are fooling? The *balabatim* [lay persons] won't agree to abolish the second day of *yom tov*. They know that you have two *sedarim* on Pesach. Do you think they will agree to say Yizkor of the seventh day of Pesach and not the eighth day?"[257] He purportedly sent a letter to the *Morgen Journal*, critical of the proposal.[258] Some suspected that Lieberman's refusal to accept an honorary doctorate from the Reform Jewish Institute of Religion was motivated by his profound disagreement with the religious positions taken by the Reform movement.

Lieberman followed the common practice of many Lithuanian rabbis of reciting their daily prayers rapidly, so as to have more time in which to study the sacred texts. He quipped that he was a devotee of the *Brisker shita* (the analytical approach to the study of Talmud developed by Rabbi Hayyim Soloveitchik of Brisk d'Lita), by which he meant that he subscribed to being "brisk" at prayer. However, his religious devotion while at prayer was impressive. On Rosh Hashanah and Yom Kippur, he would occasionally prefer standing behind a curtain in order to pray with greater concentration and devotion.[259] He was once asked why he always prayed with an open prayer book before his eyes. Why was it that he who "knew the whole of Mishnah by heart, should feel insecure in regard to the contents of the daily prayer book"? Lieberman's response was that "he feared lest his mind wander and cease for a moment to be aware that he was addressing the Lord."[260] Likewise, Lieberman always made a point of reciting the Kiddush from an open book.[261] Others recall his devotion during his recitation of the blessing for the washing of the hands prior to eating.[262]

We shall later discuss the fact that Lieberman's introductory lectures to his JTS Talmud students were frequently characterized by advocacy, if not apologetics. He sought to emphasize the wisdom of rabbinic teachings and their relevance to contemporary issues. He not only taught texts, but a positive and reverential attitude toward the texts. Lieberman was known, on occasion, to subtly (or not so subtly) chide his students for such "offenses" as neglecting to recite all of the daily prayers dealing with the sacrificial cult, or walking outdoors bareheaded. In the Seminary synagogue on *Yom Yerushalayim* (the anniversary of the liberation of Jerusalem in the 1967 war), Lieberman objected to the prayer leader's pronouncement of the benediction prior to the recitation of Hallel (a series of liturgical psalms of praise), even though this practice had the approval of several liberal Orthodox rabbis.[263] It was his practice invariably to accompany guests departing his home well beyond the door and into the street in keeping with the halakhic dictates governing hospitality. The front page of his publications feature his father's name appearing in larger-print type than his own, in keeping with the custom not to write one's own name above that of one's father.[264]

Lieberman's very traditional approach was reflected in his commitment to *taharat hamishpahah* (the laws of family purity). He made a generous financial contribution to the building of *mikvaot* (ritual baths) in Israel. Lieberman's wife, Judith, attended the *mikveh* regularly. Ruth Link-Salinger dedicated her work for a conference on Jewish law in 1979 in New York as well as the book *Jewish Law in Our Time* "to the living presence of Dean Dr. Judith Berlin Lieberman."[265] Lieberman was pleased with this reference to Judith's observance of the laws of family purity and stressed that he wanted to be known as "Orthodox."[266] It should be noted that it is only in recent years that the laws of family purity have gained somewhat wider acceptance. Lieberman enthusiastically welcomed support for this often neglected mitzvah. Dov Zlotnick, a student and intimate of Lieberman, delivered a powerful sermon entitled "Today's Met Mitzvah" at JTS in 1967 on Rosh Hashanah, advocating the observance of *taharat hamishpahah*.[267] This sermon elicited Lieberman's enthusiastic commendation and endorsement. According to Jane Calem Rosen, "[Zlotnick's] mentor, JTS professor Saul Lieberman, lauded the talk as a *kiddush Hashem* [sanctification of God's name], and Dr. Zlotnick was allowed to offer JTS's first class in the tractate Niddah."[268] Lieberman sought to educate scholars who were, or would become, religiously committed. Zlotnick, who went on to become a distinguished professor of rabbinic literature at JTS, expressed appreciation for the education that he received from Lieberman: "It was [Lieberman] who urged the study of Talmud upon me, and in a sense all that I have learned and whatever there is of value in this work I owe to him."[269]

Above and beyond his fidelity to specific halakhic observances, Lieberman's personality was that of a traditional Jew. Indeed, his somewhat ambivalent relationship with Gershom Scholem has been attributed in part to the fact that, notwithstanding their friendship and their common view of what constituted proper scientific research, "emotionally . . . they were worlds apart. Scholem remained the German Jew of assimilationist parents, and Lieberman remained the East European Jew, a descendant of a long line of Lithuanian rabbis."[270] It should be noted that another factor was Scholem's purported opposition to Lieberman's faculty appointment at the Hebrew University. Indeed, Lieberman made no secret of the fact that their relationship was not always close. At Lieberman's seventy-fifth birthday celebration at the *beit hanasi* in Jerusalem, Lieberman acknowledged Scholem's presence among the honored guests with the observation: "There were times when this man was *gershom* [a stranger] but now he is *shalom* [peace]."[271]

While Lieberman's personal religious piety seems not to have been questioned in most Orthodox circles, he was nevertheless perceived as tacitly approving certain striking halakhic leniencies emanating from the Conservative movement. Maimon, for example, congratulated Lieberman upon his receiving the Bialik Prize, and lamented that there were some who failed to appreciate Lieberman's scholarly contributions; then Maimon inquired if it was true that JTS and the Rabbinical Assembly approved of traveling to the synagogue on the Sabbath by automobile. Maimon hastened to add that he was certain that neither Lieberman nor Finkelstein would do such a thing, although rumors were circulating that they had given their approval to this enactment.[272] Maimon's letter to Lieberman reflects his relationship with the Orthodox rabbinate. Those who knew him continued to respect him as a personally observant Jew. However, they perceived him as lending support and credence to the Conservative movement by virtue of his association with JTS. It is probable that Lieberman's busy New York schedule and intimate association with the Seminary led to less frequent encounters with Orthodox colleagues in America. In Israel, however, a more leisurely schedule, along with Orthodox family connections, personal and professional friendships, and a minimal degree of institutional association with JTS most likely facilitated his relationships within the Orthodox community.

WORKS

Titles

A brief excursus into Lieberman's major compositions—their themes and significance—is in order at this point.

Al Hayerushalmi (Jerusalem, 1929)

Lieberman identifies textual corruptions in the *Talmud Yerushalmi,* provides variant readings for tractate *Sotah,* and proposes guidelines for correcting the text of the *Talmud Yerushalmi.* Yehuda Janowitz embarked on a project to translate the *Talmud Yerushalmi* into Hebrew and enlisted the assistance of noted bibliophile R. Michel Rabinowitz, who had emigrated to Palestine from Minsk in 1925. Rabinowitz, an acquaintance of Lieberman's from Lithuania, sought his assistance in this matter. Lieberman demurred, however, on the grounds that any translation would be premature, owing to the need for first establishing a corrected text.

Talmudah shel Kisrin (Jerusalem, 1931)[273]

This volume contains an analysis of the editing of the *Talmud Yerushalmi.* Lieberman proposed that *Bava Kamma, Bava Metzia,* and *Bava Batra* of *Nezikin* differ from the other tractates of the *Yerushalmi* in language and style. They were probably edited in Caesarea in the mid-fourth century, half a century before the rest of the *Yerushalmi* was composed in Tiberias.

Hayerushalmi Kifshuto (Jerusalem, 1935)

Lieberman composed a commentary on *Shabbat, Eruvin,* and *Pesahim,* the first three tractates of *Mo'ed* of the *Talmud Yerushalmi*. At this point, Lieberman suspended his plan to produce a complete, corrected text of the *Yerushalmi* with commentary. For the rest of his life, he devoted virtually all his energy to working on the Tosefta, supplemental materials to the Mishnah consisting of parallels to and repetitions of mishnaic teachings, as well as independent comments. While the Mishnah became the foundation of rabbinic study, the Tosefta was relatively neglected as a source of study over the centuries, and many corruptions entered the text. Lieberman had to cull the numerous variations that existed in different texts in libraries throughout the world, as well as make use of Geniza fragments in order to establish the authentic text.

The question of why Lieberman chose to interrupt his work on the *Talmud Yerushalmi* and devote himself to the Tosefta is intriguing. Was it because Lieberman thought it necessary first to clarify tannaitic sources—notably, the Tosefta—before commencing work on the *Yerushalmi*?[274] Or was it because Lieberman encountered procedural difficulties and dilemmas in working on the *Yerushalmi?* In support of the latter possibility, we can cite Lieberman's own words appearing in the foreword to his *Hayerushalmi Kifshuto:*

> When I began, several years ago, to prepare the material for a new edition of the *Yerushalmi,* I encountered many difficulties. On one hand, I realized that it is necessary to go into great detail in order to establish the correct interpretation of the *Yerushalmi,* and even basic matters still require much clarification and elucidation. On the other hand, I am convinced that only a short and concise commentary could penetrate the circles of Talmud students and be accepted by them.
>
> I consequently decided to publish notes and comments to the last three orders of the *Yerushalmi* (namely, nearly 75 percent of the entire work), in order to lean upon them, and refer to them briefly in my expanded commentary to the first order. At the present, I intend to publish an edition including the text of the *Yerushalmi* itself, for the first order only.

Indeed, when Lieberman commenced working on *Mo'ed,* he was amazed at the voluminous size of his writings:

> When I printed the first chapter (one out of twenty) of the tractate *Shabbat,* I saw to my astonishment that it spanned four printed signatures (sixty-four pages). I could not follow through with what I had undertaken, and from *Shabbat* chapter 2, I limited the scope. . . .
>
> Actually, it's necessary to compose two distinct types of works on the *Yerushalmi.* One would deal with all the minutiae—dot every *i* and record even the most insignificant corruptions in manuscript texts of the *Yerushalmi* and medieval quotations—an edition for specialists. Of course, a book of this type would bring little salvation to the simple reader, the intelligent layman, the nonspecialist. It would just confuse him and bother him, sometimes even mislead him. This type of reader needs a different type of book, one that would deal only with matters of manifest significance and avoid excessive quotations.[275]

It is also conceivable that Lieberman's decision to devote his efforts to the Tosefta was due (as he himself seems to hint) to the simple practical reality that there were publishers available to sponsor his work on the Tosefta![276] There were no scholarships available to Hebrew University students at that time. Many of them, Lieberman included, could afford only to take the Number 9 bus one way to the Hebrew University campus on Har Hazofim. Epstein was apparently able to arrange compensation for the impecunious Lieberman to research and index allusions to the Tosefta appearing in the writings of the rishonim. This subsidized project eventually expanded. Economic factors should therefore not be overlooked here.

Although his elucidation of the *Yerushalmi* will continue to appear in print, not only because of the intimate relationship between the two works, but because of Lieberman's great interest in explicating the *Yerushalmi,* Lieberman's primary focus for the rest of his life would be on the Tosefta.

Indeed, there is evidence from Lieberman's Jerusalem correspondence of the late 1930s that he continued to work systematically on the *Yerushalmi* with an eye toward publication. On January 21, 1938, he informed Ginzberg that he had chosen to delay publishing further volumes of his *Hayerushalmi Kifshuto* since noticing in *Bloch's Book Bulletin* that

Ginzberg's own commentary on the *Yerushalmi* would shortly appear in print. (Ginzberg's work, *A Commentary on the Palestinian Talmud: Berakhot,* was not published until three years later.) With effusive praise, Lieberman assured Ginzberg that he would surely stand to benefit greatly from Ginzberg's work, and he was, therefore, comfortable in letting Ginzberg precede him in publishing a commentary to the *Yerushalmi.* In fact, Lieberman never did publish this work, although it seems that he was ready to go to print with it in 1938. On June 9, 1939, Lieberman informed Ginzberg that he was planning to publish *Yerushalmi, Zeraim* on the basis of several manuscripts in his possession. Lieberman's earlier works on the *Yerushalmi,* as well as his exhaustive commentary on the Tosefta, were true "pioneering efforts," as most scholars had usually ignored these texts. In Haym Soloveitchik's words, "Lieberman dealt with underprivileged texts."[277]

There were good reasons for the neglect of these "underprivileged" texts. The difficulties encountered in dealing with them were already recognized by medieval scholars. The twelfth-century talmudist R. Abraham b. David of Posquieres (Raivad) noted in one of his strictures against Maimonides: "I am puzzled by the fact that [Maimonides] sought to elucidate matters according to the Tosefta and the *Yerushalmi* and failed in his effort. For the [texts of the] Tosefta and *Yerushalmi* available to us are not properly corrected and are not adequate for such purposes."[278]

Lieberman's correspondence also discloses his involvement in the preparation of a scientific edition of the Mishnah.[279] Harry Fischel had agreed to underwrite this project and had approached Lieberman, as head of the Fischel Institute, to oversee the work. Lieberman, however, was reluctant to accept the assignment, explaining to Ginzberg in a letter of May 5, 1938, that most of the responsibility would surely fall on him, since the student body of the institute was ill equipped to engage in such serious scholarship. Lieberman was also concerned about antagonizing Epstein, whom he feared might begrudge this as an intrusion into his own domain, since he had already written an introduction to the Mishnah. A smaller-scale project, also alluded to in Lieberman's correspondence with Ginzberg (June 9, 1939), concerned the possibility of Lieberman's assisting in the translation of Ginzberg's *Legends of the Jews* into Hebrew, as well as his composing an essay on this work. Neither of these ventures came to pass.

Tosefet Rishonim, **four volumes (Jerusalem, 1937-39)**

An extensive commentary on the manuscripts of the Tosefta and works of rishonim bearing on the Tosefta, along with textual corrections based on manuscripts. Lieberman proves that, contrary to public assumption, the Tosefta was an important text for the Babylonian gaonic school. It has been pointed out that such a publication rightly necessitated the labors of an entire committee of scholars, working with technical assistance; it was not a job for just one man.[280]

Tashlum Tosefta **(Jerusalem, 1938)**

An introductory essay and supplement to the second printing of Moses Samuel Zuckermandel's edition of the Tosefta, in which Lieberman analyzes more than a hundred citations of the Tosefta that appear in early rabbinic works but that are not found in the text of the Tosefta itself (originally published as a separate pamphlet in 1937).

Tosefta Kifshutah **(New York, 1955-88), twelve volumes published in Lieberman's lifetime with *kuntres tikkunim v'hashlamoth* (1982), and three volumes published posthumously.**

Lieberman's *Tosefta Kifshutah* is, in reality, a two-part commentary. There is a short commentary, briefly explaining the meaning of the text of the Tosefta, which appears with variant readings along with references to other places in rabbinical literature where the passages are cited. There is an exhaustive commentary summarizing previous attempts to understand the texts, from the earliest authorities on, and presenting Lieberman's own commentary and elucidation of the Tosefta.

Ancillary Works

"Hazanut Yannai" (1939). A lengthy essay analyzing the importance of early liturgical poetry in the elucidation of rabbinic literature.[281]

Shkiin (Jerusalem, 1939, 1970). An analysis of obscure and lost materials, many from Karaitic and non-Jewish sources, that are helpful in explaining difficult passages in rabbinic literature. Lieberman employs citations appearing in Raymond Martini's anti-Jewish tract *Pugio Fidei* as a means for determining which rabbinic texts were then extant in Spain.

Midrashei Teman (Jerusalem, 1940, 1970). A study of Yemenite exegetical materials omitted by the Rabbis from their standard works.

Midrash Devarim Rabbah (Jerusalem, 1940, 1965, 1974). An analysis of an Oxford manuscript of *Midrash Rabbah* to Deuteronomy used by Sephardic Jews, which differs significantly from similar manuscripts employed in Ashkenazic communities.

Greek in Jewish Palestine: Studies in the Life and Manners of Jewish Palestine in the II–IV Centuries, C.E. (New York, 1942). An analysis of the influence of the surrounding culture upon Jewish institutions, notably upon language. Lieberman proves that the educated classes among Palestinian Jewry knew Greek, and the Rabbis therefore cite Greek proverbs in their sermons.

Hellenism in Jewish Palestine (New York, 1950, 1962). An analysis of broader influences and interactions between the Jewish and Hellenistic worlds. Lieberman demonstrates that the alleged ban on studying Greek wisdom applied only to Jewish schoolchildren.

Hilkhot Hayerushalmi L'Harambam (New York, 1948). An analysis of an anonymous manuscript consisting of fragments pertaining to the tractates *Berakhot* and *Ketubot* that was taken to the Cambridge library from the Cairo Geniza. Lieberman establishes this to be a part of a lost treatise on the *Talmud Yerushalmi* by Moses Maimonides, akin to Isaac Alfasi's halakhic summaries of the Babylonian Talmud. This entailed remarkable detective work on Lieberman's part, notably in his analysis of *Ketubot,* where exceedingly sparse fragments had to be totally reconstructed.

Sifrei Zuta (New York, 1968). Lieberman theorizes that this halakhic midrash was edited by Bar Kappara in Lydda and contains mishnaic materials prepared by R. Nathan, rather than those collected and redacted by R. Judah Hanasi.

Texts and Studies (New York, 1974). Selected essays of Lieberman's, some originally published in Hebrew.

Studies in Palestinian Talmudic Literature (Hebrew). Edited by David Rosenthal under Lieberman's guidance and published posthumously (Jerusalem, 1991). A collection of essays, addresses, and reviews written by Lieberman.

Lieberman prepared for publication David Pardo's *Hasdei David,* a commentary of seder *Taharot* of the Tosefta, which had remained in manuscript form (Jerusalem, 1970–71).

Lieberman also composed numerous essays on a variety of topics relating to Jewish life and thought in the rabbinic era. However, he rarely involved himself in practical halakhic matters, and therefore only rarely issued rabbinic responsa. Of his more than 225 books and articles, only four are devoted to contemporary halakhic issues; only nineteen pages of the 9,500 pages he wrote—a mere 0.2 percent—address themselves to such practical matters. Although Lieberman surely responded to a number of halakhic queries on a private basis, there were only four public forays on his part in response to practical halakhic challenges:[282]

1) In October 1945, he joined Professors Ginzberg and Marx in condemning the new Sabbath prayer book issued by Mordecai Kaplan, although they decried its burning by an Orthodox rabbi, Joseph Ralbag, and Kaplan's excommunication by two hundred members of the Orthodox Agudas Harabbanim.[283]
2) As noted earlier, he took an active role in formulating a *takkanah* to the marriage contract and negotiating with Rabbi J. B. Soloveitchik over the formation of the joint *beit din.*
3) He responded to Prime Minister David Ben-Gurion's query concerning the registration of children of mixed marriages, affirming the halakhic definition of Jewish identity.
4) In February 1978, he issued a statement opposing the ordination of women as rabbis. A few words on this statement are in order. It should be noted that Lieberman's involvement in the dispute concerning the Seminary's ordination of women is itself a matter of some controversy. The debate on women's ordination had raged within the Conservative movement until the Rabbinical Assembly, at its May 1977 convention, petitioned JTS chancellor Gerson Cohen to appoint a commission to study the matter. The commission issued its report on January 30, 1979.[284] Lieberman conveyed his opin-

> ion ("responsum") in the form of a letter, dated February 28, 1979, to a number of JTS faculty members who opposed women's ordination and had for some time implored Lieberman to speak on the matter. The letter, saying that a woman could not be ordained, was sent after the conclusion of the commission's deliberations and therefore had no impact on the outcome. Nor was the letter intended to be released to the public. It was distributed to members of the JTS faculty immediately before the vote to admit female candidates to the rabbinical school in October 1983.[285]

Prior to his responsum on the subject, Lieberman had issued no written opinion on the matter and was obviously reluctant to take a public stand. Nor was he numbered among the sixteen JTS faculty members who had challenged the ordination deliberations. The Lieberman responsum was not published until 1986, when it appeared in *Tomeikh Kehalakhah*.[286] In fact, R. Wayne Allen, editor of *Tomeikh Kehalakhah,* said that a reason for publishing the letter was that "some people speculated that this responsum did not in fact exist."[287]

Lieberman opened the responsum by saying that he would have preferred not to give his opinion on the matter for "hidden reasons" that he did not wish to disclose. Dov Zlotnick explained that Lieberman was generally reluctant to take a position on controversial and political matters.[288] Indeed, Dimitrovsky commented that while Lieberman could be intense and combative in matters of scholarly dispute, he was remarkably reluctant to argue his case in areas involving religious or political controversy. He even declined to defend his own *takkanah* in the RA *ketubah* when it came under attack in Orthodox circles.[289] Perhaps Lieberman believed that if he took a stand on this particular issue, while remaining silent on others, his silence might be misinterpreted. Furthermore, he viewed acts of involvement in such issues to be a distraction from his scholarly pursuits. In any event, he clearly did not relish participating in such a political battle that might find him publicly opposing several of his prominent former students.[290] In private conversations, he seemed to indicate that there were more important issues confronting the Conservative movement. Indeed, there are those who claim that Lieberman was pressured into articulating a stand on what he personally considered to be a "losing battle."

Lieberman clearly opposed the ordination of women rabbis,[291] but his opposition may have been based more on the fear that this would further escalate tensions with the Orthodox community than on strict halakhic grounds. As a halakhic ruling, Lieberman's responsum seems to reflect lukewarm opposition to the ordination of women. He minimized the significance of rabbinic ordination by pointing out that in Lithuania, it was common practice to ordain students well before they were old enough to issue legal decisions. In his concluding statement, Lieberman reduced the matter to the following: If a woman cannot sit as a judge, "she cannot be ordained by this title";[292] but he seemed careful not to say that it is prohibited to ordain a woman. He seemed to be saying that it is essentially a matter of definition: if one defines a rabbi as a judge, and a woman cannot be a judge, a woman therefore cannot be a rabbi. However, is it possible that she would not necessarily be precluded from performing many other tasks associated with the contemporary rabbinate? Indeed, it has been pointed out that Lieberman's responsum seemed to be directed more against a woman's use of the title "rabbi" than against her actually functioning as a rabbi.[293]

To raise a basic question: in view of Lieberman's vast erudition and voluminous scholarly contributions, why did he refrain, for the most part, from engaging in *pesak halakhah,* the rendering of legal decisions? Part of the reason doubtless lay in the fact that Lieberman never viewed himself as a *posek* (legal decisor) for the Conservative movement. As he affirmed in his letter to the newspaper *Ma'ariv,* "I am not one of the heads of the Conservative movement and I am not, nor have I ever been, the vice president of the [Jewish] Theological Seminary. I teach Torah to the Jewish people."[294]

It was only on singularly rare circumstances, such as when approached concerning the permissibility of having a "women's Torah reading service" on Simhat Torah, that Lieberman took upon himself, as official rabbi of the Seminary synagogue, the role of *posek,* and in consultation with Finkelstein gave his approval to the service, albeit with clearly delineated restrictions.[295] Otherwise, Lieberman avoided involving himself in the halakhic issues confronting the Conservative movement.

More to the point, Lieberman perceived himself a teacher of Torah, not a *posek,* irrespective of the religious organization or denomination. He embraced and epitomized the traditional Lithuanian model of the *rosh yeshiva* (head of the talmudical academy) as a scholar-teacher, not a religious decisor. It is significant that the Gaon of Vilna's voluminous literary contributions are likewise virtually bereft of any responsa. Rendering legal decisions was not the responsibility of Lieberman's esteemed *roshei yeshiva* in Lithuania. The role of *posek* fell upon the shoulders of others, often less scholarly personages such as the community rabbis. Neither was the rendering of legal decisions the responsibility of JTS deans or Talmud professors. As Chancellor Ismar Schorsch of JTS notes, "The . . . Seminary . . . inherited from Breslau a tradition that abdicated the responsibility to provide halakhic guidance for its own day. The twin model of the *rosh yeshiva* and the German professor combined to raise the academic at Breslau or New York above the level of a *mere* [emphasis ours] *moreh hora'a* or halakhic decisor."[296] It is interesting to note that Louis Ginzberg did function for several decades as the official halakhic decisor of JTS, and it seems that on occasion, he would forward inquiries to Lieberman for his opinion.[297] However, responsa writing was neither part of Lieberman's job description at JTS, nor was it an area where he chose to concentrate his greatest efforts. His task was the study and elucidation of sacred texts. Once he brought clarity to the text by explaining the origin and meaning of the rabbinic discussion, the correct path to the halakhah would be easier to follow.

Approach

Lieberman's scholarship is based on a remarkable dual competence. He was a pioneer of the "historia-realia" approach to rabbinic literature. His mastery of the languages, culture, and institutions of the Greco-Roman world granted him a unique understanding of the classical rabbinic texts. He was the "comparative talmudic scholar" par excellence, in analyzing these texts against their background in the general milieu. At the same time, Lieberman was a "text-immanent scholar," skilled in the scientific analysis of texts and endowed with detective-like instincts in reconstructing lost or defective texts and a keen ear for the nuances of language while analyzing their composition and mode of transmission. Lieberman was able to provide precise definitions for more than a thousand obscure talmudic words, and he is credited with explaining 90 percent of all difficult terms in rabbinic literature.[298]

Lithuanian-Style Scholarship

In many respects, Lieberman's approach to rabbinic texts was neither as radical nor as unprecedented as it has frequently been made out to be, for he was a product of the traditional Lithuanian style of scholarship developed and exemplified by Rabbi Elijah, the Gaon of Vilna (1720–97). It was not until well into the nineteenth century that the *Wissenschaft des Judentums* circles of Western Europe first incorporated modern scientific methodology into the analysis of rabbinic texts. Decades earlier, proto-critical approaches had been exemplified by the Gaon and several of his disciples in Lithuania. Indeed, it could be said that the emphasis on the study of sacred texts, as well as the manner and mode of study characteristic of Lithuanian Jewish talmudists, bore the unmistakable imprint of the Gaon. Lieberman exemplified and perfected this mode.

To state the obvious, the study of Torah was integral to Jewish life in Lithuania, a passion of professional scholar and layperson alike. Whereas German and Hungarian Orthodoxy emphasized producing people of a certain halakhic lifestyle, Lithuanian Orthodoxy emphasized, above all, the development of academicians, masters of sophisticated halakhic discourse.[299] In Lithuania, the scholar of texts was the ultimate role model, the exemplar at the apex of the social configuration. Lieberman described a scene from his youth when he visited his maternal uncle, a rabbi. As they walked down the street together, all the Jewish residents rose from their places and stood in reverence for his uncle. Such was the veneration naturally accorded to a scholar by the townspeople. Years later, Lieberman recalled how moved he was by this homage to Torah scholarship and how inspired he was by the sight of his older cousin, the Hazon Ish, reciting by heart the tractate *Eruvin* late at night.[300]

But it was not "just" the study of Torah that was so extolled by Lithuanian Jewry. It was the creative study of Torah, the discovery of *hiddushim* (innovative interpretations). However, such novellae had to stand the test of rational analysis and examination and had to be derived from disciplined study. Although the Haskalah (enlightenment) movement, in many Orthodox circles, had become synonymous with apostasy and licentiousness, it was tolerated to a remarkable degree in Lithuanian traditional circles—not only because the early Lithuanian devotees of Haskalah were frequently learned in traditional Jewish studies and not concerned with religious reform, but because the Gaon of Vilna was himself perceived as having been a "proto-Maskil," personifying the mediation between traditional Eastern European Torah study and the scientific study of texts. It would clearly be inaccurate to refer to the Gaon as a Maskil. However, he did insist upon a disciplined methodological approach to the study of the sacred texts as well as knowledge of grammar and etymology. He eschewed *pilpul* (casuistry for the sake of casuistry) in favor of subjecting rabbinic texts to rational analysis, scientific criticism, and correction, and he also advocated the mastery of certain secular sciences.[301] Like many Western rationalists, "the Gaon believed that understanding, properly and painstakingly applied, led to unshakable truth."[302] Therefore, many rabbinical scholars in Lithuania, standing in the elongated shadow of the Gaon, were fairly comfortable employing tools of critical scholarship in the pursuit of the truth. This was, after all, a reflection of the Gaon's faith in the power of the human mind, when applied critically, to determine correct textual interpretations.

Therefore, we find certain aspects of *Hokhmat Yisrael,* the Eastern European mode of the *Wissenschaft des Judentums* that advocates the use of modern methods of research in the study of Judaism, permeating some Lithuanian yeshivot. Several nineteenth-century Lithuanian scholars produced new editions of, and commentaries on, the *Sifra, Sifrei* gaonic literature, and they displayed a renewed interest in the study of the *Talmud Yerushalmi.*[303] R. Naftali Zevi Yehudah Berlin, the grandfather of Judith Lieberman, followed the Gaon in emphasizing disciplined, critical intellectual endeavor in his commentaries on talmudic and post-talmudic works. Judith recalls his traveling to the Russian capital to procure a manuscript of *Aha* (*Ahai*) of Shabha Gaon's *She'iltot* so that he could establish a correct text for this gaonic work.[304] It was another Lithuanian talmudist, R. Isaac Halevy (1847–1914), who laid the foundations for an Orthodox-style *Wissenschaft des Judentums* with the publication of his *Dorot Harishonim.*

This is not to suggest that Lieberman's encounter with J. N. Epstein at the Hebrew University was not a "new" academic experience for him. It surely was, and he was exposed to a new methodology. It is important to note, however, that Lieberman's studies in the Lithuanian yeshivot were also characterized by a modicum of modernity in the form of critical thinking, careful textual analyses, and some exposure to secular studies. Nor should the factor of "intellectual stimulation" be minimized. Not only did Slobodka attract an intellectually gifted student body to begin with; the pedagogical gifts of R. Natan Zevi Finkel—notably, his emphasis upon each student developing his own unique potential for greatness—had a powerful impact on the student body and encouraged breadth and diversity. One has only to note the remarkable achievements of Slobodka's alumni, not only as deans of yeshivot (R. Aaron Kotler, Lakewood; R. Yaakov Kamenetsky, Torah V'-daat; R. Yaakov Ruderman, Ner Yisrael; R. Yitzhak Hutner, Chaim Berlin; R. David Leibowitz, Chafetz Hayyim; R. Abraham Kalminowich, Mir; R. Naftali Levovitz, Krementz; and R. Jacob Lesin and R. Avigdor Cyperstein, Isaac Elhanan) but as academicians at secular institutions (Harry A. Wolfson, Harvard University) and non-Orthodox rabbinic seminaries (Samuel Atlas, Hebrew Union College).

Both deans of Berlin's Orthodox Rabbinical Seminary ("Hildesheimer's Seminary"), R. Yehiel Yaakov Weinberg and R. Abraham Elijah Kaplan, were Slobodka alumni. While Kaplan may not have had the benefit of a secular education, as did Weinberg, he fully appreciated the need for "the accumulated historical and linguistic knowledge, and the like, necessary for the optimum clarification of the halakhic sources." He also emphasized the importance of adhering to the Gaon of Vilna's practice of eschewing *pilpul* in favor of a precise understanding of rabbinic texts.[305] Kaplan's premature death at the age of thirty-four cut short his plan of composing a new commentary to the Talmud, in which he planned to incorporate textual emendations from alternate manuscripts and present precise translations for obscure terminology.

Lieberman, like Ginzberg, undoubtedly preferred viewing himself not so much as an innovator breaking with the traditional past, but rather as an authentic heir to the Gaon of Vilna, continuing on the trodden path of traditional-style Lithuanian *Hokhmat Yisrael,* albeit with an expanded scope of knowledge and refined tools of scholarship.[306] Like his cousin the Hazon Ish, Lieberman followed a disciplined conservative style of textual study, emphasizing *peshat* (the simple meaning of the text) rather than the analytical method of study (notably that of R. Hayyim Soloveitchik of Brisk) in vogue at some Lithuanian yeshivot.[307]

Lieberman's breadth of knowledge may well have had its roots in his formative educational years. R. David Tevel Dinovsky, Lieberman's influential mentor at the Malch yeshiva, whom he first encountered at the impressionable age of twelve, was a remarkable pedagogue. He was a charismatic personality and avowed devotee of *musar,* having studied under R. Simhah Zissel Zev of Kelme, a disciple of R. Yisrael Salanter. R. Dinovsky, described as a Maskil in breadth of knowledge and literary skills, was trained as a bookkeeper, was a stylish dresser (hard bowler hat, a stiff colored bib and cravat), an early supporter of the Hoveve Zion Zionist movement, and a gifted linguist who knew German, composed elaborate prose and poetry in Hebrew, and quoted Scripture by heart. R. Dinovsky's son-in-law and co-leader at Malch, R. Shlomo Gavurim, was a chess master who evinced great interest in Jewish history. R. Dinovsky and R. Gavurim are credited with having instilled in another of their students, R. Yaakov Kamenetsky, an affinity for Hebrew grammar and language and an appreciation of the value of Jewish history for better understanding rabbinic texts.[308]

Another of Lieberman's teachers, R. Shlomo Polachek, the Illui of Meitshet (1877–1928), studied at Volozhin under R. Hayyim Soloveitchik of Brisk and at Slobodka, and later became head of the yeshiva at Lydda. Lieberman studied under R. Polachek when the Lydda yeshiva was forced to relocate to central Russia during World War I, and encountered in him a scholar with broad academic interests. Polachek studied mathematics, appreciated Russian and German literature, and encouraged Lieberman to share with him the medical knowledge that Lieberman was acquiring at the time in a university correspondence course.[309]

Hokhmat Yisrael

Although Lieberman's studies at the Hebrew University under J. N. Epstein exposed him to the Western *Wissenschaft* approach to Judaic scholarship, it could be argued that in nature and approach, Lieberman remained, throughout his life, more the Lithuanian *Hokhmat Yisrael* scholar than the German *Wissenschaft* professor. This was evident in a number of ways: 1) his autodidacticism—the Tosefta, the Palestine Talmud, and the midrash, texts that were the focal points of Lieberman's work, were not systematically taught at the Slobodka yeshiva;[310] 2) his reverential attitude toward the texts; 3) his micro, rather than macro, approach; 4) his being primarily a *mefaresh* (commentator) on texts, rather than a *hoker* (investigator) of texts; and 5) his eventual departure from the approach of J. N. Epstein.

Autodidacticism. To characterize Lieberman as an autodidact would not be totally accurate. However, for the first three decades of his life he was mostly self-taught in secular studies and had absolutely no Western-style university training in Jewish studies. He therefore entered the Hebrew University as a novice who, as noted earlier, had never heard of Zacharias Frankel or, presumably, other renowned names in critical Jewish scholarship. Many Eastern European *Hokhmat Yisrael* scholars were likewise not university products and could be characterized as autodidacts. In this respect, Lieberman's background differed from that of Epstein, who, although born in Brest-Litovsk (Brisk), Lithuania, and educated at home in his early years by his father and at the yeshiva of Mir, spent many years at universities in Vienna and Berne and lectured at the Hochschule für die Wissenschaft des Judentums in Berlin.

Reverential Attitude toward Texts. Lieberman approached texts as sacred, treating them reverentially. He related to them, in the words of an associate, "as living entities, not corpses to be dissected."[311] Lieberman disliked engaging in "source criticism," that is, searching for discrepancies in the early transmission of texts to account for difficulties in interpretation. Lieberman disliked correcting texts, citing Hai Gaon's admonition not to emend mishnaic and talmudic texts because of difficulties in their exposition. He made it his policy not to emend a text unless the only alternative would be a forced, contrived *pilpul*-istic explanation.

In his 1935 critique of Jacob Lauterbach's edition of the *Mekhilta,* Lieberman stressed the legitimacy of differing textual versions.[312] In his early correspondence with Finkelstein (December 31, 1938), while still living in Jerusalem, Lieberman stated, "In my view, there is no [textual] error of which we can state with absolute certainty that it is truly an error." Lieberman explained to Finkelstein his reluctance to correct any rabbinic source, even on the basis of other rabbinic sources, unless there was firm support from subsequent authoritative texts. Even then, he refused to introduce such corrections in the body of the text, preferring to present them as suggested emendations to be included in a commentary appended to the text. In his

Tosefta Kifshutah, Lieberman stated that prior to emending a text one must make every effort to center one's work "on the foundation established by our Rabbis, of blessed memory; the earlier and later authorities, namely by means of great and diligent effort to understand the issue from within the text as it is, and from the other works of our masters."[313] Lieberman affirmed, "Everyone in whose eyes the words of the Talmud are holy understands that it is forbidden to an individual to decide on his own that since a particular text is obviously faulty, it is therefore permissible to delete it from before the reader's eyes. Better to retain even obvious errors in a manuscript, for the passage of time and acquisition of knowledge may prove that the errors are not errors at all."[314]

In other words, emend only as a last resort! For even the existence of different versions of a given text is not an indication that one of the versions is necessarily in error. Several legitimate variants may exist, and they are to be preserved intact, for each may be correct according to its derivation.[315] Lieberman thus justifies his reluctance to emend texts on the basis of methodology, pointing to a distinction that he draws between historical truth and textual truth.[316] While there can be only one historical truth, it is quite possible that there may be multiple textual truths, since each text possesses its own truth, derivative from its own sources and traditions. It would thus be methodologically incorrect to emend one textual version in order to harmonize it with another, since each may be true to its own source and tradition.[317] Lieberman's conservatism vis-à-vis the emendation of texts is, no doubt, also derivative of his reverential attitude toward the texts. He was not a cold dispassionate academician dissecting literary sources. He perceived himself, rather, as a student of Torah on the continuum of traditional Lithuanian rabbinical scholarship, seeking to explicate sacred rabbinic texts. His gestalt was more *Hokhmat Yisrael* than *Wissenschaft.*

Micro Rather than Macro Approach. Notwithstanding the breadth of Lieberman's knowledge of the Greco-Roman world and his pioneering comparative approach to understanding rabbinic texts against the background of their surroundings, his writings are not all characterized by broad strokes and elaborate theorizing. Rather, they are characteristic of the attention to detail and minutiae manifested by the Gaon of Vilna and associated with

Hokhmat Yisrael scholarship.[318] Most appropriately, Yitzhak Gilat does apply to Lieberman Scholem's citation from the writings of Goethe: "Gott vohnt [*sic*] in Detail."[319]

Lieberman was not a true *Wissenschaft* scholar in the broader sense of the meaning of the word, that is, one who engages in philosophical contemplation. His was a narrow and precise philological-based *Wissenschaft* mode. It is therefore understandable that when Finkelstein asked Lieberman to deliver a lecture for Seminary alumni on a theme involving philosophy, Judith Lieberman replied on behalf of her husband, "Dr. Lieberman will lecture to the alumni, but he looks forward to it with reservation. I suppose that it is the 'philosophical' aspect that leaves him cold."[320]

R. Yehiel Yaakov Weinberg, in his correspondence with Samuel Atlas, characterized Lieberman's approach accurately: "L. is a commentator in accordance with the simple sense, and he has a feel for proper interpretation. He knows how to make use of the entire talmudic literature, the rabbinic and scientific, in his commentary. He does not have a sweep of vision nor does he consider all the problems in one survey. He confines himself to establishing texts and exact interpretation. Such a confining task is good for him and the world, for through it he contributes greatly with his many books."[321]

Not surprisingly, there were many who lamented Lieberman's confining his interests and restricting his scope, noting that he alone was qualified to write *the* book on the subject of Judaism and the Hellenistic age, but chose not to, preferring instead to devote his energies to detailed textual explications.[322] But it is possible that Lieberman's emphasis on the micro may also be a reflection of his personal reverence for the religious tradition and his reluctance to speculate on the extent to which the rabbinic perception of reality was influenced by Hellenistic civilization. Lieberman's insistence on exactitude and certainty in his work may also have been a factor here. He had an aversion to imaginative, speculative interpretations that were unsubstantiated by facts. He abhorred unfounded generalizations and the building of intellectual castles in the sky. Throughout his works, he assiduously avoided sensational theorizing, preferring simple unadorned prosaic deductions from simple indisputable facts. It is reported that on one occasion he tore up several pages of his own imaginative solutions to a difficult textual problem with the words "it's too clever." He would often remind his students that "the eraser is more important than the pencil."[323]

Lieberman was decidedly not a theoretician. He did not seek to infer principles or formulate generalizations from facts. He inferred facts from facts. Even his quasi-historical studies, such as *Redefat dat Yisrael* and *Palestine in the Third and Fourth Centuries,* are primarily descriptive in nature and lack the sort of discussions of historical forces and pressures that would have entailed theorizing. In this connection, it is instructive to recall the differentiation made by Professor Harry Gideonse between the "intellectual" and "the scholar."[324] The intellectual "lives beyond his means," that is, he theorizes, often with insufficient backing for his theories. Lieberman, by this definition, was a scholar, concerned with conclusively substantiating whatever he wrote. Macro-theorizing went against his nature. It was too risky. It was also not the *Hokhmat Yisrael* approach.

In Lieberman's introductions to his *Yerushalmi Kifshuto* and *Tosefta Kifshutah,* he stated his intentions to compose at a later date (presumably when these works would be completed) a more general analysis of the texts. Regretfully, this never came to pass.

***A* Mefaresh *Rather than a* Hoker.** Although, technically speaking, Lieberman was both a *hoker* and a *mefaresh,* his true love was the art of *parshanut.* He was a commentator-teacher in the classical, traditional sense, albeit one endowed with modern critical tools of scholarship. In this respect as well, he was more representative of the *Hokhmat Yisrael* approach than that of the *Wissenschaft* school.

The case has been made that it is considerably easier for a scholar to be a *hoker* than to be a *mefaresh.*[325] The *hoker* chooses an area of interest and develops competence in that specific area. The *mefaresh,* however, must manifest competence in all subject matter and is not free to choose for himself only those research topics for which he has an affinity. Lieberman had little regard for certain *hokrim* whom he thought lacked a broad base of knowledge and who were often incapable of locating sources in the original. He would label them derisively as "concordance scholars," or "dictionary concordance scholars."[326] Lieberman "was probably the greatest comparative talmudic scholar of all time,"[327] contributing unprecedented analyses as to the relationship of the outside Greco-Roman culture to rabbinic texts, and he was also a premier text-immanent scholar. He was, however, reluctant to speculate on the evolution and development of the texts, preferring instead to deal with textual transmission and elucidation. In other words, he chose the role of the *mefaresh,* the textual commentator.

If anything, Lieberman's commentaries at times appear to be too exhaustive and comprehensive. He admitted that the incorporation of numerous commentaries into his works was "done almost unconsciously, if not against my will, for the natural inclination of a writer is to publicize his own novellas, and not those of others."[328] This is an interesting admission on Lieberman's part. He could not help but include alongside his own commentary the commentaries of others. Furthermore, not only did he present the reader with an all-inclusive commentary; his approach, frequently, is to lead the reader, via his commentary, to explore with him, step by step, the route to a proper understanding of the text. This is the pedagogical technique that he chose to employ. Rather than proudly proclaim to the reader his personal "discovery" or "solution to the problem" and then substantiate it, Lieberman preferred prodding the reader to search along with him for the proper solution.[329] Most likely, this technique was transplanted from a classroom setting or, more accurately, a Lithuanian yeshiva lecture-study hall. According to Dimitrovsky, "Lieberman's study of the text was based on careful examination of all the earlier interpreters of the subject matter and assessment of the merits of each in the light of new insight and analysis based on the vast sources at his command."[330]

Conceivably, Lieberman preferred the approach of the *mefaresh* for methodological as well as religious reasons. Methodologically, he was convinced that a comprehensive commentary must precede any attempt at analysis or dissection of a text. However, since this was also the traditional religious approach to textual study on which he was nurtured in Lithuania, it was the style of study and teaching closest to Lieberman's heart. Indeed, Lieberman observed on many occasions that his personal works were in the spirit of the traditional mode of rabbinic study.[331] Even Lieberman's scholarly articles are composed in the style of a *mefaresh*. He rarely addresses himself to issues and topics in the abstract. His approach took a more traditional form. In the manner of a Lithuanian *rosh yeshiva,* he confronted specific textual difficulties and proceeded to solve them. General topics are discussed in an ancillary way, as derivative of the textual explication.[332]

Lieberman's approach is decidedly not that of a historian. Indeed, he has been criticized for employing "a dialectical rabbinic 'learn' method,"[333] or "a talmudic system of logical discourse, rather than proper historical, propositional discourse."[334] As noted earlier, Epstein purportedly rejected *Tosefet Rishonim,* Lieberman's proposed doctoral dissertation at the Hebrew University, on the grounds that it lacked a historical perspective. However, textual explication, not historical speculation, was Lieberman's primary concern and interest. Lieberman clearly informs us of this in the introduction to his *Hellenism in Jewish Palestine:*

> The main purpose of the book remains what it was originally: the elucidation of difficult passages in rabbinic literature which were hitherto either unexplained or misinterpreted, and sometimes unknown altogether; the examination of certain customs and practices and the treatment of the literary methods used by the rabbis. This content is discussed against the background of Hellenism in Jewish Palestine. The well-known facts are used only as a kind of cement to make the citations coherent.[335]

Lieberman informed us that writing books such as *Talmudah shel Kisrin, Shkiin, Midrashei Teman,* and *Greek in Jewish Palestine* was decidedly not his primary interest. He referred to them as being "in a series of small publications which the author felt impelled to prepare at the expense of his regular work and studies."[336] Lieberman could not be more blunt. Such writings on his part came at the expense of his true academic interest. For Lieberman, historical analyses were secondary to textual exegesis.

Nor does historical analysis always come easy for a textual scholar. As Ismar Schorsch stated, "Textually oriented thinking is essentially concrete, circumscribed and episodic. Its very specificity induces a minimal level of abstraction and a bewildering absence of systematic analysis."[337] Lieberman clearly chose to avoid theorizing. He abhorred speculation that was not grounded in solid textual analysis, and he declined involving himself in "literary problems," such as the structure, editing, and dating of texts, or the relationship between the Mishnah and the Tosefta. "I never wrote anything I cannot prove," was his guiding principle, so it was only natural for him to avoid speculative issues and historical theorizing.[338] Lieberman rarely manifested an intellectual interest in theoretical historical studies and historical reconstructions. If anything, his historical observations tended to consist of applications of common sense and pragmatic wisdom.[339]

Departure from J. N. Epstein. Lieberman's assumption of the role of the *mefaresh* over that of the *hoker* also reflects a core difference in approach between himself and his mentor, Epstein. As noted earlier, Lieberman was initially reluctant to enroll at the Hebrew University and be exposed to a Western European critical approach to traditional Jewish texts, and once there he at first resisted Epstein's approach to textual analysis. Although Epstein's origins, like Lieberman's, were in a Lithuanian yeshiva, Epstein's training took place in institutions of Western European *Wissenschaft,* an alien world to Lieberman. Eventually, Lieberman grew to appreciate Epstein's approach, and praised him as "the father of critical talmudic research," acknowledging, "I have learned very, very much from him."[340] While lecturing at Harvard University, Lieberman stated that "the foundations of modern research in rabbinic literature were laid at the Hebrew University some fifty years ago," clearly a tribute to J. N. Epstein.[341]

In some way, Epstein's disappointment that Lieberman apparently failed to pay him sufficient honor affected their relationship. As noted earlier, Epstein disapproved of Lieberman's dissertation choice of *Tosefet Rishonim,* preferring a thesis more analytical-historical in nature. Profound differences between the two men appear to have been accentuated with the passage of time. For example, Epstein disputes Lieberman's contention that Caesarea was the probable site of origin of several tractates of the *Talmud Yerushalmi,* and Lydda the locale for the redaction of the *Sifrei Zuta.*[342] Lieberman reacted strongly to Epstein's critique (published posthumously by Epstein's student E. Z. Melamed), speculating that Epstein's comments may have been mere notes that he jotted down for himself but would never have submitted for publication until they could be carefully validated. Nevertheless, Lieberman concluded his comments with praise for Epstein: "It was my privilege to have poured water on the hands of my master and teacher, R. Yaakov Nahum Epstein, of blessed memory. I knew him well. The truth was precious to him, and he showed favoritism to no scholar."[343]

The core differences between the two scholars are essentially methodological. Epstein emphasized the study of source materials for tannaitic literature while Lieberman did not. Lieberman was less concerned with origins than he was with what transpired after the appearance of tannaitic literature—the forms in which it was manifest, the interpretations it received, and the influence it came to exert.[344] Epstein's interest was in origins, in uncovering layers and sources of the Mishnah to show that there were earlier mishnaic editions. In many respects, he applied techniques of biblical criticism to talmudical research.[345] Lieberman's concern was establishing the correct text available to us, and then providing us with a full understanding of the text. In other words, Lieberman's approach was that of the *mefaresh,* the commentator; Epstein epitomizes the *hoker,* the investigator. Epstein's concern was the origin and formation of texts; Lieberman's interest was in the transmission and interpretations of the texts.

It is only to be expected that there should also be a difference in the *modus operandi* of the two scholars. As Shamma Friedman points out, Epstein, the theoretician, composed momentous introductions, while Lieberman, espousing a practical approach, worked on editions, preferring to postpone any methodological introductions, "which, due to his sad demise, we have not had the fortune to see."[346] Most revealing regarding Lieberman's attitude toward "introductions" is his amusing and self-deprecating personal recollection of his early days at the Hebrew University:

> Prior to my coming to the Hebrew University I had never heard of Zacharias Frankel. Upon hearing his name from Professor Epstein and that he was the author of a volume entitled *An Introduction to the Yerushalmi,* I was astounded, and declared: "What need is there for an introduction to the *Yerushalmi* and how would that help in the study of the *Yerushalmi?*"[347]

While Lieberman's recollection may have reflected his youthful naïveté and uncritical thinking at the time, it was also indicative of something deeper—a basic disagreement as to priorities and emphases, which continued to manifest itself throughout their lifetimes. Epstein wrote introductions; Lieberman composed commentaries.

It is not difficult to trace Lieberman's progressive distancing of himself from Epstein's approach, notably in the area of Epstein's emphasis on higher textual criticism.[348] Lieberman's earliest works, *Al Hayerushalmi* and *Talmudah shel Kisrin,* reflect Epstein's orientation, with their emphasis upon the dating of texts and the identification of editions, as well as direct textual criticism.[349] However, Lieberman soon reverted to the older (and for him, more natural) yeshiva style of *parshanut,* with the primary goal being the elucidation of the text. While he mastered Epstein's approach, he simply preferred not employing it, perhaps in part because Lieberman, as a traditionalist, preferred viewing the Talmud as a harmonious unit rather than as a collection of fragments to be analyzed and dated. Lieberman's eventual reluctance to embrace Epstein's higher textual criticism approach may be reflected in a simple statement: "We do not know exactly what part Rabbi Judah Hanasi played in the systematization of the Mishnah"[350]—the intimation possibly being that we cannot know, and therefore should not concentrate on such speculation. Thus, rather than concern himself with the composite nature of texts or their stages of historical development, Lieberman preferred to follow the traditional approach and devote himself to the understanding of the text as it was.

However, it must be emphasized that in his search for the proper understanding of a text, Lieberman fully accepted and enthusiastically embraced Epstein's comparative approach, with its emphasis upon knowing the languages, institutions, and realia of the Greco-Roman world. Lieberman took this approach to unparalleled heights and seemed perfectly comfortable employing it as an integral part of his *parshanut.*[351] It may well be that the primary contrast between Lieberman and Epstein was rooted in the inherent difference between an Eastern European traditionally inclined *mefaresh* and a Western European critically inclined *Wissenschaft hoker.* In Lieberman's thinking, there were two types of *hokrim:* the *hoker* and the *hoker lamdan,* that is, the *hoker* who is a scholar in the traditional sense of understanding texts and engaging in *parshanut.* It was the latter class that Lieberman respected, not the former.[352] In his November 1943 tribute to Ginzberg, Lieberman emphasized this contrast:

> The modern methods are only external, though excellent tools, with which to operate an independent complicated mechanism. But first of all, we have to know the exact working of that mechanism: What did the Rabbis say, and what did they mean, and then we are qualified to put the tools to work. Otherwise the application of modern tools may not only be fruitless, but very often destructive. Jewish scholars in Germany have contributed a great deal to talmudic scholarship. They were the first to apply modern methods of research to rabbinic creations. Some of them, such as Rabbi Zacharias Frankel, displayed a fine understanding of rabbinic thought and an extensive knowledge of talmudic sources. Yet their books and works diverge widely from the usual pattern of rabbinic writings. The East-European academics could never have accepted the works of the Jewish German scholars as part and parcel of rabbinic literature.
>
> The rabbinic student of the East-European academics rightly considered himself the bearer of an unbroken chain of the traditional rabbinic art of thinking and reasoning. No matter to what extremes the dialectic method was carried in the Polish yeshivot, the members of those schools nevertheless recognized the achievements of the Gaon of Vilna, who was far from the dialectic hairsplitting, as the high mark of rabbinic creativity. But the books of the Jewish German scholars in this same field, in spite of their learning and great achievements, fall far short of the genuine rabbinic tradition; they are beautiful and attractive, but belong to a strange world. If one turns from the study of the Mishnah to a reading of Frankel's admirable book *Darke Hamishnah,* "the Ways of the Mishnah," or if one leaves the study of the Palestinian Talmud to consult his excellent introduction to this Talmud, one cannot escape the feeling of a transition from Jerusalem to Berlin and from Tiberias to Breslau.[353]

In fairness, one should be careful not to create dichotomies and rigid demarcations. It is not a matter of *mefaresh* versus *hoker, Hokhmat Yisrael* versus *Wissenschaft,* Lieberman versus Epstein. Lieberman the *mefaresh* mastered the tools of the *hoker* and employed them brilliantly in bridging the Eastern European–Western European scholarship "chasm." He assimilated a great deal from Epstein and admitted as much. For all their differences, they were partners in the search for truth. As Abramson put it, "Epstein may have laid the foundation, but Lieberman built the palace."[354]

How did he build it? By means of remarkable genius and diligent application that earned for him truly hyperbolic commendation and approbation.

NOTES FOR PART I

1. Saul Lieberman, "Bimhitzat Rabbanim," in *Mehkarim b'Torat Eretz Yisrael* (*Studies in Palestinian Talmudic Literature*), ed. David Rosenthal (Jerusalem, 1991), pp. 608–11.
2. Elijah Schochet, interview with Rabbi Chaim Rogoff, a relative of Lieberman, Aug. 1997.
3. Lieberman's British passport of July 24, 1937, as well as his birth certificate, issued by the chief rabbinate of Palestine on July 26, 1940, lists May 23 as his birth date. The British passport of Sept. 30, 1947, designating his birth date as May 28, is probably in error.
4. See Zvulun Ravid, "Motele: The City Where Weizmann Was Born," *Hadoar* 42, no. 27 (May 17, 1963): 502–3. Ravid dedicated his essay to "Rabbi Saul Lieberman, a son of Motele of whom we are proud."
5. *Trial and Error: The Autobiography of Chaim Weizmann* (New York, 1949), pp. 3–4.
6. Solomon Spiro, interview with Meir Lieberman, Aug. 4, 1999.
7. See Zvulun Ravid, "Professor Azriel Shohat," *Hadoar* 56, no. 36 (Sept. 2, 1977): 622–23.
8. Yarden, who edited a journal of mathematics, explained that it was not at all surprising that a Hebrew scholar from Motol was knowledgeable in mathematics, since people from Motol excelled in that field. Indeed, Professor Lieberman's students, especially those who studied *Eizehu Neshekh* with him, will recall that he often demonstrated his mathematical acumen. See Zvulun Ravid, "Dov Yarden and His Contribution to the Study of Hebrew Poetry of the Middle Ages," *Hadoar* 49, no. 3 (Nov. 21, 1969): 39.
9. See Ravid, "Professor Azriel Shohat," p. 622, where he lists a number of other accomplished Jews who were born in Motol.
10. Most of the details of Lieberman's maternal ancestry are derived from N. Rosenstein's "Scion of Sagely Stock: Saul Lieberman in Memoriam," *Jewish Press,* Apr. 29, 1983, p. 26b. For an account of the exemplary career and character of R. Saul Katzenellenbogen, see M. Tzinovitz, "Litoldot Harabbanut Bikobrin Bimaot Hakodmot," in *Sefer Kobrin,* ed. Bezalel Schwartz and Israel Haim Biltzki (Tel Aviv, 1951), pp. 36–40.
11. Rabbi Nathan Kamenetsky, interview with Meir Lieberman, Sept. 18, 1996.
12. See Tzinovitz, "Litoldot Harabbanut Bikobrin," p. 40.

13. Moshe Zevi Neriah, ed., *Likkutei Hare'ayah* (Bene Berak, 1990), 2:338. Lieberman referred to R. Zadok as "Dodi Zekeini." See also Tuvia Preschel, "Mahalakh Hayav Udmuto shel Rav Shaul Lieberman," *Hadoar* 42, no. 23 (Apr. 5, 1963 [11 Nissan 5723]): 370.
14. R. Hayyim Soloveitchik of Brisk, the grandfather of the Rav, married Lifsha, the granddaughter of the Netziv and his first wife. Following the death of his first wife, the Netziv married a niece, Reina Batya, thirty years his junior, who gave birth to R. Meir Berlin (Bar-Ilan). Thus, R. Meir Berlin's daughter, Judith Lieberman, and R. Hayyim Soloveitchik were cousins; Judith and the Rav were cousins twice removed. R. Meir Berlin was raised by the Rav's (R. Meir Berlin's nephew) grandfather, R. Hayyim Soloveitchik of Brisk (Spiro, interview with Haym Soloveitchik, Nov. 9, 1998). See Hayyim Karlinski, *Harishon l'Shalshelet Brisk* (Jerusalem, 1984), pp. 230–32. Dr. Reuben Fink, a physician friend of Lieberman, recalls making a house call to treat Judith Lieberman, whereupon Lieberman, showing him to Judith's room, passed the sitting room in which the Rav was sitting, and said to Fink, "You must know my cousin" (Spiro, interview with Reuben Fink, Aug. 15, 1999).
15. Mark Jay Mirsky, interview with Saul Lieberman, spring 1982.
16. Shraga Abramson, "Darko shel Harav Shaul Lieberman b'Heker Hasifrut Hatalmudit," in *L'Zikhro shel Shaul Lieberman,* Israel Academy of Sciences and Humanities Annual (Jerusalem, 1984), pp. 24–25. Meir Lieberman recalls that a Rabbi Gershonowitz was studying in Motol and living (eating *kest*) with his prominent father-in-law. Meir relates that R. Gershonowitz, recognizing Lieberman's genius, not only urged him to go to Malch, but personally brought him there. R. Gershonowitz later served as rabbi in Jabenke and eventually in B'nai Brak (Spiro, interview with Meir Lieberman, Aug. 10, 1999).
17. Mirsky, interview with Lieberman, spring 1982. According to Lieberman, the cost of traveling from Malch to Motol by train at that time was a prohibitive thirty rubles; he therefore went instead to Kosov for his bar mitzvah. Preschel, "Mahalakh Hayav," p. 370.
18. Abramson, "Darko shel Harav," p. 27.
19. Kamenetsky, interview with S. Abramson, Oct. 4, 1991.
20. Spiro, interview with Meir Lieberman, Aug. 10, 1999. Lieberman was later to write an exceedingly laudatory review of Silberg's *Talmudic Law and the Modern State* (New York, 1973) in *Shana b'Shana* (Jerusalem, 5735 [1974]), pp. 342–44, following the publication of the English translation. Lieberman gave his review copy to Solomon Spiro with the observation, "Silberg begged me to review the book, and despite the fact that I was very busy, I could not refuse him." Many similar illustrations could be cited of Lieberman's loyalty to old friends and individuals who helped him in his time of need.
21. Spiro, interview with Yitzhak Herzog, Aug. 4, 1999.
22. Spiro, interview with Haym Soloveitchik, Feb. 4, 1996.
23. Spiro, interview with Meir Lieberman, Aug. 10, 1999; Mirsky, interview with Lieberman, spring 1982.
24. Abraham Goldberg, "Professor Lieberman's 'Uncompleted' Literary Legacy," in *Saul Lieberman, 1898–1983: Talmudic Scholar,* ed. Meir Lubetski (Lewiston, N.Y., 2002), p. 46.

25. Kamenetsky, interview with Abramson, Oct. 4, 1991.
26. Abramson, "Darko shel Harav," pp. 25–26; Lieberman, "Bimhitzat Rabbanim," p. 609; Kamenetsky, interview with Abramson, Oct. 4, 1991; Kamenetsky, interview with Meir Lieberman, Sept. 18, 1996; Spiro, interview with Meir Lieberman, Aug. 10, 1999.
27. Slobodka yeshiva did not generally bestow rabbinic ordination on its own students; students desirous of acquiring ordination would present themselves to local rabbis for examination and certification. This could take place at any time during their tenure at Slobodka, for such "practical" studies would usually take place on the student's own time. In a document entitled "Professional Recommendation" on the letterhead of the Committee on International Education Cooperation, completed and signed by Lieberman in late 1976 or early 1977, he states that he was ordained at Slobodka Theological Seminary in 1916. It is not clear whether he used a convenient shorthand in mentioning the name of the institution over the name of a particular rabbi who may have given him ordination or whether his ordination was granted by the institution as such and not by any particular rabbi. Had Lieberman displayed his ordination certificate in his office, the answer to this question might have been clear.
28. Lieberman, letter to Louis Ginzberg, Jan. 11, 1930.
29. As a consequence of Lieberman's marriage to Rachel Rabinowitz, he acquired a number of prominent relatives, among them R. Abraham Dubner Kahana Shapiro, rabbi and *av beit din* of Kovne (his wife's uncle), and R. Mendel Gluskin (the husband of Lieberman's wife's sister, Freidel), who, upon his father-in-law's death, succeeded him as rabbi of Minsk. Lieberman was also related to R. Gluskin through his grandfather, R. Saul Katzenellenbogen, rabbi of Kosov and Kobrin. R. Katzenellenbogen and R. Perelmann were intimate friends. See Meir Halperin, *Hagadol Miminsk: R. Yerucham Yehuda Leib Perelmann,* ed. Shlomo Slonim (Jerusalem, 1991) (ms., ca. 1915), pp. 208–9. The above text was brought to our attention by Dr. Tibor Juda of Toronto.
30. Mirsky, interview with Saul Lieberman, spring 1982.
31. Kamenetsky, interview with Meir Lieberman, Sept. 18, 1996.
32. Mirsky, interview with Saul Lieberman, spring 1982.
33. Nissin Wachsman, "Lidmuto shel Hagaon Rav Shlomo Polachek z'l," *Talpiot* 1–2 (1953): 17.
34. Kamenetsky, interview with Meir Lieberman, Sept. 18, 1996; Preschel, "Mahalakh Hayav," p. 370.
35. Spiro, interview with Meir Lieberman, Aug. 10, 1999.
36. Abramson, "Darko shel Harav," p. 26. Michel Rabinowitz was the son-in-law of R. Meir Halperin, who taught R. Perelmann's sons and prepared the manuscript for the book *Hagadol Miminsk.* R. Halperin eventually opened a bookstore in Minsk to sell rabbinic texts, for which Michel Rabinowitz handled the business matters. Rabinowitz, trained in the finest Lithuanian yeshivot, was also a modern enlightened scholar. When he emigrated to Jerusalem, he brought many rare books with him and founded a bookstore named Darome, which served as a meeting place for Lieberman and his fellow scholars. (*Minsk Ir Va'em,* ed. Shelomoh Even-Shoshan [Tel Aviv, 1974], pp.

447–48; and *Hagadol Miminsk*, p. 16, citing *Minsk Ir Va'em*, p. 524. The latter contains a memorial essay for Rabinowitz by President Zalman Shazar.) Probably only a *landsman*, a close friend of his wife's family, as well as one deeply rooted in talmudic studies, could have persuaded Lieberman to enroll in the Hebrew University and later to initiate his study of the *Talmud Yerushalmi*.

37. David Weiss Halivni, "Professor Saul Lieberman," *Conservative Judaism* 38, no. 3 (spring 1986): 6.
38. Spiro, interview with Abraham Goldberg, Aug. 22, 1999.
39. Lieberman's diploma is dated Feb. 13, 1932. According to Halivni ("Professor Saul Lieberman," p. 5), Lieberman's master's dissertation was in talmudic geography, possibly prepared under the influence and guidance of Professor Samuel Klein.
40. Yaacov Sussmann, "Mesoret Limud Umesoret Nusah shel Hatalmud Hayerushalmi," in *Mehkarim Basifrut Hatalmudit: Yom Iyun l'Regel m'Lot Shmonim Shana l'Shaul Lieberman* (Jerusalem, 1983), p. 12.
41. Spiro, interview with David Rosenthal, Aug. 8, 1998.
42. Spiro, interview with Meir Lieberman, Aug. 10, 1999.
43. Judah Magnes, letter to Harry Fischel, Nov. 24, 1931 (Hebrew University Library, file no. 201).
44. Minutes of the meeting of the Hebrew University board of directors, Feb. 25, 1937. Only J. N. Epstein opposed the resolution to drop Lieberman's class.
45. Spiro, interview with A. Goldberg, Aug. 22, 1999; Spiro, interview with Itamar Aviad, Aug. 12, 1999.
46. Spiro, interview with Halivni, Jan. 31, 1996. Lieberman believed that *Talmudah shel Kisrin* deserved consideration as a Ph.D. dissertation. After describing the thesis of *Talmudah shel Kisrin* in a letter to L. Ginzberg on June 1, 1930, Lieberman asked him to suggest dissertation topics and asked whether Ginzberg believed that the work "On the Redaction of the Bavot of the Yerushalmi" (*Talmudah shel Kisrin*) would satisfy the Ph.D. requirement. He offered to send Ginzberg the results of his research. See below, section entitled "Traditional Ambiance." Lieberman was never awarded a doctorate. He did, however, receive a number of doctorates *honoris causa*. For a list of honorary degrees, see below, section entitled "Honors, Affiliations, and Invitations."
47. Yitzhak Raphael, "Point of View: In the Company of the Great," *Jewish Press*, May 22, 1981, p. 4.
48. Spiro, interview with Halivni, Jan. 31, 1996.
49. Lieberman was appointed dean in 1935 (Preschel, "Mahalakh Hayav," p. 370) and served until the summer of 1940, when he moved to New York to join the JTS faculty.
50. Spiro, interview with I. Aviad, Aug. 12, 1999.
51. R. Kook, *Halakhah Berurah* (Jerusalem, 1940).
52. Lieberman, preface to *Tosefet Rishonim*, Harry Fischel Institute Publications (Jerusalem, 1937), pp. vi–vii. Lieberman's preface provides an excellent statement of the objectives of Talmud scholarship, in his typically concise and lucid style. Lieberman's Hebrew introduction includes considerable interpre-

tation and explanation of difficult texts. Chief Rabbi Abraham Isaac Kook, a prime mover in the founding of the institute, remained at its helm until his death, in 1935. The institute embarked on the study of the rishonim on *Mo'ed Katan,* the tractate dealing with the laws of mourning, as a response to the death of the chief rabbi. While *Tosefet Rishonim* includes comparison of texts and variant readings, its significance to the directors of the institute lies in the attempt to relate the halakhah to the Talmud text.

53. Lieberman believed that Epstein would view any involvement in the preparation of a scientific edition of the Mishnah as an infringement on his area of expertise. Although Epstein was not engaged in preparing a scientific edition of the Mishnah at the time, he was then working on his *Mavo l'Nusah Hamishnah,* which Lieberman viewed as quite distinct from a scientific edition of the Mishnah. Lieberman, letter to Ginzberg, May 5, 1938. Lieberman feared that his heading a scientific Mishnah project under the auspices of the Harry Fischel Institute would profoundly upset Epstein. Lieberman's correspondence with Ginzberg (to be discussed below) reflects this anxiety.
54. Spiro, interview with Meir Lieberman, Aug. 10, 1999. Meir rightly credits Saul with saving his life and those of his wife and daughter, describing it as a "miracle." They were among the last in the area to receive British visas to Palestine. It is a tribute to Saul Lieberman that he obtained such visas for his brother's family, when immigration to Palestine was so restrictive. It must have taken much of Saul's ingenuity and a considerable sum of money. Since Saul left Palestine on Aug. 20, 1940, Meir did not see him upon his arrival. It is unlikely that they met again until after the war.
55. Letter from Meir Lieberman to his sister in Europe, June 7, 1946, in response to a letter that she had sent him through someone in the U.S. This was apparently the first communication between brother and sister since the end of the war. Meir told his sister, "Saul lives . . . very well—he is a professor of Talmud," and gave her Saul's address.
56. N. Rosenstein, *Jewish Press,* Apr. 29, 1983; Florence Bar-Ilan, letter to Schochet, Apr. 29, 1996.
57. Kamenetsky, interview with Beverly Gribetz, Dec. 1998; Schochet, interview with Rogoff, Aug. 1997; and Spiro, interview with A. Goldberg, Aug. 2, 1999. Some believe that Lieberman's wife had an ectopic pregnancy (Spiro, interview with Alice Zlotnick, May 15, 2001).
58. J. N. Epstein, letter to Ginzberg, July 30, 1931.
59. Spiro, interview with I. Aviad, Aug. 12, 1999.
60. Tuvia Preschel, "Something about the Shulamith School," *Hadoar* 48, no. 28 (May 30, 1969): 472–73.
61. Francine Klagsbrun, "Reunion Brings Back Memories," *Jewish Week,* Jan. 11, 2002, p. 19. Gerson Cohen, Nehama Cohen's son, later became chancellor of JTS.
62. Spiro, interview with Hannah Urbach, Aug. 10, 1999.
63. This is clear from a review of the correspondence in *Pirkei Nehama: Prof. Nehama Leibowitz Memorial Volume,* ed. Moshe Arend, Ruth Ben-Meir, and Gavriel Haim Cohen (Jerusalem, 2001), pp. 21–23.
64. Ibid., pp. 22–23.

65. Spiro, interview with Moshe Zwick, May 1, 2002.
66. Schochet, interview with Moshe Tendler, Mar. 1990.
67. Hillel Goldberg, *Between Berlin and Slobodka: Jewish Transition Figures from Eastern Europe* (Hoboken, N.J., 1988), pp. 79–80.
68. Lieberman, letter to Anita Shapira, May 31, 1982.
69. Lieberman, "Bimhitzat Rabbanim," pp. 610–11.
70. Kamenetsky, interview with Meir Lieberman, Sept. 18, 1996. Those who say that Lieberman's wife died in childbirth contend that her inadequate diet was a contributing factor.
71. Florence Bar-Ilan, letter to Schochet, Apr. 1, 1996.
72. Spiro, interview with David Novak, Oct. 26, 1999.
73. Aaron Halevi Pizenic, "Ishim Degulim Shehekarti," in *Shana b'Shana: L'Halakhah, l'Mahshava Ulba'ayot Hayahadut,* ed. Pizenic (Jerusalem, 1986), pp. 404–5. R. Meir Bar-Ilan explained that Lieberman had to leave Jerusalem because he was a scholar of great genius and was lacking the conditions to facilitate his program of study and writing.
74. Judah Avida, "Tannah Yerushalmi v'Tannah Tosefa'ah," *Hadoar* (11 Nissan 5723 [1963]): 8–9. Avida, a Slobodka alumnus, was a noted author in both Yiddish and Hebrew as well as an accomplished orator. In 1957, two years following the publication of the first three volumes of the *Tosefta Kifshutah, Zera'im,* Avida prepared an essay on Lieberman to commemorate the event. Following the publication of the three volumes of *Tosefta Kifshutah, Mo'ed* in 1962, *Hadoar* planned the special issue honoring Lieberman on the publication of these volumes. Avida was to update his essay for this issue, but he was unable to prepare the update because of an illness, which resulted in his death in 1962. *Hadoar* therefore published his original 1957 article, explaining the matter in an editorial note at the conclusion of Avida's essay. An additional note disclosing a communication from Moshe Chovev, a young writer who assisted Avida in organizing his literary work, is added to the *Hadoar* essay as an example of the extent of Avida's admiration and respect for Lieberman. Chovev relates that Avida insisted on speaking at an occasion in Jerusalem to honor Lieberman, although he was weak and ill. The next day, Avida related to Chovev that, difficult as it was for him to prepare and deliver his remarks, "I was very pleased that when I descended from the speaker's platform for the last time, it was after having spoken in honor of one of the greatest people of our generation." Ibid., p. 9.
75. Lieberman, letter to Anita Shapira, May 31, 1982. This may have been the case during Lieberman's early years in Palestine, but it would appear that after his marriage to Judith, earning a livelihood was not a problem. Itamar Aviad, whose family arrived in Palestine in 1933, recalls Lieberman bringing expensive gifts to their apartment and providing funds in advance for his and his brother's education. Both earned income and, not having children, their expenses were relatively modest. Lieberman's problem was not that his employment generated insufficient income for his needs, but that it was not conducive to his aspirations as a scholar (Spiro, interviews with Itamar and Yakov Aviad and Abraham Goldberg).

76. Yaacov Sussmann, "Schechter Hahoker," in *Mada'ei Hayahadut* (Jerusalem, 1998), 38:213–29. See also Jonathan D. Sarna, "Two Traditions of Seminary Scholarship," in *Tradition Renewed: A History of the Jewish Theological Seminary of America,* ed. Jack Wertheimer (New York, 1997), 2:59; and Robert Liberles, "Wissenschaft des Judentum Comes to America," in *Tradition Renewed,* 1:335–36. Liberles points out that JTS likewise had a propensity toward hiring Lithuanian-born scholars.
77. Lieberman, letter to Scholem, Mar. 2, 1941.
78. Judith Lieberman, letter to Scholem, Aug. 26, 1941. In the same letter, she explained that they chose to live in a furnished apartment instead of establishing a permanent residence, presumably because they hoped to return to Jerusalem. Similarly, Saul Lieberman, in a letter to Scholem, Mar. 2, 1941, expressed his reluctance to take a permanent appointment at JTS. These sentiments indicate the conflicting forces tugging at the Liebermans as they settled in New York.
79. David Landau, "The Talmud's Rising Prestige," *Jerusalem Post* interview, Aug. 25, 1970.
80. Lieberman, letter to Scholem, Mar. 2, 1941; Judith Lieberman, letter to Scholem, Aug. 26, 1941.
81. Spiro, interview with Menahem Schmelzer, Mar. 22, 1996.
82. Spiro, interview with Bernard Mandelbaum, June 7, 1996.
83. Finkelstein related this incident to David Lieber. Samuel Dresner relates: "[W]hen the important chair in Talmud [at JTS] became available in the 1930s, with an eye on the eventual retirement of Rabbi Louis Ginzberg, the three most important candidates who applied were, according to Wolfe Kelman, J. B. Soloveitchik, Samuel Belkin, and Saul Lieberman" (Samuel Dresner, *Heschel, Hasidism, and Halakha* [New York, 2002], p. 119 n. 25).
84. Jack Wertheimer, "JTS and the Conservative Movement," in *Tradition Renewed,* 2:406.
85. Cited in Mel Scult, "Schechter's Seminary," in *Tradition Renewed,* 1:85.
86. Ibid., 1:85–86, 88.
87. Cited in *Tradition Renewed,* ed. Wertheimer, 1:101 n. 166.
88. See, for example, Jeffrey S. Gurock, "Another Look at the Proposed Merger: Lay Perspectives on Yeshiva–Jewish Theological Seminary Relations in the 1920s," in *Hazon Nahum: Studies in Jewish Law, Thought, and History Presented to Dr. Norman Lamm on the Occasion of His Seventieth Birthday,* ed. Yaakov Elman and Jeffrey Gurock (New York, 1997), pp. 729–42.
89. Cyrus Adler, letter to Jacob Schiff, Nov. 11, 1919 (Cyrus Adler's papers, box 24); cited in Ira Robinson, "Cyrus Adler: President of JTS, 1915–1940," in *Tradition Renewed,* 1:131.
90. Aaron Rothkoff, *Bernard Revel: Builder of American Jewish Orthodoxy* (Philadelphia, 1972), pp. 99–103.
91. Louis Finkelstein, eulogy for Ginzberg and Marx, "Our Teachers," *Proceedings of the Rabbinical Assembly of America* 18 (1955): 174.
92. Finkelstein, "Doctor Saul Lieberman: An Appreciation," *United Synagogue Review* (fall 1983): 3. The excerpt is from Finkelstein's eulogy for Lieberman.

93. Louis Ginzberg, *On Jewish Law and Lore* (Philadelphia, 1955), pp. 48–49.
94. Cited in Harvey Goldberg, "Becoming History: Perspectives on the Seminary Faculty at Mid-Century," in *Tradition Renewed,* 1:359.
95. Eli Ginzberg, *Keeper of the Law: Louis Ginzberg* (Philadelphia, 1966), p. 141.
96. Lieberman, letters to Ginzberg, Jan. 31, 1930, and Mar. 28, 1938.
97. Copies of the cables were provided by the Joseph and Miriam Ratner Center for the Study of Conservative Judaism.
98. Finkelstein, letter to A. M. Warren, chief of visa division, Washington, D.C., June 24, 1940.
99. Michael Greenbaum, "Finkelstein and His Critics," *Conservative Judaism* 47, no. 4 (Sept. 1995): 29.
100. Cited in ibid., p. 22.
101. Ibid., pp. 55–56.
102. Finkelstein, letter to Arthur Hays Sulzberger. Cited in Greenbaum, "Finkelstein and His Critics," p. 29.
103. Jeffrey S. Gurock, "Yeshiva Students at JTS," in *Tradition Renewed,* 1:471–514.
104. Greenbaum, "Finkelstein and His Critics," pp. 35–36.
105. Spiro, interview with Halivni, Jan. 28, 1996.
106. Ezra Finkelstein claims that while his father, Louis Finkelstein, relied on Lieberman for guidance and direction, he did not always adopt Lieberman's views, valuing his own independence. However, Finkelstein gave Lieberman free rein in certain areas with the hope that his wisdom would guide the Conservative movement and JTS, i.e., "keep them on the traditional path" (Spiro, interview with Ezra Finkelstein, May 11, 1998).
107 Spiro, interview with David Kogen, Sept. 8, 1998.
108. Cited in Baila R. Shargel, "Texture of Seminary Life," in *Tradition Renewed,* 1:532.
109. Spiro, interview with Emunah Katzenstein, Aug. 3, 1999.
110. Finkelstein, letter to Judith Lieberman, Sept. 23, 1946 (RG I-C 50/25).
111. Finkelstein, letters to Lieberman, Aug. 9, 1946; Dec. 28, 1950; Nov. 22, 1955; and May 18, 1967.
112. L. Finkelstein, "The Pharisees: Their Origin and Their Philosophy," *Harvard Theological Review* 22 (1929): 185–261; idem, *The Pharisees: The Sociological Background of Their Faith* (Philadelphia, 1938).
113. See Louis Ginzberg, "The Significance of the Halachah for Jewish History," in *On Jewish Law and Lore,* pp. 77–126. This was a lecture delivered in 1929–30 at the Hebrew University, and later published by the Hebrew University Press. It is not inconceivable that Lieberman might have heard it from Ginzberg at the Hebrew University at that time. Indeed, Ginzberg asked that Lieberman prepare the lecture for publication.
114. Lawrence Schiffman, "The Pharisees Revisited: Louis Finkelstein on the Second Temple Period," in *Yakar Le'Mordecai: Jubilee Volume in Honor of Rabbi Mordecai Waxman,* ed. Zvia Ginor (New York, 1998), pp. 85–101. Schiffman presents a fine analysis of these concerns on Finkelstein's part and how he sought to address them through his scholarship. We are grateful to Robert Chazan for bringing this essay to our attention.

115. Louis Finkelstein, *The Pharisees: The Sociological Background of Their Faith,* rev. ed. (Philadelphia, 1962), 2:636.
116. Ibid., 1:cxxiii.
117. Ibid., 1:xliv–xlv.
118. Finkelstein, letter to Lieberman, May 18, 1967.
119. Spiro, interview with A. Goldberg, Aug. 2, 1999.
120. Spiro, interview with Emunah Katzenstein, Aug. 2, 1999.
121. L. Finkelstein, "Emendations of the Sifrei," *Tarbiz* 3, no. 2 (Jan. 1932): 198–204.
122. "Od l'Tikkunei Girsaot b'Sifrei," *Tarbiz* 3, no. 4 (July 1932): 466–67.
123. Louis Finkelstein, *Akiba: Scholar, Saint, and Martyr* (New York, 1936), pp. 47–49. Finkelstein's depiction of the Sage is indeed exceedingly negative, with character indictments that would seem difficult to justify on the basis of historical evidence. Both Finkelstein's *Akiba* and *The Pharisees* stem from a period when he attributed great importance to sociological and socioeconomic factors in his historical analyses, clearly favoring some practices and practitioners over others.
124. Lieberman, letter to Finkelstein, Jan. 1938. Finkelstein replies at length on Mar. 23, 1938.
125. Finkelstein, *Akiba* (Northvale, N.J., 1990), pp. xxvi–xxvii.
126. Finkelstein references Lieberman's essay "Persecution of the Jewish Religion," published in the Jubilee volume (Hebrew volume) in honor of Professor Salo Baron (1975), 3:213 ff. Finkelstein cites Lieberman's explanation that R. Akiba's death was not an execution, but was brought about instead by R. Akiba's recitation of the Shema, which was viewed by the Romans as an act of defiance toward the emperor and his pretensions of divinity. The Romans beat the courageous Rabbi in order to stop him from reciting the prayer, and when R. Akiba refused to cease, he was beaten and flayed to death.
127. See below, part 2, section entitled "Detective Sense," for a brief discussion of Lieberman's essay on the Hadrianic persecutions.
128. Finkelstein, *Akiba,* p. 48.
129. Lieberman, letter to Finkelstein, May 31, 1937.
130. As Ginzberg's health deteriorated in the 1940s, Lieberman came to replace him as Finkelstein's adviser and confidante (Spiro, interview with E. Finkelstein, May 11, 1998).
131. Stanley Fuld, letter to Lieberman, Nov. 5, 1971.
132. Finkelstein, letter to Lieberman, Aug. 4, 1944. Several months earlier (June 20, 1944), Finkelstein had written to Lieberman, asking him to write a chapter in the proposed volume (*Judaism and the Jews*), to be titled "The Talmud and Midrash as Cultural Monuments." No volume containing that chapter title appears in print. A two-volume work entitled *The Jews: Their History, Culture, and Religion* (ed. Finkelstein) was published in 1949 but does not contain essays contributed by Ginzberg or Lieberman. William Foxwell Albright and Judah Goldin wrote on the biblical and talmudic periods, respectively.
133. Lieberman, letters to JTS faculty, Feb. 15, 1957, and Apr. 9, 1957.
134. Greenbaum, "Finkelstein and His Critics," pp. 35–36.
135. Report of Rabbi David H. Panitz, chairman of the Rabbinical Assembly Com-

mittee on Regions, Jan. 5, 1962; and Lieberman, letter addressed to Rabbi Sidney Greenberg, Nov. 14, 1961, pp. 2–3.

136. Finkelstein, letter to Lieberman, May 13, 1946 (RGI-C 50/25).
137. Lieberman, letter to Finkelstein, June 21, 1950.
138. Spiro, interview with A. Goldberg, Aug. 2, 1999.
139. Finkelstein, letter to Lieberman, Aug. 14, 1947. Cited in H. Goldberg, "Becoming History," 1:366.
140. Finkelstein's 4½-page single-spaced letter to Lieberman, July 22, 1955.
141. Cited in H. Goldberg, "Becoming History," 1:374.
142. Spiro, interview with Kogen, Sept. 8, 1998.
143. Ibid.
144. Ibid.
145. E.g., Finkelstein, letter to Lieberman, Mar. 27, 1938.
146. See below, part 2, section entitled "Honors, Affiliations, and Invitations." Spiro, interview with Emunah Katzenstein, Aug. 3, 1999.
147. Finkelstein, letter to Lieberman, Aug. 8, 1954: "Moshe Davis just arrived and I went to his house to get the Tephilin, which are astonishingly beautiful. They make me feel so good that I had to write at once to thank you for getting them for me. It will be a joy each day to put them on and will make saying my prayers even more delightful than it normally can be."
148. Apr. 13, 1949. Finkelstein had given to Lieberman a tallit, which was subsequently stolen. On the eve of Passover, Finkelstein presented Lieberman with a new tallit. Lieberman's thank-you letter includes a humorous comment to the effect that on every Shabbat he was angry to think that a thief had desired his particular tallit.
149. Spiro, interview with E. Finkelstein, May 11, 1998.
150. Finkelstein, letters to Lieberman, Aug. 29, 1951, and Aug. 17, 1954.
151. Lieberman, letter to Finkelstein, July 31, 1949.
152. Finkelstein, letter to Lieberman, Aug. 24, 1942.
153. Finkelstein, letter to Lieberman, May 28, 1977.
154. Spiro, interview with E. Finkelstein, May 11, 1998.
155. Finkelstein, letter to Judith Lieberman, Mar. 13, 1951.
156. Judith Lieberman, letter to Finkelstein, July 20, 1948. Finkelstein's remarks concerning Ezra were likely related to Ezra's not having written home often enough while away. Such concerns are also later expressed in a letter that Finkelstein wrote the following summer to Lieberman, Aug. 23, 1949.
157. Lieberman, letter to Finkelstein, July 26, 1951. Quoted in H. Goldberg, "Becoming History," 1:377.
158. Lieberman, letter to Finkelstein, Nov. 11, 1938.
159. Lieberman, letter to Finkelstein, cited in H. Goldberg, "Becoming History," 1:373.
160. Cited in H. Goldberg, "Becoming History," 1:422–23.
161. Spiro, interview with E. Finkelstein, Nov. 5, 1998.
162. Schochet, interview with Eli Ginzberg, Aug. 5, 1997.
163. Lieberman, letter to the editor of *Ma'ariv,* Sept. 16, 1974, in response to the report that Lieberman had met with Golda Meir and that she had implored him as a leader of the Conservative movement and vice president of JTS to

persuade the Conservative movement to support a compromise on the issues of immigration and registration of converts. See David Golinkin, "The Influence of Seminary Professors on Halakha in the Conservative Movement: 1902–1968," in *Tradition Renewed,* 2:452, and nn. 55 and 57. In an undated *Jerusalem Post* interview, Lieberman explicitly stated that he himself was not a Conservative Jew; however, he praised Conservative Jews for their sincerity and their success in appealing to young people.

164. Lieberman wrote to Yaakov Vainstein on behalf of Rabbi Theodore Friedman, Oct. 31, 1971.
165. Maimon, letter to Lieberman, Jan. 15, 1958. Since the law committee did not unanimously approve travel by automobile on the Sabbath, the policy did not receive the approval of the Rabbinical Assembly and thus did not constitute official policy. Mordecai Waxman, ed., *Tradition and Change: The Development of the Conservative Movement* (New York, 1958), pp. 351 ff.
166. Finkelstein, letter to Lieberman, Mar. 25, 1952 (RGI-H 108/6).
167. *Proceedings of the Rabbinical Assembly of America* 17 (1953): 75–77.
168. Irving A. Breitowitz, *Between Civil and Religious Law: The Plight of the Agunah in American Society* (London, 1993), p. 97.
169. Ibid., p. 98. See also Linda S. Kahan, *Jewish Divorce and Secular Courts: The Promise of Avitzur,* 73 Georgetown Law Journal 193 (1984); and Elizabeth Lieberman, *Avitzur v. Avitzur: The Constitutional Implications of Judicially Enforcing Religious Agreements,* 33 Catholic Law Review 219 (1983), cited in Breitowitz, p. 393.
170. Spiro, interview with Emanuel Rackman, June 6, 1996. See also E. Rackman, "Political Conflict and Cooperation: Political Considerations in Jewish Interdenominational Relations 1955–56," Bar-Ilan University Political Science Series.
171. Rackman, ibid., pp. 120–21. Five years later, Norman Lamm of Yeshiva University, in a critique of "the Conservative amendment" to the *ketubah,* reiterated the claim that the document was "by nature, so vague and indeterminate that it fails to satisfy the minimal subjective requirements for valid contracts." In other words, it is invalid precisely because it is an *asmakhta* (Norman Lamm, "Recent Additions to the Ketuba: A Halakhic Critique," *Tradition* 2, no. 1 [fall 1959]: 93–118). Interestingly, Lamm's rabbinical colleague Cecil Walkenfeld takes issue with him, contending that the amendment is decidedly not an *asmakhta* (C. Walkenfeld, "Communications . . . The Conservative Ketuba," *Tradition* 3, no. 1 [fall 1960]: 103–5). R. Lamm's response, pp. 105–6.
172. Louis Bernstein, interviews with Wolfe Kelman and David Hollander in Louis Bernstein, *Challenge and Mission: The Emergence of the English-Speaking Rabbinate* (New York, 1982), p. 67.
173. "The Steering Committee of the Joint Law Committee (1953–54)," *Proceedings of the Rabbinical Assembly of America* 17 (1955): 64. The report was submitted by Theodore Friedman.
174. Ibid.
175. Letter from Israel Klavin to Simon Dolgin in Bernstein, *Challenge and Mission,* pp. 67–68, 76.
176. See Rackman, "Political Conflict and Cooperation," pp. 121–22; and Bernstein, *Challenge and Mission,* pp. 68–69.

177. Bernstein, *Challenge and Mission,* p. 69. According to Rackman, "Political Conflict and Cooperation," p. 124, the vote was 7–5.
178. Bernstein, *Challenge and Mission,* p. 70.
179. Cited by Wolfe Kelman, letter to *Jewish Week,* May 14, 1987.
180. Rackman, who served as president of the RC, 1958–60, viewed the story of the defeat of the proposed *beit din* as a "painful" episode. One may speculate that if the efforts of Lieberman and Soloveitchik bore fruit in the formation of a joint *beit din,* the further collaboration of these two great men, who respected each other, would have had a tremendous positive impact on the future development of the two movements and on Jewish unity.
181. Spiro, interview with Rackman, June 6, 1996.
182. Rackman, "Political Conflict and Cooperation," p. 122.
183. Landau, "The Talmud's Rising Prestige."
184. Spiro, interview with Rabbi Emanuel Gettinger, Feb. 2, 1996.
185. Alexander Marx, "Dr. Lieberman's Contribution to Jewish Scholarship," *Proceedings of the Rabbinical Assembly of America* 12 (1948): 259–71.
186. Lieberman, "Response," *Proceedings of the Rabbinical Assembly of America* 12 (1948): 288–89. The student in question was Hillel E. Silverman, who recalls: "Saturday night, before my Sunday examination, I was studying until the early hours of the morning in my dormitory room on the fourth floor. In traditional talmudic sing-song, I was chanting the Talmud at the top of my lungs. I finished studying at 2 A.M. and prepared for bed. To my horror, there was a loud knock on the door; there stood Professor Lieberman! I was distraught. 'Forgive me, Professor, I must have disturbed you. I completely forgot that your study on the fifth floor was directly above my dormitory room.' 'No, Silverman, I heard you studying and then you stopped; I thought perhaps you had a problem with the text!' 'No, no, Professor, I finished my studies and was preparing for bed. I'm terribly sorry that I disturbed you.'"

    In an interesting postscript, Silverman records hearing of Lieberman's reaction to the episode from his uncle, Rabbi Herman Hailperin, at whose synagogue Lieberman delivered a lecture. In the course of his comments, Lieberman related the story to the audience, concluding with this observation: "I can't believe that here was a young man, born in the United States, parents also born in this country, late on a Saturday night, and rather than attend a play or frolic on Broadway in Times Square, was in his Seminary dormitory room, singing aloud in traditional Gemara sing-song as he studied the Talmud. And when his voice reached me on the fifth floor, it occurred to me that when the voices of the students on the fourth floor blend with the voices of the professors on the fifth floor, there is a future for Judaism in the United States." *Proceedings of the Rabbinical Assembly of America* 62 (2000): 34.
187. Gedalyahu Alon, "The Lithuanian Yeshivas," in *The Jewish Expression,* ed. Judah Goldin (New York, 1970), pp. 451–52; originally from *Mehkarim Betoledot Yisrael* (*Studies in the History of Israel*), vol. 1 (Jerusalem, 1957).
188. E. Ginzberg, *Keeper of the Law: Louis Ginzberg,* p. 46.
189. Cited in Michael Shashar, "Oseh Torah Kol Yamav," *Hatzofeh,* Mar. 26, 1993.
190. Michael Shashar, "Fanaticism, a Difficult Competitor and a Cheap Substitute

for Torah: A Conversation with Professor Saul Lieberman" (Heb.), *Ha'aretz* interview, May 7, 1965.

191. Robert Liberles, *Salo Wittmayer Baron: Architect of Jewish History* (New York, 1995), p. 358.
192. Scult, "Schechter's Seminary," 1:68. The citation is from the Mordecai Kaplan journal, Feb. 4, 1917.
193. Richard L. Rubenstein, *Power Struggle* (New York, 1974), pp. 128–29.
194. The attribution is to William Greenfield. Cited in H. Goldberg, "Becoming History," 1:428 n. 70.
195. Kamenetsky, interview with Abramson, Oct. 4, 1991. See Nathan Kamenetsky, *Making of a Godol: A Study of Episodes in the Lives of Great Torah Personalities* (Jerusalem, 2002), 1:1190 n. c, which cites a story attributed to R. Ruderman about R. Epstein asking Lieberman to leave the Slobodka yeshiva while the Alter was away.
196. "Rabbi Yaakov Yitzchak Ruderman as Remembered by His Students," *Jewish Observer,* Nov. 1987, pp. 14–15. Lieberman is not identified by name in this article.
197. Schochet, interview with R. Yaakov Kamenetsky, July 1979.
198. Neriah, ed., *Likkutei Hare'ayah,* 1:459, 2:338–39. Lieberman explained that if he prepared for the session, Rav Kook would do likewise, and the session would then be so extended that they would not achieve their objective of reviewing a considerable portion of the text. Needless to say, they would take the time to deal with issues and questions that arose in the course of the session.
199. Ibid., 1:460.
200. Ibid., 2:339.
201. Yehuda Leib Hakohen Maimon, ed., *Azkarah l'Nishmat Hagaon Hatzadik Harav Rabi Avraham Yitzhak Hakohen Kook z'l* (Jerusalem, 1937–38).
202. Yitzhak Raphael, ed., *Yovel Sinai* (Jerusalem, 1987), 1:606. Dr. Aaron M. Nussbaum and Dr. Tibor Juda, both of Toronto, brought this story and its source to our attention.
203. Pinchas Peli (P. Ben-Yair, pseudonym), "Hagaon Kifshuto," *Panim el Panim,* no. 517 (Apr. 18, 1969): 10.
204. Lieberman, letter to Menahem Zulay, Dec. 30, 1939. The Netziv's sister was the grandmother of Penina Herzog's grandparents.
205. Chaim Herzog, in *In Praise of a Master: Tributes to Professor Saul Lieberman,* American Jewish Heritage Committee, ed. William Berkowitz (New York, 1987).
206. Eli Lederhendler, "The Ongoing Dialogue: The Seminary and the Challenge of Israel," in *Tradition Renewed,* 2:196.
207. Spiro, interview with Meir Benayahu, Aug. 13, 1999.
208. Yisrael Dubitsky, communication to Spiro, Apr. 13, 2000. Dubitsky is the public services librarian at JTS.
209. Yitzhak Raphael, "Professor Rabbi Shaul Lieberman," eulogy, *Sinai* 93 (5743 [Apr./May 1983]): 91–92.
210. Raphael, "Point of View: In the Company of the Great," *Jewish Press,* May 22, 1981, p. 4.

211. June 20, 1962 (Nissin); May 27, 1971 (Unterman); Mar. 29, 1971 (Goren); Oct. 23, 1965 (Walkin); Aug. 1, 1960 (Kook); Dec. 5, 1971 (Hutner); Feb. 9, 1965 (Riff); Sept. 9, 1963 (Price); two undated letters were sent to Lieberman under the letterheads of Kerem Monthly Publication and Tvuno Rabbinical College (Zimmerman); and Sept. 12, 1971 (Belkin).
212. Spiro, interview with Rackman, June 6, 1996. R. Rackman said that R. Joseph Lookstein, his predecessor as chancellor of Bar-Ilan University, relied on Lieberman as the spiritual leader of the university. He added that Lookstein always went to Lieberman for counsel and guidance: "We did follow his advice. No president, dean, or rector [of Bar-Ilan University] would have acted against him." See below, section entitled "Honors, Affiliations, and Invitations," for a discussion of Lieberman's collaboration with Lookstein in guiding the development of Bar-Ilan University.
213. When Rackman was approached regarding the presidency of Bar-Ilan University, he did not want to meet with the search committee; but when he was asked whether he would meet with Professor Lieberman, he replied that he would consider that an opportunity. Rackman wanted his personal advice as to whether he was the right man for the job, and whether he could better serve *klal Yisrael* as president of Bar-Ilan or as rabbi of the Fifth Avenue Synagogue. Lieberman urged him to accept the appointment as president of Bar-Ilan.
214. Weinberg letters, Aug. 3, 1954, and Oct. 27, 1956.
215. Schochet, interview with R. Jordan Hoffman, June 6, 1998.
216. Spiro, interview with Tibor Juda, a son-in-law of R. Hirschprung, Oct. 28, 1999. Juda provided us with a copy of a publication, *Ohel Torah* (1930), which included a laudatory review by Hirschprung of Lieberman's first published work, *Al Hayerushalmi,* in which he praised the attainments of "Harav Hagaon R. Shaul Lieberman," whom he described as one of the exceptional young men of the Lithuanian yeshivot. In a time when yeshiva scholars were not studying the *Yerushalmi,* Hirschprung marveled at the way Lieberman mastered the *Yerushalmi* and commended him for his commentary on the tractate *Sotah,* wherein he listed the categories of errors that fell into the text, clarifying what had until then been misunderstood. In the late 1940s, Lieberman urged Hirschprung to join the JTS faculty, pointing out that he could achieve much more than in Montreal, where he served as chief rabbi. Lieberman was impressed with Hirschprung's encyclopedic knowledge of rabbinic texts and his analytical skills, as well as with his warm, unassuming personality. His appointment to the faculty would have been consistent with the plans of Finkelstein and Lieberman to enhance the reputation of JTS as a traditional institution (Spiro, interview with Chaya Hirschprung, Aug. 25, 2001).
217. Jeffrey Gurock, letter to Schochet, Apr. 14, 1997. For example, Herschel Schachter, in *Nefesh Harav* (Jerusalem, 1944), p. 248, reports that Soloveitchik told him of having met Lieberman at a *brit* and having discussed gaonic responsa dealing with the subject of priestly uncleanliness due to contact with corpses.
218. Raphael, "Point of View: In the Company of the Great," p. 50.
219. Chaim Dalfin, *Conversations with the Rebbe* (Los Angeles, 1996), p. 54. We

are grateful to Rabbi Sol Majersdorf, copy cataloger, JTS library, for drawing our attention to this interview. Regarding Lieberman's relationship to Lubavitch, see part 2, section entitled "Support for Scholars."

220. Florence Bar-Ilan, letter to Schochet, Apr. 24, 1996; Meir Bar-Ilan, letter to Lieberman, Jan. 17, 1945. Early in 1943, Finkelstein and his children were invited by the Liebermans to join them and R. Meir Bar-Ilan for lunch. Finkelstein says in a letter to Mrs. Lieberman (Feb. 1, 1943) that the luncheon "gave me the chance to have so free and frank a talk with your father, whom I have revered for so many years."
221. Cited in Pizenic, "Ishim Degulim Shehekarti," p. 404. The talmudic passage quoted by R. Bar-Ilan is from *Berakhot* 28a.
222. "Open Letter" (no author given), *Hapardes* 19, no. 6 (Sept. 1945): 31. Rabbi Tuvia Preschel kindly brought this article to our attention.
223. *Hapardes* 19, no. 7 (Oct. 1945).
224. Marc B. Shapiro, ed., *Collected Writings of Rabbi Yehiel Yaakov Weinberg* (Scranton, 2003), appendix, 2:449–50. The letter was found in the archives of Rabbi Dovid Lifshitz, at Yeshiva University.
225. See below, part 2, section entitled "Personality Integration," p. 223, and part 2, n. 480, for Lieberman's view of academic competitiveness.
226. See n. 216 above.
227. This letter bears a remarkable resemblance to a similar anonymous letter sent by "an Orthodox critic" to Louis Ginzberg in 1948. It has been suggested that in the case of Ginzberg, the letter proved so upsetting that it triggered a chronic illness! See E. Ginzberg, *Keeper of the Law: Louis Ginzberg,* pp. 145–46.
228. Yaakov Gil, letter in *Ma'ariv,* May 28, 1958.
229. Yedidiah Cohen, *Amudim* (Iyar 5743 [Apr./May 1983]): 285–86.
230. Lieberman, letter to Scholem, Mar. 2, 1941. Both Meir Lieberman and Penina Herzog commented that this was the rationale that Lieberman provided to them for choosing to come to JTS (Spiro, interviews with Meir Lieberman, Aug. 10, 1999; with Penina Herzog, Aug. 9 1999; and with Yehuda Shapira, Aug. 12, 1999).
231. Spiro, interview with Aaron M. Nussbaum, Sept. 9, 1996.
232. Lieberman, letter to Jacob David Abramsky, Feb. 18, 1965.
233. Lieberman, letter to Finkelstein, Aug. 12, 1956. Cited in H. Goldberg, "Becoming History," 1:427 n. 51.
234. Ibid.
235. Spiro, interview with Shashar, Aug. 11, 1999; Schochet, interview with Rabbi F. E. Rottenberg, Sept. 1994.
236. Dresner, *Heschel, Hasidism, and Halakha,* p. 99.
237. Spiro, interview with Joel Roth, Sept. 23, 1999.
238. Marc B. Shapiro, "Scholars and Friends: Rabbi Yehiel Yaakov Weinberg and Professor Samuel Atlas," *The Torah U-Madda Journal* 7 (1997): 105. Weinberg continued to enjoy a close friendship characterized by warm correspondence with his former Slobodka colleague Samuel Atlas, long after the latter accepted a teaching position at the Reform Hebrew Union College in Cincinnati.

239. Lieberman, letter to Chaim Levanon, mayor of Tel Aviv, Oct. 2, 1957.
240. Shashar, "Fanaticism, a Difficult Competitor and a Cheap Substitute for Torah." The quotation is from pp. 7–8 of a draft English translation of Lieberman's interview prepared for JTS.
241. Gary Rendsburg, "The Demise of Rabbi Saul Lieberman," letter to the *Jewish Press,* Apr. 22, 1983.
242. Schochet, interview with Hillel Goldberg, Mar. 20, 1998.
243. Shashar, "Oseh Torah Kol Yamav."
244. Tibor Juda, citing Pinhas Hirschprung (Spiro, interview with Juda, Oct. 28, 1999).
245. R. Berel Wein, *The Wein Press* 4, no. 7 (Oct. 1998): 5.
246. Emanuel Rackman, "Don't Repeat This Attack on Jewish Unity," *Jewish Week,* May 8, 1987, p. 28.
247. Wolfe Kelman, letter to the *Jewish Week,* May 14, 1987. See above, section entitled "The Joint *Beit Din,*" for the context of this statement, which was made in the course of the joint *beit din* negotiation.
248. Lieberman, letter to Scholem, Apr. 17, 1966. Lieberman would sign a check made out to charity on every Hol Hamoed (the intermediate days of a festival) so that his tradition of not writing on Hol Hamoed would not harden into a rule of law (*neder*) (Spiro, interview with Juda, May 31, 2003).
249. Nathan Kamenetsky, interview with Beverly Gribetz, Dec. 1998.
250. Lieberman, letter to B. Rivlin concerning his acceptance of the Israel Prize, Apr. 14, 1971.
251. It appears that it was Lieberman's practice to decline invitations to dine at people's homes until it could be confirmed that the highest standards of kashrut were observed. For example, sometime after Judith's death, Erica Jesselson (wife of Ludwig) invited Lieberman for a meal at her home on Passover. A few days later, he responded: "I don't eat outside my home on Passover, but I will accept your invitation." Erica replied, "That's quite a compliment! How did you arrive at your decision?" Lieberman said that he had asked his brother, Meir, whether he could rely on the kashrut in the Jesselson home. Meir exclaimed, "You wouldn't eat at the home of Pappenheim's grandchild?" (Spiro, interview with Erica Jesselson, June 6, 1996).
252. N. Kamenetsky, interview with Shamma Friedman, Oct. 4, 1997.
253. Spiro, interview with Tibor Juda, Oct. 28, 1999. On a related issue, Alice Zlotnick (wife of Dov) asked Lieberman whether she was permitted, under Jewish law, to recite the Kaddish in the synagogue after her father's death, in view of the fact that she had no brothers to say Kaddish. Lieberman told her that she was permitted to say Kaddish if there was a male worshiper reciting it in the synagogue at the same time, so that the other worshipers would be responding to his Kaddish (with "amen" and other responses).
254. Spiro, interview with Emunah Katzenstein. Aug. 3, 1999.
255. Spiro, interview with Dov Zlotnick, Sept. 21, 1995.
256. Shashar, "Fanaticism, a Difficult Opponent and a Cheap Substitute for Torah." The citation is from p. 9 of a draft English translation of Lieberman's interview prepared for JTS.
257. Spiro, interview with A. Goldberg, Aug. 2, 1999.

258. Ibid.
259. Spiro, interview with Kogen, Sept. 8, 1998.
260. Simon Greenberg, remarks at Mincha services at JTS in memory of Lieberman, Mar. 24, 1983.
261. Spiro, interview with Yakov Aviad, Aug. 14, 1999.
262. Spiro, interview with Gettinger, Mar. 21, 1996.
263. Lederhendler, "The Ongoing Dialogue," 2:198. Simon Greenberg's reflections on the incident to his grandson are instructive: "Professor Lieberman, like I, who did not recall that this was the anniversary of the capture of the Old City in 1967, at first objected. Even after he was told [why the Hallel was being inserted into the service], he still thought that the *berakha* should not be made . . . and so the hazan did not recite the closing *berakha*." What was a matter of *klal Yisrael* (ideological-ethnic) identification for the students was, for their teacher, a matter of "the law not yet [having] been fixed [so that] it is preferable to perform the act but not recite the *berakha* so that God's name not be taken in vain."
264. Raphael, "Professor Rabbi Shaul Lieberman," eulogy for Lieberman, p. 91. Raphael refers to Lieberman's practice of recording his name, on the cover page of his books, "Shaul B. R. Moshe Z'L," insisting that the letters of his and his father's name be of the identical size, e.g., *Al Hayerushalmi, Hayerushalmi Kifshuto*. Eventually, he came to insist that his father's name be in larger type than his own, e.g., *Tosefta Kifshutah*. See below, part 2, section entitled "Simplicity, Modesty, Kindness, and Generosity," and part 2, n. 295.
265. "Our paths crossed often: in *mikveh,* in synagogue. . . .," Ruth Link-Salinger, ed., *Jewish Law in Our Time* (New York, 1982), p. 107.
266. Spiro, interview with Ruth Link-Salinger and Arthur Hyman, Mar. 1997.
267. Dov Zlotnick, "Today's Met Mitzvah," in *Best Jewish Sermons of 5727–28,* ed. Saul Teplitz (New York, 1968), pp. 225–32.
268. Jane Calem Rosen, "A Modern-Day Tanna," *JTS Magazine* 10, no. 3 (spring 2001): 24.
269. Dov Zlotnick, introduction to *The Tractate Mourning: Regulations Relating to Death, Burial, and Mourning,* trans. and notes (New Haven and London, 1966).
270. Halivni, "Professor Saul Lieberman," p. 6.
271. Judge David Bartov, letter to Spiro, Dec. 9, 1999.
272. Maimon, letter to Lieberman, Jan. 15, 1958.
273. Supplement to *Tarbiz* 2, no. 4 (1931).
274. Spiro, interview with D. Zlotnick, Sept. 21, 1995.
275. Cited in Shamma Friedman, trans., "From Prodigy to Master: An Introduction to the Scholarship of Saul Lieberman," Saul Lieberman Institute of Talmudic Research (lecture delivered by Friedman at JTS, Feb. 1987).
276. H. Z. Dimitrovsky, "Miparshanut l'Mehkar," in *L'Zikhro,* p. 44; in the English version (translated by Baruch Feldstern) of this essay, "From Commentary to Scholarship" (which appears for the first time as appendix III in this volume), p. 289.
277. Spiro, interview with Haym Soloveitchik, Nov. 9, 1998.

278. *Hilkhot Ma'aser Sheini* 1:10
279. It is likely that Lieberman's essay "The Publication of the Mishna," in *Hellenism in Jewish Palestine* (New York, 1950, 1962), pp. 83–99, was to serve as the introduction to a scientific edition of the Mishnah.
280. Spiro, interview with Edward Gershfield, Nov. 7, 1995.
281. Lieberman, "Hazanut Yannai," *Sinai* 4 (1939): 221–50.
282. Golinkin, "The Influence of Seminary Professors," 2:450.
283. In his personal diary, Kaplan describes Lieberman's conduct toward him, following his excommunication and the burning of his book: "As I entered the room, I noticed that Prof. Liberman [*sic*] did not give the slightest sign of recognizing my presence. I was a bit flustered for a moment, but soon adjusted myself to the situation, because I had always known him to be violently antagonistic to me and my works. At the table later, I noticed that he sat at the very end together with Davis, instead of at a place near the head of the table, according to his status on the faculty. When the luncheon was over, and I was waiting for the elevator to take me downstairs, Liberman was coming in my direction. As soon as he noticed me, he lowered his eyes and hastened his steps. 'Why are you angry with me?' I said in all innocence. 'I am not angry,' he replied, and ran on. Later, it occurred to me that possibly he regarded it his duty to obey the *herem* of the Rabbis. Sure enough, when I was at the Seminary on Friday, I learned that that was actually the case." Mel Scult, "Kaplan's Heschel: A View from the Kaplan Diary," *Conservative Judaism* 54, no. 4 (summer 2002): 3, 9.
284. Simon Greenberg, ed., *The Ordination of Women as Rabbis: Studies and Responsa* (New York, 1988), pp. 5–6. Elijah Schochet served as a member of the commission.
285. Spiro, interview with D. Zlotnick, Jan. 29, 1999.
286. R. Wayne Allen, ed., *Tomeikh Kehalakhah,* responsa of the panel of halakhic inquiry, Union for Traditional Judaism (New York, 1986), 1:14–22 for Hebrew text and translation by Allen. One would have expected the volume published by JTS, *The Ordination of Women as Rabbis,* to include Lieberman's responsum, but it did not.
287. Ibid., 1:20.
288. Spiro, interview with D. Zlotnick, Jan. 29, 1999.
289. According to Dimitrovsky, "Lieberman was not combative." When a colleague would differ with him at a faculty meeting, Lieberman would usually not respond to the challenge (Spiro, interview with Dimitrovsky, Aug. 2, 1999).
290. E.g., Gerson Cohen and Seymour Siegel. A brief discussion of Lieberman's reluctance to criticize former students will follow. Rabbi Ronald Price recalls that during Lieberman's initial silence on the issue, a memorandum was circulated implying that Lieberman might be supportive of JTS ordaining women. Upon reading the memorandum, Lieberman declared to Price, "This is not something with which I would be involved, but once they are mentioning my name. . . ." A few days later, Lieberman sent Price and some of Price's traditionalist colleagues a one-sentence handwritten note, stating, "I

send my blessings for success to you who represent the last ember of halakhah in the movement." Ronald D. Price, "Remembering the Grash," *Jewish Standard,* Mar. 20, 2001, p. 5.

291. Spiro, interview with D. Zlotnick, Jan. 29, 1999.
292. Lieberman, in *Tomeikh Kehalakhah,* 1:22 n. 4.
293. Such is Judith Hauptman's interpretation of Lieberman's responsum. Hauptman is convinced that Lieberman's long silence in the face of the women's ordination controversy is best explained by his positive attitude toward an enhanced role for women in Jewish life—particularly, in education and talmudic studies. In Lieberman's lifetime, women were not admitted to JTS rabbinical school. When Hauptman was a student in the Seminary College of Jewish Studies, a division of JTS, she approached Lieberman with a request that he admit her to his rabbinical school Talmud class. Without hesitation, Lieberman admitted her and another female student; shortly thereafter, he also gave permission to Lynn Gottlieb to attend his Talmud class. (This was before divisions between the various schools were eliminated, which enabled those attending other schools to be admitted to classes in the rabbinical school.) Lieberman could easily have rejected the applications of females out of fear that their admission would begin the descent down a slippery slope toward the ordination of women rabbis. However, he was not constrained by such concerns, as his desire was to encourage any serious student, male or female, who wanted to study Torah. Hauptman concludes that Lieberman was intellectually and emotionally in favor of women seeking "intellectual expression," and notes that he did not speak out publicly against women's ordination nor did he publicly attack its proponents. She suggests that he believed it was not contrary to halakhah. However, being a traditionalist and fearing the loss of his support among the Orthodox, he could not bring himself to approve it, either, and Lieberman's long silence and "weak" responsum reflect the ambivalence of his response to the women's ordination issue (Spiro, interview with Hauptman, Oct. 20, 1999). Needless to say, there are other explanations for Lieberman's long silence and somewhat hesitant responsum.
294. Cited in Golinkin, "The Influence of Seminary Professors," 2:452.
295. Kamenetsky, interview with Gribetz, Dec. 1998.
296. I. Schorsch, "Centenary Thoughts: Conservatism Revisited," *Proceedings of the Rabbinical Assembly of America* 48 (1986): 83.
297. On one occasion, Ginzberg mentioned his intention to forward to Lieberman a query he received on the subject of fellatio! See David Golinkin, *The Responsa of Professor Louis Ginzberg* (New York, 1996), p. 216.
298. Yehezkel Kutscher, "Prof. Saul Lieberman and His Linguistic Achievement" (Heb.), *Hadoar* 42, no. 23 (Apr. 5, 1963): 377–79.
299. Jay Michael Harris, *How Do We Know This? Midrash and the Fragmentation of Modern Judaism* (Albany, 1995), pp. 249–50.
300. Lieberman, "Bimhitzat Rabbanim," p. 608.
301. Elijah Judah Schochet, *The Hasidic Movement and the Gaon of Vilna* (Northvale, N.J., 1994), pp. 149–52.

302. Harris, *How Do We Know This?,* p. 239.
303. See Louis Ginzberg, *A Commentary to the Palestinian Talmud* (New York, 1941), 1:lix–lxiv.
304. The incident is referred to in Judith Lieberman's autobiographical essay appearing in *Thirteen Americans: Their Spiritual Autobiographies,* ed. L. Finkelstein (New York, 1953), pp. 159–76; see p. 161.
305. Abraham Elijah Kaplan, *B'ikvot Hayirah,* 2d ed. (Jerusalem, 1988), pp. 74, 208. We are indebted to Rabbi Shmuel Jacobs of Los Angeles for bringing these citations to our attention.
306. Shamma Friedman, "Kavim Lidmuto Hamada'it shel Profesor Shaul Lieberman z'l," *Newsletter of the World Union of Jewish Studies,* no. 23 (winter 1984): 23.
307. Lawrence Kaplan, "The Hazon Ish: Haredi Critic of Traditional Orthodoxy," in *The Uses of Tradition: Jewish Continuity in the Modern Era,* ed. J. Wertheimer (New York, 1992), pp. 153–54.
308. Schochet, interview with Kamenetsky, May 1997.
309. Wachsman, "Lidmuto shel Hagaon Rav Shlomo Polachek, z'l," pp. 16–17.
310. Dimitrovsky, letter to Spiro, June 29, 2002.
311. Michael Shashar, "Keter Torah, Veketer Hokhma," *Hadoar* 56, no. 15 (Feb. 11, 1977): 228–29; see also idem, "Oseh Torah Kol Yamav."
312. Lieberman, "Mekhilta de Rabi Yishmael, Lauterbach, Ed.," *Kiryat Sefer* 12 (1934–35): 54–65; *Mehkarim b'Torat Eretz Yisrael,* pp. 540–51.
313. *Tosefta Kifshutah, Zera'im,* pt. 1, p. 22; *Mo'ed,* pt. 3, p. 16.
314. Lieberman, "Ha'arot l'Masekhet Nedarim," in *Mehkarim b'Torat Eretz Yisrael,* p. 32.
315. Lieberman, *Tosefet Rishonim* (Jerusalem, 1939), 4:12–13, 15.
316. Lieberman's review of Finkelstein's edition of *Sifrei Devarim,* which appeared in *Kiryat Sefer* 14 (1937–38): 323–24; *Mehkarim b'Torat Eretz Yisrael,* pp. 566–67. Lieberman, *Tosefet Rishonim,* 4:15. See Dimitrovsky, "Miparshanut l'Mehkar," pp. 39, 45–47 ("From Commentary to Scholarship," appendix III to this volume, pp. 289–292), for an excellent discussion about "textual truth" and "historical truth."
317. See previous n., Lieberman's review of *Sifrei Devarim.* Dov Zlotnick, "The Methodology of Professor Saul Lieberman in Determining the Correct Reading of a Text," in *Saul Lieberman,* ed. Lubetski, p. 4, discusses Lieberman's approach to emending texts as explained in Lieberman's review of Finkelstein's edition of the *Sifrei.*
318. In addition to the Gaon of Vilna, whom he emulated, Lieberman was influenced by the work of the Rogochover Illui (R. Joseph Rosen, author of *Tsafenat Pane'a al Arba'a Helkei Harambam*), and he greatly valued the *Or Same'ah* of Meir Simha Hakohen of Dvinsk, a commentary on Maimonides' Code (Dimitrovsky, letter to Spiro, July 1, 2002). Dimitrovsky relates that Lieberman often expressed his admiration for the *Or Same'ah,* urging him to study it. Lieberman remarked that Meir Simha's commentary illuminated the text in a truthful way. Without demonstrating his intellectual acuity in a self-indulgent way, he explained what Maimonides had said and intended (Spiro, interview with Dimitrovsky, Aug. 2, 1999). For Lieberman, that was the task of the *mefaresh,* the commentator or interpreter.

319. Yitzhak Gilat, "The Life's Work of Professor Saul Lieberman" (Heb.), *Bitzaron,* n.s., 9, nos. 35–36 (Sept. 1987): 51.
320. Cited in H. Goldberg, "Becoming History," 1:379. Judith Lieberman to Jessica Feingold, June 2, 1959.
321. Cited in Shapiro, "Scholars and Friends," p. 10. Letter from Weinberg to Atlas, Mar. 7, 1956.
322. Gerson Cohen, communication to R. Joel Rembaum, 1979; Schochet, interview with Amos Funkenstein, Apr. 1985; and Schochet, interview with Arnold Band, May 1997.
323. Dov Zlotnick, "Hametadologia shel Shaul Lieberman b'Yevanut v'Yevanit b'Eretz Yisrael," in *Divrei Hakongres Hale'umi Ha'ahad Asar l'Mada'ei Hayahadut* (Jerusalem, 1984), p. 10. Also, idem, introduction to Saul Lieberman's *Greek in Jewish Palestine / Hellenism in Jewish Palestine* (New York and Jerusalem, 1994), p. xiii.
324. Aaron Kirschenbaum, letter to E. Schochet, June 10, 1997.
325. H. Z. Dimitrovsky, "Devarim al Gedol Hakhmei Doreinu," *Hadoar* 56, no. 15 (Feb. 11, 1977): 227–28.
326. Ibid., p. 227. Lieberman's rigorous insistence on an intimate familiarity with the full range of primary rabbinic sources rather than merely an acquaintance with selective secondary sources was noted by Dov Zlotnick: "From [Lieberman] I learned that the greatest textual discovery is the *peshat*—the simple meaning; that every dictum of the Rabbis and the smallest detail of a text is inextricably bound with the whole; and that only by acquiring some understanding of the whole can one hope to hear those Rabbinic echoes and to make those textual associations that will shed light on a difficult reading." Zlotnick, trans., *The Tractate Mourning,* p. 30.
327. Halivni, *The Book and the Sword* (New York, 1996), p. 137.
328. Lieberman, introduction to *Hayerushalmi Kifshuto.* See E. S. Rosenthal, "Hamoreh," *Proceedings of the American Academy for Jewish Research* 31 (1963): 7; and Shamma Friedman, "Shaul Lieberman: Hora'ato Be'al Peh Uviktav," in *L'Zikhro,* p. 51.
329. Rosenthal, "Hamoreh," pp. 2–3.
330. Dimitrovsky, letter to Spiro, June 29, 2002.
331. See, for example, Lieberman's introduction to *Sifrei Zuta.*
332. See Dimitrovsky, "Miparshanut l'Mehkar," p. 48 ("From Commentary to Scholarship," appendix III to this volume, pp. 292–293).
333. Luitpold Wallach, review of *Greek in Jewish Palestine,* by S. Lieberman, *Review of Religion* 8, no. 1 (Nov. 1943): 63.
334. Jacob Neusner, *Wrong Ways and Right Ways in the Study of Formative Judaism: Critical Method and Literature, History, and the History of Religion* (Atlanta, 1988), pp. 9–10.
335. Lieberman, *Hellenism in Jewish Palestine,* 2d ed. (New York, 1962), p. xiii.
336. Lieberman, preface to *Greek in Jewish Palestine* (New York, 1942), p. vii.
337. Ismar Schorsch, *From Text to Context* (Hanover, N.H., 1994), p. 172.
338. Spiro, interview with J. Hauptman, Oct. 12, 1999.
339. Spiro, interview with Robert Chazan, Apr. 4, 2000.
340. Lieberman, *Sifrei Zuta,* p. 135. See also introduction to *Talmudah shel Kisrin,*

p. viii, where Lieberman thanks Epstein for guiding him on the path of proper research and scientific analysis. See also Lieberman's *Al Hayerushalmi* (Jerusalem, 1929), 2d sec. of bk., entitled *Nusha'ot Miktav Yad Roma l'Yerushalmi, Mesekhet Sotah,* pp. 51, 54 (unnumbered); note of thanks to Epstein for access to *Yerushalmi* manuscripts.

341. See Lieberman, "Achievements and Aspirations of Modern Jewish Scholarship," *Proceedings of the American Academy for Jewish Research* 44–45 (1979–80): 369.
342. J. N. Epstein, *Mevo'ot Lesifrut Ha'amoraim: Bavli v'Yerushalmi* (Jerusalem, 1962), pp. 279–87.
343. Lieberman defends his *Talmudah shel Kisrin* in the *Sefer Hama'asim* lecture at Kinus l'Mada'ei Hayahadut, 1973.
344. Lieberman, introduction to *Tosefta Kifshutah, Mo'ed,* pt. 3, p. 16. See Abramson, "Darko shel Harav," p. 28.
345. Spiro, interview with Dimitrovsky, Aug. 2, 1999. See also Dimitrovsky, "Miparshanut l'Mehkar," p. 41 ("From Commentary to Scholarship," appendix III to this volume, pp. 285–286).
346. Shamma Friedman, "Saul Lieberman and the Study of the Tosefta," *Proceedings of the American Academy for Jewish Research* 31 (1963): 4. See also Dimitrovsky, "Miparshanut l'Mehkar," p. 35 ("From Commentary to Scholarship," appendix III to this volume, p. 280).
347. Cited in Dimitrovsky, "Miparshanut l'Mehkar," p. 38 ("From Commentary to Scholarship," appendix III to this volume, p. 283). Our discussion owes a great deal to this essay by Dimitrovsky, in which he presents an incisive analysis of the growth and development of Lieberman's scholarship. Whereas Lieberman follows Epstein's methodology in his earlier works, he gradually forges his own style, reaching the apex of his intellectual attainment with the publication of *Tosefta Kifshutah,* a work free of the constraints of Epstein's approach. See "Miparshanut l'Mehkar," pp. 42–46 ("From Commentary to Scholarship" appendix III to this volume, pp. 287–292).
348. Rosenthal traces this move on Lieberman's part in "Hamoreh," p. 34.
349. See Dimitrovsky, "Miparshanut l'Mehkar," pp. 35–38 ("From Commentary to Scholarship," appendix III to this volume, pp. 280–282).
350. Lieberman, "The Publication of the Mishna," p. 96.
351. Abramson, "Darko shel Harav," p. 30.
352. Dimitrovsky, "Miparshanut l'Mehkar," p. 39 ("From Commentary to Scholarship," appendix III to this volume, p. 284).
353. Lieberman, "The Role of Professor Louis Ginzberg in Jewish Scholarship," an address given on Nov. 28, 1943.
354. Abramson, "Darko shel Harav," p. 32.

Saul Lieberman enjoying a cigar in his study, 1952. Photograph by Grace Goldin.

Saul Lieberman making *Hamotzi* at the wedding of Dov and Alice Zlotnick (Judith Lieberman in the background), 1953. Photograph by Valeche.

The avuncular Saul Lieberman on Martha's Vineyard, 1959, with Karen Zlotnick (now Karen Kirshenbaum). Photograph by Alice Zlotnick

Saul Lieberman, portrait by Grace Goldin, 1960.

Lieberman with Louis Finkelstein at a Seminary farewell marking the appointment of Judah Goldin to the faculty of Yale University, 1958. Photograph by Alice Zlotnick.

Golda Meir and Louis Finkelstein seated at a table in the Seminary Sukkah; Saul Lieberman speaking, 1961. Courtesy of the Ratner Center for the Study of Conservative Judaism, Jewish Theological Seminary.

Lieberman at work in the study of his Jerusalem home, 1981. Photograph by Alice Zlotnick.

Saul Lieberman, portrait by Alice Zlotnick, 1979.

Judith Lieberman, portrait by Alice Zlotnick, 1979.

Saul and Judith Lieberman in front of their Jerusalem home, 1979.
Photograph by Alice Zlotnick.

Saul Lieberman, Louis Finkelstein, Gerson Cohen, and a scribe celebrating the completion of a *Sefer Torah,* Jerusalem, 1981. Photograph by Alice Zlotnick.

Lieberman is featured on the April 18, 1969, cover of *Panim el Panim* to celebrate his return to Jerusalem.

Nahum Sarna, David Weiss Halivni, Louis Finkelstein and Saul Lieberman in Seminary courtyard, 1965. Courtesy of the Ratner Center for the Study of Conservative Judaism, Jewish Theological Seminary.

Moshe Lieberman, Saul's father. Photo, *Panim el Panim*.

Hazon Ish (Avraham Yeshayahu Karelitz), Saul Lieberman's cousin. Photo, *Panim el Panim*.

Lieberman making a point. Photo, *Panim el Panim*

Lieberman in front of JTS.

J. N. Epstein, Lieberman's teacher at the Hebrew University. Photo, courtesy Hebrew University.

Saul Lieberman with Louis Finkelstein, in Seminary courtyard, 1960s. Courtesy of the Ratner Center for the Study of Conservative Judaism, Jewish Theological Seminary.

Portrait of Saul Lieberman, undated. Courtesy of the Ratner Center for the Study of Conservative Judasim, Jewish Theological Seminary.

Saul Lieberman speaking with men in former Library reading room, Schiff building, at Convocation of Law as a Moral Force, 1959. Courtesy of the Ratner Center for the Study of Conservative Judasim, Jewish Theological Seminary.

Gerson Cohen and Saul Lieberman holding a Torah together in Israel, 1976. Courtesy of the Ratner Center for the Study of Conservative Judaism, Jewish Theological Seminary.

PART II

APPROBATION

Uniqueness of Acclaim

The approbation received by Saul Lieberman during his lifetime takes a consistent form. He is frequently described not as *one* of the greatest, but as *the* greatest—not only as the greatest of his generation, but also as the greatest of *many* generations. The acclaim comes from America, Israel, and Europe; from scholar and journalist; and from student and colleague. The following sampling of citations is representative:

> Eliezer Shimshon Rosenthal: "Saul Lieberman is indisputably the greatest in the world; in his way—the greatest who ever lived."[1]
>
> David Weiss Halivni: "Professor Lieberman was not only unique in his generation but unique in all generations; he was the greatest *baki* since the Gaon of Vilna."[2]
>
> Michael Shashar: "He is the high priest of postbiblical literature. . . . He is . . . unique among the scholars of Israel."[3]
>
> Haim Zalman Dimitrovsky: "He is the greatest of the scholars of our generation."[4]
>
> Mordecai Margulies: "He is the *gaon shebegeonim* . . . the preeminent Jewish scholar of our generation."[5]
>
> The editors of *Hadoar*: "Rav Shaul Lieberman, the greatest of all great Jewish scholars . . ."[6]
>
> Joseph Klausner: "[T]here does not remain in Israel a talmudic scholar of his magnitude."[7]

> Yitzhak Gilat: "In order to be able to follow in Lieberman's path, one must be a Professor Lieberman, and lo, he has not left behind anyone like unto him."[8]

> Meir Benayahu, son of Chief Rabbi Yitzhak Nissim: "Lieberman was the greatest of the great; he knew it all, *Bavli* and *Yerushalmi*."[9]

> R. Yaakov Kamenetsky: "Lieberman is an extraordinarily erudite and expert scholar. I never met anyone with such *biki'ut*, such breadth of knowledge."[10]

Jacob Neusner stated in a letter to him, "You are the greatest exegete of rabbinic texts of the twentieth century and among the true greats . . . of all time." Emphasizing the sincerity of his accolade, Neusner concludes the letter with the assurance: "I am not famous as a flatterer, so I hope you will take seriously these words of appreciation."[11]

Eli Ginzberg, in speaking of the intimate associations of his father (Louis Ginzberg) with the outstanding scholars of his era, stated: "No one impressed my father as much as Lieberman."[12]

Chief Rabbi Isaac Herzog is cited by his son, President Chaim Herzog, as designating Lieberman "the greatest authority on the Jerusalem Talmud."[13] Other Israeli leaders who venerated Lieberman include Yitzhak Raphael, former minister of religion of the State of Israel, who proclaimed: "In my own estimation, [Lieberman] is the greatest scholar of the present generation, a man of unique attainment."[14] On the thirty-day anniversary of Saul Lieberman's death, Raphael stated: "I am neither qualified, nor am I so arrogant to declare that Professor Saul Lieberman *z'l* was the greatest of all the *hokrim,* the scholars of talmudic literature who have arisen in recent generations. However, it appears that none is to be found who would challenge this assertion."[15]

It is therefore not surprising, writes Yitzhak Gilat, that Saul Lieberman left no one student truly qualified to follow in his path. No one is his equal, and therefore, there is none capable of making contributions such as his.[16] Likewise, when the issue is raised as to who is able to evaluate Saul Lieberman's scholarship, Eliezer Shimshon Rosenthal states:

> Were I to undertake here a comprehensive evaluation worthy, in itself, and befitting Lieberman's immense talmudic undertaking, not

> only would I have to go on forever, but I would not be worthy of the task. For indeed, such a review requires someone like Lieberman himself, who has learned and absorbed the entire length and breadth of talmudic literature, without overlooking even one Mishnah or Tosefta, or any detail from the Talmud, Palestinian and Babylonian, laws and legends, minutiae of the Torah or the scribes, arguments *a fortiori* or *gezera shava,* proverbs of the launderers and wolf proverbs, conversations of the ministering angels and demons' twaddle. For indeed, Lieberman himself has not left over any single passage of talmudic literature, great or small, whose textual readings he has not examined, whose language and style he has not plummeted [*sic*], or whose content he has not elucidated. None of all these things I have said here about Lieberman was said in hyperbole, as is well known by all those who have read from his books and articles.[17]

Other prominent scholars echoing Rosenthal's sentiment were Yehezkel Kutscher and Shraga Abramson. Kutscher stated, "There is no one scholar today qualified to write a broad critique from all aspects on any one of the books of Professor Lieberman."[18] According to Abramson, "Should one seek to describe [Lieberman's] greatness, one must be exceedingly great in Torah scholarship, extraordinary in textual analysis, in the understanding of the Hebrew language and the classical languages, and so on. Can such a one be found?"[19] In a similar vein, Morton Smith commences his review of Saul Lieberman's *Hellenism in Jewish Palestine* with the observation, "When Dean Lieberman speaks *ex cathedra* on matters of rabbinic literature, there are only three or four people in the world who have any right to question his statements."[20]

Saul Lieberman's work elicits unrestrained praise. Upon receiving the first three volumes of the *Tosefta Kifshutah,* R. Yehiel Yaakov Weinberg, rector of the Berlin Orthodox Rabbinical Seminary, said of Lieberman: "He and he alone is equipped for such a great scientific undertaking."[21] Abraham Goldberg stated, "Professor Saul Lieberman's new edition of the Tosefta, together with his comprehensive commentary, is easily the greatest single contribution to Jewish scholarship of our generation,"[22] a sentiment echoed by Neusner: "Saul Lieberman's *Tosefta Kifshutah* and *Tosefet Rishonim* constitute the greatest commentaries to mishnaic literature ever written. . . . This sage reserve and close attention to internal evidence, not to mention the extraordinary thoroughness, exegetical lucidity, stylistic taste, and prudent judgment, set Lieberman's work apart from anything ever done or ever likely to be done. He has raised scholarship on Mishnah-Tosefta to an entirely new level of achievement."[23]

Menahem Schmelzer, the JTS librarian who drew on the library's vast resources to respond to Lieberman's needs, said, "If the JTS library had been created just for his scholarship—*dayenu*."[24] Kutscher, in assessing Lieberman's ability as a linguist, stated, "As a result of Saul Lieberman's research, all talmudic dictionaries are obsolete."[25] After receiving a letter from Lieberman, the noted classicist Erwin Goodenough replied on April 1, 1957, "To be able to sit down and write out of one's head so extraordinary a collection of references, fills me with grief and envy." We cite these words of gratitude to Saul Lieberman by Daniel E. Gershenson and Daniel A. Greenberg, authors of *Anaxagoras and the Birth of Physics:*

> We wish to thank our teachers and colleagues, as well as many students in the Departments of Greek and Latin and of Physics in Barnard College and Columbia University, whose interest and sympathy have been a source of encouragement to us throughout. We are especially grateful to Professor Saul Lieberman of the Jewish Theological Seminary of America, whose students we have been for some three years. If there is merit in this book, much of it is due to our having learned in the course of our studies with him fundamental methods of dealing with ancient texts, as well as the basic frame of mind in which texts must be approached if antiquarianism and adumbrationism both are to be avoided.[26]

Lieberman's remarkable gifts were apparent in his youth, when as a child prodigy, he performed amazing feats of memory. Early in his yeshiva career, he became known as the "Illui of Motele," the genius of Motol. Upon his arrival at Slobodka, not long after the celebration of his bar mitzvah, R. Natan Zevi Finkel declared: "He'll not become a *gaon* [genius], because he is one already."[27]

As mentioned above, R. Yaakov Kamenetsky, a fellow student at Slobodka, extolled Lieberman's comprehensive scholarship. During the Slobodka yeshiva's relocation in Minsk, Lieberman was among the ten students chosen to receive the extravagant scholarship stipend of 40 rubles per month![28] R. Kamenetsky recalled how R. Eliezer Rabinowitz of Minsk, the son-in-law of R. Yerucham Yehuda Leib Perelmann, the "Minsker Godol," approached the *rosh yeshiva* of Slobodka in search of a husband for his daughter. When he asked who the most brilliant student was, Lieberman was mentioned, and soon became the son-in-law of R. Rabinowitz.[29]

While a young man, Lieberman was befriended by some of the most prominent rabbinic scholars of his time, each of whom was impressed by his scholarship. R. Baruch Baer of Kamenetz referred to him as "Shaulke, my best student."[30] Lieberman was privileged to spend considerable time in the home of his *rosh yeshiva,* R. Natan Zevi Finkel,[31] and was later befriended by Rabbi Yosef Yosel of Novogrudok (Novaredok) and stayed in his home for an extended period as well.[32]

Lieberman's genius was so esteemed that, when ill with scarlet fever, he was taken into the home of R. Shlomo Polachek, the Illui of Meitshet and a student of R. Hayyim Soloveitchik of Brisk; hence, his appellation "Der Tzveiter Reb Chaim" (the second Reb Chaim).[33] When the Illui's wife complained, "But what will happen to us and our children?" the Illui's response to her was: "You will have to move out!" Lieberman remained in R. Polachek's home for several weeks, until he recovered fully.[34] Lieberman later explained his privileged status in his teachers' homes as simply the normal practice in Lithuania. "[The yeshiva heads] treated a *ba'al kisharon* [capable student] like a son."[35]

Lieberman enjoyed a special relationship with R. Polachek. He became a part of his household as well as one of his chess-playing companions. In striving to understand the outside world, the Illui (R. Polachek) taught himself Russian and German, as well as algebra, geometry, and trigonometry. He was also a devotee of classical literature. When his children were young, he would read to them from Victor Hugo's *Les Misérables*. As they grew older, he took an active interest in their literary pursuits. When Lieberman was studying with the Illui in Yelizavetgrad, in the Ukraine, Lieberman was enrolled in a correspondence course in medicine. Consequently, throughout the course of their studies, the Illui strove to learn medical insights from Lieberman. He succeeded to the extent that his physician was astounded when he once correctly diagnosed his own daughter's illness. Indeed, the Illui, a great Talmud scholar whose vision and interest encompassed knowledge of the secular world, provided an example that Lieberman would later emulate.[36]

Lieberman visited R. Hayyim Ozer Grodzinski in Vilna before leaving Lithuania. They discussed R. Menahem HaMeiri's opinion regarding a statement in the Tosefta concerning a blemished priest.[37] When Grodzinski was unable to recall the relevant passage in the Tosefta, he requested Lieberman's assistance. When Lieberman provided the correct reference and explanation,[38] Grodzinski declared, "Indeed, this appears to be the statement referenced by the Meiri. However, in order to identify it, one needs to be Saul Lieberman."[39] In 1938, while on a trip to Vilna from Jerusalem, Lieberman impressed Vilna's chief rabbi, Hayyim Ozer Grodzinski, with his knowledge of the *Sifrei*. This was one example offered by Meir Lieberman as proof that his brother was a *mutslah* (one blessed with good fortune), because just prior to the meeting with R. Grodzinski, Lieberman had been studying that text, and, by coincidence, upon entering R. Grodzinski's study, Lieberman noted the volume of the *Sifrei* upon his study table.

"He has all the tools," was the Hazon Ish's evaluation of his cousin.[40] When Lieberman wrote to the Hazon Ish requesting the source of an obscure reference in rabbinic literature, the latter responded with a postcard asking why Lieberman would turn to him for such information. "In our family, you are the scholar. If you don't know, no one knows." Lieberman later wryly observed, "If I had known that the Hazon Ish would become so famous, I would have framed and kept that postcard." As it was, he left the postcard somewhere in one of his many books.[41] According to Lieberman's brother-in-law, Abraham Halkin (Halkin's wife, Shulamit, was Judith Lieberman's sister), "Any field he would have undertaken, he would have mastered quickly and excelled in to the point of premier prominence."[42] While still in Palestine, Lieberman corresponded with leading scholars of the era as an equal—offering suggestions and not hesitating to point out corrections to A. M. Habermann,[43] Louis Finkelstein,[44] and Louis Ginzberg,[45] among others. The correspondence with the last two was most notable and extensive.

Manifestations of Genius

Breadth of Knowledge

Lieberman mastered the traditional Jewish sources as well as the languages of antiquity—notably, Greek and Latin. When Professor Sara Mandell, of the University of Southern Florida in Tampa, once questioned his proficiency in Greek and Latin, several classical literature and language scholars affirmed Lieberman's mastery in this field.[46] Rejoinders came from Professors Howard Jacobson of the University of Illinois and Howard Marblestone of Lafayette College. Jacobson defended Lieberman against Mandell's critiques, stating, "When we use Lieberman's work on rabbinic texts, I think we can feel confident that he will be a reliable and responsible guide in his application of Greco-Latin sources, and we need not worry that the Greekless and Latinless will be led astray."[47] Marblestone extolled Lieberman's knowledge of Greek and Latin:

> To the question then, "Did Saul Lieberman Know Latin or Greek?" my answer is that *he knew them both broadly and profoundly*. His knowledge thereof was close, precise, and uncannily perceptive. He would encounter a text in these two, as in many other languages, directly and on its own native terms, and best of all, with profound respect for its context. His brilliant insights carried him far beyond the need for standard dictionaries and lexica, for he eschewed in this area as well what he called "the routine method of investigation in ancient Hebrew and Aramaic texts" (*Texts and Studies,* p. 222).[48]

In a paper entitled "Professor Saul Lieberman as Lexicologist and Philologist: Hebrew, Greek, Latin," Marblestone says: "What Mandell alleges to be Professor Lieberman's mistakes in Greek and Latin most often amount to differences of interpretation that reputable scholars may have with each other."[49] Professor Marblestone summarizes his view: "Indeed, Professor Lieberman's knowledge of the classical languages was broad, deep and subtle."[50]

Henri Gregoire marveled at Lieberman's mastery of the languages, texts, and "realia" of the Greco-Roman world, and Ephraim Urbach refers to Gregoire and Johanan Lewy's praise of Lieberman's remarkable ability to define obscure terms whose true meaning had eluded generations of scholars.[51] For example, in the preface to *Greek in Jewish Palestine,* Urbach cites Gregoire's response to Lieberman's statement: "While one of the principal aims of the book is the explanation and elucidation of rabbinic texts in the frame of the cultural conditions of the Mediterranean world, light is *incidentally* shed upon many a Greek and Latin text [emphasis ours]." Gregoire states that one is seldom able to find in encyclopedias, dictionaries, or reference books the definitions and identifications that Lieberman supplied for so many unclear passages. Whereas many scholars despaired of ever understanding a difficult text, Lieberman was able to offer plausible and convincing explanations. Johanan Lewy, an authority on Hellenism, offers a similar evaluation. Lieberman, he writes, brings otherwise obscure formulations to the fore, purging them of error, so that they may be presented with pristine clarity.

Remarkably, Lieberman's mastery of Greek and Latin may not have been the result of formal, systematic university studies, as he was very much the autodidact. He apparently knew Latin from his student days in Russia before coming to Palestine (according to Florence Bar-Ilan, he prided himself on being able to quote Newton's laws of physics in Latin);[52] he likewise acquired a rudimentary knowledge of Greek while still in Eastern Europe.[53] Lieberman undoubtedly had a natural affinity for languages and a sophisticated appreciation for nuance and style. Elie Wiesel declared in a tribute to Lieberman: "I do not send a manuscript to my publisher in Paris before our guest of honor [Lieberman] has seen it. Sometimes he corrects an expression or a flaw in style or a carelessly written sentence. His mastery of the French language arouses in me surprise and enthusiasm."[54] According to Lieberman's brother, Meir, he knew French while still in Russia, having lived for three months in a French-speaking household.

When one of Lieberman's guests on Martha's Vineyard saw a boat with old French markings in the Edgartown harbor, Lieberman immediately translated them, launching into a discourse on the nuances of medieval French dialects.[55] He was a master not only of contemporary French, but of medieval French dialects as well, and he enjoyed the companionship of Abraham Dov Daff, a professor of French literature at the Hebrew University and an authority on medieval French.[56]

Lieberman deeply appreciated good literature. He was a connoisseur of fine writing and enjoyed the friendship of several prominent contemporary writers. Dov Zlotnick said of Lieberman:

> I consider him the greatest textual scholar of the twentieth century, a textual scholar who had a real flair and feeling for literature. He really loved it. I am speaking not only of his command of rabbinic literature and all the midrashim, but also of his expertise in Greek literature. He was a very close friend to a number of important writers who were frequent visitors in his home, such as Agnon and Hazaz. He had an enormous amount of respect for Chaim Grade,[57] a fellow alumnus of the Slobodka yeshiva, whom he believed would be recognized in the future as belonging in the class of the other two, Agnon and Hazaz; and of, course, Elie Wiesel, who attended Lieberman's classes at JTS. It is interesting that two of the four were Nobel Laureates.[58]

Lieberman's only published work written in Yiddish was an essay on Chaim Grade, entitled "An Eyduss" (A Testimonial).[59] While Lieberman went to great lengths to disclaim any expertise as a literary critic, it is obvious that he brought to bear a fine appreciation of Grade's work. Lieberman was first introduced to the works of Grade in 1946 by his brother, Meir, who had studied with Grade under the Hazon Ish in Vilna. Judith later reintroduced him to Grade's writings when they were serialized in New York's Yiddish daily newspaper, *Der Morgen Journal.* Lieberman became an avid reader of the serial episodes of Grade's work, and often felt challenged to project his own resolution of the plot, which always turned out to be different from that of the author. He brought Grade's work to the attention of Finkelstein (who was particularly interested in the Lithuanian yeshivot), urging him to read Grade's stories, and assuring him that he would thereby feel as if he, too, had been at those yeshivot.[60] In particular, Lieberman praised Grade's gift for character development and for portraying the complexity of his subjects' personalities.

Interestingly, Lieberman declined to write about his friend Chaim Grade in Hebrew because he complained that he did not have adequate time to write a rigorous piece in Hebrew.[61] When Hayim Leaf prepared a Hebrew translation of the essay, Lieberman proposed several stylistic revisions and provided his own Hebrew translation of the first paragraph.[62] Lieberman may have insisted on translating into Hebrew the first paragraph of his Yiddish essay precisely because he wanted his disclaimer of expertise in literary criticism to be perfectly clear. His pretensions of modesty and inadequacy notwithstanding, Lieberman's essay on Grade, along with his personal correspondence, displays great power of expression and lyrical beauty.[63]

Lieberman could recite by heart extensive selections of Russian and German poetry and prose[64] and analyze the literary qualities differentiating Russian from British literature.[65] He would spend hours with Leah Shapira, wife of Moshe Hayyim Shapira, president of the world Mizrachi movement and prominent member of Ben-Gurion's cabinet, discussing Russian literature in Russian, notably the works of Pushkin and Lermontov.[66] Lieberman was interested in the writings of Isaac Babel[67] and was observed reading Alexander Solzhenitsyn's *Gulag Archipelago* in Russian.[68] He could quote extensively from *The Iliad* and *The Odyssey*,[69] and read five hundred volumes of the writings of the church fathers in Greek and Latin.[70]

Apparently, Lieberman once angered Agnon by telling him that Agnon's "Bilev Yamim" (In the Heart of the Seas) was remarkably similar to a short story by Tolstoy; a piqued Agnon refused to speak to Lieberman for several days thereafter. Lieberman also observed that several Gogol short stories had mysteriously reappeared over the signature of contemporary authors.[71]

There were other authors, such as Isaac Bashevis Singer, for whom Lieberman had no use, as he considered their writings to be "pornographic."[72] When informed that Bar-Ilan University was considering granting an honorary degree to Singer, Lieberman told Rabbi Joseph Lookstein, the chancellor of Bar-Ilan:

> You can go ahead and do it, but you will have to find a new chairman of the Committee on Academic Honors. I would not associate myself with an honor for a man who so disparaged Eastern European Jewry and besmirched their reputation. There isn't a single book of his that doesn't contain one or more characters who are bizarre or who possess very unflattering qualities.[73]

It is not surprising that, when Singer was awarded the Nobel prize for literature, Lieberman's reaction was, "I come from the old world; I know the old world, and Singer did not."[74] Lieberman professed, perhaps far too modestly, his own inadequacy as a writer. He frequently referred to himself as a sufferer from the affliction of "writing-phobia" and admitted to being a poor correspondent.[75] With self-deprecating humor, he once told the linguist Hanoch Yalon (Distenfeld) to feel free to make all necessary stylistic changes in certain of his written comments, asking, "Are they poetry set to meter, or the words of an oracle?"[76] Yet when literary Nobel prizewinner Agnon addressed the closing banquet of the Rabbinical Assembly convention in Washington, D.C., in June 1967, Lieberman introduced him with such poetic power, sweep, and humor, that the audience felt blessed with two magnificent literary presentations.

Philosophy was decidedly not one of Lieberman's interests; he had little use or patience for philosophical speculation. On November 9, 1952, Lieberman recounted to Scholem, with obvious glee, that following a lecture by the philosopher Martin Buber, someone in the audience had asked Buber, "Would his honor be so kind as to translate into *lashon enushit* [understandable human language] the contents of the lecture?"

Moshe Greenberg recalls that, during his student years at JTS, Fritz Rothschild once noted that Lieberman's copy of Maimonides' *Guide for the Perplexed* contained numerous marginal notes penned by Lieberman. When he evinced surprise that Lieberman would be so interested in studying a work of philosophy, Lieberman responded, "I am not a *navokh* [perplexed one], but there are statements in the *Guide* that have application to halakhah."[77]

Lieberman did evince curiosity about philosophy, even if he personally felt far removed from philosophical speculation. In Jerusalem, he frequently engaged in philosophical discussions with Dr. Isaiah (Wolfsberg) Aviad, a pediatrician, distinguished writer, past president of the Mizrachi in Germany, later Israel's ambassador to Switzerland, and an associate of Lieberman's father-in-law, R. Meir Berlin, while still in Germany.[78]

Lieberman considered himself knowledgeable in medical science. Because of his brief sojourn in medical school, he boasted of his expertise on the workings of the human body[79] and was a generous source of medical advice for friends, suggesting, for example, to Gershom Scholem, how his wife, Fannie, should best treat her phlebitis.[80]

As is well known, Lieberman's acumen extended to finance,[81] which generated impressive profits in the stock market. The financial hardship Lieberman endured in his youth and in Jerusalem probably motivated him to take time off "to play the market" in New York, where he was most successful with his financial investments. Although financiers such as Maxwell Abbell and Alan M. Stroock guided him in his investments,[82] financial experts are said to have marveled at his own financial acumen. Lieberman took pride in his financial savvy, thus taking offense at newspaper reports that he had pledged his *last* funds to Israel in 1967. His market holdings and profits far exceeded the $25,000 he had pledged! Upon his death, Lieberman's holdings in Exxon stock alone were valued at $400,000.[83]

Speed of Assimilation

Lieberman's genius further manifested itself in the remarkable speed with which he was able to synthesize and master materials. He claimed to have absorbed all that the Hebrew University had to offer him in a remarkably short period of time, complaining to Louis Ginzberg in a letter of January 1, 1930, that "there is hardly anything left for me to learn here at the university." Within a year of commencing the study of Greek with Professor Schwabe, he audaciously claimed to know the language as well as his professor.[84] Indeed, Schwabe corroborated this claim, because he told Lieberman, "It is a waste of time for you to come to class, because I already taught you all that I know."[85] Yaacov Sussmann mentioned a letter that Schwabe had written in the late 1920s in which he said that he had a bad feeling about the faculty of the Hebrew University and that the only scientific scholar on the faculty was J. N. Epstein, who had one student in particular, Saul Lieberman, who was similar to him—and that Lieberman would go very far.[86]

While in Lithuania, Lieberman did not study the Palestinian Talmud, as it was not generally part of the yeshiva curriculum.[87] So when Michel Rabinowitz asked Lieberman in 1927–28 to translate the Palestinian Talmud into Hebrew, Lieberman commenced, for the very first time, a study of the Palestinian Talmud, and after only a year and a half of nighttime study ("For me, it is *Noctes Hierosolymitanae*"),[88] he had mastered it. By the summer of 1929, he advised Rabinowitz that a translation of the Palestinian Talmud, though greatly desirable, would be ill advised, owing to the numerous textual difficulties and inaccuracies.[89]

Apparently, however, this eighteen-month intense and thorough study of the Palestinian Talmud led Lieberman to a lifetime of work in its uncharted waters. In 1929, he published *Al Hayerushalmi,* illustrating an approach to dealing with the Palestinian Talmud's textual problems. In a January 11, 1930, letter to Louis Ginzberg, Lieberman described, with eloquence and excitement, his discovery concerning the redaction of the Palestinian Talmud tractate *Nezikin*. This discovery was the subject of Lieberman's *Talmudah shel Kisrin*. In this letter to Ginzberg, Lieberman states that he is embarking on his major work on the Palestinian Talmud, explaining that it is impossible to work on *Berakhot* without knowledge of the entire Palestinian Talmud: "It was only this summer [1929] after I finished studying the entire Palestinian Talmud that I was able to return once again to the study of *Berakhot*."

Urbach marveled how, less than four years after publishing *Talmudah shel Kisrin,* Lieberman was able to produce over five hundred pages of text and commentary to the tractates *Shabbat, Eruvin,* and *Pesahim* of the Palestinian Talmud, as well as several scholarly articles in *Tarbiz*.[90] Personal testimonies to Lieberman's amazing speed of assimilation are astonishing. Pinchas Peli recounts that Lieberman was able to review a lengthy essay of his in a few moments and immediately subject it to detailed analysis and critique.[91] Lieberman's correspondence reflects several occasions when he hurriedly sight-read essays submitted to him, and instantly proposed corrections or suggested further elucidations.[92] Elijah Schochet visited Lieberman on Martha's Vineyard, bringing with him the two volumes of the responsa of Rabbi Joel Sirkes, the *BaH* (containing 254 responsa), to consult with Lieberman regarding a forthcoming study of Sirkes and his works. In less than one and a half hours, Lieberman read the entire responsa collection and proceeded to analyze the contents.

Once a scholar approached Lieberman concerning the sequence of the phrase that concludes the second blessing of the wedding service, *seder erusin: al yedei huppa v'kiddushin* (through the wedding canopy and betrothal). Would it not be more logical, Lieberman was asked, for the order to be *al yedei kiddushin v'huppa* (through betrothal and the wedding canopy)? The scholar theorized that the present version might have been selected because it was musically felicitous. Lieberman leaned his head on his hand for two minutes and said, "*Ein stirah babavli*" (there is no contradiction to anything in the Babylonian Talmud). Then he again leaned his head on his hand and said, "*Ein stirah bayerushalmi*" (there is no contradiction to anything in the Palestinian Talmud).[93] Lieberman concluded that there was no problem, by means of a four-minute trip through the two Talmuds!

One final anecdote underscores the power of Lieberman's perception and memory. In a bookstore in England, Louis Finkelstein had discovered three rare volumes of Talmud tractates printed from plates in Spain, prior to the 1492 expulsion, which contained several variant readings. Although Finkelstein wanted to purchase them for the JTS library, the proprietor's asking price was far too high at the time. However, several years later, the Seminary library did purchase the volumes, and Finkelstein immediately brought them to Lieberman so that he could consult them for his work on the Tosefta. Lieberman politely declined Finkelstein's offer, explaining to him that when he had heard of the existence of the volumes he had flown to London, visited the bookstore, and was granted permission by the proprietor to spend several hours perusing the books. Lieberman memorized all the variant readings in the volumes on the spot and was able to use them later in *Tosefta Kifshutah*.[94]

Power of Recall

The aforementioned episode points to Saul Lieberman's remarkable powers of recall. He may well have been endowed with a near-perfect photographic memory that complemented his mental acuity.

David Weiss Halivni stated that Saul Lieberman knew the Palestine (Jerusalem) Talmud by heart, complete with all textual variations.[95] Ephraim Urbach cites an observation made by Lieberman to the effect that a particular phrase "is found, it seems to me, only once in the Palestine Talmud," adding that at the time Lieberman made that statement, the concordance had not yet been published, and when it appeared, it only confirmed Lieberman's recollection. He indeed knew the Palestinian Talmud by heart.[96] Pinchas Peli's account of Lieberman correcting M. Kossovsky's concordance of the Palestinian Talmud from memory is as amusing as it is impressive.[97]

Although Lieberman was aware of the danger of relying solely on one's memory (he once remarked to Eliezer Rosenthal, "I had no time to [look it up] and naturally one should not rely on memory alone"),[98] he felt quite comfortable in trusting his own powers of recall. Early in his academic career, Saul Lieberman confessed to Louis Ginzberg (on May 5, 1932): "I do my writing virtually without texts before me." While composing his commentary on the Tosefta, Lieberman worked from memory or directly from manuscripts, without employing notes.[99] In an eight-page undated document (clearly from his later years) with detailed references and explanations, he said, "I am not as fluent in my studies as I was when I was younger. I must now consult the text and sometimes even search for references." However, according to Haym Soloveitchik, even in advanced years Lieberman frequently worked on articles while in Israel, without any texts before him, and when checking references upon returning to his New York study, he would find that his work was almost invariably correct.

We find in Lieberman's writings sweeping statements such as these, which reflect his confidence in his powers of recall: "Greek philosophic terms are absent from the entire ancient rabbinic literature;"[100] "[T]he early rabbinic literature never mentions a single Greek 'philosophic' term used by the Gnostics";[101] "[N]ot the slightest allusion is extant in rabbinic literature to the symbols and formulas of the heathen mysteries to their phallic rites and licentiousness";[102] and "Nothing can be found in the entire rabbinic literature of the third and fourth centuries from which we might legitimately conclude that the Roman government deliberately persecuted the Jewish religion during that time."[103]

Here is Elie Wiesel's account of his first meeting with Lieberman, in which he encountered the latter's prodigious memory:

> Finally, almost in passing, [Lieberman] came to the subject I yearned to speak of. "Toward the end of the first half of your lecture," he said, "you explained an apparent conflict concerning a text of the *Mekhilta*. Was that explanation your own find?" "I think so," I stammered. "I see," he said. "You think so." He stood up,

> took a dusty volume from the very top of a bookshelf and flipped through it, until he found a certain page. "Look," he said. "Your finding dates back . . . six centuries." I told him I was pleased to walk in such footsteps, but the impish look on his face suggested he only half believed me. He returned to the attack: "A little before the conclusion you presented a solution to the problem raised by Maimonides with regard to Aristotle. Did you think this solution was your own finding?" I nodded. "All right," he said. "Let's see." This time he opened an even older and dustier volume and pointed to an annotated page: "Here it is." Disappointed?[104]

An extraordinary memory can be a curse as well as a blessing. Judith Lieberman commented that her husband refrained from reading the daily newspaper, as he did not want his retentive mind to become a storehouse for ephemeral matters.[105] Indeed, Saul Lieberman once told a JTS secretary that he did not read novels, not only because "the Torah is a jealous mistress," but because "I remember all the characters and what they did. A pity to fill my mind with all these details." However, as noted earlier, this was not entirely true, for Lieberman did read and appreciate good literature, although he once informed Agnon (in a letter dated July 12, 1947) that he permitted himself the luxury of reading mysteries only while on vacation on Martha's Vineyard.

Detective Sense

Lieberman is frequently praised for his remarkable "detective work" in scholarship. Preschel analyzed Lieberman's method of discerning the original meaning of obscure words and phrases. Lieberman shed light on the meaning of words that had been misunderstood or were not understood at all. He offered meanings different from the commonly accepted meaning and rediscovered meanings that had been lost. He also referred to variant texts to find the original meaning of a word or phrase. The key was often found in a midrashic text that was long lost, but that was referred to in whole or in part by a rishon (rabbinic commentator of the early Middle Ages). Preschel suggests that Lieberman, employing the skills of Sherlock Holmes, was a detective of the Hebrew language, for, like the famous creation of Sir Arthur

Conan Doyle, Lieberman followed a series of apparently unrelated clues to solve difficult cases. Indeed, Preschel correctly assumed that Lieberman would have read detective stories in his rare moments of leisure.[106] Perhaps most noteworthy in this regard is *Hilkhot Hayerushalmi,*[107] in which Lieberman proved that four unattributed fragments taken from the Cairo Geniza ninety years earlier by Solomon Schechter that pertain to *Berakhot* and *Ketubot* were in reality the works of Maimonides.

Lieberman wrote in the introduction to the *Hilkhot Hayerushalmi* that Louis Ginzberg had published a collection of fragments from the Palestinian Talmud that were found in the Cairo Geniza.[108] Ginzberg's book, which, according to Lieberman's assessment, opened avenues toward a greater understanding of the Palestinian Talmud, included parts of a summary of sections from *Berakhot.* Lieberman noted that twenty years later, J. N. Epstein published several pages of a summary of sections from the Palestinian Talmud, *Ketubot,* which were in poor condition, that is, numerous words were missing or blurred. Epstein quite correctly pointed out that those manuscripts must have been written by the same author as those brought to light by Ginzberg.[109] Upon close examination, Lieberman concluded that they were intended to constitute a code, along the lines of that of Isaac Alfasi,[110] who had written a code on the Babylonian Talmud, and that none other than Maimonides was the author. Lieberman recounted that Ginzberg, some six years earlier, had speculated that these fragments were from a Maimonidean code, but he remained uncertain. After close study of the texts, Lieberman was able conclusively to identify them as those of Maimonides. A handwriting expert, Morris Lutzki, confirmed Lieberman's conclusion.[111] Lieberman's remarkable forensic skills are very much in evidence here, for he was forced to reconstruct texts of *Ketubot* on the basis of exceedingly sparse fragments. It is noteworthy that, until 1947, this may have been the only previously unpublished manuscript by Maimonides discovered in modern times.

Eliezer S. Rosenthal marveled at Lieberman's forensic skills and the manner in which he would make sense out of seemingly incomprehensible words and passages and could reconstruct lost segments of the Palestinian Talmud in their proper sequence—reconstructions that were validated by subsequent discoveries in the Cairo Geniza and elsewhere.[112] Kutscher speaks of him as a master conductor bringing into play many disciplines to determine the correct meaning of words. These disciplines include a mastery of Semitic languages, Greek and Latin, along with a comprehensive knowledge of rabbinic literature and a remarkable ear for nuances of language.[113] In the words of Abraham Goldberg, "No one has a keener ear for the nuances of language or a more sensitive feeling for text."[114]

Lieberman employs commonsense principles to determine the veracity of statements appearing in rabbinic literature. For example, when analyzing the accounts in rabbinic literature of the death of two saintly Rabbis, Rabbi Hananiah ben Teradyon and Rabbi Akiba, he "discriminates between 'authentic texts,' recording events that occurred in the author or editor's own time, and later midrashim which are *post facto* literary creations," typical of the genre of martyrology literature produced by many nations.[115] Lieberman described his methodology:

> The simple rule should be followed that the Talmud may serve as a good historical document when it deals in contemporary matters within its own locality. . . . The Palestinian Talmud (and some of the early midrashim) whose material was produced in the third and fourth centuries contains valuable information regarding Palestine during that period. . . . The evidence is all the more trustworthy *since the facts are often recorded incidentally and casually.*[116]

The latter principle ascribes authenticity to "aside statements," that is, statements made *meisiah lifi tumo* (spoken in innocence), which are not essential to the object of the text. For example, the *Sifrei* focuses on passages in the Torah portion of *Ha'azinu* relating to martyrs who are to be executed, and incidentally introduces a sketchy account of the arrest of Rabbi Hananiah ben Teradyon during the Hadrianic persecutions.[117] The account in the *Sifrei* and the one appearing in the Babylonian Talmud are necessarily reliable because they are consistent with the political and judicial practices of the Romans of that time.[118] For example, when arrested, Rabbi Hananiah was asked a trick question, presuming his guilt: "Why did you teach Torah?" This was in keeping with the practice of the Roman judges and interrogators at the time.[119] When the Romans strove to eradicate Christianity, they would sentence the

Christian martyrs (teachers) to death by incinerating them together with their sacred texts. Rabbi Hananiah was likewise sentenced to death by fire and wrapped in a scroll of the Torah. Rabbi Hananiah's wife was sentenced to death along with her husband, consistent with the Roman practice of executing the family of a political prisoner.[120]

Before advancing a particular interpretation or explanation, Lieberman demanded overwhelming corroborative evidence. Even when he would adduce firm support for his view, his students recall the frequency with which he would cautiously add the phrase, "It is a plausible hypothesis." Often, Lieberman would preface compelling interpretations with the observation *karov b'einai* ("it seems to me").[121] Theories put forward with a higher level of certainty are described as *karov livadai* ("close to certain"), while the *vadai* ("certainly correct") designation is reserved for unassailable arguments such as the identification of certain Palestinian Talmud fragments as being authored by Maimonides.[122]

Application, Diligence, and Tenacity

Lieberman's genius was matched by his remarkable diligence and tenacity—a near-total absorption in study. Meir Lieberman relates that during the turbulent years under the Bolsheviks, his brother "would be seized with a passion for learning, lasting two to three months at a time, which found him learning day and night, not eating unless reminded to do so, and not being aware of what he was eating. It was similar to the legends about great scholars of the earlier generations—he knew no difference whether the food was bitter or sour."[123] So preoccupied was Lieberman with his studies that he would frequently become oblivious to his surroundings. One anecdote depicts him waiting in line to board a bus in Jerusalem with a woman standing behind him. Once aboard the bus, he took a seat, with the woman behind him seating herself next to him. When people on the bus began to laugh, Lieberman realized the identity of the woman. He had been totally unaware that it was his wife, Judith, because he was thinking through a problem in the Talmud.[124] His focus and concentration were so intense that he often forgot to greet students in the street.

Lieberman was both admired and envied for his ability to discipline himself, fend off distractions, and concentrate considerable time and energy on his studies. R. Chaim Heller stated, "I have known many untiring scholars in my time, but I have never met a man who husbanded his time so assiduously as Rabbi Lieberman does for the Torah."[125] Moshe Zucker, of the JTS faculty, said that no one had understood Talmud as Lieberman did, since the Gaon of Vilna,[126] and that "one can marvel at his scholarship but I most marvel at his *hatmada*—never in my life have I seen such a *matmid*."[127] Rosenthal's article on Lieberman concludes with a tribute to Lieberman's patience, diligence, and painstaking attention to detail.[128]

Lieberman compulsively availed himself of every opportunity to study, being careful to use all the "in-between" times that others might overlook. He explained to Professor Isaac Twersky of Harvard University that, in Palestine in the 1920s and 1930s, the transportation system was primitive, and travel even over a short distance was time-consuming. While traveling by train or bus, he would invariably put the time to good use by studying from the *Horev,* a small-print, compact-size, one-volume edition of the Mishnah that he always carried in his pocket.[129]

David Weiss Halivni recalls that Lieberman reviewed the Palestinian Talmud over 101 times and as a matter of habit reviewed numerous texts in his mind as he walked to and from JTS.[130] This appears also to have been his practice while riding in automobiles. Shamma Friedman, Lieberman's student and frequently his "chauffeur" to and from Ben-Gurion airport, describes how Lieberman would spend virtually the entire trip in silence, reciting by heart to himself sections of the Mishnah. On one occasion, when Friedman left the highway and reduced his speed as he approached the airport, Lieberman, not believing they had already arrived at the airport, asked Friedman why he was preparing to stop. When Friedman explained that they were already near the airport, Lieberman was incredulous, exclaiming that they must have been traveling at a higher speed than usual, because on these trips he repeated to himself (he, of course, knew mishnayot by heart) the mishnah *Taharot,* and knew exactly the point in his review that would coincide with his arrival at the airport—and they had arrived at the airport in advance of reaching that point.[131]

Upon their first meeting, Halivni claims to having been able to recall a Tosafot to the tractate *Hullin* more accurately than did Lieberman, and when leaving Lieberman's office, Halivni saw Lieberman commencing the study of that tractate. When asked, "Why *Hullin?*" Lieberman replied, "If I forgot one Tosafot, who knows how many others I may also have forgotten?"[132]

Lieberman's relatively minimal teaching and administrative duties at JTS afforded him many hours of leisure time, which he transformed into an uninterrupted eight-hour period of daily study, lasting into the early hours of the morning. He was zealous in protecting these hours of study from intrusion. Lieberman purportedly kept his rooms unheated in the winter to discourage visitors, and books piled high on his sofa and chairs precluded visitors from enjoying a lengthy comfortable stay in his study. One suspected that his rapid gait also helped him avoid unnecessary conversations, as did his habit of assiduously reading his mail as he rode the Seminary elevator. As Lieberman put it in a letter to Louis Finkelstein, "Although people bother me a great deal, I see that when there is a will there is a way to get rid of many disturbances."[133]

Upon receiving a telephone call from Rabbi Solomon Joseph Zevin one evening in his Jerusalem home, Lieberman insisted to his caller, "*No, no, ich vill kumen ba eich*" (I will come to your home). What was the problem? Zevin had wanted to visit Lieberman in his home to discuss his *Encyclopedia Talmudit.* "Zevin is a Hasid," explained Lieberman. "If he comes to me, he will stay and talk all night and I cannot possibly chase him out. Better I should go to him. After ten minutes, I will be able to get up and leave and come back here to work."

Although Lieberman had a gregarious side and loved being a raconteur regaling his audience with anecdotes, he denied himself many opportunities for socializing. In his early years at JTS, he hardly socialized with his faculty colleagues; Louis Ginzberg, in particular, was keenly disappointed by the infrequency of their contacts shortly after Lieberman's arrival in New York.[134]

Lieberman's correspondence testifies to frequent refusals on his part to "waste time" by accepting invitations to lecture or compose essays for publication (on assigned topics). He politely declined Professor Heiko Oberman's invitation to lecture at the Harvard Divinity School, as he lacked time to prepare a fitting lecture. Lieberman explained, "Rabbi Akiba never read the Torah in public before speaking it to himself two or three times. To come not fully prepared is to slight the audience."[135] On February 21, 1978, Lieberman turned down a request of Professor Wolfgang Haase of the University of Tübingen in Germany: "Regretfully, at the present time I am overcommitted and barely have the time to fulfill promises already made." He declined an invitation to spend a year at Oxford University because of the need to work on his *Tosefta*[136] and regretted that he did not have time to review articles for the *Standard Reference Encyclopedia*.[137] One has the impression that Lieberman must have declined many invitations to deliver lectures or to submit articles for publication. Apparently, he never accepted Arthur Darby Nock's invitation to publish articles in the prestigious *Harvard Theological Review*.[138]

Sometimes, Lieberman's refusals reflected his dry, acerbic sense of humor. For example, he declined to submit an article for the *Israel Elfenbein Jubilee Volume,* claiming that "the great names of the participants in the volume in your honor frighten me out of my mind, and I really think I am neither worthy nor qualified to participate in the volume in your honor."[139] One wonders how Elfenbein reacted to this self-deprecating statement. In a similar vein, Lieberman responded to the invitation to spend a year at Oxford with a humorous reference to the stipend that he might obtain: "A year free of administrative worries would be quite a blessing. To spend this year in the company of the luminaries of Oxford University would be a double blessing. However, it is rather awkward for a man in my position to apply for a stipend—you know, human vanity! I therefore do not see the feasibility of this proposition." Then, turning serious, he concluded, "I want to assure you that I deeply appreciate your compliment and your extremely kind action."[140] On another occasion, Lieberman, upon receiving a letter inviting him to speak in Philadelphia, was heard to exclaim, "*Ai, ai, ai, bitul torah, bitul torah!*" ("neglect of Torah"). When told that all he had to do was write and explain that he could not be there, Lieberman replied, "Of course I will not go there. My regret is for the *bitul torah* forced upon me by my having to read the letter."[141]

Bernard Mandelbaum recalls Lieberman and Finkelstein engaged in the following dialogue:

Lieberman: You heard of a Clifton Fadiman and something called *Invitation to Learning?*

Finkelstein: It has very distinguished scholars and writers discussing important books and ideas on radio.

Lieberman: I don't know what to do. He invited me, but who wants to waste the time?

> *Finkelstein:* Look, Professor, write them a letter and tell them no.
>
> *Lieberman:* Professor, you don't understand. Saying no was never a question for me. The trouble is, I don't want to waste the time writing a letter!
>
> [Some weeks later] *Lieberman:* Can you imagine? I wrote them and said no, and guess what? They tried to bribe me.
>
> *Finkelstein:* Tried to bribe you?
>
> *Lieberman:* Sure. I received a call from a representative of Mr. Fadiman who asked if I would come if they gave me $500![142]

Financial inducements can well constitute an impediment to scholarship, and this Lieberman knew full well from his youth. While living in Palestine, Lieberman once functioned as Rabbi Yehuda Leib Hakohen Maimon's legal representative and succeeded in procuring for him a handsome settlement in resolving a dispute with the Mizrachi Bank. In gratitude, Maimon paid Lieberman generously for his services, enough for Lieberman to pay his personal living expenses for several months. When informed of the matter, Rabbi Abraham Isaac Kook told Lieberman to desist from matters involving financial gain. "You have all the qualities for success [in Torah scholarship]; however, you are in need of money. There is therefore great danger that you will end up taking leave of the world of Torah! Distance yourself therefore from matters such as these." Lieberman concluded, "To this day, I am grateful to the rav for his sage counsel."[143]

Lieberman's love for the study of Torah was evident to all who knew him. On May 17, 1942, not long after arriving in New York, he wrote to Gershom Scholem, "I sit in the tent of the Torah, and were it not for the evil inclination and Satan, I would sit all day engrossed in Torah study. . . . I refrain from socializing lest I neglect the work of the Torah." On November 12, 1960, Lieberman apologized to the Scholems for a long delay in writing to them: "The truth is that following my return from Israel, I was stuck on Martha's Vineyard, where I immersed myself in the pleasures of the sea of Talmud and therefore had no time to write." On October 29, 1962, Lieberman wrote Scholem of his desire to return to live in Israel so as to be able "to devote my time solely to the study of Torah."

In his correspondence with Finkelstein, Lieberman routinely referred to his good fortune in having uninterrupted hours of study. "You can study all day without being disturbed" is the main benefit Lieberman derived from spending his summers in the country; and, once delayed in Marseilles for several weeks while en route to Palestine, Lieberman rejoiced that "we are staying in a hotel near the shore in a quiet area where it is possible to study undisturbed."[144] On August 25, 1950, while vacationing on Martha's Vineyard, Judith wrote Finkelstein that "Dr. Lieberman, I am afraid, has treated our summer place as a retreat for intensive work and study." Not that Lieberman was indifferent to the temptations of nature's beauty. He wrote to Finkelstein from his summer home:

> Just a few lines to inform you that there are wonderful places in this world where you are almost bound to interrupt your studies and exclaim: *mah na'e ilan zeh, mah na'e nir zeh* [how beautiful is this tree, how beautiful is this field]. Or if you look at it from another angle, you realize the truth of *retsonkha lehakir et mi she'amar vehaya ha'olam, histakel bema'asav* [if you wish to come to perceive (know) Him who spoke and the world came into being, then contemplate His deeds (Creation)].[145]

For the most part, Lieberman was able to resist interrupting his studies. Judith Lieberman described the varied distractions and impositions upon his time that her husband had to contend with while in Jerusalem:

> But here the "pressures" are so overwhelming that you cease to be the master of your own time. To give you some insight into our doings . . . the phone begins ringing after seven in the morning, and the voice tells you that the caller is from Tel Aviv or some settlement with the request to consult Mr. L. on "difficult passages in the Talmud" or needed assistance to publish "a memoriam [*sic*] volume of deceased communities in Eastern Europe" and so on. The archaeologist also needs assistance in deciphering inscriptions and realia found (made usually of earthenware).[146]

Lieberman describes his cousin the Hazon Ish's early years in Minsk as being his "best years" because of the privacy afforded him then to study all day without interruption. "He was associated with no institutions, no yeshiva, he taught no one, he visited no one. He sat all the time by himself at home and studied."[147] No doubt Lieberman was accurate in designating this period of the Hazon Ish's life as his "best years" because he had not yet attained recognition and therefore was able to study undisturbed. One suspects that Lieberman would say the same about himself—that his own "best years" similarly were those prior to his worldwide renown as an academician, when he could spend all his hours of study undisturbed and fully engaged in doing what he loved most.[148]

"Doing what he loved most" was in evidence most dramatically on the festival day of Simhat Torah. Whereas others celebrated the completion of the reading of the Torah cycle with song and dance in the JTS synagogue, Lieberman would spend these hours before an open book engaged in study. He loved to celebrate Simhat Torah not with his feet, but rather with his head; not by dancing but by studying Talmud.[149]

In recalling the loss of his wife, Judith, Lieberman declared his love for his sacred texts. "The Palestinian Talmud owes me nothing, but I owe all my life to it. Even when my most precious companion was taken from me, the Palestinian Talmud did not forsake me. It comforted and sustained me and it will not, I hope, abandon me in old age."[150] In describing his last study session with Lieberman, shortly before Lieberman's death, Elie Wiesel wrote:

> Lieberman had acted strangely when I saw him last. At the end of our lesson he had stood up and embraced me. He was to leave that afternoon for Jerusalem, to celebrate Passover with his older[151] brother. I was in a hurry. I was giving a lecture at Yale that afternoon. He walked me to the door, but suddenly exclaimed, "Would you like to come back, Reb Eliezer?" We went back and reimmersed ourselves in study. I remember the passage. It was the one about an anonymous corpse discovered in a public place. The Law demands that the community elders expiate with a sacrifice. My master's commentary on assigning the blame: They

> allowed a lone visitor to depart without protection. Never was Lieberman more brilliant than on that day. He was inspired by Palestinian sages, and by his adored Radak, the Gaon of Vilna.
>
> An hour went by. Once again he accompanied me to the hallway, we embraced, and I got into the elevator, but my friend and master took me by the arm and said, "We still have time, Reb Eliezer, don't we still have time?" We went back to his desk, took our places, and opened the Talmud for another hour. It was by then one o'clock in the afternoon. This time no delay was possible.[152]

Wiesel concludes his recollection with the affirmation that Lieberman had a premonition that his death was imminent, an observation echoed by Judith Hauptman.[153] He would naturally want to spend his last hours in the study of his sacred and beloved texts.

Even his solitary, private approach to his scholarship—"He worked without assistants, without file cards or computers. Alone, he produced marvels of scholarship and learning"[154]—bespeaks a love for learning that Lieberman expressed in his unique way. The study of Torah is, after all, a *hiyuv gavrah* (personal obligation) and cannot be delegated.

Gaon of Vilna: Affinities and Similarities

Louis Ginzberg took great pride in the fact that he was a great-great-great-grandson of Abraham, the brother of the Gaon of Vilna.[155] Ginzberg dedicated his *Perushim v'Hiddushim b'Yerushalmi* to the Gaon, spoke most deferentially of his illustrious ancestor ("When I think of the phenomenal achievements of the Gaon of Vilna . . . my own achievements look to me rather picayune"),[156] and clearly looked upon himself as treading upon the intellectual path blazed by the Gaon.[157]

We alluded earlier that Lieberman also viewed himself as an authentic link in a distinguished line of Lithuanian rabbinic scholars exemplified by Rabbi Elijah, the Gaon of Vilna. If there is any single personage with whom Lieberman may be compared, it is the Gaon, with one important qualification. Whereas the Gaon was the preeminent kabbalah scholar of his age, as well as an avid kabbalist, Lieberman had little interest in kabbalah or mysticism. Considering his voluminous literary productivity, Lieberman's articles on kabbalah are extremely few.[158] Witness his introduction for Gershom Scholem when the latter was due to lecture at JTS on the subject of mysticism. Lieberman said, "Mysticism is . . . nonsense. . . . Nonsense is nonsense, but the history of nonsense is scholarship."[159] In many other respects, however, Lieberman was similar to the Gaon, and took great pride when the similarities between the two were noted.

Lieberman reputedly treasured and often carried with him a letter he received from Professor Immanuel Loew (the one Hungarian scholar whom Lieberman respected), in which Loew lauded Lieberman: "In the depth of your writings there are to be found many sparks of the spirit of the Gaon of Vilna." The letter is reproduced in appendix V to this volume.[160] In his 1943 tribute to Louis Ginzberg, Lieberman said that the many achievements of the Gaon of Vilna were recognized by the yeshivot "as the high mark of rabbinic creativity."[161]

David Weiss Halivni recalls how Lieberman once boasted that he had "made a Litvak out of him." Halivni writes: "I took this statement as a compliment, meaning that despite my Hungarian background, I had adapted well to the scientific study of Talmud, which in his eyes was identical with the classical Lithuanian style of learning, tracing back to the Gaon of Vilna, shunning *pilpul,* the convoluted reasoning I had encountered in my youth."[162]

Indeed, the Gaon eschewed *pilpul,* stressing the need to determine the plain meaning of the text and the true intent of the Rabbis;[163] he disdained "those who tried to 'show off' by engaging in *pilpul* without acquiring a proper educational foundation. . . . The GRA [Gaon] also castigated teachers of Torah who were imprecise in their teachings and, as noted earlier, frowned upon those who encouraged fanciful *pilpul* as a means of talmudic exegesis."[164] The Gaon's rigorous scholarly approach constituted a pioneering effort. In Solomon Schechter's words, "With this great contribution [of the Gaon's] the foundations for textual criticism were laid."[165]

Both the Gaon and Lieberman labored at reconstructing fragmented and faulty texts and determining authentic versions on the basis of philology, reasoning, and learned conjecture. The Gaon, like Lieberman, devoted himself to establishing the correct text as well as the correct interpretation.

And the Gaon criticized those who failed to consult the Palestinian Talmud and the Tosefta, those oft-neglected texts that Lieberman elucidated. The following articulates an approach to scholarship akin to that of Lieberman:

> The GRA believed that there was one authentic and decisive legal text, the text of the Talmud; all subsequent texts were only interpretative and regardless of the greatness of their authors, were open to challenge. Since for the GRA "truth" was the ultimate goal and purpose of all study, he forthrightly challenged any and all legal decisions of the savants of previous generations, regardless of their status and acclaim, if he felt that their view ran counter to the "truth." The GRA was neither reticent nor subtle[166] in leveling criticism against those whose views he disputed. He pointed out, for example, that even the Geonim and Maimonides failed to pay sufficient attention to the Jerusalem Talmud and to the Tosefta because of their preoccupation with practical legislation.[167]

Both the Gaon and Lieberman exemplified rigorous intellectual honesty and independence in their work, extolling the truth above all else. As noted earlier, Lieberman has been rightly compared with his cousin the Hazon Ish "in his exceptionally comprehensive, text-centered *peshat* approach, as well as in his avoidance of analytic *lomdut*"—both reflecting the conservatism of the Gaon of Vilna.[168]

The Gaon, like Lieberman, employed unconventional sources in his search to elucidate texts. Thus he encouraged certain secular studies on the grounds that, "If one is ignorant of the secular sciences in this regard, one is a hundredfold more ignorant of the wisdom of the Torah, for the two are inseparable."[169] According to the Gaon: "To gain a deeper understanding of the wisdom of the Torah, which is part of divine wisdom, it is important to learn the seven wisdoms inherent in our world, the natural world."[170] Furthermore, "If one lacks knowledge of the laws of nature, his Torah knowledge will lack a hundredfold, while if a Torah scholar understands the laws of nature, his Torah wisdom will gain a hundredfold."[171] Therefore, the Gaon urged the translation of Josephus's writings into Hebrew so that "we will thereby be better able to understand the meaning of our rabbis in many areas of the Talmud and midrashim as pertains to our Holy Land in ancient times."[172] It was in this spirit that Lieberman sought to master the study of the realia of the Greco-Roman world:

> I have thus resolved not to be guided by the words of the "learned ones," but instead to myself explore and traverse the pathways and streets of the land [Palestine], alleys and side streets of Syria, and those of Pumbedita and Nehardea in Babylonia; to see and to listen to the sounds of the street. And thus I wandered from place to place traversing a span of hundreds of years.[173]

Lieberman's need to master the culture of the Greco-Roman world is reflected in his introduction to *Hellenism in Jewish Palestine:*

> Rabbinic literature is replete with valuable information about the life, manners and customs of the ancients. Many passages in it can be properly understood only in the general frame of its environment. The Jews of Palestine were by no means isolated from the ancient Mediterranean civilized world. They shared many of its general beliefs, conceptions and patterns of behavior.[174]

In the same way that the Gaon continually emphasized diligent rational study and unceasing application in study (according to the Gaon, this was preferable even to receiving divine revelation of textual truth),[175] so Lieberman writes that rather than pride oneself on one's God-given intellectual gifts, one should take pride only in one's toiling to persevere in scholarship.[176] In the process of their toil, both men denied themselves sleep and were indifferent to luxury. An account of Lieberman studying the Palestinian Talmud late at night in Jerusalem, with his feet in a pail of water so as not to fall asleep, is reminiscent of the report depicting the Gaon as striving to stay awake at night by placing his feet in a container of cold water.[177]

Lieberman's correspondence reflects all manner of inquiries concerning scholarly matters from such fellow academics as Hanoch Albeck, Avigdor

Aptowitzer, Simha Assaf, Abraham Meir Habermann, Arthur Darby Nock, Ephraim E. Urbach, Morton Smith, William Braude, Yitzhak Baer, and E. J. Bickerman.[178]

Lieberman was frequently consulted concerning academic awards and academic appointments. He recommended Ephraim Urbach and Zeev Ben-Haim for the Rothschild Prize[179] of 1971, and was consulted concerning the appointments of Urbach and S. Safrai as associate professor at the Hebrew University and Tel Aviv University, respectively.[180] Jacob Katz, of the Hebrew University, referring to his praise of an essay by Haym Soloveitchik, requested his help in publishing it,[181] and Lieberman was asked by Gershom Scholem about the merits of Heinemann's *Darkhei ha'Aggadah*.[182]

He also received occasional halakhic inquiries. R. Yehiel Yaakov Weinberg asked Lieberman to supply him with gaonic sources or Palestinian Talmud variants, which would be helpful in his resolution of a case involving a levirate widow.[183] In a letter of March 28, 1967, Lieberman asked the Israeli ambassador to the U.S., Abraham Harman, to convey to Premier Levi Eshkol that it would be exceedingly improper for the State of Israel to perform autopsies without the permission of the family of the deceased.[184] When the "who is a Jew?" controversy arose in Israel, Lieberman wrote to Ben-Gurion, in response to his inquiry, to advise him that "it is perfectly clear and without a shadow of doubt that a son born to a Jew by a non-Jewish wife is not called his son and is considered a non-Jew in all respects. . . . The son must meet all the traditional legal requirements to be considered a proselyte."[185]

Honors, Affiliations, and Invitations

Lieberman received the following honorary degrees:

- D.H.L., Jewish Theological Seminary of America, 1942
- Ph.D., Hebrew University, 1962
- Litt.D., Harvard University, 1966
- LL.D., Dropsie University, 1969
- LL.D., Bar-Ilan University, 1971

In 1980, a chair in the Palestinian Talmud was established at Bar-Ilan University in Lieberman's honor.

Lieberman served as an editor or as editor in chief of the following *Festschrift* and Jubilee volumes:

- The Alexander Marx volumes, 1950
- The Louis Ginzberg Jubilee volumes, 1954
- The Harry A. Wolfson Jubilee volume, 1965
- The Salo W. Baron Jubilee volume, 1974
- The Hanoch Yalon volume, 1963

Lieberman received the following awards:

- The Kook Prize (1956–57), which he declined because of protests in some Orthodox circles[186]
- The Bialik Prize in *Hokhmat Yisrael* (Tel Aviv, 1958)[187]
- The State of Israel Prize, 1971. Lieberman was the first non-Israeli citizen to receive this award.
- The International Harvey Prize for Sciences and Literature (1976), known as Israel's Nobel Prize, the highest award granted by the State of Israel, with a cash award of $35,000[188]

Lieberman was active in the following academic organizations:

- He was a pivotal leader of the American Academy for Jewish Research (AAJR), serving as chairman of the budget committee, and as president 1950–53, 1954–58.
- He was an honorary member of the Academy for the Hebrew Language.
- He was a fellow of the American Academy of Arts and Sciences.
- He was a fellow of the Israel Academy of Sciences and Humanities.
- He was a trustee of the Alexander Kohut Memorial Foundation.
- He served, along with Salo Baron, Theodor Gaster, and Jacob Marcus, on the advisory council of the Jewish Information Bureau.

Lieberman also involved himself in Israel's Bar-Ilan University, not only because it bore the name of his father-in-law, but because he viewed it approvingly as an institution combining a deeply religious approach to Jewish learning with that of broad-minded modern scholarship. Rabbi Joseph H. Lookstein, the chancellor of Bar-Ilan, frequently turned to Lieberman for assistance, and expressed confidence in Lieberman's ability to solve difficult problems, describing him as "a man of wide experience and of unusual sagacity."[189] In the spring of 1966, when Rabbi Lookstein was dealing with questions of authority and academic policy in the context of the drafting of a constitution, he persuaded Lieberman to schedule a visit to Israel to help solve the school's problems. As Lookstein explained to Professor O. Schachter of Bar-Ilan in a letter of May 9, 1966:

> Because Professor Lieberman is so vitally concerned, he is prepared to come to Israel on June 26 [1966] and to remain, if necessary, for two weeks in order to take up on the spot with the Senate and the Executive Council the various aspects of the question of authority. His devotion to the institution, as you know, is great. His experience in academic matters is vast. He is thoroughly familiar with the American pattern, as well as with Israeli and continental pattern. . . . I think his presence in Israel for that purpose will enable us to solve all the problems.

Some years later, Lookstein again addressed Bar-Ilan problems in a letter to Lieberman: "I hope to discuss these matters with you when I visit you, prior to your departure for Israel."[190] Lieberman spent considerable time over the years in meetings and discussions with Rabbi Lookstein and others concerning the administrative structure at Bar-Ilan University.

The correspondence between Lookstein and Lieberman from 1961 to 1976 reflects the efforts of two political allies working on behalf of Bar-Ilan. In the course of his efforts, Lieberman attended meetings and wrote detailed letters to Bar-Ilan officials and Mizrachi leaders, including Schachter,[191] Moshe Hayyim Shapira (Israel's minister of the interior), and Zerah Warhaftig (Israel's minister of religion).[192] Lieberman was most sympathetic to Lookstein's contention (in a letter to Lieberman of August 6, 1976) that in his role as chancellor of Bar-Ilan, he was reduced to a figurehead who spoke at public events but who had no authority when it came to formulating academic policy. Lieberman insisted that in fairness, his close friend Rabbi Lookstein should be given a meaningful role in the university's administration. Lieberman reminded Schachter that Lookstein assumed a responsibility following the death of Pinkhos Churgin (1957), when the university was in disarray, and he nurtured and cared for it with great devotion.[193] Accordingly, Lieberman contended, Lookstein must be the head of the faculty committee and share the duties with a resident president.

However, the selection of a president proved difficult and dominated the efforts of Lookstein and Lieberman over a long period. Following years of maneuvering and a stalemate in the effort to find a president agreeable to all factions, Lieberman finally lost patience and said, "I am sick and tired of the whole business, and if we do not succeed in getting a president, I shall resign from the committee and perhaps from the board of governors." If Lieberman lost his patience, he retained his sense of humor. In a letter of May 23, 1976, to Lookstein, he offered reasons that each of three key persons opposed a particular choice of a president, and said of one, he "is against on principle of always being against." Lieberman's intense and time-consuming involvement in the politics of Bar-Ilan occurred while he was working on the *Tosefta Kifshutah*. He persevered in his efforts because of his commitment to the school, which was identified with his father-in-law, and because of a principle that was always close to his heart: the university must not forget one who extended himself and stepped into the breach in the troubled times when it was left without a leader.

Lieberman was also involved, though to a lesser degree, in the affairs of the Hebrew University. Samuel Rothberg (chairman of the board of governors of the Hebrew University and chairman of the board of directors of the American Friends of the Hebrew University) invited him to attend a meeting of the university's board of governors in March 1972. Lieberman, accepting the invitation, added: "I am interested in the Student Affairs and the Research and Development Committees."[194]

For over four decades, Lieberman remained at JTS, although in the interim he received attractive offers to relocate. In 1950, ten years after his arrival at JTS, Simha Assaf, rector of the Hebrew University, invited Lieberman to return to the university and occupy J. N. Epstein's chair upon his imminent retirement. Assaf assured Lieberman that he was the unanimous choice for the position and that all Jerusalem would rejoice in his return. Although the salary of 150 lirot per month did not compare with Lieberman's salary at JTS, Assaf assured Lieberman that it would afford him a comfortable life in Israel, and added that even a government minister in Israel was paid only 75 lirot a month. Assaf concluded his letter of January 1, 1950: "I am anxiously awaiting your reply in the hope that it will be a positive one and you will not delay in coming." Obviously, Lieberman's response was not in the affirmative.

Speculation and rumor centered on Lieberman's also being offered a position at Harvard University, which he declined. In one version of the events, Harvard withdrew the offer after it was tentatively tendered to Lieberman. Frank Moore Cross, Hancock Professor of Hebrew and other Oriental languages at Harvard, clarified the issue:

> When Professor Wolfson retired, my department at Harvard (of which I was then chairman) voted to invite Professor Lieberman to assume his chair. We had our eyes on a young scholar—Isadore Twersky—who needed some years of publication before advancement, and the interval called for a distinguished scholar. I went down to JTS to visit, and spent some hours with Lieberman. I was deep in the Dead Sea Scrolls at the time and took the opportunity to pick his brain. I also issued the invitation, and to my delight he appeared open to the possibility of coming to Harvard. Later he wrote to me that he would like to come up to Harvard to visit. I assumed—wrongly, as it turned out—that he wished to negotiate with Dean Bundy—his peer—and not with a youngster (which I once was).
>
> The visit proved disastrous. The two men, with me present, grew increasingly cool as the discussion continued. Bundy asked what title Professor Lieberman thought appropriate. Lieberman replied, "Professor of Rabbinics." The Brahmin Bundy turned red, and said no one was going to train rabbis in his college. I intervened and described rabbinic literature as a field. Bundy's comment was that if he didn't understand what rabbinics was, others would also be confused. I then proposed that Lieberman take the

> title of his chair at JTS—I knew what it was, Professor of Palestinian Institutions, if my memory serves me correctly—and Lieberman decided that would be fair if a bit esoteric in the university context. Bundy subsided. Next, Lieberman stated that he would wish to remain rabbi to the JTS community while at Harvard. The interview quickly and coolly ended, and it was clear to me that neither man had warmed to the other. When I returned to my office, Bundy was on the phone, and asked me to withdraw the invitation—that Harvard did not allow faculty to have joint appointments at institutions outside of Cambridge, or live at a distance.
>
> Later I learned, to my utter dismay, that Professor Lieberman, an exquisite gentleman, had asked to come to Cambridge as a courtesy to me, returning my visit, and had no intent to parley with the dean. So the affair ended in a flurry of misunderstandings between Bundy and Lieberman over issues that need not have come up, and Harvard and our department missed out on having him in his senior years.[195]

After serving briefly as a visiting professor at Harvard, Lieberman returned to JTS, most happy to be back and, according to Eli Ginzberg, "more or less totally unimpressed that he had spent time at what was probably the world's outstanding institution of higher learning."[196]

Contributions

Textual Explications

We shall briefly note some of the accolades received by Lieberman in tribute to his textual contributions.

When Harvard University conferred an honorary degree on Lieberman, on June 16, 1966, the citation described him as a "rabbi . . . whose patient learning illumines treasured ancient texts for modern man." He was indeed an illuminator, one who emphasized to his students, "My task as a teacher is to simplify that which appears complicated, instead of complicating that which is simple." In this spirit, Lieberman proposed, in a discussion with Dov

Zlotnick, a simple test for determining the accuracy of an interpretation: "After you have explained something that no one else has explained, it must sound so reasonable that someone else who hears it will say, 'So what? What's the *hiddush* [novelty]? It is obviously so!' Then you know you have it."[197] In this way, Lieberman established correct texts and interpreted texts, mindful always that the text must make sense and speak to us with clarity, so that there should be no need to impose upon it convoluted and unintended meanings. Dimitrovsky describes Lieberman as a premier philological and lexicographical master who elucidated obscure words and passages in the hundreds (according to Kutscher, in the thousands) that were previously not correctly understood.[198]

Likewise, Lieberman identified texts used in various epochs in Jewish history. As a member of the Committee of Censors of Hebrew Books, Raymond Martini had access to many manuscripts in thirteenth-century Spain, from which he quotes.[199] By analyzing Martini's writings, Lieberman was able to determine the nature of these texts and their versions in existence at that time.[200]

Historical Realia

Lieberman was a pioneer in relating the rabbinic literature to the historical, social, and economic realities of the civilization in which it arose. Lieberman stressed that philology was not enough; one needs knowledge of realia, because Israel was not isolated. Jews lived and interacted with the Greco-Roman world. One must first understand the realia of that world to fully understand Jewish literature of the time. According to Jacob Neusner, "That talmudic literature evolved in creative symbiosis in the Hellenistic-Roman world was proved in a most masterful manner by Saul Lieberman."[201]

The following topics are illustrative of the broad range of Lieberman's writings: the alleged ban on Greek wisdom; the persecution of the Jewish religion, dealing with the impact of the Hadrianic restrictions; the phenomenon of the *bat kol;*[202] and support from the *Talmud Yerushalmi* that midrashim are not to be taken literally.[203]

Tosefta

As discussed earlier, the Tosefta, like the *Yerushalmi,* was among the "disadvantaged texts"[204] on which Lieberman concentrated his efforts to produce the definitive edition and commentary. Even though the Tosefta was excluded from the corpus of the Mishnah, it was studied during the post-rabbinic period, and Lieberman proved that it was diligently and systematically studied during the gaonic period.[205] Through Lieberman's efforts, it may be studied and understood today as perhaps never before.

CHARACTER

Complex *Musar* Typology

It is easy to misinterpret the behavior and misunderstand the personalities of those of a different culture and environment from our own. What appears to be criticism can be in reality a statement of interest in, concern about, and praise for a person. To understand Lieberman, one has to understand his milieu, upbringing, and the social and cultural world in which he grew to maturity. For the most part, that world is unfamiliar to us, and therefore Lieberman is not an easy figure to understand. His style in teaching was, to a certain degree, that of another age and culture. He was a product of the *musar* world of late-nineteenth- and early-twentieth-century Lithuania. This was a world of paradox and complexity, a world of toughness and softness.

Toughness

Home Environment. Lieberman was clearly the product of what we call today a "tough-love" upbringing at home. In the words of a distant cousin, "while he inherited compassion and generosity from his mother, he inherited strictness and discipline from his father."[206] Indeed, he was driven hard to excel by his father, who, disappointed that young Saul was not thoroughly versed in Talmud, sent him away before his bar mitzvah to study in the yeshiva of Malch, as it was difficult to find teachers in Motol who were able to challenge him. Apparently, young Saul thought otherwise, because when asked upon his arrival in Malch, "Boy, do you need a rebbe?" Lieberman's response reputedly was, "Rebbe? I don't need a rebbe; perhaps I am in need of a student."[207]

Lieberman's brother, Meir, explained that his father's strict and hyper-critical approach to young Saul was due to his father's awareness of his son's genius. To ensure that he not become arrogant, the father employed an approach of strictness and caustic criticism as a tool to instill humility in the youth. Once, when Lieberman's father showed Saul a certain book (that happened to be written by a relative), it evoked the desired response: Saul said, "It's humbling to read a book that tells me so much that I didn't know." Another depiction of Lieberman's departure for Malch portrays a family friend, Rabbi Gershonowitz, literally abducting him from his Motol home and bringing him to Malch to a school better suited for stimulating the young boy's genius.[208]

Lieberman's bar mitzvah was celebrated in Kosov, in the synagogue presided over by Rabbi Shmaryahu Yosef Karelitz, his uncle. R. Karelitz was deeply impressed with young Lieberman's bar mitzvah speech and subsequently sent him a letter complimenting him on his address and predicting greatness for the youth. Lieberman, letter in hand, approached his father and inquired innocently, "Father, who is greater in Torah, you or Uncle Shmarya?" Replied his father, "Uncle Shmarya." "I thought so, too," agreed young Saul. "Uncle Shmarya understands matters better than you do," and he presented his father the laudatory letter he had received. Lieberman's father read the letter and laughed. "Saul, my son, until now I was convinced that you were an ignoramus, but I did feel that you had some common sense. Now I see that you have no sense, either. Did your uncle really write you this letter in truth to praise you? He merely wrote these words to flatter you and help you to feel good about yourself. Do you honestly feel that there is any truth to his words? Such a fool you are." And Lieberman's father tore his son's prized letter to bits before his eyes.[209]

Another version of the episode (or perhaps a similar story) portrays young Saul sending off some of his insights on rabbinic texts together with questions to a noted scholar and receiving a reply praising his erudition and addressing him as an adult with full honorific titles. His father, however, discounted the praise, claiming that the scholar was merely joking.[210]

The talmudic ideal of students "being in awe (or fear) of their teachers" and humble with respect to their own attainments was clearly Lieberman's desire for his own students at the Seminary. Thus, he followed the accepted practice of many Lithuanian *musar* yeshivot to avoid offering praise to a student even if that student was worthy of commendation. Only indirectly and subtly would he bestow accolades upon the deserving. As for offering critiques, Lieberman was far more direct, but here, too, he could employ subtlety and ambiguity. Richard Rubenstein writes most negatively of encounters he had at JTS with a certain professor "Kleinman" (likely a pseudonym for Lieberman). Rubenstein records one such dialogue between the two of them:

> I told him that I wanted to continue my studies after graduation in the hope of eventually becoming a scholar. In ancient times, the Hebrew word for one ignorant of rabbinic literature was an *am ha'aretz*. When I told Kleinman of my hopes and my willingness for further sacrifice to achieve a solid foundation in Jewish learning, he responded: "Rubenstein, if you study for fifteen years, maybe you'll reach the level of an ancient *am ha'aretz*."
>
> The term *am ha'aretz* is one of contempt and opprobrium in rabbinic Judaism. I had a very good idea of the vastness of the subject matter. I also had a realistic idea of my own limitations. I was not a poor student by seminary standards; in spite of my personal difficulties and the deficient background with which I began, I completed the seminary's course in the minimum time and was graduated *cum laude*. This made no difference to Kleinman. Like most of his students, I was an unworthy *am ha'aretz* in his eyes.[211]

Technically speaking, Rubenstein may be correct in writing that "the term *am ha'aretz* is one of contempt and opprobrium in rabbinic Judaism." However, this was not always the case in the learned circles of Lithuanian Jewry in which Lieberman grew to maturity. Rabbi Yaakov Kamenetsky observed, "In Lithuania, unless someone knew the entire Babylonian Talmud, he lacked even the most basic prerequisite for being considered a *talmid hakham*. Whether he was actually recognized as such depended on his ability to bring that vast knowledge to bear in analyzing any topic at hand and on the depth of his understanding." If by these criteria a scholar did not merit that designation, the alternative label, under certain circumstances, might well be *am ha'aretz!*[212] As Abramson explains, among scholars of Torah the phrase *am ha'aretz* was applied to a scholar, as if to say, "Indeed you are a scholar, but you have not mastered this matter. One who was not a scholar did not merit being called an *am ha'aretz!*"[213] In such a way, Lieberman's father used the idiom in addressing his son. It is not impossible that Lieberman similarly would employ the phrase—and be misunderstood in the process.

How easy it is to misinterpret. A phrase within a specific context that may have had one meaning within one culture may be completely misunderstood in another. However, the user of the phrase may choose to employ the phrase to make a point. The circumstances surrounding the use of the phrase are important. Indeed, the *am ha'aretz* designation is typical of Lieberman's tendency to engage in the use of double entendres. On one level, the phrase means an ignoramus; on another level, it means one who is studying Torah but has not yet attained the highest degree of proficiency that is expected before one can be viewed as a *ben torah*—a man of learning, or a *lamdan*—a scholar. Which is the intended meaning? Depending on the context, it is difficult to be certain.

Although Lieberman would surely have tried to live up to his own description of Eastern European *b'nai torah,* striving "to be overly demanding upon myself and exceedingly forbearing and forgiving toward others,"[214] his early environment may have caused him to develop a critical nature, an uncompromising demand for excellence, a deep disdain for mediocrity, and a lack of subtlety in the process. This is the way it was done back in Lithuania, and others in that context took little offense. However, in another age and locale, such a style could be insulting and demeaning. Indeed, a number of Lieberman's students characterized his teaching style in those terms.

Lieberman elaborated on his approach to criticism in his introduction to *Sifrei Zuta.*[215] He said that although he frequently took serious issue with contemporary scholars in the volume, he did not want to deride great scholars. His critiques are rhetorical flourishes intended to enhance and sharpen the analysis, akin to young voices joining the Holy Temple choir in order to add sweetness (spice) to the melody.[216] Lieberman said that his criticisms are offered only to substantial scholars, because "I do not pay any attention whatsoever to small foxes." The analogy is instructive because it reveals the nature of the academic criticism that Lieberman deplored.[217] He describes a particular species of fox that would sleep camouflaged in a tree during the day and suck the juices from the fruit at night. Lieberman quotes from the Song of Songs (2:15), which speaks of "the little foxes that ruin the vineyards" in blossom, as well as Aristotle's *History of Animals,* which describes "the little foxes that spoil the grapes."[218] We note further that the Rabbis made disparaging remarks about the fox. The Rabbis speak of the "bite of the fox" (*Avot* 2:10), and R. Mattia ben Charash asserts that it is "better to be a tail among lions than the head among foxes" (*Avot* 4:15). Thus, Lieberman uses "little foxes" to aptly describe clever, parasitic, destructive, and ultimately inconsequential critics. The Talmud also uses the word "fox" to describe an insubstantial person. When Rabbi Judah commiserates over the rejection of his arguments by Rabbi Elazar (ben Shimon), his father says, quite modestly, that Rabbi Elazar is a lion—the son of a lion—while Rabbi Judah is a lion, the son of a fox.[219] That is to say that his father is an insignificant person who does not have the intellectual strength of the lion. Lieberman ignores the fox, preferring to engage only the lion in debate. Criticism should therefore be viewed as part of scholarly dialogue carried on among reputable scholars designed to enhance the understanding of a text, thesis, or argument; challenging and debating are reflections of mutual respect and affection.

Lieberman also frequently criticized his students as a pedagogic tool to motivate them to study diligently. If he had to embarrass students into preparing the Talmud text thoroughly, so be it. However, after careful examination of a considerable volume of Lieberman's intra-Seminary correspondence with Finkelstein and other Seminary faculty and administrators, over a long period, including the period when he served as dean of the rabbinical school, and later as rector, as well as his correspondence with scholars, educators, and friends outside the Seminary, we are not able to find even a hint of criticism of his Talmud students, or, for that matter, of any member of the Rabbinical Assembly. On the contrary, according to Emanuel Gettinger (a prominent Orthodox rabbi on New York's West Side and a relative of Judith Lieberman), Lieberman always expressed pride in the achievements of his students and boasted that they could hold their own against yeshiva students.[220] His critiques were "in-house" critiques for private ears, not for public consumption.

Academic Environment. During his early education, Lieberman came under the influence of three outstanding *musar* personalities: Rabbi David Tevel Dinovsky of Malch, Rabbi Natan Zevi Finkel of Slobodka, and Rabbi Yosef Yosel Hurwitz of Novogrudok (Novaredok).

Malch. Although Lieberman was only twelve or thirteen years old when he studied at Malch, he apparently considered R. Dinovsky to be his principal rebbe.[221] R. Dinovsky, a student of R. Simhah Zissel Zev of Kelme, who was a disciple of Yisrael (Lipkin) Salanter, was an avowed *musarnik,* affirming the Kelme ideal of the non-clergy ethicist. He was a charismatic speaker who would sermonize for hours at a time, mesmerizing his audience.

Slobodka. Lieberman's stay at Slobodka was only about three years, but there he was first exposed to arguably one of the most influential of all *roshei yeshiva* in Lithuania—R. Natan Zevi Finkel, the Alter of Slobodka (1849–1927). R. Finkel, also a disciple of R. Simhah Zissel Zev of Kelme, was an outstanding educator and a penetrating psychologist who related to each of his students on an individual basis, treating each according to his needs and potential. He emphasized *gadlut ha'adam,* the "inherent greatness of Man," the fulfillment of one's full potential through constant self-improvement. His *musar* lectures stressed the need for integrity and truth. Lieberman would later recall his teacher's perceptiveness and wisdom in judging people.[222] Slobodka's other *rosh yeshiva,* R. Moshe Mordechai Epstein, a prodigy of the Volozhin yeshiva, emphasized the study of such obscure sources as the *Talmud Yerushalmi* and the Tosefta.[223] Interestingly, Lieberman's choice of a *musar* text at Slobodka was the more philosophical work *Hovot Halevavot* by Bahya ibn Pakuda.[224]

Novogrudok (Novaredok). As a result of the upheavals that followed World War I, the Slobodka yeshiva was forced to relocate in Russia.[225] R. Yosef Yosel Hurwitz (1848–1919), the Alter of Novaredok, was Lieberman's third *musar* mentor, a singularly demanding personality who stressed a regimen of self-discipline and self-denial. The intensity of Lieberman's study in Jerusalem following the death of his first wife, Rachel, is reminiscent of how R. Hurwitz locked himself in a cabin for a year and a half, immersed in study, after his own wife had died in childbirth. Indeed, *shivti* (Ps. 27:4: that I may dwell in the house of the Lord all the days of my life) was the Novaredok credo denoting the need for perpetually engaging oneself in the study of Torah.

This is not the place for a detailed analysis of the *musar* movement. However, such phrases as "rigorous intellectual and moral training," "self-examination," "self-discipline," "self-criticism," "self-improvement," "self-abnegation," "fulfillment of one's potential," and an almost obsessive concern with integrity aptly describe the *musar* environment that nurtured Lieberman.[226]

Integrity

One facet of Lieberman's personality attributable to his *musar* upbringing was his emphasis on living a life of integrity. Lieberman possessed a love for the truth and a hatred for dishonesty that are vividly reflected in his thought and action. His personal correspondence includes many references to his contempt for falsehood and deception. In a letter to Anita Shapira, he thanks her for sending him her biography of Berl Katznelson and reminisces about his own early years in Palestine. In reflecting on what might have happened had he chosen to join a kibbutz, Lieberman writes, "I would not have been enticed to embark on a career in politics because of my natural hatred for mendacity and hypocrisy, and thus would have remained in the kibbutz for all of my life."[227]

Lieberman thanked Gershom Scholem for sending him his article on Joseph Ashkenazi, and said that he identified with Ashkenazi as a fellow "seeker after the truth." "He is a man after my own heart. . . . He is not ashamed to say what he thinks," wrote Lieberman.[228] Indeed, knowing of Lieberman's commitment to the qualities that Ashkenazi exemplifies, Scholem dedicated "New Contributions to the Biography of Rabbi Joseph Ashkenazi of Safed" to Lieberman.[229] Lieberman confessed that he admired Ashkenazi, not only for his critical analysis of mishnaic texts and his astute original interpretations, but for his love of truth and, therefore, his rejection of false and distorted interpretations of rabbinic texts. Likewise, Lieberman praised David Pardo as a "seeker after the truth."[230] Despite his rivalry with J. N. Epstein, he praised him because "the truth was precious to [Epstein], and he never showed favoritism toward any scholars."[231]

Lieberman's personal choice for a prayer with which to conclude his introduction to his commentary on the Tosefta speaks volumes: "May it be thy will that He who knows the truth, He whose seal is the truth, will reveal unto us the truth." Lieberman's scholarly works are not sermons. They are objective and dispassionate studies without any personal agenda. However, Lieberman emphasized in his writings the deep sense of integrity of the Rabbis of the Talmud.[232] Lieberman resented the tendency on the part of some secular elements in Palestine in the 1920s and 1930s to deride the Sages, and to claim that

> the Sages, ensconced in the precincts of the academy, fabricated all kinds of questions and problems completely unrelated to the real world; they constructed castles in the air, and fashioned for themselves a unique and peculiar kind of literature, unlike any other. It is no wonder that a large number of students approached the subject [Talmud] with levity and derision.[233]

Lieberman took every opportunity to illustrate the sensitivity of the Rabbis to issues of integrity. The Rabbis saw the Roman government as attempting to cloak its deviousness and dishonesty in a mantle of idealistic piety. The Rabbis "were not unaware of the fact that the Romans tried to put a face of legality on their robberies. A Rabbi of the third century summarized it in the following phrase: 'This wicked government robs and extorts and makes it appear as though it were holding court.'"[234] Therefore "the Rabbis did not criticize the justice of the Hellenistic or the Roman laws per se but condemned the cruelties in capital punishment, the legal procedure in practice, the catch questions, the forced confessions, briberies, and so on."[235] In other words, it was not only the immoralities and cruelties of the Roman world that were to be condemned, but also the deceitful pious pretense that accompanied these activities.

Abhorrent as many of the practices of the Gentiles appeared to be, the Rabbis, according to Lieberman, were careful not to exaggerate or distort such activities even while condemning them. He made a striking declaration to this effect: "I have not found in all the talmudic literature accusations against the Gentiles that I am not aware of from the literature of the Gentiles themselves."[233] In other words, Lieberman claims that the Rabbis' sense of integrity dictated that they refrain from fabricating any indictments with which to condemn their neighbors. To the contrary, even when discussing an instance of a Gentile engaging in perverse sexual relations, the Rabbis would refrain from generalizing and condemning Gentiles for such immoralities.[237] Indeed, on occasion, they commended Gentiles for their virtuous behavior.[238] This was a major point of contention between Lieberman and Gedalyahu Alon, with the latter arguing that Lieberman's claim that "the attitude of the Rabbis toward the Gentiles who remained faithful to their religion was very tolerant and liberal"[239] was not a fair appraisal of the situation. Alon polemicized on this issue in an extensive and harsh review of Lieberman's *Greek in Jewish Palestine*.[240]

It constituted high praise, indeed, when Lieberman would say of a person, *er iz an emmeser* ("he is a truthful person"), for, as any of his students can testify—some from bitter experience—he also expected a high standard of honesty from others: "He did not tolerate hypocrisy or deceit. There was no shame involved when a student or colleague failed to know or understand a source or a passage, but to create the impression that one knows something he really does not understand was reprehensible."[241]

Lieberman's response to a request regarding two candidates competing for the 1971 Rothschild Prize in Jewish studies reveals the moral depth of his character. In a December 20, 1971, letter, Gershom Scholem, chairman of the Rothschild Prizes Organization in Israel, informed Lieberman that his committee was considering Professor Ephraim Urbach and Professor Zeev Ben-Haim in the Jewish studies category. Scholem asked Lieberman for a

> comparative evaluation of the works of Professor Urbach and Professor Ben-Haim. However, should you find it impossible to let us have a comparative opinion on the works of the above two candidates, we would appreciate receiving your opinion on the work of Prof. Urbach, *Hazal: Pirkei Emunot Vedayot* [*The Sages: Their Concepts and Beliefs*].

On January 6, 1972, Lieberman wrote a separate letter to Scholem on each of the two candidates. In the Urbach letter, he said that he had read all of the books and most of the articles of Urbach. He concluded that all of his work is "distinguished with erudition on the highest level, sound method and independent thinking. His most recent book [*The Sages*] is unique in its field. It fills an evident gap. He certainly deserves the Rothschild Prize for his works." In the Ben-Haim letter, he said that his work on Samaritan literature and institutions has

> opened new vistas for the scholars in the field. . . . [T]he results of his investigations shed new light on the Western Aramaic . . . and no scholar in the field of Palestinian Semitic dialects in the time of the Talmud can do anything without consulting the indices of his three volumes. . . . All his works are distinguished with an exact philological method combined with a native sense for languages. It goes without saying that he deserves a Rothschild Prize.

Lieberman refused to assess the two scholars relative to each other. It is clear, however, that Ben-Haim's work would have had a greater impact on Lieberman's scholarship than Urbach's, especially in connection with their shared passion for philology and the Hebrew language. Ben-Haim's work included: "The Literary and Oral Tradition of Hebrew and Aramaic amongst the Samaritans"; "The Struggle for a Language" (dealing with the revival of Hebrew as well as its grammar); "A Collection of Samaritan Midrashim"; and "Studies in the Traditions of the Hebrew Language." That Lieberman chose to write a separate letter for each reveals his deep hesitation to provide a "comparative evaluation" of one over the other.

On February 16, 1972, more than five weeks after his initial letters to Scholem, Lieberman sent him a handwritten note to "ease my conscience with respect to my recommendations regarding the Rothschild Prize." Lieberman wrote that there was no doubt that Urbach's book (*The Sages*) deserved a prize and that the other two leading texts in the field cannot be compared with Urbach's book in methodology or substance. Lieberman then made a startling admission: "I have tried to be objective, although Urbach and I have a strong friendship,[242] whereas Professor Ben-Haim and I have met only in passing." If there must be only one prize for Jewish studies, he concedes that Ben-Haim would be his choice. Ben-Haim, wrote Lieberman, excels in his mature critical sense (as his studies are based on primary sources) and in his awareness of the limits of his own knowledge. In his initial letters to Scholem, Lieberman did not make this explicit, as he did not feel comfortable ranking one scholar in relation to another, especially when one was a very close friend. Lieberman continued to hope that it might not be necessary for the committee to choose between the two, as it could choose to award a prize to each. Lieberman concluded by reflecting that his friendship with Urbach may have caused him to withhold a well-deserved endorsement of Ben-Haim over Urbach. Whether his friendship with Urbach interfered with his assessment of the merits of his scholarship relative to Ben-Haim's deeply troubled Lieberman. The handwritten letter to Scholem poignantly reveals the depth of Lieberman's inner struggle.

On occasions when Lieberman believed he had no choice but to recommend people for recognition, he did so by using ambiguous terms—thereby hoping to avoid falsehoods.[243] Needless to say, speaking the unadulterated truth openly and bluntly is not always conducive to maintaining amicable social relationships. In a March 8, 1960, letter to Salman Schocken's (1877–1959) son, Gershom, Lieberman reflected on how his "Russian" style of "speaking the truth to a person's face, a truth unsweetened and unadulterated," would sometimes be unpleasant to Schocken, a gentleman bred on proper Western European manners. Indeed, Lieberman observed that Schocken once refused to speak to him, apart from exchanging greetings, for weeks after receiving a blunt letter from Lieberman telling the truth as he saw it.

At times, however, Lieberman sought to tone down a harsh truth to spare the other party pain. Thus, on January 21, 1940, he wrote to Ginzberg from Jerusalem, saying that Michael Higger had misquoted him, Lieberman, in the *AAJR Proceedings*. Lieberman suggested that Ginzberg might write a "gentle" letter in his, Lieberman's, name pointing out the inaccuracies. Obviously, a response from a third party of Ginzberg's stature would be most effective. Lieberman was also concerned lest he offend Higger by writing a letter of his own that would be more strident than Ginzberg's.[244] To complicate matters further, Higger was a scholar associated with the institution at which Lieberman would soon be teaching, and Lieberman did not want to offend a future colleague.

Just before Passover 1940, Lieberman explained in a letter to Ginzberg that he had chosen to allude subtly to the matter that the *Sheur Komah* may be based on external sources (i.e., Greek art and sculpture forms), rather than to state so blatantly, as he did not want to offend the religious sensitivities of the pious Jews who may believe in the sanctity of the *Sheur Komah*. Likewise, in *Hellenism in Jewish Palestine,* Lieberman preferred not to emphasize that certain principles of logic by means of which the Torah is expounded might have parallels in Greco-Roman legal principles.[245] Despite such illustrations, Lieberman tended to be blunt and direct in speech and correspondence, preferring the unadorned truth of Eastern Europe to the refined manner of Western Europe.

Lieberman once complained (on January 4, 1961) to Scholem that he had not received any correspondence from him in quite a long time. Lieberman asked if Scholem was angry with him and, if this were the case, would he let him know what was bothering him: "If you are correct, I will admit to you as much. If you are mistaken, I will correct you." Lieberman, one day later, again wrote to Scholem, this time apologizing for his letter of the previous day—because he had just received correspondence from Scholem and realized that there was no problem; Scholem bore no grudge against him.

On April 22, 1963, Lieberman wrote a contrite letter to Samuel Mirsky, apologizing for being curt with him because of his mistaken assumption that Mirsky had seen his written comments on a particular matter. Apparently, Mirsky had phrased a question to Lieberman, giving him the impression that Mirsky had seen his discussion of a particular term in his *Yerushalmi Kifshuto*. It therefore appeared to Lieberman that it was a taunting question, and he responded angrily, "It can all be found in my text." Lieberman's apology began, "I want to ask your forgiveness and pardon for suspecting the innocent." Lieberman explained that it was wrong of him to have assumed that Mirsky had read his text: "This is simply vacuous arrogance of an author who is certain that everybody reads his work." Lieberman admitted to Mirsky that "by nature I am incapable of speaking with anyone heart to heart. . . . I behaved improperly and I am deeply pained over this matter." He concluded by saying that he would have sent him a copy of his *Yerushalmi Kifshuto;* however, since it was out of print, he promised instead to send him the volumes of the *Tosefta Kifshutah, Nashim.*

Most revealing is the letter referred to earlier, sent by Lieberman to Anita Shapira, author of *Berl Katznelson: A Biography.*[246] Lieberman reminisced about his early days as an immigrant to Palestine in the 1920s, admitting candidly that he was totally ignorant of the Zionist movement and had no appreciation of its role in the building of the State of Israel. He admitted that he knew more about the Palestine of two thousand years earlier than contemporary Palestine, and could have learned much from Berl Katznelson. It was quite possible, mused Lieberman, that had he then developed an appreciation for Zionist ideology he might have spent his life on a kibbutz.[247]

Although Lieberman could be remarkably subtle and oblique in offering criticism, and at times delighted in the use of double entendres, there were occasions when he was brutally direct and acerbic in his rebukes. He frequently was reticent to apologize verbally—especially to students. He was more comfortable expressing his regrets in the form of magnanimous behavior than verbal contrition.

For example, Lieberman was greatly displeased by a senior sermon[248] delivered on December 11, 1954, *parshat Vayishlah,* in the Seminary synagogue by one of his students, Baruch Levine, in which Levine criticized the Patriarch Jacob for his deviousness.[249] Lieberman was particularly distressed when Levine, dealing with the etymology of "Yaakov," described Jacob as "the crooked one." Lieberman responded by spending the entire ensuing Talmud class publicly rebuking Levine for his critique of the Patriarch, implying that, like the ancient Greek hero who burned down the palace of Apollo to gain fame, Levine may have been motivated by vainglory in denigrating the sacred. Deeply hurt by Lieberman's castigation, Levine sought a private audience with Lieberman a month later to say how unfair he thought his mentor's accusations to be, and how deeply hurt he had been by them. Levine stressed the purity of his motives and that Lieberman did not know him well enough to impugn his character in such a manner. Levine pointed to his record as a serious and respectful student of rabbinic texts who devoted many hours to the extracurricular study of Talmud and would frequently present himself to Lieberman for examination in this subject matter. Finally, Levine suggested that Lieberman may have misunderstood the primary thrust of his sermon—a tribute to Jacob's positive growth from one who used deceit for self-advancement to one who is capable of admitting his unworthiness and confronting his adversary directly in order to become Israel. Lieberman countered that Jacob was a "tragic figure" who endured many misfortunes (Laban's trickery, Esau's hostile behavior, the angel's attempt to kill him, the violation of his only daughter, Dinah, the death of his favored wife, the Joseph episode) and who deserves our understanding instead of condemnation.

Although Lieberman issued no formal apology to Levine after this conversation, it is obvious that Lieberman subsequently exerted substantial effort to make amends in the matter. At JTS commencement exercises, Levine was honored as the co-recipient of the homiletics prize, a prize he could not have been awarded without Lieberman's approval as dean of the rabbinical school. Thus, the very sermon that Lieberman criticized so severely was implicitly granted the highest possible commendation. Immediately after the graduation, Lieberman invited Levine's parents (fellow Litvaks) to join him in his office, where he played the role of an extremely cordial host, praising Levine for his academic achievements, which reflected honor upon Levine's distinguished Lithuanian rabbinic ancestry.

Some five years later, Lieberman visited Brandeis University for the opening of the Philip W. Lown Institute of Advanced Jewish Studies. Levine, by then a doctoral student at Brandeis, also attended the opening events. When Lieberman saw Levine, he casually inquired, "What about *Yaakov avinu* [our father Jacob]?" Levine replied, with a slight change in one word in a passage in Isaiah (40:4) so that it read, "*V'haya Yaakov l'meshor*" ("Jacob shall be straight," namely, that which was crooked shall become straight). Levine intended a second meaning, namely, that his own understanding of Jacob had been straightened out, due to Lieberman's explanation—whereupon Lieberman responded, enjoying the pun and appreciating the change in attitude, "Very good Levine."

Whatever tension existed between the two had been resolved, and the closeness of their relationship was such that in ensuing years, Levine was invited by Lieberman to join him in several small-group study sessions in Lieberman's Jerusalem home. Did Levine ever hear a formal apology? No;

that was not Lieberman's *musar* style. One maintained a stern demeanor, preferring to let one's deeds speak volumes of apologies. Bernard Mandelbaum, among others, even suggested to Levine at the time of Lieberman's public rebuke (perhaps to comfort him) that he should have been flattered to be castigated by Lieberman, for Lieberman critiqued him precisely because he thought so highly of him. One makes greater demands upon greater people. A scholar bears a special responsibility for his words. Whether or not this had any bearing in the matter, such was the *musar* approach. One might theorize that Lieberman's commitment to the truth enabled him to be surprisingly comfortable with criticism—self-criticism as well as criticism of others. His tendency was to be open, straightforward, and uninhibited in his response to others.

Self-Criticism. In his younger years, Lieberman tended to be overly harsh on himself, insisting on stridently criticizing himself for his errors and publicly confessing his mistakes. When R. Hayim Heller pointed out an error in Lieberman's *Yerushalmi Kifshuto,* Lieberman promptly brought the matter to public attention by publishing an article in *Tarbiz,*[250] in which he proclaimed, "All my words regarding this matter in the *Yerushalmi Kifshuto* are null and void."[251]

Lieberman admitted to having erred in his *Tosefta Kifshutah* with respect to the *Hemdat Yamim* of Shalom Shabazi: "My note is the fruit of imaginary scholarship."[252] In a footnote in his edition of *Devarim Rabbah,* Lieberman criticized A. Epstein for misciting the form in which the midrash *Devarim Rabbah* is referred to in the *Pugio Fidei* of Raymond Martini; Lieberman then acknowledged that he had made the same mistake in his book *Shkiin.*[253] In the second edition of *Devarim Rabbah,* he stated, "All that I wrote (in the latter portion of a footnote in the first edition) is useless and the correct interpretation is. . . ."[254] In his introduction to the last published volume of the *Tosefta Kifshutah,*[255] Lieberman confessed, "I did not fulfill my duty" in locating the source of a citation by R. Menahem Hameiri purporting to be from the Tosefta, but not to be found in extant editions of the Tosefta. Lieberman expresses his gratitude to fellow scholars whose insights helped him to belatedly solve the dilemma.[253]

Reportedly, J. N. Epstein, Lieberman's Jerusalem mentor, was disturbed by his student's hyper-modesty and penchant for public admission of personal errors; Epstein suggested that such excessive modesty on the part of a youth might be, in truth, an indication of just the opposite—arrogance.[257] There may be some truth to Epstein's observation, for the youthful Lieberman was exceedingly self-confident and well aware of his abilities; however, Epstein may have failed to appreciate the depth of Lieberman's commitment to seek the truth and therefore, the importance of his admitting to error. In this, there may also be a reflection of an important aspect of the *musar* ideology absorbed by Lieberman in his youth. Great scholars were not only willing, but eager, to admit their errors. R. Perelmann (grandfather of Lieberman's first wife, Rachel), the "Minsker Gadol," was known to welcome criticism from those of lesser academic stature and to publicly concede that he had erred.[258]

Throughout his life, Lieberman was never embarrassed to assert that he had changed his thinking on an issue, even if it meant revising earlier essays. In summer 1942, Finkelstein discussed with Lieberman a lecture that Lieberman was to deliver at the Seminary's Institute of Post-Biblical Studies in November 1942, entitled "The Jewish Attitude toward the Christian Martyrs in Caesarea."[259] Lieberman's essay "The Martyrs of Caesarea," which consisted of a refinement of the material, was published in 1944,[260] and upon receipt of the essay based on the lecture, Finkelstein commented in a July 10, 1944, letter to Lieberman, "I see that you have added an enormous amount of new material." It is instructive to compare this essay with an extensive revision of the material appearing in his 1974 essay "The Persecution of the Jewish Religion."[261] Lieberman chose not to include "The Martyrs of Caesarea" in his 1974 collection of essays, *Texts and Studies,* precisely because it was "completely reworked with many additions and modifications."[262] Indeed, the 1974 essay includes modifications and expansions on the early piece as well as Lieberman's response to the critiques of Yitzhak Baer. Thus, the 1974 essay was the culmination of a process of analysis over a thirty-year period, during which Lieberman revised and refined his earlier thinking on the subject.

Lieberman demonstrated an extraordinary ability to reconsider his longstanding views; an example would be his approach to the Leiden manuscript of the Palestinian Talmud.[263] Yaacov Sussmann explains that in his early work, Lieberman did not rely on the Leiden manuscript as a basic tool in determining the correct text.[264] Sussmann quotes a statement by Lieberman in *Hayerushalmi Kifshuto:* "R. Zacharias Frankel was correct in his assessment that the Leiden manuscript is not of great value."[265] In his early work, Lieberman attempted to establish the correct text of difficult sections of the Palestinian Talmud. Sussmann observes that, in so doing, he used several sources, only occasionally referring to the Leiden manuscript. Sussmann notes that when Lieberman did refer to it, the references were from secondary sources. Over the years, Lieberman grew to appreciate the importance of the Leiden manuscript and changed his opinion of its value. Sussmann cites Lieberman's introduction to the publication of a facsimile edition of the Leiden manuscript in which Lieberman conceded, "One cannot establish the text of the Palestinian Talmud without careful study of the Leiden manuscript."[266]

A gathering was convened on June 13–14, 1978, in honor of Lieberman's eightieth birthday. In responding to the laudatory speeches and lectures, Lieberman remarked that a scholar who had reached the age of seventy or eighty should write his own Jubilee volume to correct all the errors in his earlier publications. He would also invite colleagues and students to contribute their corrections.[267] Although a humorous remark, it reflects Lieberman's very real concern about the declining quality of scholarship and, of course, his own fear of errors in the interpretation of the sacred texts. He was therefore careful to provide a body of evidence to support each hypothesis that he advanced. As he was constantly engaged in study and analysis, he could not help but compare new insights with early assumptions and interpretations. This would lead either to additional support of a proposition stated in an earlier work or some adjustment, variation, or revision of the original proposition. Lieberman was conscientious about updating his explanations and diligent about informing his readers of such changes through his ubiquitous *hosafot vitikkunim* (revisions and corrections). Subsequent editions of his books invariably included a section entitled *hosafot vitikkunim* or *hashlamot*[268] or "Additions and Corrections."[269]

Mehkarim b'Torat Eretz Yisrael is the posthumous publication of many of Lieberman's numerous essays, articles, and lectures, written over a period of approximately fifty years.[270] In the final years of Lieberman's life, David

Rosenthal gathered most of Lieberman's essays, with a view to publishing them with additional notes prepared by Lieberman. Rosenthal expected Lieberman to draw on the marginal notes that he had added over the years in his personal copy of each publication. Lieberman, however, did not find the time to devote to this effort, as he concentrated on the *Tosefta Kifshutah* and on his commentary and notes to Ephraim Rosenthal's edition of *Yerushalmi, Nezikin*.

Criticism from Others. While Lieberman may have employed modern scientific techniques in his scholarship, his objective was to fulfill the simple traditional religious commandment of teaching Torah by revealing the true *peshat,* the correct interpretation of the text. If the critiques of others would eventually lead to the true *peshat,* then the critiques were to be welcomed, not resented. In an undated letter to Miklishansky, Lieberman advised him not to critique prominent scholars because "you will thereby attract enemies." Lieberman continued, "Thank God, I have written much, and, necessarily many have written against me." For the most part, Lieberman bore no grudge toward his serious critics; on the contrary, he would respond positively to criticism, even when he doubted its validity, provided it was offered with honesty and sincerity. However, he excluded from his consideration those who offered criticism not as part of a search for the truth, but rather *lekanter* (to reproach and rebuke others). For Lieberman, the study of Torah should comprise a search for the true *peshat,* not a means for self-aggrandizement. In Lieberman's words, "My constant prayer is that the Merciful One should save us from study for the sake of gaining fame."

At the close of Lieberman's lengthy response to J. N. Epstein's posthumously published criticism of his *Talmudah shel Kisrin,* Lieberman warned the reader to approach the work of a critic with a skeptical eye. He called attention to the fact that E. Z. Melamed, editor of the posthumous publication of Epstein's work, expressed doubt that he had correctly reproduced Epstein's critiques. Lieberman stated, "These honest words serve as a warning to the reader that he must examine carefully the sources cited by the critic, especially when they are words written in the heat of polemics."[271] In a footnote, he formulates a principle that may even cast doubt on his own polemics: "It is generally better at all times not to rely completely on the critics (and I also include myself among them) and instead to carefully investigate the words of the author, because sometimes the "judge" sees only what he wishes to see."[272]

Lieberman discusses his response to criticism in correspondence with Ginzberg written in the decade prior to his coming to the U.S.:

> Believe me . . . that I am very happy to be corrected, even by lesser personages, how much more so by those greater than I, and I am so greatly pleased by your work [of correction] that I read [the corrections] repeatedly [May 18, 1932]. . . . As one grows older and learns more from others as well as from oneself, it becomes evident to him that matters which seemed clear and obvious may not be the case, and vice versa [Lieberman then expressed regrets for errors he had made earlier; January 22, 1934]. . . . Your critiques are sweeter to me than the acclaim and accolades of others [January 21, 1938].

Lieberman offered such affirmations of humility and fallibility not only to the eminent Professor Louis Ginzberg, to whom he would later be indebted for his role in Lieberman's appointment at JTS, but to others as well. He assured Avigdor Aptowitzer, "Let his honor believe me, I am not at all ashamed to admit that I have erred."[273]

However, should Lieberman consider the critic to be inept as a scholar, he preferred to ignore the criticism and to pass over the matter in silence, or to vent his frustration by communicating his ire in private correspondence with close friends.[274] We shall let the following excerpt from Lieberman's correspondence with Scholem speak for itself:

> I feel that I must be getting old. The proof of the matter is that when I received the last issue of *Kiryat Sefer*, I did not get angry (as would have been the case in my youth) but rather found myself amused and entertained when reading the words of the "the fair-haired unfortunate youth" and perceiving how one who does not know the difference between his right [hand] and his left

> [hand] presumes to stick his nose into the matter and attempt to teach me the principles of methodology in research.[275]

Prominent critics deemed to be mistaken or unfair had to be confronted publicly, and Lieberman did so on several occasions. He responded to Luitpold Wallach's generally unfavorable review of his *Greek in Jewish Palestine* with a vigorous defense of the book and a caustic critique of the reviewer, commenting, "with how little care the reviewer read the book." Lieberman concluded, "I am duly appreciative of the good intentions of Dr. Wallach, who magnanimously volunteered to help me. But, in all truthfulness, it must be added that the achievement falls so far short of the intention that I should not have taken notice of it had it not been published in so reputable a journal as *The Review of Religion*."[276]

When Isaiah Sonne offered detailed criticism of Lieberman's methodology and conclusions in "The Martyrs of Caesarea," Lieberman responded, and later reacted again to Sonne's subsequent response.[277] Their exchanges were intense but lacking in personal invective.[278] On another occasion, Lieberman tried to assuage Sonne's hurt feelings when the latter failed to receive minutes of the American Academy for Jewish Research meeting, by sending a letter of explanation and apology to Baron regarding the matter, with the intention that the letter be forwarded by Baron to Sonne.[279]

In general, Lieberman's responses to what he considered unfair scholarly criticism are remarkably restrained. When Baron directed a harsh footnote to Lieberman, he did not reply in kind, preferring to gently note an omission on Baron's part.[280] It was in reply to Baron's subsequent letter, which contained a detailed discussion of the issue, that Lieberman commented, "There is nothing more that I appreciate than friendly criticism, because I deem it the only way of establishing the truth by continuous consideration and reconsideration."[281] When Michael Higger[282] claimed that Lieberman was in error in stating that the baraita of Levi is to be found only once in the Palestinian Talmud, Lieberman complained to Finkelstein and Ginzberg[283] that Higger had suggested that he had said something that he did not say. He was concerned that this matter had become the subject of discussion in the "small city of Jerusalem." He felt that, if not handled properly, the American Academy for Jewish Research (publisher of the journal that carried the Higger article) and Jewish scholarship itself would be subject to ridicule and rebuke. However, Lieberman did not want to enter into an angry debate with Higger on the issue, and under no circumstances did he want to embarrass Higger by publicly pointing out his mistakes.[284] Lieberman asked Finkelstein to speak privately with Higger and explain matters to him, with the hope that he would issue a clarification. However, some ten weeks later, on April 7, 1940, Finkelstein replied that he had consulted with Ginzberg and Marx on the matter, and that they were all in agreement that it was best not to pursue the issue at all. The letters to Finkelstein and Ginzberg reflected Lieberman's inner struggle. He was deeply hurt by Higger's attributing an incorrect statement to him and wanted someone to set the record straight, preferably Ginzberg or Higger. At the same time, he said in the letter to Finkelstein that he did not want to see Higger's reputation suffer because, after all, he studied Torah and engaged in scholarship. In his letter to Ginzberg of January 21, 1940, Lieberman showed concern for Higger's material well-being. It must be pointed out, however, that this exchange of correspondence took place while Lieberman was still in Palestine, prior to coming to JTS, and may have also reflected his concern not to offend a scholar associated with that institution.

Lieberman's reaction to Gedalyahu Alon's scathing critical review of his *Greek in Jewish Palestine* illustrates how a personal rivalry can lend harshness to scholarly discourse.[285] Alon and Lieberman were fellow students at the Hebrew University in the early 1930s, and they were appointed at the same time to teach Talmud in the preparatory division, with Lieberman teaching the advanced group. As noted above, after five years, enrollment in Alon's class remained high while that in Lieberman's advanced class dwindled and he was subsequently dismissed. Despite Lieberman's ill fortune at the Hebrew University, his prestige rose rapidly in the decade following his dismissal, and the publication of *Greek in Jewish Palestine* represented a high point in his tenure at JTS. It would be understandable for Lieberman to perceive this negative review as a personal attack, or, as he often described such reviews, *lekanter*, as being for the sake of creating controversy and damaging a reputation rather than an attempt to discern the truth. Lieberman's initial response was anger, and his personal copy of Alon's review contains his own marginal notes in which he condemned

Alon's critiques as "lies and falsehoods" and "only in the critic's imagination." Alon's criticism was especially painful and perplexing to Lieberman because it came from a fellow Slobodka alumnus whom Lieberman recognized as a knowledgeable scholar. Lieberman said that "all of the pages [of the review] are based upon the author's false premise." Furthermore, he complained to Scholem of the unfairness of Alon's critique, describing him as a Don Quixote, one who set up a *golem,* a straw man, who bore no relationship to Lieberman, and then proceeded to tear him apart.[286] However, in the second edition of *Greek in Jewish Palestine,* in "Additions and Corrections," Lieberman writes charitably of Alon, seeking to excuse Alon's errors on the basis of the difficult conditions under which he labored and that Alon's comprehension of the English language was poor.[287] Lieberman theorized that it was for these reasons that Alon imputed to him statements that he never made and theories that he never espoused. In the "Corrections" section, Lieberman included Alon's name along with those of critics whom he admired and took seriously, such as Nock and Gregoire. Furthermore, Lieberman contributed "Six Words from Koheleth Rabbah," to a memorial volume for Gedalyahu Alon.[288]

In his "Hazanut Yannai," Lieberman expressed appreciation to Menaham Zulay for his book *Piyyutai Yannai,* while offering criticisms, including his disappointment that Zulay failed to provide citations for the sources used by Yannai.[289] Lieberman seemed to have underestimated the impact of his comments. Zulay was apparently distressed over Lieberman's criticism, so Lieberman wrote him a long letter. He went to great lengths to tell Zulay how much he appreciated his achievement, reminding him that he had credited Zulay with revealing the poetry of Yannai by piecing together manuscript fragments. Lieberman continued: "Believe me that I value your work far more than you can imagine."[290] Lieberman mentioned that he had promised Rabbi Yehuda Leib Hakohen Maimon a short essay, and added: "When I saw your book among a group of new books, I realized that I must study this book intensively, and accordingly I studied it, spending the entire Sabbath day on it, and I found many wonderful things in it, more than what I mentioned in my essay, and I therefore expanded my essay." Lieberman continued with a detailed discussion of several issues raised by the work of Yannai, the Zulay book, and his own essay. Although we could count only three erasures in Lieberman's letter, he apologized profusely for the "many" erasures, explaining, "This is because I am writing you late at night, when I have much work before me [to complete]." Despite the pressures of his own scholarship, Lieberman devoted time and effort to make Zulay feel better about his essay. The letter concludes on a friendly note, with an invitation to Zulay to visit Lieberman on a Friday night.[291] One suspects, however, that magnanimity on Lieberman's part toward his critics was not always forthcoming. His paternalistic attitude toward *his* texts, that is, the *Talmud Yerushalmi* and Tosefta, apparently resulted in harsh responses to scholars who, in his eyes, misinterpreted these texts, even if they were not critical of him.[292]

Simplicity, Modesty, Kindness, and Generosity

The *musar* emphasis on humility, reticence, and the avoidance of ostentatious attire permeated even non-*musar* yeshiva circles in Lithuania. This is reflected in Lieberman's account of a visit paid by his cousin the Hazon Ish to a small synagogue in Minsk.[293] With his simple style of dress and unassuming manner, the Hazon Ish appeared "like a small-town tailor," and his extreme nearsightedness made him appear uncertain, if not ill equipped, to understand the Talmud volume he had picked up and was holding close to his face. Thus, when the synagogue's Talmud study session was about to begin, the shammash did not hesitate to take the volume from the Hazon Ish's hands, saying: "A simple Jew should read Psalms and not peruse such books. We need the Talmud for our studies." The Hazon Ish nodded in agreement and surrendered the volume. The following day, when he learned the Hazon Ish's identity, the shammash profusely apologized for having insulted him. Lieberman described his cousin's perplexity: Why is the shammash so apologetic? He was perfectly correct in acting as he did. The tome of the Talmud is indeed synagogue property and was to be used by those who were participating in the Talmud study group. The shammash was likewise correct in his observation that it is proper for a Jew to recite Psalms. The Hazon Ish had no problem with what had transpired the previous day, nor did he entertain the possibility that his simple garb was somehow inappropriate to his status as a scholar.

Lieberman's clothing was the simple, unadorned style of Western dress characteristic of the Slobodka yeshiva student. He was not "rabbinical" in any conspicuous way, and his demeanor and behavior were likewise unpretentious. In fact, Haym Soloveitchik, who was well acquainted with Lieberman, observed that if one visited the Jerusalem dry-goods store of Lieberman's brother, Meir, when both men were present, one would not know which of the two was the proprietor of the store and which was the scholarly author of the monumental work *Tosefta Kifshutah*.[294] Lieberman insisted on having his father's name appear in larger print than his own in his publications[295] and left instructions to have a simple tombstone erected over his grave, with no mention of his scholarly achievements, only the words *shalshelet hayuhasin,* signifying his descent from notable ancestors.[296] As Lieberman put it, very much in the *musar* spirit: "Nothing elevates one and makes one greater than does *hitapkut* [self-restraint]."[297]

David Rosenthal recalled the words of praise of his father (Eliezer Shimshon Rosenthal) for Lieberman: "His ego never came before his Torah." According to Dimitrovsky, Lieberman would often respond to effusive praise for his erudition with the statement, "I simply know where to look for things." How convincing were Lieberman's protestations of modesty? Can one be totally modest about one's genius? We noted how, in his early years, Lieberman practiced modesty and self-criticism to such an extent that he was told that excessive modesty in a youth may indicate just the opposite. How can one understand a September 25, 1933, letter to Ginzberg in which Lieberman promised Ginzberg that in exchange for a book, Lieberman would send him "a full line of notations on sources that were unknown" to Ginzberg? Such confidence, even arrogance, on the part of a young man in writing to an older scholar hardly reflects modesty. We may conclude that Lieberman was secure enough to admit his errors because of his confidence in his ability to correct them.

Lieberman was clearly aware of his competence—indeed, his greatness—at an early age. How could he not be, with the preferential treatment that he was receiving from his revered Lithuanian mentors? However, as Rabbi Moses Feinstein said, "An *anav* [modest person] is not one who does not know his own greatness. It is one who expects nothing from others."[298] Lieberman expected a great deal, but not from others; only from himself. The key to Lieberman's attitude toward his gifts may be found in his response to Yaakov Kenaani, whom Lieberman had complimented for his hard work in preparing the volumes that Kenaani had sent him. When Kenaani expressed disappointment that Lieberman praised him only for his hard work, Lieberman responded: "When I wrote that there is much hard work and toil in your books, I did not mean to detract from your achievement, but rather to give credence to it. One does not need to take credit for something that is given to him from Heaven. However, hard work and toil are solely in the control of the individual, and for that he deserves praise."[299] Although Lieberman may have drawn this distinction to ease the author's disappointment, it reflects his view that the intellect is a divine gift for which a human being deserves no praise or acclaim, and surely is not a justification for arrogance. Recognition, however, is deserved if one makes use of God's gift with diligence, discipline, and morality.

Lieberman's penchant for self-criticism was probably derived from his drive for perfection and his search for the truth, rather than from a sense of modesty. True, Lieberman consistently manifested modesty in deference to the scholars of earlier generations, but this was undoubtedly due in part to his personal religious sensitivities vis-à-vis the veneration for scholars of the past.

In his introduction to *Tosefta Kifshutah, Zera'im,* Lieberman acknowledges his indebtedness to the early commentators: "the first pioneers . . . upon whose shoulders we stand and from whose wine we drink."[300] Lieberman attributed errors on their part to the conditions of their time and to the lack of manuscripts that are available today. In particular, Lieberman calls our attention to the difficult working conditions of Moses Samuel Zuckermandel, the first scholar to publish a scientific edition of the Tosefta.[301] Yet in the interest of truth, Lieberman points out the limitations that constrained the scholarship of previous generations.

- They possessed little knowledge of the Greco-Roman world.
- They failed to understand or appreciate the uniqueness of the *Talmud Yerushalmi*'s style and language.
- They failed to appreciate how the traditions of the Jews in Palestine differed from those of Babylon.
- They lacked manuscripts of the *Talmud Yerushalmi.*

- They did not pay sufficient attention to gaonic writings in order to determine accurate texts of the *Talmud Yerushalmi*.[302]

Lieberman informs us of how shockingly full of errors is our text of the *Talmud Yerushalmi,* and how great the need is for one to painstakingly and properly elucidate the text—and he clearly had every confidence in himself and his abilities to be the one to do so.[303]

His tough, acerbic exterior notwithstanding, Lieberman possessed an inner softness and deep compassion, although, in characteristic *musar* style, he seemed at times reluctant to show it in public. As Finkelstein expressed it, Lieberman "was also a warm human being, a trait never more evident than in the company of his beloved wife, Judith."[304] Lieberman's consideration for Judith, who was most supportive of her husband's arduous schedule, rarely seeing him except on the Sabbath, is reflected in many of his letters. He asked Simha Assaf not to mention to anyone that a box of his own books was lost because he did not want Judith to be upset about the loss.[305] He asked Scholem not to mention anything to her about Alon's searing critique of his *Greek in Jewish Palestine* because it would aggravate her.[306] In a letter of March 17, 1977, he cautioned Scholem not to mention to Judith that while visiting Jerusalem, Lieberman accidentally swallowed a gold tooth. Apparently, Lieberman was also reluctant to have Judith know that he gave financial support on several occasions to an author who was a member of the family of his first wife, Rachel.[307] Mandelbaum described Lieberman's living quarters in Israel:

> [Lieberman] acquired two apartments [in Jerusalem] adjacent to each other. One was beautifully furnished; the other was practically empty, with only a long table, chair, and some bookshelves. It was in the latter that he studied. [Lieberman explained]: "If I'm at home, with all the calls I receive in Jerusalem, I'll never get anything done, and I don't want my wife to have to lie. So when she says, 'He's not at home,' I'm not: I'm next door."[308]

During Judith's illness, Lieberman spent many hours at the hospital at her bedside, and she asked, "Why are you here? Shouldn't you be studying?"

Lieberman's responded, "Now I see that you are a granddaughter of the Netziv!"[309] Upon Judith's death, Lieberman was inconsolable; his uncontrollable weeping made it difficult for him to eulogize her at the funeral.

"All of us could see what influence he had on children, whom he loved so dearly," wrote Finkelstein.[310] Indeed, Lieberman devoted considerable attention and showed deep concern for children and young people, especially children of friends and fellow faculty members. He arranged for Dudi, the ten-year-old grandson of Simha Assaf, to attend Camp Ramah, a JTS summer camp. Lieberman described to Assaf the wonderful impact of Camp Ramah on Dudi, and suggested that he write a letter of thanks to R. Bernard Segal for his role in facilitating Dudi's enrollment in the camp and his special kindness to Dudi.[311] Later, Lieberman wrote to Assaf, "About Dudi, he is a wise and beloved child. I have grown to love him very much. He often speaks with the maturity of an adult and surprises me with his observations."[312] Lieberman frequently conducted informal study sessions with children, paying them about a dollar for each chapter of Mishnah studied and memorized. Jonathan Sarna relates that when he was eight years old, Lieberman examined him and his older brother, usually on Sundays, with the examination and discussion always carried on entirely in Hebrew.[313]

Lieberman developed a number of avuncular relationships with children in Israel. After the untimely death of Yaakov Herzog (son of Chief Rabbi Isaac Herzog and a distinguished diplomat and scholar who served for many years as Israel's ambassador to Canada), on March 10, 1972, Lieberman bestowed much time and attention upon young Yitzhak Herzog, which included frequent gifts from the U.S.[314] Lieberman developed a particularly close relationship with Itamar and Yakov Aviad, the children of Isaiah and Sonja (Wolfsberg) Aviad, entertaining them regularly in his home on Sabbath afternoons, and occasionally bringing them two pears—at that time, a rare and most appreciated gift. In 1940, on the morning of the Liebermans' departure from Jerusalem to New York, at 5:45 A.M., the Aviad boys, ages twelve and fifteen, appeared on their doorstep, presenting flowers and tearfully bidding farewell to their "uncle" and "aunt." Judith Lieberman recalled the moment vividly and fondly in a letter to their mother written almost a quarter century later.[315] Needless to say, Lieberman was affectionately known as *der dod* (the uncle) to his own eight grandnephews and grandnieces, the grandchildren of his brother, Meir.[316]

Sylvia Heschel describes Lieberman's deep affection for her daughter, Susannah, who was a welcome summertime guest in Lieberman's Jerusalem home.[317] Susannah recalls warm childhood memories of the Liebermans, who lived in the same apartment building (425 Riverside Drive), with Mrs. Lieberman baking Susannah's favorite cake as a breakfast treat. When Susannah was five years old and Lieberman heard that her parents were taking her to the circus in Manhattan, he asked if he could join them, and spent the afternoon with Susannah, enjoying the spectacle. Lieberman's own sense of playfulness probably found natural expression in his encounter with children. "He may have been a cold analyst, but he was a warm person . . . and he treated me like a son," states Dimitrovsky, recalling a leisure afternoon Lieberman spent at the Bronx Zoo with him and his fiancée.

We referred earlier to a letter from Lieberman to Finkelstein in which Lieberman attempted to make life easier for Finkelstein's children during the hot summer by appealing to their father to relax his strict stand vis-à-vis their swimming during the "Nine Days."

> Mrs. Lieberman contends that the prohibition of bathing during the "Nine Days" (before the fast of *Tishah Be-av*) does not apply to the country since it is not pleasure-bathing but natural escape from the heat. She maintains therefore that there is no good reason for Muni to postpone the visit till after *Tishah Be-av* and meanwhile be rosted [*sic*] in the heat of New York.[318]

Although Lieberman frequently played the role of an austere, demanding, and demeaning professor in the classroom, he cared deeply for his students. His style of teaching, which could be condescending at times, was not dissimilar to that of other scholars such as Rabbi J. B. Soloveitchik, who reportedly treated his students in a similar fashion.

Shortly after arriving in the U.S. and beginning his teaching duties at JTS, Lieberman wrote to Gershom Scholem (March 2, 1941) of his confidence in understanding the psychology of his American students, and that a proper educational approach would result in "their being brought closer to Torah and Judaism." A few months later, on August 26, 1941, Judith described to the Scholems how exceedingly touched Lieberman was by the affection shown him by his students, emphasizing that this meant more to him than all the formal, more superficial, manifestations of appreciation bestowed upon him—honorary degrees, salary raises, and so on. Lieberman took his teaching responsibilities seriously and, as discussed above, took great pride in the achievements of his students. He made a special effort to capture the interest of his class, stating that "to teach Torah, you must be an actor," and he accordingly spiced his classroom lectures with humor, anecdotes, and drama.[319]

Several of Lieberman's students achieved significant success as scholars and published essays and books dealing with rabbinic literature and Jewish law. Lieberman once told Seymour Siegel that he would never put into writing a critique of his students' work, a principle he seems to have honored with only a few notable exceptions[320]—although at times he seems to have adhered to the "letter of the law," if not the "spirit of the law." In expressing to his students his dislike for source criticism ("you don't have to operate on the Talmud"), in class lectures he would never mention David Weiss Halivni by name, as a proponent of that approach, and even his scathing critique of Jacob Neusner's translation of several tractates of the Palestinian Talmud does not refer to Neusner by name.[321]

Lieberman once permitted a senior student who had failed a final exam to retake the exam in order to graduate with his class because Lieberman had received a letter from the failing student's mother: "I am a widow and getting on in years. It is for this *naches* that I live. All my life I have looked forward to this day, and who knows whether I will be here next year."[322]

Lieberman's graciousness toward his colleagues, both senior and junior, is much in evidence. When he believed that a scholar had made a meaningful contribution and had approached the material with honesty and integrity, he was pleased to respond with approbation. When Louis Ginzberg requested that the youthful Lieberman write a *bikorate* (critique) of his *Legends of the Jews,* Lieberman replied, in a letter of August 9, 1939, that a work of that magnitude deserved a *ma'amar* (essay) in its honor, not a critique.

Lieberman's extensive correspondence with Jacob David Abramsky displays remarkable personal concern and affection for the young scholar. Not only was Lieberman able to grant Abramsky financial assistance; he gave him sage advice and empathetic commiseration as a caring mentor, if not surrogate parent. Thus, he cautioned him not to feel hatred for those "unworthy of it," for they deserve pity, not hatred, and not to be crushed as a result of humiliation, for it is better to be embarrassed than to embarrass others. If a person who has embarrassed you has no conscience and is undisturbed by his behavior, why should you feel such hurt? This is an individual who does not deserve to be taken seriously! Lieberman likewise cautioned Abramsky concerning the dangers of succumbing to depression and bitterness, urging him to confront life's bitter challenges and rise above them. Not surprisingly, Lieberman observed that the study of Torah was the best antidote for feelings of despair over the sad state of affairs in the world. Lieberman advised Abramsky not to be critical of a certain individual for his incessant pursuit of "honor." "I know this individual very well," said Lieberman. "His need for honor is understandable because he has had an exceedingly difficult life. How can you find fault with him for pursuing honor—who among us despises honor? . . .

After all, the pursuit of honor may not be all that terrible, because in the process, you end up honoring the very people who honor you as you value the honor they pay you!" On several occasions, Lieberman functioned as a *musar* pedagogue, prefacing his admonitions with the classical stylistic formulation, "I may not be worthy of chastising you, but. . . ."[323]

Very much in the *musar* spirit, Lieberman rebuked an acquaintance for declining an invitation (presumably to attend a special function and accept an honor) tendered by the president of Israel, telling him that he had thereby committed a sin. Lieberman explained: "If a person wants to honor you, you are not permitted to suspect him of evil motives." It appears that Lieberman viewed his correspondent as being overly concerned with what others would think of him, and being easily slighted if others failed to pay him the proper respect and honor. Lieberman stated:

> Our sages have taught us that a person's happiness does not depend on others but on himself alone. . . . A wise man is not one to whom everybody comes to learn; a wealthy person is not one

> with money whom people honor because of his wealth; a strong man is not one whom everybody fears because of his strength and power; an honorable person is not one whom everybody honors. Every single thing that depends upon the opinions or response of others cannot be true or genuine, but is rather half a fraud (forgery). All the good qualities and attributes that a person desires are within his capacity to attain, and are not at all dependent on the opinions and assessments of others, as the first mishnah in *Pirkei Avot,* chapter 4 teaches.[324]

Lieberman implored his correspondent to respect every person, while at the same time not to expect perfection in people. He justified doubts and inner conflicts when he asserted that the human being who appears to have no inner conflicts is not a living being, but a robot.

Lieberman seems to have been an active facilitator for others. As early as 1938, he wrote to Finkelstein, giving an unqualified recommendation to Moshe Davis, presumably for admission to the JTS rabbinical school, praising him as a diligent student at the Harry Fischel Institute.[325] He often wrote letters of recommendation for his students to pursue graduate studies and for colleagues to receive university appointments[326] and was approached with requests from Mordecai Margulies and Aaron Halevi Zimmerman, among others, to assist in securing teaching positions.[327]

Lieberman was actively involved in assisting refugees from Europe to immigrate to the U.S. and receive financial support. Abraham Schreiber, chief rabbi of Greece, asked Lieberman in a letter of March 4, 1948, to submit a statement from JTS attesting to his scientific and scholarly research so that he might obtain a visa to come to the United States. Long before David Weiss Halivni attended JTS, Lieberman signed the requisite legal papers guaranteeing that Halivni would not become a public charge, thereby enabling him to remain in New York and to pursue his studies at an institution of his choosing.[328]

In his capacity as president of the American Academy for Jewish Research, Lieberman was able to assist the Roman law expert Adolph Berger (a refugee from Italy) by choosing him to translate Jean Juster's *Les Juifs dans l'empire romain,* with a portion of the funds allocated by the Conference on Jewish Material Claims against Germany.[329] Lieberman assisted other refugees from Europe—for example, Rabbi Osias Babad, Adolph Kober, and Menasha Unger—to obtain stipends for their academic projects.[330]

Lieberman allocated funds from the American Academy for Jewish Research to create projects for several scholars and assist them in obtaining formal financial aid. He helped Yaakov Polock procure a grant from the National Institute for the Humanities for the publication of a manuscript on the Palestinian Talmud by the Poltaver Illui.[331] In 1964, he arranged for J. D. Abramsky to receive a grant-in-aid for the publication of his *Jews in Russia* and provided him with financial assistance.[332] In 1963, he arranged JTS support for the continuation of Tuvia Preschel's research fellowship with the AAJR. Lieberman raised funds for Chaim Grade,[333] Hayim Hazzaz,[334] Mordecai Margulies,[335] and the aforementioned Abraham Schreiber.[336] Lieberman urged Leo Jung of the Jewish Center to assist Rabbi Z. H. Kanel in the publication of his *Otsar Hageonim,*[337] and sought financial aid for Rabbi Zvi Kaplan's publication of the Netziv's commentary to the *Sifrei.*[338] Indeed, Lieberman's astute management of the finances of the American Academy for Jewish Research facilitated the funding of many worthy scholarly projects.[339]

Lieberman also undertook to raise funds for the establishment of a scholarship in memory of the son of Professor E. E. Urbach, who died in the defense of the State of Israel.[340] For these, and many other projects, Lieberman turned to prominent pulpit rabbis who had been his students and Rabbinical Assembly members who were close friends[341] as well as to charitable foundations.[342] Lieberman could be charmingly persuasive in fund-raising endeavors. He once solicited Anshel Rothschild for a generous donation, explaining that the term "GeMaRA" is an abbreviation for "*G*ett *M*ehr, *R*eb *A*nshel" (Give more, Reb Anshel).[343] An interesting paradox characterizes Lieberman's personal spending habits. Largesse and frugality coexisted comfortably in his personality. Bernard Mandelbaum writes of Lieberman:

> When I once paid a toll, instead of taking a slightly extended bypass, it became the occasion for this insight into life: "You see, that's why you'll never be a rich man. People with money watch their pennies. *Kabtzanim* [poor people] like you are big shots

with a dollar!" His generosity in big things (support of scholars and members of his and his wife's family) also prevailed in little things. I was the official purchaser of the toys for his nieces and nephews in Israel: "Something nice!" However, he was most discriminating and frugal when shopping in the general store. "Watch for the sales." And he hated to be "taken" by anyone.[344]

There is, of course, a broader principle here: personal thriftiness toward self (as may be characteristic of one whose youth was spent in poverty), great generosity toward others, and, as befits one trained in *musar* ideology, generosity accompanied by a cloak of anonymity. Lieberman was exceedingly generous to his family, purchasing apartments in Israel for relatives and supporting his nephew Meir Bar-Ilan's schooling.[345]

He also manifested great generosity to institutions. Upon being informed that he was awarded the Bialik Prize, Lieberman thanked the committee, and asked that the money be donated to the Hebrew University.[346] He provided scholarships for students of the Shulamith School for Girls, where his wife served as dean[347] and for students of the Manhattan Hebrew High School.[348] Nor did he overlook JTS, the school that brought him from Palestine in 1940 and provided him with the atmosphere and facilities that enabled him to do what he loved most—to study, to write, and to teach Torah. In 1971, he donated several valuable manuscripts to the Seminary library with a value in excess of $1,500,[349] and eventually his personal library, with its many rare books and manuscripts (known as the Stroock/Lieberman Collection), to JTS. It is now located in the library of the Schocken Institute in Jerusalem. On January 3, 1977, Lieberman transferred $100,000 of U.S. Treasury Bonds to JTS, executing a trust agreement reserving an income interest for life.

Lieberman had discretionary authority to distribute funds on behalf of several charitable organizations. Bernard Heller, a wealthy Reform rabbi who frequently attended services in the JTS synagogue and who had great respect and admiration for Lieberman, formed the Baruch Ben Chaim Foundation, on September 16, 1965, with Lieberman as one of three trustees. This foundation has provided considerable funds to the Seminary, including the Judith and Saul Lieberman Fellowships in Talmud.[350]

Support for Scholars. Lieberman frequently sent money to needy scholars[351] and supplied them with vital goods as well, once arranging for a Philco refrigerator to be delivered to an Israeli rabbi.[352] Simha Assaf, who was ill upon his arrival in New York, later wrote Lieberman thanking him for personally meeting him at the airport, providing medical help, and taking care of his other needs.

Daniel Sperber recounts that in the 1970s, he traveled to New York from Israel to seek medical attention for his sister, who had a brain tumor. Sperber encountered Lieberman at religious services at JTS, and when the latter expressed concern over Sperber's troubled appearance, Sperber explained his sister's medical emergency, adding that his family was experiencing financial difficulty because of the expenses. Lieberman disappeared for a moment, promptly returning with a personal check for a thousand dollars, which he presented to Sperber while hurriedly ushering him out so as not to hear his words of gratitude. Sperber later commented: "[Lieberman's] deeds of charity were many but little known, as I afterward learned from others."[353]

Lieberman performed many kindnesses under conditions of anonymity. When Yosef Hayim Yerushalmi, a senior student in the JTS rabbinical school, was sitting in Lieberman's office late at night, having just completed his oral comprehensive examination in Talmud, Lieberman asked him about his plans following ordination. Yerushalmi said that he had hoped to enroll in Columbia University to study with Salo Baron, but that it was too late to apply for a fellowship. Lieberman responded by volunteering that the AAJR would surely provide a fellowship to enable him to pursue his studies in Jewish history, stipulating only that Yerushalmi continue to attend his Talmud class at JTS, to which Yerushalmi readily agreed. Yerushalmi became a prominent scholar, eventually succeeding Salo Baron as head of the Jewish history department at Columbia University. Twenty years after the fateful meeting in Lieberman's office, Yerushalmi learned the true story—that the AAJR did not provide the fellowship that he believed had been extended to him, and that it was Lieberman who provided the "fellowship" funds personally![354] Yerushalmi added that Lieberman performed numerous similar unpublicized acts of *tzedakah,* and it has been corroborated that Lieberman provided scholarships enabling many JTS students to pursue their studies.[355]

On October 31, 1973, Lieberman wrote to Judah Nadich, president of the Rabbinical Assembly: "I appeal through you to all the members of our congregations: Please, double and triple your efforts on behalf of the State of Israel. Our brethren in Israel are bleeding. For us as well. Be part of them!" With the letter, Lieberman enclosed a personal check for $50,000 to the Israel Emergency Fund.

Lieberman's generosity encompassed Orthodox institutions. He did not allow a Litvak's negative orientation toward the hasidic movement to affect his admiration for the achievements of Lubavitch or to withhold financial support from Chabad activities.[356] Lieberman often recalled that in the late 1920s, Lubavitch achieved a great deal while fostering Jewish education in Eastern Europe,[357] and it is possible that Lieberman was personally acquainted with R. Menahem Mendel Schneerson, the Lubavitcher rebbe, as they both studied at the Sorbonne in the 1920s.[358] Indeed, Lieberman was generous in supporting organizations and institutions that condemned and ostracized him because of his association with JTS. He contributed to the American Committee for Taharas Hamishpacha in Israel for the construction of *mikvaot* in "the poor kibbutzim of Eretz Yisroel."[359] He saw to it that JTS was listed as an accredited institution accepting credits from the Beth Medrash Govoha of Lakewood, New Jersey (pursuant to the request of the Immigration and Naturalization Service); the dean of that institution, Rabbi Aaron Kotler, was an older colleague of Lieberman's from Slobodka.[360]

The anonymity surrounding Lieberman's donations was particularly in evidence when the beneficiaries were Orthodox individuals and Orthodox institutions that might have been embarrassed or even declined to accept money, had they known the identity of the donor—one associated with JTS. Lieberman often used Rabbi Naftali Riff (a cousin of Judith's) and Riff's son-in-law, Rabbi Emanuel Gettinger, as conduits for his donations to Orthodox causes and institutions.[361]

The following episodes provide insights into Lieberman's state of mind while giving. Florence Bar-Ilan, Lieberman's sister-in-law, recalls Lieberman being honored with an aliyah at a synagogue in Holon. He pledged a sum of money and donated well in excess of the amount pledged, explaining that one is obligated to fulfill the admonition to "say little and do much."[362] In allocating funds to be distributed on Purim, in fulfillment of the religious obligation of *matanot l'evyonim* (gifts to the needy), Lieberman stipulated that they must be given to poor people living in Brooklyn; he claimed that he was unaware of any truly poor people on Manhattan's Upper West Side![363] Lieberman made it a practice to send flowers to Shirley Kushner, the JTS switchboard operator, every year on the anniversary of the death of her husband, who died on D-Day.[364] In a letter dated August 8, 1971, Judith Lieberman described to Jessica Feingold an episode in which two representatives of the *neturei karta* visited Lieberman in his Jerusalem home, with the elder of the two introducing himself as the minister of foreign affairs of that organization, and requesting a donation. Judith recorded, "His excellency succeeded in his mission. A substantial sum was given him to hasten the marriage of a poor girl—a very big mitzvah."

Impressive as was Lieberman's generosity with his funds, far more impressive was his generosity with his time, for his moments were far more precious to him than his dollars. The extraordinary scope and ambitious scale of his scholarly work necessitated his devoting as many hours as possible to his studies and writing, for he was running a race with the angel of death to complete as much of his *Tosefta Kifshutah* as possible. It is therefore important to note how generous he was in sharing his time and expertise with others. It was the common experience of most JTS students that, busy as he may have been, Lieberman always made time to answer his students' queries. No question remained unanswered, and even students who appeared at his office door unannounced found him generously responding to their queries.[365]

Eli Ginzberg thanked Lieberman for being "always ready to help" in the preparation of Louis Ginzberg's *An Unknown Sect* for publication and expressed his gratitude to Lieberman for being so generous with his time in assisting him in writing his father's biography, *Keeper of the Law*.[366] Apparently, Lieberman spent many hours explaining to him the nature of the Lithuanian Jewish world in which his father grew up. "Without Lieberman's help," wrote Eli Ginzberg, "I would never have been able to bring that book to completion . . . [and] I doubt that the *Unbekente* would have ever seen the light of day but for Lieberman."[367]

Lieberman spent "three to four days, eight to ten hours each day, at the beginning and the end of the summer for some ten years," guiding and assisting Bernard Mandelbaum in preparing his edition of the *Pesikta deRav*

Kahana for publication.[368] Not long before his death, Lieberman devoted several hours a day, twice a week, to assisting Yosef Ciechanover in the preparation of a comprehensive study of the Jewish, Christian, and Islamic treatment of the issue of suicide.[369]

Numerous scholars, including Margulies, Goitein,[370] Baron,[371] Haym Soloveitchik,[372] and Twersky,[373] express their indebtedness to Lieberman for his time and suggestions. A perusal of the bibliography of Lieberman's writings discloses his contribution of annotations, observations, and critiques to more than forty scholarly books and texts published by colleagues and students.

The genesis of many of Lieberman's literary "observations," appended to the works of other scholars, stemmed from Lieberman's careful review of their publications. One cannot exaggerate the number of books and essays sent to Lieberman by authors who hoped to receive encouragement, endorsement, and approval. Lieberman somehow found the time to examine these and respond to the work of such scholars, with varying degrees of enthusiasm, always trying to supply accolades and/or constructive criticism.

When a book had considerable merit, Lieberman would carefully read it and send the author detailed comments. Thus, when Hanoch Yalon sent him his *Mavo Linikud Hamishnah* (Introduction to the Vocalization of the Mishnah), a collection of essays on that topic, Lieberman responded by writing the author a lengthy letter including several scholarly "comments."[374] He explained that he couldn't wait to give the text a close reading, and took it with him to Martha's Vineyard. He offered Yalon the highest praise: "I never imagined that *nikud* [vocalization] is in reality a kind of a commentator or interpreter of the text. . . . It is not my intention to simply praise you, but to express my appreciation to you, because it is a long time since I have learned so much from one book." Lieberman added: "I wish to comment on a few minor points which occurred to me when I read your precious book." Lieberman's comments consist of about three pages of notes that he claimed indicated how carefully he had delved into the author's words and that his words of praise were not collected "out of thin air" merely to fulfill an obligation. Yalon responded with a request that he be granted permission to reproduce Lieberman's comments as a unit in an essay, with the assurance that he would make absolutely no changes to his comments. Lieberman responded, with the suggestion that his comments be integrated with Yalon's text so as to make it easier for the reader.[375] In a humorous vein, Lieberman said (as cited earlier), "Are my notes poetry set to meter or the words of an oracle?"[376] He thanked Yalon in advance for any improvements that Yalon would make in Lieberman's literary style. Lieberman explained, "My letters are, for the most part, written at night, or, more accurately, early in the morning, in an informal style and not intended for publication—it's obvious that it's acceptable to improve the style." In fact, the Lieberman notes were published as a unit, with very insignificant changes.[377] Thus, a few pages of a letter written late at night became a series of important comments constituting a formal essay. No doubt many of the famous Lieberman "comments" that were added to a text or to its subsequent editions emerged initially as casual comments in a letter of response to the author who sent him the manuscript or the text for his comment.

It is no secret that Lieberman frequently put the academic priorities of others above his own best interests. His correspondence with Scholem of January 10, 1960, discloses Lieberman's urging Finkelstein not to translate into English his own essay slated for the appendix of Scholem's book, since that would result in delaying the publication of the book until "the days of the Messiah." "Better to publish Scholem's work promptly and delay the publication of my own piece," was his declaration to Finkelstein.[378] When Lieberman sent Scholem the text of his appendix on February 1, 1959, he told Scholem to add or delete from the text as Scholem wished, because he was no longer immersed in that particular material. Probably the most striking example of Lieberman's sacrificing his time for study and publication to assist colleagues in their own research relates to Professor Eliezer Shimshon Rosenthal of the Talmud department of the Hebrew University, who also taught at the Seminary for several years and was the first director of the Seminary's Schocken Institute for Research in Jerusalem. According to Mandelbaum,

> Professor Lieberman probably could have completed his *Tosefta Kifshutah*. . . . [He] was diverted from his course because of his admiration of and devotion to Professor Shimshon Rosenthal *z'l*. . . . For almost a year, Professor Lieberman worked intensively on an important study, launched by Professor Rosenthal, of an aspect

> of the Jerusalem Talmud, but he was taken to the *olam ha'emet* long before it was ready for publication.[379]

Rosenthal had identified a manuscript as tractate *Nezikin* of the Palestinian Talmud (the Escorial Manuscript) and was involved in preparing a critical edition of the manuscript upon his death in 1977.[380] In the words of Rosenthal's sons Avraham and David, Lieberman "agreed to take upon himself the task of completing the edition. He added an introduction to the manuscript, in which he describes its importance, and wrote a detailed commentary, elucidating the passages where the text of the manuscript differs from that of the printed editions as well as clarifying obscure passages in the entire tractate."

Yitzhak Raphael claims that Lieberman neglected his own work for most of his last two years to work on the Rosenthal manuscripts. When Raphael pointed out to Lieberman that these labors were at the expense of his own research on the Tosefta, Lieberman replied that he felt a "moral obligation" toward his departed friend and colleague.[381] Indeed, Lieberman had the highest regard and admiration for his good friend. He wrote to Scholem concerning Rosenthal on the eve of his return to the Hebrew University (October 6, 1962) following his teaching term at JTS: "This year, you are privileged to have Dr. Rosenthal, who is an erudite talmudist and a great technical scholar as well as an exceptional human being. I am certain that you will be pleased to have him [at the Hebrew University]." Lieberman viewed Rosenthal's achievement as a milestone in the study of the Palestinian Talmud. In his address "A Talmud Written by the People in Their Own Land," Lieberman listed the publication of the Escorial manuscript of the Palestinian Talmud *Nezikin* as one of the "[t]hree important events [that] have taken place in the last two years with regard to the Palestinian Talmud. First, a very important manuscript was discovered by the late Professor Rosental [*sic*] of blessed memory of the Hebrew University, a manuscript of a part of the Palestinian Talmud that will greatly enhance our knowledge and understanding of that Talmud in general. Second, a concordance of that [Palestinian] Talmud is now being published in Jerusalem by the Israel Academy of Sciences and the Jewish Theological Seminary of America, an undertaking made possible by the generosity of Mr. Howard Holzman of

New York. Third, an international assembly of Orthodox rabbis has suggested that the Palestinian Talmud should be studied daily by all Jews who study the Babylonian Talmud."[382]

Lieberman made a special point of accepting invitations to the life-cycle events of his colleagues and students—weddings, circumcisions, and so on, even though the travel time involved may have been lengthy. He was particularly solicitous of the needs of widows, empathetic of their loneliness, noting that upon her husband's death, the wife often finds herself neglected, if not forgotten, by those in her social circle. He would frequently visit Alexander Marx's widow and Penina Herzog after her husband's death.[383] On his summer trips to Israel, he often visited Sonja (Wolfsberg) Aviad and Leah, the widow of Moshe Hayyim Shapira, who happened to be a friend of Lieberman's first wife, Rachel.[384]

An interesting paradox presents itself with respect to Lieberman's socialization patterns. The conventional portrait of him as an indefatigable workaholic, relentlessly driven by his studies to spend most of his daily hours in isolation with texts and manuscripts for his constant companions is undoubtedly accurate. Would this explain why Lieberman had little time for socializing with many of his JTS colleagues? Eli Ginzberg said that Lieberman had very few close friends, and that his father, Louis Ginzberg, bemoaned the fact that Lieberman spent very little time with him upon coming to JTS.

There is no evidence that in his early days at JTS, Lieberman spent time with any other talmudists and academics on the JTS faculty, with the possible exception of Shalom Spiegel, a close friend of Scholem with whom Lieberman established a social bond upon arriving at the Seminary. Lieberman found Spiegel and his wife endearing people, commenting that they were devoted friends to Scholem, and Judith Lieberman wrote of the wonderful reception the Spiegels made for them. But Lieberman complained of the many receptions, official and unofficial, tendered in honor of Judith and him upon their arrival, which left them fatigued. Lieberman understood such socializing to be an American requirement, and, much as he did not want to surrender to it, he resigned himself to the fact that one simply could not escape social obligations but must set aside at least one evening a week for socializing.[385] However, Judith's subsequent letters to the Scholems contain scant references to any such regular social gatherings. Apparently, Lieberman succeeded in avoiding social events for the most part.

Lieberman's relationship with Heschel has been the subject of much speculation and analysis.[386] Lieberman was instrumental in bringing Heschel to JTS.[387] In late 1962, Heschel wrote a warm letter to Lieberman, expressing great appreciation for his comments, presumably on a book recently written by Heschel. (It is well known that Lieberman prepared comments for an author only when he truly valued the work and believed the author to be a competent scholar.)[388] In response, Heschel said that Lieberman already knew how much he admired the strength of his "Torah" and the splendor of his wisdom. He thanked Lieberman from the bottom of his heart for every single comment, adding that even where he may have differed with Lieberman's view, he did so with the greatest respect.[389] What volume was the object of Lieberman's comments? Probably Heschel's *Torah min Hashamayim* (*Theology of Ancient Judaism*), volume 1, published in 1962, a book that marshals considerable rabbinic sources and would therefore have been of interest to Lieberman. Moshe Greenberg, a student of Lieberman, is convinced that Heschel, in effect, addressed the entire lengthy introduction to *Torah min Hashamayim* to Lieberman for two purposes: to serve as a defense of the aggadah (the nonlegal part of the rabbinic literature) in response to Lieberman's reputed disdain for theology; and to demonstrate that he was not a lightweight in rabbinic scholarship.[390] Significantly, Lieberman, in a letter to Scholem, lavishly praised one of Heschel's recent works. Given the date of the letter, we may assume that the book was *Torah min Hashamayim*. Lieberman read it in the summer while in the country and described it as "unique unto itself. . . . I know of no comparable work. . . . When I returned to New York I wanted to purchase Heschel's book for you so that you too would enjoy it, but the author assured me that he would himself send you a copy."[391]

More than a decade later, Lieberman sent Heschel's book on the Kotzker (R. Menahem Mendel of Kotzk) to Scholem, assuring him that he would find it appealing.[392] Lieberman retained a basic respect for Heschel and his achievements as a scholar, particularly when his work was not exclusively based on hasidic sources, and when he drew on rabbinic sources and espoused institutions and rituals that were central to normative Judaism.

Sylvia Heschel recalls that some time after her husband's death, she saw Lieberman at the Seminary, and he remarked that *The Sabbath* was Heschel's best book.[393]

Notwithstanding Lieberman's praise for Heschel, the relationship between the two scholars seems to have been distant, owing, no doubt, to basic differences in background, temperament, and scholarly interests. Heschel was a passionate Hasid while Lieberman was the stereotypical Litvak—a Mitnagged, an opponent of Hasidism. For Lieberman, Talmud study, not philosophical speculation, was the essence of Judaism and should constitute the core curriculum of the rabbinical school.

Some have theorized that Lieberman's conservative political views were at variance with Heschel's liberalism, and Lieberman was uncomfortable with Heschel's political assertiveness as well as with his vocal opposition to certain policies of the United States government. It may not be difficult to understand the perspective from which Lieberman assessed Heschel's political activities, for Lieberman had a strong patriotic commitment to the U.S. and its government. Less than two years after arriving in the United States, Lieberman purchased a $1,000 U.S. Savings Bond out of "a sense of duty toward this beloved country."[394] In a letter to Lieberman, Maxwell Abbell, a prominent Republican Party activist, stated, "I am exceedingly happy to find that your high regard for the president [Dwight Eisenhower] coincides with mine." However, fully realizing Lieberman's reluctance to make public statements about political matters, Abbell concluded, "I respect your desire to refrain from any publicity for your views."[395]

One should not underestimate Lieberman's strong commitment to good citizenship and American values. As one who experienced post–World War I anarchy and tyranny under Bolshevik rule, as well as the oppressive British Mandatory rule in prewar Palestine, Lieberman had great appreciation for American democracy. To expedite the grant of citizenship, he wrote to the Immigration and Naturalization Service on November 5, 1952: "I have been in this country more than twelve years, enjoying almost all the privileges of a citizen, without being able to discharge the duties of a citizen." He was conscientious about his civic duties and apparently devoted time to serious reading about the United States. In a letter to Jessica Feingold, Finkelstein's executive assistant, Judith thanked her for sending Lieberman reading material about the history and institutions of the United States, adding, "I found my husband engrossed in *Look at America*."[396] When Governor Theodor McKeldin of Maryland, a prominent Republican, gave him *Washington Bowed,* Lieberman responded in a letter of May 3, 1960, saying that he read the book "last Saturday, and I was simply charmed by it." Lieberman went on to discuss Washington's great achievement at Valley Forge, impressed that, after having won the battle for independence, Washington had no intention of ruling the country. Lieberman continued his carefully considered response: "At the moment of Washington's resignation of his commission, the American people realized how great was the man whom Providence had chosen to be the deliverer of our country."

It is thus conceivable that tensions between Lieberman and Heschel arose in the later years of Heschel's life, when Heschel publicly and aggressively opposed continued U.S. involvement in the Vietnam War. One can only speculate as to other reasons for Lieberman reacting negatively to Heschel's political activities. Perhaps it was his conservatism that led him to believe that one must not give comfort to America's enemies when she is at war with them, and his *musar* personality that would advocate the performance of one's duties quietly and without fanfare; that would lead him to view Heschel's public advocacy as unwise, a form of grandstanding.[397] Quite possibly, Lieberman may have also perceived Heschel to be more of a popularizer than a serious academician and textual scholar.[398]

Reports of ill feeling, if not animosity, between the two men may well have been unfounded. It is significant that Heschel's widow, Sylvia, chose Lieberman to eulogize her husband in her home on Heschel's first Yahrzeit. She also credits Lieberman with assisting her in several important matters following her husband's death.[399] Susannah Heschel deplores the "falsification and rewriting of history" that portrays her father and Lieberman as adversaries. She describes them as "sharing mutual respect for each other and enjoying informal family warmth and friendliness." She was a guest in Lieberman's Jerusalem home when her parents were traveling, and recalls how "totally shaken Lieberman was when he rushed to their apartment upon hearing of Heschel's death."[400] When approached during a conference on March 23, 1998, at JTS commemorating the twenty-fifth Yahrzeit of Heschel, Susannah Heschel had an immediate positive response concerning Lieberman and his relationship with the Heschel family. She stressed that the Liebermans, who lived in the same apartment building in New York as the Heschels, were very good neighbors and often visited each other on Shabbat afternoons.[401] Sylvia Heschel recalled accompanying Lieberman and Heschel during strolls down Riverside Drive, when the two seemed to speak together in the manner of a secret code, as they good-naturedly exchanged quotations and interpretations of rabbinic statements and texts. Judith Lieberman said that she and Mrs. Heschel formed a very close and sincere relationship, noting that Heschel's wife was a professional musician.[402] In the late sixties, recalls Yakov Aviad, the Heschels and Liebermans could be seen enjoying meals together in the Seminary sukkah, while engaged in animated and warm conversation.[403]

Lieberman was at the helm of the American Academy for Jewish Research for many years, where Heschel was a member of the executive committee in the 1960s and early 70s. The committee of the *Louis Ginzberg Jubilee Volume,* of which Lieberman was a leading member, invited Heschel to contribute an essay, the result being Heschel's seminal Hebrew article "Did Maimonides Strive for Prophetic Inspiration?"[404] Some years later, when Lieberman served as editor of the Marx Jubilee volume, Heschel contributed another major essay, "The Holy Spirit in the Middle Ages," which included additional notes prepared by Lieberman.[405] Most likely, when Lieberman received the Heschel essay, he noted his comments on the text before returning it to Heschel, whereupon the latter requested that the Lieberman notes appear in print, added to his own. Such a level of collaboration supports the view that Heschel and Lieberman respected each other.

Commitment to his scholarly work notwithstanding, Lieberman was decidedly not the solitary, cloistered academician. He frequently showed his gregarious, genial side. His Friday evening table was invariably crowded with guests, and it was said that with his conviviality and popularity, "he could easily have been elected mayor of Martha's Vineyard," his summer home.[406] His social circle was broad, ranging from General David Sarnoff, his Passover seder guest,[407] to secular Labor Party members in Israel,[408] to sailors on Martha's Vineyard.[409] According to Yehuda Shapira, "Lieberman mingled with people with whom one would have thought he had nothing in common. He liked talking with *amkha* [the common man], those he met in the course of daily life, such as the storekeeper. . . . Lieberman was not a snob."[410] In Haym Soloveitchik's words, "There was no fusion between [Lieberman's] intellectual status and his personality. In meeting him or seeing him in ordinary conversation, one would never have guessed his towering intellect."

Many who ventured out to Martha's Vineyard uninvited and unannounced found themselves greeted and hosted warmly by Lieberman at his summer vacation home. For example, Judith Lieberman wrote to Louis Finkelstein on July 19, 1953: "Dr. Lieberman maintains a rigid schedule of his own. However, his studies do not deter my husband from taking a personal interest in his former students. When we heard that Rabbi Kreitman (whom I had not met before) came singly to the island my husband set out in search of him lest the rabbi remain over Shabbat without a proper meal." When Eli and Penina Schochet visited Martha's Vineyard in the second week of July 1965 and phoned Lieberman to announce their unexpected arrival, lodging was procured for them; they were guests in Lieberman's home for a Shabbat meal, and were taken for an extensive tour of the island the following day.

Lieberman had an earthy side. He enjoyed a good cigar, a good joke, and was a connoisseur of fine wine. Once Lieberman challenged Nock to a drinking contest and won.[411] Frank Moore Cross commented on how Lieberman gallantly partook of the sweet kosher wine provided by Harvard University even though his palate was accustomed to select drier libations.[412] When Jessica Feingold sent Lieberman a gift of vodka in 1954, he responded, "Your sweetness added a special flavor to the bitter vodka. I think I have now a supply for a whole year, and can go on quietly with my studies without worrying for the rest of the year." Once at a JTS ordination party, he was observed downing eight ounces of vodka "as if it were water."[413]

It would appear that Lieberman preferred the leisure-time companionship of nonacademicians, or noncompetitive scholars, to that of his colleagues. Perhaps there was a measure of relaxation for him in partaking of worlds other than his own during the time he took off from his studies.

Lieberman probably possessed an earthy, nonacademic side as a youth. For example, he prided himself on his noncerebral achievements, recalling his physical stamina in the years following the Russian revolution, when he worked alongside Gentiles engaged in cutting down timber for transport to Kiev. Lieberman reminisced:

> You know the *koach,* strength, I got from that work probably kept me alive until today. I learned to endure, hunger, bitter cold. How cold it was in Kiev. They decided to pull down houses, cut lumber, in order to warm the students. They asked for volunteers. I was the only Jew. I wanted to show them that a Jew was not afraid of manual labor. . . . You had to cut the trees just so. I had a good eye. So I could tell whether a tree was leaning in one direction or another. If you cut from the direction it was leaning, it would break the saw. The work of sawing the trees down was easy, as was sawing them in pieces, but the splitting of the lumber was hard. The hammers weighed about fifteen pounds. After a while, I couldn't do it. However, I had such a good eye that they asked me to go from group to group and identify the way the trees should be sawed. But I didn't want a Jew to be identified as an overseer. Instead, I asked to be able to do the cutting down, the felling of the trees, and the sawing. But the splitting I would be exempt from. They agreed and were delighted at my attitude.
>
> We used to tell one another stories. They were from Caucasus. They would tell me what they thought of Jews. Terrible stuff. And I would tell them what I thought of them, but with laughter so that the other one could take it. We were very frank with one another. And they liked me. They had meat, it was *treif,* so they agreed that for my portion of meat, they would give me eggs, cheese, milk, and bread. It was all very fresh and good.
>
> On Saturdays, I would walk into town for Shabbas. It took me from six in the morning until twelve o'clock, but I didn't break the *eruv* because there were houses all the way. . . . I volunteered for another two weeks. Four weeks later, when I came back, I had muscles on my arms.[414]

Lieberman's childhood in Motol probably proved invaluable in equipping him for such tasks. Many Motol Jewish merchants earned their livelihood from the timber trade, cutting timber and then transporting it on rafts across the rivers to Danzig. A particular expertise was involved in selecting the proper trees to be felled and in determining the best angle by which to fell them.[415]

Louis Finkelstein, Saul Lieberman, and Talmudic Ethics. As is well known, Finkelstein dedicated much effort to the formulation of a system of ethics to be extrapolated from the rabbinic literature. He was convinced that before one can look to rabbinic literature for guidance for ethical decision making, one must first possess a comprehensive knowledge and deep understanding of the literature itself. It would seem that Lieberman became the key person to guide and assist Finkelstein in achieving his objective. On July 22, 1955, Finkelstein wrote a five-page, single-spaced letter detailing his proposal to develop a fifth *Shulhan Arukh,* that is, the ethics of the Talmud. It appears from Finkelstein's letter that this was an issue that the two men had discussed frequently. Finkelstein praised Lieberman: "I owe whatever insights I have in this field to conversations with you, studies of your work and watching your life. What I am trying to work out is Professor Lieberman as an institution, having the same relationship to you that the Torah of Yavneh had to its founder."

Lieberman's response reflects his view that Judaism provides a sliding scale of ethical standards, with the obligation to maintain the most stringent standards—in keeping with *musar* tradition—the responsibility of the most learned. They are the most accountable precisely because of their scholarship. Lieberman writes:

> I might have stated to you my position on Jewish law and legal ethics. I believe that they are only the minimum without which no society can exist. The real legal ethics begin beyond this minimum. Each individual is legally bound by an ethical system conditioned to his individual character, temperament and general stature. A certain behavior on the part of an ordinary man may rightly be considered blameless under the circumstances, but the same behavior on the part of a learned man should be considered

> ethically criminal. In between the ignorant small man and the learned great man there are number less [numerous] gradations of ethical principles which correspondingly should [bind or guide?] the individual according to his status. Rabbinic literature abounds in episodes which highly illuminate the particular ethical principles with which we are concerned. The general idea is that none is exempt from the moral duty to *aspire* for perfection, thus raising the standards of the ethical principles required by the law from the particular individual.
>
> A detailed and analytical study of the entire rabbinic literature must be specifically undertaken in order to discover the rules of a systematic code of rabbinic ethics. I believe I can be of some help in periodic meetings with you alone, where we can discuss the results and conclusions in your group meetings. I hope to discuss with you the matter when we meet in New York or perhaps on this island.[416]

Apart from Finkelstein's prodigious writing on the ethical dimension of the rabbinic worldview, he organized several conferences and institutes dedicated to the study of ethics. "The Law as a Moral Force" conference held at JTS on September 13–15, 1957, featured Earl Warren, chief justice of the U.S. Supreme Court, along with other prominent business and political leaders, participating in a three-day intensive course in Jewish ethics taught by various Seminary professors, including Lieberman, who taught chapter 4 of *Sanhedrin* at one session. It would be logical to infer that Lieberman collaborated with Finkelstein in formulating the theoretical basis for the subject of the conference. A highlight of the conference, which culminated in a convocation at which Earl Warren received an honorary degree from the Seminary, was the publication of Lieberman's *Tosefta Kifshutah, Zera'im.* Finkelstein included in the convocation program his analysis of the significance of Lieberman's edition of, and commentary on, the Tosefta. Finkelstein referred to the ethical issues concerning the value of human life, and the saving of lives, all discussed in Lieberman's commentary: "Judaism was far more than merely a ritualistic and juristic system. It is a system of discovering what is right and mastering methods for such discovery. Professor

Lieberman's commentary, like the great work it illumines, is a real contribution to this aspect of Judaism."[417] While Finkelstein encouraged Lieberman in his scholarly endeavors out of sincere personal regard and profound respect for his genius, we may assume, in addition, that Lieberman served Finkelstein well as the "theoretician" providing the foundation and the premise for extrapolating ethical principles from the rabbinic imperatives.[418]

Finkelstein launched the Herbert Lehman Institute of Ethics (HLIE) at the same time that JTS convened the Warren convocation. The HLIE was a three-year program for rabbinical students who had already completed three years of study, and was designed to deepen the student's knowledge of the texts and enhance his appreciation of the ethics of the Rabbis. Lieberman was involved in this program as well, meeting with students and explaining the Ph.D. requirements. The students were invited by Lieberman to participate in a Talmud seminar and to consult with him individually if they had questions concerning the assigned material. Not surprisingly, the study of Talmud was a prerequisite for all courses of study, because it "is a comprehensive record of the Jewish life of antiquity containing history, economics, and the personal moral behavior of the Rabbis."[419]

Exceedingly poignant are Lieberman's comments to Finkelstein during World War II, when Finkelstein invited him to deliver a lecture, "The Jewish Attitude toward the Christian Martyrs in Caesarea":

> I thank you very much for your proposal to have me deliver a lecture on the Jewish attitude toward the Christian martyrs in Caesarea. I do not like to confuse apologetics with science, but in this case I am fully convinced that both the Rabbis and the Jewish masses did not remain indifferent to the tortures of the Christians. In that age of darkness and religious fanaticism, the Jews reacted to the pains of scores of Christians in a more humane way than do the contemporary enlightened Christians to the mass executions of hundreds of thousands [of] innocent Jewish men, women and children. Thus, such a lecture seems to be in time [timely].[420]

In the private, personal realm, can examples be adduced of Lieberman taking upon himself demanding standards of ethical behavior, in keeping with the principle of *lifnim mishurat hadin* ("within" or "beyond the line of the law") and *minhag hasidut* ("standards" or "practices of piety")? In other words, did Lieberman personally exemplify the higher pietistic standard for a scholar that he refers to in the Finkelstein correspondence? In *Greek in Jewish Palestine,* Lieberman writes:

> The Palestinian Talmud related an episode about R. Jonathan, who was renowned as a just judge. It happened that the branches of a tree belonging to R. Jonathan spread into the territory of a Roman Gentile whose house and field adjoined his. Once a case of a tree spreading in somebody else's premises came before R. Jonathan, and he put off the decision to the following day. The Roman said: "It is on account of me that the decision was postponed; tomorrow I shall waste the whole day to see what decision will be rendered. If he judges others but does not judge himself he cannot be called a man." At nightfall R. Jonathan had all the branches of his tree which spread into the Roman's premises cut off. . . . Upon discovering that the tree was cut down, he said: "Blessed be the God of the Jews."[421]

Dov Zlotnick relates that Lieberman was once involved in a similar circumstance. A Jew approached him inquiring whether it was permissible to enter into a partnership in a nonkosher restaurant. It so happened that at the time, Lieberman owned stock in a hotel that had a nonkosher restaurant on its premises. Before rendering a decision in the matter, Lieberman did something that was unheard of in the investment community: "He returned the stock, which had grown considerably in value, and asked that he be reimbursed with only its initial cost."[422] Only afterward did Lieberman feel qualified to respond objectively to the query he had received.

The relationship between Lieberman and J. N. Epstein casts an interesting light on Lieberman's ethical sensitivities. As noted earlier, Epstein and Lieberman had strong differences of opinion as academicians, and Epstein's correspondence with L. Ginzberg displays the competitiveness that Epstein felt toward his student.[423] Lieberman, however, writes deferentially of Epstein, referring to him as the teacher "from whom I have learned so very much," and attempts to shelter him from the criticisms of others, notably Albeck and Zeitlin.[424] As noted earlier, when Lieberman's *Talmudah shel Kisrin* came under strong criticism in J. N. Epstein's posthumously published *Mavo Lesifrut Ha'amoraim,*[425] Lieberman, while defending his thesis, took great pains to make excuses for his mentor, pointing out that Epstein's posthumous works were merely tentative notes, hence their unevenness and lack of thoroughness.[426]

In truth, their relationship was impaired by more than scholarly differences or personality clashes. In a most revealing letter from Lieberman to Ginzberg, Lieberman lamented that Epstein's bitterness and anger toward him "knows no bounds," that Epstein hated him because he disagreed with him and occasionally extolled the works of other scholars, and that Epstein maligned him at every opportunity.[427] However, Lieberman emphasized that he had deep compassion for Epstein and felt badly that such a great scholar was unappreciated and ignored by the scholarly world, and that Epstein's sixtieth birthday was passed over in silence by the Jerusalem academic community. Epstein deserved to be shown appreciation and honor because he had devoted his life to Jewish scholarship. As for his character flaws, one should not pass judgment upon him, for there were mitigating factors: his bitterness and anger stemmed from the painful experiences life had inflicted upon him, and he deserved compassion, not censure or condemnation.

There are reports that Epstein was resentful of Lieberman for not having given him and the Hebrew University sufficient recognition for the publication of his *Tosefet Rishonim,* since a good part of the work was done while Lieberman was at the Hebrew University.[428] It is also claimed that Epstein, fearing that Lieberman would surpass him as a scholar, wanted him to leave the Hebrew University, and he reputedly came before the Hebrew University board, asking for Lieberman's dismissal.[429] It is claimed that Lieberman received an additional dismissal letter from the Hebrew University, this one bearing Epstein's signature with the demeaning comment, "Many good people have applied, but I had to choose the best."[430]

To the credit of both men, the passage of time brought about a degree of reconciliation, and their relationship warmed. Lieberman praised Epstein publicly at every opportunity, and David Rosenthal was impressed that Lieberman carried Epstein's picture in his wallet.[431] In 1947, Lieberman sent a generous gift to Epstein's son, Hayyim, with the stipulation that he study

Talmud with his father. Lieberman received a thank-you letter from Hayyim, and his mother, Tzipora, together with a very friendly letter from Epstein that included a response to technical talmudic issues raised in Lieberman's last letter to him.[432] Lieberman, as editor of the Marx Jubilee volume, subsequently invited Epstein to contribute an essay, and their correspondence deals with Epstein's choice of topic and the editing of his essay.[433] The geniality and cordiality of their relationship is to the credit of both scholars. Speaking at a Hebrew University–sponsored function on the anniversary of Epstein's death, Lieberman praised his teacher profusely, declaring that nothing gave him more pleasure than to read Epstein's *Mavo Lenusah Hamishnah* page by page.[434]

Lieberman's tenure at JTS extended many years beyond what he wished it to be. It would appear that this was due to Lieberman's sense of moral obligation toward Finkelstein to remain at the institution even though Lieberman yearned to leave the Seminary and return to Jerusalem. In a letter of November 27, 1962, to Gershom Scholem, Lieberman informed him that he was trying to persuade Finkelstein to free him from his obligation to JTS so that he could return to Israel. However, Finkelstein did not want him to go, and Lieberman said that he could not leave without Finkelstein's blessing. After the Six-Day War, Lieberman again wrote Scholem (December 6, 1967) of his desire to return to Israel to reside. However, he was unable to do so because he could not bring himself to leave Finkelstein alone: "There was a time when I needed [Finkelstein] and it is not pleasant [*arev*] to leave him at a time when he needs me." Lieberman never forgot the dire straits that he had been in when Finkelstein brought him to America, bestowing upon him friendship and respect, together with the working conditions that facilitated his great achievements. This sense of loyalty resulted in Lieberman spending all his remaining years at JTS.

We shall cite one final observation, arcane as it may sound, as to Lieberman's advocacy of higher pietistic standards. He was known to have remonstrated repeatedly against the accepted practice of New York City pedestrians crossing against red lights. He viewed this as a violation of Jewish law, even if the act did not pose danger to the pedestrian and the police were indifferent to the matter. Why? Because of *gezel* (theft). Such behavior, on the part of pedestrians, might force oncoming drivers to apply their brakes, and it was therefore an unfair imposition adding to their fuel costs, not to mention stress and aggravation.[435]

Love for Israel. After Lieberman's death, Finkelstein wrote a revealing paragraph about Lieberman's love for Israel:

> I did not know, until recently, how difficult it was for Professor Lieberman to make up his mind to come to us. Of course, I was aware that it was not easy for him to leave the Holy Land and that, in fact, after having accepted an invitation to come here, he withdrew the acceptance and then withdrew the withdrawal. He loved every stone of the Holy Land and it was hard for him to leave it. A few weeks before he left America on his final trip, he told me that the pressure of friends not to come to the Seminary and his inner struggle were so great that he stopped eating.[436]

Indeed, a recurrent theme in Lieberman's correspondence is his love for Israel, his yearning to return there, and his guilt in not being there to share in its tribulations.

On August 26, 1941, Judith Lieberman wrote to the Scholems, detailing the degree to which she missed the city of Jerusalem. She wrote that they were not establishing a permanent abode in the U.S., but were only taking a furnished apartment for the coming year, for their hope was to return soon to Jerusalem. Her husband echoed her sentiments; in a letter of March 2, 1941, he had explained to Scholem that he wished to renew his contract at JTS for one year only, while the Seminary was holding out for a permanent appointment. In other letters to Scholem, Lieberman spoke of how much he missed the sound of the shofar on Friday afternoons. "Here in the U.S., there is no Sabbath and no festivals," wrote Lieberman, and he informed him that he had recently renewed his passport so as to be able to return to Jerusalem. In one letter to Scholem, Lieberman described his state of mind: "I sit and I learn and I yearn for the Land of Israel. My yearnings rise within me whenever dangers present themselves to our Holy Land, and

I sometimes feel like a deserter." Shortly after the establishment of the State of Israel, Lieberman openly declared his guilt in being in the U.S. and not in Israel, sharing in "the pain of the Jerusalem community." This was to become a recurrent theme in Lieberman's correspondence through the years. After the 1967 war, Lieberman lamented, "I was not privileged to share in the pain of the community," and he tried to take comfort in the fact that he was able to raise substantial funds for Israel while in New York. On another occasion, he told Scholem that he was not in the mood to write because of the pain he experienced in being so far away from Israel. "We were not privileged to be together with our brethren in Eretz [Yisrael] and to help them bear their burden." Although periodically, Lieberman expressed the hope that he would soon be able to return to Israel and settle there permanently, this was never to be. He was only able to partake of eagerly awaited visits. "I am counting the days until I will be able to return to the holy city of Jerusalem."[437]

Finkelstein was concerned that on one of Lieberman's trips to Jerusalem, he might decide to remain there and not return to JTS. Finkelstein wrote to Alexander Marx: "I hope that the Palestinians will not persuade him to stay in Palestine. His failure to return here would be, indeed, a frightful loss to us all."[438] On one occasion, Finkelstein even considered having a private plane sent to Israel to bring Lieberman back to New York.[439]

In the letter of May 31, 1982, to Anita Shapira (referred to earlier), Lieberman emphasized his love for Israel. He professed great admiration for the pioneers of the Second Aliyah, who risked their lives in the building of the Jewish state. Lieberman recalled his first arrival in Israel, a refugee who fled persecution in Russia, but one who knew nothing about Zionist ideology and its true meaning. His sole concern was making a living. Years later, Lieberman mused that had he then truly appreciated the kibbutz movement, he probably would have become part of it and would never have left the Land of Israel. In his later years, his love of the modern Hebrew language and of the State of Israel led him to learn all the *rashei teivot* ("abbreviations") employed by the Israeli army. He wanted to be a full Israeli and expressed that desire through language, striving to use in his conversations the slang expressions of young Israelis.[440]

Teaching as a Religious Mission

Several months after his arrival in New York to assume his position at JTS, Lieberman wrote his friends in Israel relating, with apparent pleasure, that he was required to teach only four to five hours per week.[441] This could reflect the fact that research and writing were of primary importance to Lieberman, and that he considered teaching to be somewhat of a chore, a duty to be tolerated; however, this was not the case. Lieberman's classroom teaching was very important to him. Although a request to give up teaching would probably have been granted by Finkelstein because of Lieberman's prestige, he never made such a request.

Lieberman enjoyed participating in the formation of the policies of JTS and, by virtue of his position at the Seminary, affecting the course of Judaic studies and Judaism in North America. One way to influence the future of an institution is through the power of appointment. Lieberman's class consisted of seniors and a select number of students from other classes who displayed exceptional aptitude in Talmud studies. Every rabbi ordained by JTS during Lieberman's tenure had been his student. Since the JTS faculty was staffed largely by its own graduates, Lieberman was in a position to place selected students in a position to be candidates for the faculty. Faculty members taught by Lieberman who served as faculty include Gerson Cohen (later JTS chancellor), David Weiss Halivni, Bernard Mandelbaum, and Seymour Siegel. Among the students of Lieberman who currently serve on the JTS faculty are Israel Francus, Shamma Friedman, Edward M. Gershfield (since July 2002, emeritus), Neil Gillman, Judith Hauptman, Avraham Holtz, Joel Roth, Raymond P. Scheindlin, Burton Visotzky, and Dov Zlotnick. Many of these appointees were Lieberman's personal choices, while others were selected with his approval.

Indeed, Lieberman used the classroom as a recruiting ground, encouraging promising students to choose Talmud as their major field of study. Moshe Greenberg was a special student at JTS, enrolled in a program to prepare him for a career in Bible studies. Lieberman tried to persuade him to specialize in rabbinics, contending that it is more challenging than Bible while offering greater variety. Lieberman also tried to encourage Yochanan Muffs, another Bible scholar, to devote himself to rabbinic studies. While both remained committed to biblical scholarship, their work reflects their interest and skill in rabbinics.[442]

Most of Lieberman's students went on to serve as pulpit rabbis. One reason Lieberman gave for leaving Jerusalem in 1940 to join JTS was that he would thereby have the opportunity to train future leaders of the American Jewish community. When his devoutly Orthodox brother, Meir, questioned his acceptance of an appointment to the "Conservative" JTS, Lieberman explained that this would give him an opportunity to cultivate select students who would ensure the survival of traditional Judaism. In a letter to Scholem after his arrival in New York, Lieberman wrote that Epstein had told Shlomo Zalman Schocken, "Lieberman is the right person for America." While this was likely a backhanded compliment, Lieberman chose to take it as well-intentioned praise. He went on to write that he indeed "understands well the psychology of the 'boys' in America" and that it seemed to him that "by means of the proper approach, it is possible to draw them to Torah and Judaism." This is the key to understanding Lieberman's approach to classroom teaching. He was a passionate exponent of rabbinic literature, motivated to strengthen his students' commitment to traditional Judaism by demonstrating, as he did in his writings, that the Rabbis of the Talmud were men of their world who understood human nature, culture, society, and economics—not ivory-tower figures constructing theories in thin air.[443] Lieberman emphasized that the Rabbis reacted against the corrupt societies in which the Jewish people lived by formulating principles of an ethical life, which continue to guide us to this day. Needless to say, Finkelstein shared this conviction.

As discussed above, Lieberman taught each year from one of six tractates: *Sanhedrin, Bava Metzia, Avodah Zarah, Ketubot, Gittin,* and *Nedarim*. The first three are in *Nezikin* (damages), and the last three are in *Nashim* (women). The curriculum in the Lithuanian yeshivot was also drawn from these *sedarim* (orders). According to Gedalyahu Alon: "In practice, only six or seven talmudic tractates [from *Nashim* and *Nezikin*] were studied in the Lithuanian yeshivas."[444] While following the tradition in which he was trained, these tractates offered Lieberman the opportunity to transmit to his rabbinical students the values of Torah. Indeed, each tractate that Lieberman taught was selected for a reason. *Sanhedrin* prescribes the court system and describes the sophisticated and ethically sensitive principles underlying the Mosaic administration of justice. *Bava Metzia,* with its chapter *Eizehu Neshekh,* which deals with complex commercial transactions, articulates the ethical principles governing business transactions, and it places constraints on exacting interest, in order to prevent the oppression of the poor. *Avodah Zarah* was not generally studied in the Lithuanian yeshivot because it includes a significant component of aggadah (nonlegal sections). This was precisely one of Lieberman's reasons for teaching that tractate.[445] *Avodah Zarah* focuses on the Jewish response to idol worship, guiding Jews in their relationship with non-Jews, a matter of contemporary relevance. *Ketubot* and *Gittin* set out principles of family relations, the mutual responsibilities of spouses, and rules concerning witnesses and evidence. *Nedarim* deals with the rules regarding oaths and promises, emphasizing the sanctity of the word, teaching the importance of integrity in interpersonal relations. These tractates offer detailed guidance on how to manage disputes and litigation. They deal with situations where people interact in commercial dealings; where they are governed by different religious practices; where husband and wife interact; and where people make commitments to one another. Lieberman was, in effect, transmitting an important principle of the *musar* movement, which teaches that Jewish tradition is not confined to ritual practice but governs all aspects of interpersonal relations as well, placing emphasis on the latter.

Lieberman would generally devote the first two or three sessions of the year to an elaborate introduction, developing the recurring themes of the tractate. This series of lectures was designed to explain the basic concepts of the Talmud, while demonstrating their lofty ethical character. Although Lieberman delivered these lectures with neither text nor notes, these lectures were carefully organized and prepared. Indeed, Lieberman, in his preparation, used 3" by 5" index cards to list the rabbinic texts, each card referring to the text to be discussed and occasionally including a brief heading or phrase as a reminder to deal with a particular topic. For example, he included the phrase "torture in antiquity" in his introduction to *Sanhedrin,* regarding the use of torture to extract confessions. Lieberman used these notes to guide him in his lecture and discussion. However, he did not refer to these or any other notes during his lecture. The concepts that he advanced and the sources that he used in his introduction to *Sanhedrin,* as well as in the course of the study of *Bava Metzia,* helped the students understand his approach.

The following explanations are based on notes taken during Lieberman's classes (not tape recordings). We also draw on Lieberman's index cards, which are found in the JTS library archives. Any inaccuracies are the responsibility of the authors.

Introduction to Sanhedrin

Lieberman discussed elements of the talmudic judicial system, illustrating the values of justice and fairness, sensitivity to the supreme value of life, common sense, effectiveness, and efficiency. Lieberman's personal *Sanhedrin* index-card notes bear the heading "Difference [between our laws and those] of other nations." This was a major theme in his *Sanhedrin* lectures. The Torah introduced compassionate, sensitive, sensible legal principles and public policies designed to civilize a primitive society.

In contrast to ancient societies, which often inflicted severe physical or capital punishment for theft and robbery, Jewish law confined itself to financial sanctions in those circumstances, with a view to compensating the victim for his loss. Robbery, theft, and property damage were not criminal offenses punishable by death. As Jewish law did not distinguish between civil and criminal offenses, Lieberman used the term "criminal" to denote the imposition of physical punishment or incarceration.[446] This is in marked contrast to capital punishment for property offenses, imposed by the laws of many of the ancient peoples. Lieberman would say that to condemn a person to death for stealing property is as barbaric as it is ridiculous. Instead, Jewish law prescribes that the thief must pay a fine that effects restitution and that often includes an amount in excess of the value of the property stolen for purposes of deterrence.

Lieberman related an account of one of the Rabbis who had a debate with a robber. The robber prevailed, for when a robber has logic and law on his side, he will prevail. Resh Lakish was once guarding an orchard when someone came along and helped himself to some figs: Resh Lakish shouted at him, but the fellow ignored him, whereupon he said: "Let that fellow be under a *shammetha* [form of excommunication]!" The fellow replied: "On the contrary, let Resh Lakish be under a *shammetha!* If I have incurred a pecuniary liability toward you, did I incur excommunication?" Resh Lakish went to the academy and reported the incident. They said: "His excommunication of you is justified. Your excommunication of him is not."[447] Resh Lakish was advised to visit the robber to be absolved from his excommunication, but since he did not know the robber's identity, he had to appear before the *nasi* (prince or senior religious authority) for absolution. The robber's position was that Resh Lakish could require him to pay money, but had no right to excommunicate him.

This aggadah illustrates the principle that a robber is subject only to financial sanctions; Resh Lakish could compel him to appear before the court but could not excommunicate him. Furthermore, explained Lieberman, the Talmud expresses an important principle—that when he knows the law, even a robber's position prevails over that of a rabbi, for authority and rank do not override the application of the law to all. This constitutes the basis of the "rule of law" later adopted by English common law. Likewise, the Torah's rejection of excessive punishment for a robber is echoed in other legal systems.

How is society to discourage theft and other interference with private property rights? Lieberman found a solution to the problem in the Talmud's emphasis on moral education. He explained the section of the Talmud that describes the true *neturei karta* (guardians of the city) as *saferin umatnayanin* (teachers of the written and oral tradition), to indicate that the teachers of morality guard the city by ensuring honesty.[448] Proper education will go a long way to protect society from crime; police power alone, without moral education, is inadequate, and can be a destructive force.

Lieberman also discussed the rule against self-incrimination, which provides that one is neither competent nor compellable to testify against oneself.[449] That is, one cannot confess voluntarily. The purpose of the rule was to eliminate the possibility of forced confessions and testimony motivated by fear.[450] Lieberman then cited the *Sifrei,* which, in the course of formulating a *kal vehomer* (an *a fortiori* argument), states the following as a self-evident proposition: "Rabbi Jose says, just as one's own confession cannot be counted together with that of a single witness as evidence for the death penalty. . . ."[451] Rabbi Jose employs the *kal vehomer* in an attempt to prove that the testimony of a single witness, while not sufficient to prove liability, is sufficient to impose the requirement of an oath upon the defendant. The *kal vehomer* fails, and Rabbi Jose thus must derive the rule from a biblical passage.[452] The general rule is that a fact can be established only by the testimony of two witnesses. One would have thought that an admission by an accused murderer corroborating the testimony of one witness would be equivalent to the evidence of two witnesses; however, according to the *Sifrei,* such testimony lacks probative value. Lieberman noted that this principle was later cited as a matter of fact in a second-century text. In so doing, he disproved the view of those who dated these texts considerably later in an attempt to diminish the achievement of early Jewish law that insisted on a strict standard for the admission of evidence and eliminated the possibility of torture to compel confessions at a time when torture and other cruel practices prevailed in the Roman courts.[453]

Continuing his discussion of selected elements of the talmudic judicial system, Lieberman explained that witnesses generally do not take an oath. The only oath in connection with witnesses takes place when the plaintiff demands that all those with information about his claim come forward. At that point, the prospective witness would respond with an oath that he has no knowledge of the matter. This *shevu'at ha'eidut* (oath of the witness; Lev. 5:1) is the only oath to which a witness responds. There is no oath, however, which relates to the truth of the testimony. As Lieberman explained, if the witness can lie to the court in giving his evidence, he can also swear falsely when taking an oath.

Another principle of *dinei nefashot* (criminal law) stipulates that circumstantial evidence has no probative value in capital cases.[454] Maimonides justifies the strict rules of evidence in capital cases with the proposition that it is better to acquit a thousand guilty people (sinners) than to kill one innocent person, as the Torah states (Exod. 27:7): "You shall not execute the innocent and righteous."[455] This compassionate yet rigorous approach must be balanced by an exceptional provision for dealing with habitual and dangerous killers. Lieberman explained that in capital cases the king, as well as the court, was empowered to override the strict requirements of the rules of evidence and to impose the death penalty, and that the court was similarly empowered to dispense with the strict rules of evidence.[456] Lieberman explained the mishnah dealing with a case in which a murderer had intimidated potential witnesses so that they would be afraid to give the *hatra'ah* (advance legal warning) to a potential offender.[457] In that case, the witnesses viewed the crime in hiding, without giving the requisite warning, and the punishment imposed was life imprisonment.[458]

As one would expect, Lieberman often referred his students to relevant interpretations and comments found in his own publications. In the course of one lecture, Lieberman explained and elaborated upon his commentary in *Tosefet Rishonim* on the statement in the Tosefta regarding the king's authority to impose the death penalty: "The authority is given only to execute by the sword."[459] Continuing the discussion of what he cited in *Tosefet Rishonim,* he explained the case of Joab (1 Kings 2:28–34), King David's general who killed two people and who believed that he could escape the death penalty because of the requirements of *eidim v'hatra'ah* (witnesses and advance legal warning). However, Joab failed to consider the king's extraordinary authority to execute him in the absence of "witnesses and advance legal warning."

In this manner, Lieberman attempted to deal with the problem of conflicting values in crime and punishment—namely, justice based on compassion for the perpetrator of a crime, on the one hand, and the protection of society, on the other. He then commenced a discussion of an aggadic mishnah that expressed this tension in sensitive poetic terms. "R. Meir said, When a man undergoes suffering (because of his sins), what does God say (as it were)? *Kalani meroshi kalani mizero'i* (My head is in pain, my arm is heavy)."[460] The term *kalani* is generally taken to mean "heavy." However, Lieberman, citing Maimonides' commentary on the Mishnah, translates *kalani* to mean "disgrace" or "shame," so that God says, "I am ashamed if I punish, and I am ashamed if I do not." Yochanan Muffs, a former student of Lieberman, describes Lieberman's depiction of the agonizing conflict confronting God:

> Saul Lieberman in his lectures often depicted the Lord as a tragic figure, torn between His feelings of love, prompting Him to pardon the wicked, and His feelings of righteous indignation, prompting Him to punish them. The inner battle raging in the di-

> vine mind is between *middat ha-din,* "the quality of justice," and *middat ha-rahamim,* "the quality of love and forgiveness." The most dramatic expression of this divine tension and God's basic reluctance to punish is found in the well-known passage in *m. Sanhedrin* 6:5: *qeloni meroshi qeloni mizro'i;* this is explained by Lieberman [personal letter, Feb. 20, 1974] as follows: "My disgrace from my head, my disgrace from my arm. Maimonides explains the passage, "When a man (i.e., a sinner) is in sorrow, because he is about to be punished, what does the *Shekhinah* say? 'My disgrace from my head, my disgrace from my arm,' i.e., I will be ashamed if I do not use my head and punish the man, and I will be ashamed if I do not use my arm and pardon the man."[461]

In the course of his introductory lecture on *Sanhedrin,* Lieberman grappled with the difficult issue of how far freedom of speech extends before it becomes a threat to society. Lieberman suggested that an examination of the law of the *zaken mamreh* (the Rebellious Elder) helps us to understand this issue. One's initial reaction is that it is harsh to say that the "Rebellious Elder" deserves the death penalty.[462] However, Zlotnick's recollection is that Lieberman said that the only one to attract the death penalty would be a "martyr," since we also require both "warning" and the testimony of two eyewitnesses. Lieberman discussed two additional conditions required in the case of a "Rebellious Elder," which would render such a conviction exceedingly rare. Lieberman translated *zaken mamreh* as "a judge who defies the law." In other words, this law applies only to a judge—one who is in a position of authority. Furthermore, it applies only where the judge urges the disobedience of a ruling issued by the Beit Din Hagadol (the High Court or the Sanhedrin). If a judge simply says, "I disagree with the court's ruling," he is not a *zaken mamreh.* To become liable for such a penalty, the judge must counsel or advocate a particular course of action or behavior, that is, he must contend, "Act as I say." Lieberman viewed this as a powerful assertion of freedom to speak and to teach, provided it is within the framework of "While we must obey the law, we are nevertheless free to disagree with it and to advocate repeal or amendment."

Lieberman quoted a mishnah in *Eduyot,* 5:6, to support the proposition that the halakhah values independent opinions. Akavia ben Mahalalel maintained his minority position on four issues in the face of the Rabbis, who were in the majority and who urged him to change his position in exchange for an appointment to a high office. This mishnah asserts that one should teach what one believes to be right and just, and Akavia ben Mahalalel therefore had a duty to defend his position without fear of the majority.

Lieberman continued his lecture with a discussion of the mishnah of *Perek Helek* (chapter 10 of *Sanhedrin*), which deals with the type of conduct that causes a Jew to lose his share in *Ha'olam Haba* (the World to Come). After explaining selected portions of the chapter, he introduced three quotations from rabbinic literature that suggest ideas central to Lieberman's theology.

The first quotation is from *Kiddushin* 1:10: "Whoever performs a single commandment shall enjoy a good and a long life and shall inherit the land." "The land" refers to *Ha'olam Haba* (see Rashi ad loc.). Lieberman relates the citation to the above mishnayot in *Sanhedrin, Perek Helek*, emphasizing that even one mitzvah can be decisive, for if one's deeds are evenly balanced between good and evil, one additional good deed is sufficient to tip the balance in favor of the good deeds; that person is judged favorably. Lieberman quoted the Palestinian Talmud on the mishnah in *Kiddushin* in which Rabbi Yosi Bei Rabi (A)bun states that "performing one mitzvah" refers to *mi sheyiheid lo mitzvah velo 'avar aleha miyamav* (one who concentrated his efforts on a particular mitzvah and never transgressed its imperatives in all his days); an example of such a mitzvah is honoring one's parents.[463] This teaches that one's deeds are of ultimate importance and that even a single deed can have far-reaching consequences.

The second quotation discussed by Lieberman asserts that faith can make a decisive difference. The pious of the nations—when they carry out the seven Noahide commandments with all their details, they are called "pious ones." When is that said? When they observe the Commandments and acknowledge that they do so "because Noah commanded us to adhere to these Commandments on the instruction of God—that is why we observe them!" If this is what they do, behold they inherit (acquire) the World to Come as does an Israelite (Jew). That is so, even though they do not observe the Sabbaths and the festivals, because they were never commanded to do so. However, if they observe the Seven Commandments, and they say "we heard them from so-and-so, or arrived at them through our own reasoning because they are logical," or they associated them with the name of idol worship, even if they were to observe the entire Torah their reward is only in this world.[464]

Lieberman explained that Maimonides codified the principle of the midrash, that is, this midrash was the basis for his legal ruling.[465] While Maimonides adopted the liberal position of the midrash in declaring that the Gentile will have a share in the World to Come, he did not reproduce the word *k'Yisroel* (as an Israelite). (It is conceivable that Maimonides' text of this midrash may not have included this word.)

This midrash highlights the important principle that a Gentile who observes the seven basic Commandments of God based on a belief that they were commanded by God is, like a Jew, rewarded with a share in the World to Come; thus, where two Gentiles perform the same good deed, one out of belief in God, and the other without faith in God, the latter enjoys his reward only in this world. It is the additional element of faith that merits the greater reward of the World to Come. The principle of this midrash is that faith, belief in God, is the proper basis for the performance of the mitzvot. These are the basic components of Lieberman's credo—faith in God and the carrying out of the mitzvot commanded by the Torah, which God gave to the Jewish people. By adhering to the Torah, we sanctify God and our existence.

The third quotation, which served as Lieberman's conclusion to his introductory series of lectures on *Sanhedrin,* is the following midrash:

> You shall be holy because I your God am holy. If you consecrate yourself, I consider it as though you sanctified Me. And if you do not sanctify yourself, I consider it as though you did not sanctify Me. But do not say that I am sanctified only if you sanctify Me, and if not, I am not sanctified—therefore the passage says, "For I am Holy"—I am sanctified whether you sanctify Me or not.[466]

Central to Lieberman's approach was the conviction that we sanctify God by our behavior. We study Torah to learn how to act—what to do and what not to do. Holiness is expressed through deeds, and we sanctify God through the good deeds done at His behest. Even one single mitzvah, performed because God commanded it, serves to sanctify God.

Ethical Issues in Bava Metzia

When Lieberman taught *Eizehu Neshekh,* the fifth chapter of *Bava Metzia,* which deals with laws concerning interest, credit, and usury, he explained in his introductory lectures numerous features of the commercial society confronting the Rabbis. During the term, Lieberman concentrated on ethical issues discussed in *Eizehu Neshekh.* For example, the Talmud explains that a person transgresses the commandment against stealing when he takes another's property, even with the intention of returning it.[467] Lieberman stressed that this is a serious transgression even if it is assumed that the moment when the victim discovers the loss, he suffers pain for only a short time. This constitutes a transgression even if the motives of the "thief" are positive and he wishes only to teach the person to guard his possessions; and even if the victim can be said to enjoy the relief attendant upon the recovery of his possession. Lieberman emphasized that this illustrates the seriousness of causing pain to another person even for a moment.

Another violation of the law occurs when the vendor is *tomein mishkelotav b'melah* (buries the weight in salt) in order to reduce the amount of produce the purchaser receives.[468] Lieberman explained that the *agoranomus* (market inspector) would place a stamp on the weight so that it would be difficult for the merchant to tamper with it. Thus, to deceive the customer, the vendor would bury the weight in salt, thereby corroding it and reducing the weight in such a way that the unsuspecting victim would never notice.

Lieberman dealt with the well-known moral issue of the container of water held by one of two companions wandering in the desert. The quantity of water is sufficient to keep only one person alive. Ben-Peturah suggests that the two should share the contents and, if need be, both would die; while R. Akiba says that the owner should drink all the water, basing his ruling on the passage *v'hei ahikha imakh* (your brother shall live *with you*).[469] With his knowledge of ancient literature, Lieberman elucidated R. Akiba's reasoning, explaining that this genre of ethical problem is also found in Stoic literature. Indeed, Cicero refers to the case of a shipwreck that leaves two survivors, but only one board for flotation. The utilitarian solution of the Stoics is that the person most valuable to society should live. This approach is offensive to Judaism for, according to the Rabbis, a person is *karov etsel atsmo* (close to himself), that is, entitled to protect his own interest and not required to judge another person as more valuable than himself. The more "useful" person who is told by the Stoics to take the board from the other is committing murder. In the case of the two men in the desert with enough water for only one, R. Akiba's view is that the one who has the water is not required to share it or to give it to the other person. He is not permitted to take his own life and remains passive as he retains possession of the water. Furthermore, if the one who possesses the water was required to give it to the other, the other would then be required to give it back to the first, and so on, in a continuing cycle, resulting in the death of both individuals. Lieberman sought to demonstrate the sophistication, sensitivity, and superiority of rabbinic ethics to those of other ethical systems in the ancient world. In 1963, he published an article, "How Much Greek in Jewish Palestine?" in which he analyzed the moral principles applied by the Talmud in the case of the two companions in the desert. Lieberman compared them to the approach taken by Stoic literature.[470]

Teaching Technique

In teaching students to understand ancient texts, Lieberman drew on his knowledge of legal reasoning, philology, history, and social and cultural forces. Yet, as discussed above, he did not see himself as a pure academic. He had a mission: to teach Torah and strengthen the students' commitment to Torah and mitzvot. This was often done with considerable subtlety in the context of teaching the text.

Sometimes his advocacy was more explicit, and he departed from the ancient texts to confront contemporary events. One such example was in connection with a sermon delivered by one of Lieberman's students. To be eligible for graduation from JTS, each student in his senior year was required to deliver a sermon in the Seminary synagogue, with faculty and students in attendance. As noted earlier, on Saturday, December 11, 1954, Baruch Levine delivered a sermon criticizing the Patriarch Jacob for his deceitful behavior in appropriating the blessings of Isaac that were intended for Esau. Levine and his classmates were astounded the following Monday morning when Lieberman, upon entering the classroom, did not open the Talmud or call upon anyone to read from the text. Instead, he launched into a discussion of Levine's senior sermon, devoting the entire session to attacking him for vilifying Jacob. Lieberman stated that a rabbi must not "debunk" the heroes of our people. After all, would an American politician vilify Abraham Lincoln?

It should be noted that Lieberman's admonition was delivered two days after Levine's Sabbath sermon. It was not a response delivered in the heat of spontaneous anger, but was a carefully planned and organized presentation, and perhaps reflected Finkelstein's own displeasure with the sermon and the concern he shared with Lieberman that JTS-trained rabbis ought not speak to their congregants about the Patriarchs in negative terms. Quite possibly, Lieberman's comments were given with Finkelstein's full approval, if not instigation. As for the lecture itself, in many respects it was directed to the student body as much as to Levine. It would not have sufficed for Lieberman simply to speak to Levine alone, for he wanted the entire senior class, as well as several students from the other classes, to hear his comments, since they had heard Levine's sermon. Seemingly, he was concerned that some students were not showing sufficient regard for the Patriarchs and Rabbis of the Talmud. Lieberman was aware that some students engaged in intense scholarly criticism of the Bible and the Talmud, while others had a tendency to substitute their own views for those of the Rabbis, setting themselves up as iconoclasts.

Lieberman could not tolerate Levine's characterization of Jacob, because respect for our biblical ancestors and our Rabbis was sacred to Lieberman. He pronounced the names of the Rabbis with respect and veneration at all times, and in class he would not tolerate any slight of the Rabbis. If a student spoke of "Akiba" or "Tarfon" without prefacing their names with the title "Rabbi," Lieberman would sarcastically inquire, "Is he known to you personally?" Lieberman's respect for the Rabbis of the Talmud parallels his reverence for the Talmud itself as a text that is logical and makes sense. He emphasized that if we fail to understand something in the text, we should assume that it is only *mikotser sikhleinu* (because of the limitations of our own intellect). When a section of the Talmud seemed incomprehensible, Lieberman would turn to the realia (the cultural context of everyday life, language, and customs of the ancient world) to make sense of the text. He generally deferred to the rishonim (recognized authorities, commentators, and interpreters of the Talmud from about the mid-eleventh to the mid-fifteenth century), and was reluctant to differ with them. According to Dov Zlotnick:

> What compelled him to adopt their point of view was that he thought that they were correct and that they understood the text better than he did! I knew that his respect for the Raivad and Rabbeinu Tam was boundless, and, in all innocence, I once asked: "Did they really know more of rabbinic literature than you?" And he replied: "They never went to the theater!" That said it all! There were distractions in his life that were thrust upon him, and others that he chose for himself, such as reading the *Wall Street Journal.* A member of the stock exchange once told me—after a conversation with the "Grash" [Lieberman]: "That man knows more about the market than I do!" The rishonim did not have such distractions.

Despite his great respect for the rishonim, Lieberman would always reject an interpretation when he believed it to be incorrect.

As noted above, Lieberman's reverence for the sages of the past led him to severely criticize Finkelstein's book *Akiba: Scholar, Saint, and Martyr* where Finkelstein was especially harsh in his assessment of Rabban Simeon ben Gamliel I. Indeed, Lieberman asked Finkelstein to delete the objectionable section on Rabban Simeon ben Gamliel I. In no other place in his correspondence with Finkelstein is Lieberman so critical of him and so vociferous in imploring him to revise his work..

As any of his students can testify, Lieberman was hardly a cold dispassionate teacher of rabbinic texts. His deference to and reverence for the Rabbis led to his constant advocacy on their behalf—striving to demonstrate that their teaching was grounded in reality and their guidance, in wisdom. He was enthusiastic and indefatigable in explaining their commentaries and interpretations.

Lieberman had great confidence in his own ability to motivate students and was known in Israel, in the decade prior to his becoming a professor at JTS in New York, as a "tough" teacher. While teaching in the Mizrachi Teachers Institute in Israel, Lieberman scheduled an exam in Mishnah. One of Lieberman's students, the son of a faculty member who taught geography, was found in his father's geography class, with a Mishnah text on his lap, preparing for Lieberman's exam. The father was at once happy and sad—happy that his son was studying Mishnah, and sad that he was not listening to his lecture.[471]

It was Lieberman's practice not to bring outlines or notes to class. He would enter the classroom carrying only his volume of the Talmud, which he would place on the lecturer's desk. He would sit at the desk on the first or second day of class while he called the roll, requesting that students keep the same seats as on the first day. Since he memorized the seating plan and the names of all the students, there was no need for him to call the roll after the first or second session. Instead, at the beginning of each session, Lieberman would survey the class, quickly noting in his roll book the one or two absences, and promptly commence the session. He seldom sat at the desk that was on a raised platform, preferring to descend from the platform, stand on the same level as the students, and then pace up and down the aisles, maintaining close eye contact with his students. On the rare occasions when he referred to the text, he would step up to the platform to take a quick glance at it.[472]

These techniques reflect Lieberman's control of the class. As Moshe Greenberg points out, learning the names of the students in the first two sessions made it clear that no one would be anonymous, in contrast to the reality that most teachers in a university, even after a year, still do not know who their students are.[473] Lieberman's objectives were to encourage his students to prepare for class carefully and thoroughly, and to command his students' undivided attention during the session. The motivation for thorough preparation was twofold, one negative and one positive. Students would be called upon to recite the Talmud aloud and explain the text, with Lieberman exposing, with surgical precision, any lack of preparation on the student's part. The other motivation was to be sufficiently prepared to benefit from Lieberman's analysis of the text. His clear and lucid explanations, which obviated difficulties raised by the rishonim, were greatly understated. Lieberman never prefaced his own "problem-solving" explanation with a statement that he was about to offer a great *hiddush* (a novel interpretation), since, as he would frequently say, "There is no *hiddush* when you simply say the *peshat*." Students who failed to prepare adequately could not possibly appreciate the precision and elegance of Lieberman's formulations.[474]

It was a challenge for Lieberman to ensure that all his students remained alert, focusing on the subject matter. This was difficult in part because the class was composed of graduate students, many of whom were married and served as part-time rabbis or teachers, leaving them little time for in-depth preparation. Some students simply resisted the imposition of discipline: Lieberman therefore employed certain pedagogic techniques to overcome this resistance. He had a remarkable ability when looking at a student to discern whether he was following the discussion or daydreaming; when he sensed that a student's mind was wandering, he would frequently call upon him to read and explain the text. Moshe Greenberg marveled at Lieberman's ability to penetrate the psyche of a student: "He had an uncanny way of calling on you when you were not prepared. And he would say with a smile, 'If you are not prepared just tell me, say so—you don't have to prove it.'"[475] While lecturing, Lieberman would frequently call on a student to finish his sentence or his thought: "And therefore, 'Goldberg' [the pseudonym "Goldberg" is used throughout this section], Rabbi Akiba concludes that the reason is. . . ." Thus, every student was constrained to be attentive because at any moment he could be called upon to read the text, complete a sentence, or answer a question.

Occasionally, Lieberman would call on a particular student to read at every session when he thought that the student was capable, but failed to spend adequate time studying the Talmud. For example, in his first year in Lieberman's class, Aaron Singer (a student in Lieberman's class from his freshman year, in 1954, until his ordination, who currently teaches midrash at the Schechter Institute of Jewish Studies, one of the JTS schools in Jerusalem) was one of those asked to read the text in five consecutive sessions. Singer had taken on considerable outside commitments that did not allow him time to prepare adequately for Lieberman's Talmud class. When Singer subsequently relinquished some of his other responsibilities and prepared the text more carefully, Lieberman did not call on him again, and after the second year complimented him: "Zinger, you have greatly improved your preparation for class!"[476]

Lieberman frequently used humor as a blunt instrument of control, some suggesting that his "spontaneous" humorous remarks and jokes were carefully prepared beforehand.[477] When a student mistook *rabbah* (spelled with *hey* at the end) for *rava* (spelled with *alef* at the end), Lieberman asked the student, "Is it *rabbah* with a *hey* or *rava* with an *alef?*" The student, giving the wrong answer, said, "*Rabbah* with a *hey,*" whereupon Lieberman quickly said, "And I say to you *lo* with an *alef!*" Lieberman would not tolerate the incorrect vocalization of words. When a student cited the "*Tosafot yesheinim*" (*yashein,* sleep) instead of *yeshanim* (*yashan,* old), Lieberman responded with a question: "So tell me, 'Goldberg,' why were the Tosafot sleeping?" Lieberman similarly could not tolerate the incorrect pronunciation of words from a biblical passage. A student once read the Talmud's citation of the passage from Psalms wherein the Psalmist declares that if he forgets Jerusalem, *tidbak leshoni lehiki* (let my tongue cleave to my *palate;* Ps. 137:6). Instead of *lehiki,* the student read *leheiki* (to my *bosom*), whereupon Lieberman asked the hapless student how a tongue could cleave to one's bosom—the passage must be referring to a very long tongue?

On the other hand, extensive preparation that was motivated by intellectual arrogance was not tolerated and frequently was met with a caustic response. Thus, when a student once translated a word and noted that it was of Persian origin, Lieberman exclaimed, "Since when is it known to you Persian?"

Lieberman used humor to advance his own views about Jewish studies and observance. A student who was known to concentrate on philosophy and theology failed to explain the text with precision. When Lieberman pressed him to try again, the student responded, "Professor, I imagine that the Gemara is saying . . . ," whereupon Lieberman immediately said, "'Goldberg,' this is not philosophy, where you can use your imagination. This is halakhah, where you must be exact and precise!" In another instance, a student was having difficulty explaining a text relating to the *korbanot* (the ritual of sacrificial offerings). Lieberman, exasperated, said, "'Goldberg,' if you recited *Eizehu Mekoman* [mishnayot that relate to the sacrificial ritual and are part of the of the daily prayers] every day, you would be able to explain this Gemara!"

Lieberman also conducted seminars in the midrash and the Tosefta. In the early years of his tenure at JTS, Lieberman held the seminars in his apartment on Riverside Drive, and in later years, in his large office. Sometime after the commencement of the academic year, the rabbinical school bulletin board was filled with announcements of seminars offered by various professors, with space for students to sign up. There was no announcement for Lieberman's seminar, as he handpicked ten to fifteen students to join. Following a regular class session, Lieberman would put his arm around a student, and say, "'Goldberg,' you will come to the 'Seminahr.'" The seminar, meeting every other week, was held from 9 to 11 P.M. and would be followed by a *shmoose,* or general discussion, which would last until 1 A.M. This setting provided Lieberman the opportunity to transmit some of his own values to the students gathered around his table. For example, he once told a story of an incident that he had witnessed in his hometown synagogue in Motol. While visiting there in 1938, an uneducated man led the congregation in the Mincha service on Shabbat Hanukkah. In the *Al Hanisim* prayer, the leader misplaced the commas so that he read unintelligible phrases, *mosarta giborim b'yad, halashim v'rabim b'yad* (You handed over the mighty into the hands of, the weak and numerous into the hands of). Lieberman was amazed when he looked around at the great scholars who were in attendance and noted that not one of them appeared to take notice or protest when the leader made these serious mistakes. His stories frequently emphasized a moral message representative of the *musar* tradition.

Lieberman's teaching at JTS was of singular importance to him. It was a reason that he gave for living in America rather than Israel. His mission in New York was to influence a group of students who would have a positive impact on the development of Judaism in America. If not for that, he could have remained in Israel. When Penina Herzog once asked Lieberman why he did not return to Israel, he replied that "he was among the last of the European scholars schooled in halakhah, and it was his task to train American Jews to make a commitment to study and observe the mitzvot."

Lieberman's desire to influence JTS students was intertwined with his own gregarious tendencies, for he enjoyed social interactions. He was not an ivory-tower scholar, but enjoyed relating to people, discussing and responding to questions, and would delight in sitting and chatting with his seminar group for hours after the conclusion of textual study.

That he took great pride in his relationship with his students is reflected in a September 1941 letter from Judith to the Scholems, early in Lieberman's tenure at JTS. She wrote that her husband was exceedingly moved not by "the external manifestations which indicate certain successes, such as employment security, honorary titles bestowed upon him, salary increases but rather by the profound expressions of respect and honor which the students articulated on various occasions before the conclusion of the sessions. I also derived much satisfaction from this." Lieberman clearly valued the appreciation and affection shown him by his students, although his *musar* style of behavior rarely made this apparent to them, perhaps out of concern that it might make him emotionally vulnerable or instill in the students a sense of arrogance.

Personality Integration

The observation has been made by some that Lieberman had a dark side: that he was cynical and bitter, toyed with people, and often made students the objects of laughter and derision in his class. To an extent, these accusations are true; however, they must be viewed within the broader context of Lieberman's personality.

Whereas Finkelstein was a romantic, Lieberman was a realist.[478] Lieberman would have agreed with this assessment; indeed, he once good-naturedly said that Finkelstein sought out what was "nice" but not necessarily true.[479] Lieberman faced truths, often bitter and unpleasant ones. He brought with him to America a history of struggle, rejection, and tribulation, experienced in both Europe and Palestine. Lieberman's towering intellect was a factor in his cynicism, as his great intellect and constant study widened the gap between himself and other scholars. Haym Soloveitchik's image of Lieberman standing at the top of the Empire State Building and looking down at the street where all the people below appeared as pygmies to him is apt. Lieberman had to function in a world of scholars, many of whom were mediocre compared with himself, and he witnessed many an *am ha'aretz* honored as a sage. Academic competitiveness, characterized by pretension, jealousy, and arrogance, led scholars to destroy one another's reputation to the point where Lieberman feared that the scholarly community was bringing disrepute and embarrassment upon itself.[480] Perhaps he could best relieve his own pain by responding with sarcasm, and Lieberman's sharply honed sense of humor served him well, helping him cope with problems confronting a realist who perhaps envied Finkelstein for his optimistic romanticism.

Lieberman's background was a significant factor here. Lithuanian yeshivot were not polite finishing schools; they were notorious for verbal jousting and acerbic putdowns, with students competing keenly for their teachers' praise and a prestigious family in which to marry, and teachers employing whatever techniques would work in order to sharpen their students' intellects. The *musar* movement, an important influence on Lieberman in his student years, emphasized the existence of a dark side of human nature and the need to confront such temptations as arrogance, falsehood, and pretense. In stereotypical Litvak fashion, Lieberman responded with a combination of a whimsical, biting sense of humor and brutal, frank honesty.

Lieberman also had a mischievous side, and in his youth he enjoyed a reputation for being a prankster. As a schoolchild in Motol, he once locked his teacher in the outhouse, knowing full well that his teacher's deaf wife would not hear his screams for help. When the teacher finally made his way out and returned to the classroom, he had no hesitation in identifying the culprit, whereupon he smacked Lieberman, who was again punished by his father.[481] On another occasion, Lieberman ate a great deal of onions just before being examined in Talmud by his teacher, knowing of the latter's inability to tolerate the odor of onions. As contemplated, the examination was exceedingly brief.[482]

Lieberman once related that as a youngster, he was angry with his father and wanted "to get even with him." Since he had heard rumors of some great embarrassing incident in his father's ancestry, he was determined to discover what it was so as to raise it with his father. On a cold winter morning, he beheld the synagogue beadle outdoors drawing water, and with his superior strength he was able to hold the man's head beneath the freezing water until the beadle revealed the Lieberman family embarrassment: that there was a Hasid among the family members. "Not only a Hasid," Lieberman would laugh, "but a hasidisher rebbe yet." The hasidic rebbe was none other than R. Zadok Hakohen of Lublin, and young Saul put the information to good use.[483]

Upon paying a visit to a renowned family member, R. Baruch Halevi Epstein, for the first time, Lieberman was confronted by a note on Epstein's door: "Do not knock or disturb under any circumstances." Nevertheless, Lieberman knocked on the door, and when a perturbed R. Epstein rebuked him, "Did you not read the note on the door?" Lieberman replied impishly, "Listen, I don't obey every law written in the *Shulhan Arukh,* so why should I be so scrupulous as to follow what is written on your door?" Lieberman recalled, "Epstein liked my *chutzpah* and invited me in."[484]

Assuming the guise of subtle and derogatory allusions to some of his critics, Lieberman's caustic humor also appears at times in his writings. As indicated above, Lieberman did not find B. Benedikt's criticisms of his writings sufficiently worthy to merit a public response. However, in a footnote in his introduction to *Tosefta Kifshutah, Zera'im* is the following brief discussion concerning his view of his critics:

> I have not entered into debates with the ignorant and illiterate, and have not paid any attention whatsoever to their words. Although they are in error and also mislead others, note that they trip up only those like themselves, and that is not our responsibility. Moreover, some of them engage in work that is helpful to scholars, *uvrukhim yihyu* [emphasis our own], and may they be blessed.[485]

The Hebrew word *uvrukhim* may be taken to refer to "Benedikt," the Latin term for blessing, thus including him among his critics whom he does not choose to debate.[486]

A similarly unflattering reference may be concealed in an essay that Lieberman published in 1940, concerning the rabbinic view that Job did not exist and that the Book of Job is an allegory. Lieberman concludes the essay by referring to those, like Job, "whose tribulations do not defeat them and even the satan [*v'af satan*] whose intentions are for the sake of heaven is in the end subservient to the will of the righteous ones whose actions are for the sake of heaven, in order to enhance and glorify Torah."[487] *V'af satan* might be taken as a veiled reference to J. N. Epstein. Lieberman purportedly explained such allusions, "in confidence," to an individual in Jerusalem who was certain to spread the word among those in the scholarly community.[488]

How many academicians would respond to the question of the authenticity of certain *hagahot* (comments) attributed to R. Yosef Ashkenazi, author of the *Shita Mekubetset,* with such diffidence as Lieberman?: "To the best of my knowledge, we have not yet found a scholar capable of writing *Hagahot* after his death. If we therefore know that one was not alive at a particular time, it seems certain that the writings were not his."[489]

However, Lieberman was more playful than malicious. The mental jousting, intellectual repartee, and putdowns were part of his sense of humor and personality; in many instances, these responses were a means of relieving boredom rather than manifestations of a malicious and cruel mind. When Lieberman would say of a scholar who had not published that "he hasn't misled anyone yet," it was his way of articulating a truth. Likewise, Lieberman loved the use of the double entendre. When one of his students was having great difficulty explaining a passage and deciphering an abbreviation, Lieberman launched into a discussion of abbreviations, concluding that the same abbreviation, "A.H.," can mean either *Ha'olam Haba* (the World to Come) or *am ha'aretz* (ignoramus).[490]

The Israeli novelist Aharon Appelfeld described the quintessential quality of Litvaks as "they love a contradiction, a paradox."[491] This was surely true of Saul Lieberman, and, as we have noted, his personality undoubtedly embodied contradictions and paradoxes. Yet it seems to have been a thoroughly integrated personality. The question has sometimes been posed: Did Lieberman's approach to scholarship have a detrimental effect on his personal religious piety? Not at all, as elucidated by David Weiss Halivni:

> Was Professor Lieberman an unhappy person? Was he suffering from intellectual schizophrenia? Did he have a split personality?

Nothing of the sort! He was childless. He missed children very much, so he always surrounded himself with children. He was patient with them. Sometimes he had no time for a father, but he always had time for the child, son or daughter. Other than this privation, I found him to be one of the most fulfilled people I knew. He ate well, slept well and almost sensually enjoyed learning.

Was he not troubled by a lack of synthesis between his emotional commitment and intellectual strivings, between his simple beliefs and scrupulous observance and his classical sophistication and sense of historical development? Not at all! The truly great need no synthesis. They absorb whatever experience offers them. Their intensely creative personalities act like a fiery furnace, melting away contradictions. What emerges is either a harmonious whole or a creative parallelism with parts that mutually fructify and supplement each other. The truly great do not need to trim edges, as it were, to make genuine experiences fit with each other. They preserve them intact. And if their experiences appear contradictory, they build an emotional bridge spanning them allowing both the landscape and the water to be seen.

Lesser mortals resort to logical means of harmonization. They are constrained to show that the contradictions are not as acute as they appear, that there is nothing that compromise cannot reconcile. In the process they deprive one side, or both, of some of the basic qualities that seemed to be causing the contradictions. What is left is often a mutilated version of its former being, heavily dosed with apologetics and make-believe.

Professor Lieberman hated apologetics and make-believe. He accepted his experiences, religious and intellectual, as they were, enjoyed them to the fullest and transcended whatever contradictions they contained by the sheer force of his towering personality. The personality that made him cry for hours during the Avodah service on Yom Kippur in the synagogue made him write and lecture on the Jewish imitations of Christian martyrology. Those who watched him knew that there was no contradiction in his soul between the two.[492]

Elie Wiesel marvels at Lieberman's success in integrating two seemingly contradictory tendencies:

> If there is a man who uplifted the love of the Torah to the level of scientific truth and Torah scholarship to the level of love; if there is a man who merged together in the Torah of Israel truth and beauty and discovered in it not only eternal values but also an aesthetic literary dimension of first-rate—it is Rabbenu Shaul.[493]

This integration of personality between the religious and intellectual dimension did not come without a struggle. In the letter of advice referred to earlier, sent by Lieberman to one who demonstratively turned down an honor tendered by the president of Israel, he said, "When a person appears well integrated, and without inner contradictions, we must examine him carefully, lest he not be alive at all, but is merely an advanced robot."[494]

In the final analysis, Lieberman, like his older colleague, Louis Ginzberg, perceived himself not as a radical innovator, rejecting traditional Jewish study and practice patterns. Quite the contrary: he saw himself on the path followed by Rabbi Elijah, the Gaon of Vilna, testifying that sophisticated textual analysis can coexist with deep religious piety, and critical historical study is no impediment to a traditional lifestyle. If anything, Lieberman would have proclaimed that the opposite was true. The following paragraph by Lieberman from *Greek in Jewish Palestine* could be applied to himself:

> The Rabbis of Palestine were familiar with the fashionable style of the civilized world of that time. Many of them were highly educated in Greek literature as has been proved above. But they were conscious of the superiority of Judaism. They used their learning to spread Judaism among the Gentiles, to enlighten the pagans and open their eyes to see the truth.[495]

CONCLUSION

In the mid-1960s, Lieberman experienced heart problems; he visited his cardiologist in the first week of August 1965 on Martha's Vineyard, and on August 12, 1965, Jessica Feingold wrote to Judith Lieberman that Finkelstein "was distressed to find [Lieberman] a bit depressed" over his failing health. He was prohibited from carrying heavy objects and thus no longer carried the Torah scroll in the Seminary synagogue. Finkelstein was deeply perturbed that Lieberman sometimes neglected to take his heart medication, and expressed amazement that Lieberman would so endanger his health.[496] Apparently, Lieberman suffered from eye problems that interfered with his studies; he attributed the difficulty to the pills he had been taking—so he stopped taking them!

Whatever his physical limitations may have been in the ensuing years, they were apparently unaccompanied by diminished intellectual capacity. Yaacov Sussmann recalls that on one occasion, in the last years of his life, Lieberman was in a state of great agitation because he was unable to locate a particular reference in *Devarim Rabbah*. The next morning, at 6:00, a relieved Lieberman telephoned to say that the reference was indeed there, but in a different edition of the text. His memory had not failed him. E. E. Urbach observed, "Until the last moment, he remained with the full power of his intellectual vigor, memory, and grasp. I, who have known him for forty-five years, could sense no difference . . . between his first days and his last days, as others will similarly testify."[497]

Impact and Influence

For the many students required to take his Talmud course who never truly knew him and had little interest in rabbinic literature, Lieberman may have been no more than a "tyrannical professor," with little impact on their lives. However for those, like Elie Wiesel, who chose to be his student, his impact was remarkable. According to Wiesel:

> What I learned from him is what, of all my knowledge, I value most. He made me aware that to be a Jew is to place the greatest store in knowledge and loyalty, that it is because he recognizes divine justice that he speaks out against human injustice. That it is because a Jew remains attached to his God that he is permitted to question Him. It is because the prophets loved the people of Israel that they admonished them and reprimanded their kings. Everything depends on where you stand, my master used to say. With God anything can be said. Without God nothing is heard. Without God what is said is not said.
>
> As I said, we met at least twice a week. Almost without preliminaries, we would sit down on opposite sides of his desk, the Babylonian and Palestinian Talmuds open before us, along with the corresponding books of commentary. Each session lasted three hours. Some subjects were familiar to me, for I had already studied them, though badly and hastily. That was true even of my studies with Shushani. Shushani was an *illui,* a genius of immense knowledge, but not a methodical teacher. Only at the end of his presentation would his perspective become clear to his students. Lieberman was an *illui,* too, but also a *harif* and a *baki,* a man whose brain encompasses everything and dissects it before your eyes. He would lead you and excite your imagination, but at every step you knew where he was taking you, at each turn you understood his intent. Where Shushani's teaching was intense but disjointed, Lieberman's was highly structured. With Shushani it was his erudition that fascinated you, while with Lieberman there was that and much more, including the beauty of his reasoning. He showed how everything is linked, how Greek culture and Latin culture are integral to the Tal-

> mud, that you could not appreciate the sages of Tzippori if you were ignorant of the ancients of Athens. (He had mastered ancient Greek and Latin and was fluent in French.) Thus, he could read my writings in the original French. He often returned what I gave him annotated and corrected. *Everything I write about the Bible and the Talmud, and even about Hasidism, bears his stamp, including the novels.*[498]

Indeed, there is much to learn from the character of Lieberman. He exemplified the assertion that a great man is like a Torah scroll—an object for study. He mastered the classical languages and the social, cultural, and economic history of the ancient Mediterranean world, in order to understand the Talmud in the context of the surrounding civilizations. He taught that the Rabbis were not ivory-tower meditators who speculated on and formulated idle questions, and he demonstrated that they understood the world they lived in, interacted with it, and, indeed, maintained their principles in the face of its challenges.

Lieberman was a pedagogue who valued clarity and precision in articulating the talmudic discussion, because for him, the talmudic argument was clear and lucid—its logic was airtight. Lieberman could not tolerate students who twisted its logic and engaged in circumlocutions. When a student purported to explain the Talmud text by saying, "Professor, I imagine that Rava's position is . . . ," he would stop him and say, "This is not philosophy, where you can replace knowledge and understanding with imagination! This is halakhah, the law, where you must know the reasoning precisely." He would not allow his students to lose sight of the golden thread running through the talmudic argument. In fact, he taught them to summarize many pages of Talmud in the form of two, three, or four basic concepts. One left his class with the most profound appreciation, awe, and respect for the greatness of the talmudic text. He pronounced the words of the text with love and affection, and the names of Rabbi Akiba and Rabbi Tarfon as those of scholars and saints whom he knew intimately, revered, and venerated.

In spite of Lieberman's towering intellect and scholarship, he was able to remain humble. He did not ask for respect, but gave it in great measure, and taught his students that to hurt another's feelings was a most serious infraction. A student in his class dare not even appear to laugh at an error made by another student in reciting the Talmud. He was sensitive to the feelings of his students, and never exhibited the self-centeredness that so often impedes communication between teacher and student. Lieberman met the world with a smile and a twinkle in his eyes, as he served God with love and joy. He lavished his love and attention on God's Torah, as he revealed its secrets. He similarly expressed his love and respect for people. Though he worked against the clock of mortality to complete the scholarly work that only he could complete, he would extend himself, whether for a student, a colleague, or a needy scholar who required assistance to publish a book or simply to subsist.

Lieberman loved the Land of Israel. He studied and taught in Palestine from 1928 to 1940 and, even after assuming his teaching position at JTS, divided his time between Jerusalem and New York. He brought light and clarity to the Palestinian Talmud, which we could not begin to understand without the aid of his scholarly work. He was deeply attached to the Land of Israel and its people. He knew what had occurred in that land throughout history—how the great ideas of the Talmud were forged by the Rabbis who walked the streets of Jerusalem, Caesarea, and Tiberias. This land, he believed, must again be a center of learning and insights to dispel the ignorance, corruption, and immorality that grip the world—as in the days of old, when the beacon of Jewish ethics and morality shone through the murky pretense and pomposity of the hypocritical and arrogant piety and sanctimony exhibited by Rome.

On Thursday, March 17, 1983, Louis Finkelstein sent a letter to Lieberman in anticipation of his forthcoming trip to Israel to celebrate Passover with his brother, Meir, in Jerusalem:

> I am sorry that you cannot come Friday night, but I do hope to see you before you leave. I am enclosing herewith a check for $50. $30 is for the children, as usual, and $20 for your brother to give away to some good cause.
>
> With best wishes for a pleasant trip and hoping to see you on your return.

Six days later, on March 23, Lieberman was flying to Israel. As the plane traveled through the heavens toward the land that he loved, the now elderly traveler told the stewardess that he would take a nap. He never awoke. Lieberman died in his sleep, probably from a thrombosis of the leg.[499] It was the sort of death described by the Talmud as "death by a kiss" reserved for the righteous, akin to "a hair being removed from milk."[500]

The El Al plane bore Lieberman to his burial place in Israel, where his beloved Judith was buried, and where the ancient Rabbis whom he loved and revered were buried. Lieberman, who died somewhere in the heavens as he traveled to the Promised Land, is the one who put the fear and love of heaven in the hearts of his students. He continues to live through the impact he had on people as a great human being and through his monumental books and essays, interpretations, and commentaries. He lives on in the hearts and minds of his students, colleagues, friends, and relatives, who will never forget him.

In the same way that R. Elijah the Gaon of Vilna stood as a transitional figure between traditional modes of scholarship and critical textual analyses, so Lieberman might best be viewed as a towering transitional figure in modern rabbinic scholarship. Lieberman epitomized the archetypal *talmid hakham* of the traditional Eastern European Lithuanian mode, with a deep reverence for his beloved texts. At the same time, he was a pioneer in the revolution advocating new methodological and scientific procedures, the espousing of an objective historical approach, and the possession of a comprehensive knowledge of the Hellenistic world and its realia. Indeed, Lieberman's methodology and approach to rabbinic scholarship have proven to be dominant, and most contemporary talmudic research bears his imprint.[501] Who will succeed Saul Lieberman? Most probably no one individual, but rather a team of interdisciplinary computer-wielding academicians[502] of whom many, perhaps most, would apply to themselves the characterization of "dwarfs standing on the shoulders of giants."[503] Saul Lieberman was and remains the giant among giants.

Epilogue

Two incidents involving Lieberman especially merit recounting: the widow of Alexander Marx was critically ill and was advised by her physician, Dr. Rapp, to eat on Yom Kippur. When she adamantly refused to hear of it, Dr. Rapp and the widow's friends turned to Lieberman, asking him to convince her that she *must* eat on Yom Kippur. Lieberman said that he would take care of the matter. He visited her on the eve of Yom Kippur and discussed everything *except* the issue of eating on Yom Kippur. Just as Lieberman was about to leave, he turned back and said, "When you eat tonight, be sure to include *Ya'ale Veyavo* when you *bentsch*." Mrs. Marx ate on Yom Kippur and recited the proper grace after meals.[504]

The other incident has to do with Rabbi J. B. Soloveitchik, who suffered the bereavement of his mother, brother, and wife within a three-month period. During the *shiva* for his wife, observed in his Brookline, Massachusetts, home, R. Soloveitchik, extremely sad and very depressed, sat on the floor with his visitors forced to remain silent for long periods because of the custom of refraining from speaking until the mourner first speaks. Lieberman, who traveled from New York, arrived at the home, and when R. Soloveitchik acknowledged his presence, Lieberman immediately engaged R. Soloveitchik in a vigorous, spirited halakhic debate concerning the laws of mourning, specifically the laws of mourning applicable to the high priest. According to Rabbi Haskel Lookstein:

> The discussion became extremely animated and was conducted in Yiddish and English interchangeably with, of course, a lot of Hebrew thrown in as well. It required referencing in certain books. Rabbi Aharon Lichtenstein, a son-in-law of the Rav, had to go up and down the stairs several times, bringing down *s'forim* that then were piled up on a coffee table in front of the Rav.
>
> The entire experience helped to draw the Rav from his state of great sadness and gave him a respite from his depressed feelings. It was a marvelous example of a combination of Rabbi Lieberman's key knowledge of Jewish law—including the fact that the only subject of halakhic discussion that the Rav could engage in during this period was the laws of mourning—and Rabbi Lieberman's sensitivity and *hesed* in trying to help Rabbi Soloveitchik emerge, if only temporarily, from his deep experience of mourning.[505]

As an eyewitness recalled the incident, "Lieberman knew exactly what he was doing. Every move was calculated precisely. This was a brilliant performance, psychologically astute, and done with great sensitivity. By involving R. Soloveitchik in an intense halakhic dispute, Lieberman was able to pull the Rav, at least temporarily, out of his depression."[506]

NOTES FOR PART II

1. E. S. Rosenthal, "Hamoreh," *Proceedings of the American Academy for Jewish Research* 31 (1963): 1–71; Heb. sec., p. 1.
2. The first reference is from David Weiss Halivni, "Professor Saul Lieberman," *Conservative Judaism* 38, no. 3 (spring 1986): 5; the second is from a lecture delivered by Halivni on Apr. 10, 2003, Lieberman's twentieth Yahrzeit, at a program sponsored by the Union for Traditional Judaism entitled "The Wisdom and Knowledge of the G'RaSh, the Greatest Baki since the Gaon of Vilna."
3. Michael Shashar, "Keter Torah, Veketer Hokhma," *Hadoar* 56, no. 15 (Feb. 11, 1977): 228.
4. Cited in Dimitrovsky, "Devarim al Gedol Hakhmei Doreinu," *Hadoar* 56, no. 15 (Feb. 11, 1977): 227.
5. Mordecai Margulies, "Rosh Hakhmei Yisrael Bedoreinu," *Hadoar* 42, no. 23 (Apr. 5, 1963): 373.
6. Ibid., p. 370.
7. This statement appears over Klausner's signature as well as those of Ephraim Shmueli and G. Kressel. It is a brief press release issued by the Bialik Prize judges committee, Jan. 2, 1958.
8. Yitzhak Gilat, "The Life's Work of Professor Saul Lieberman" (Heb.), *Bitzaron,* n.s., 9, nos. 35–36 (Sept. 1987): 53.
9. S. Spiro, interview with Meir Benayahu, Aug. 13, 1999. Benayahu praised Lieberman for his personal qualities, calling him *ish naim meod* (a very sweet man), *ratsui l'briyot, ish haviv,* and *ohev talmidei hahamim* (pleasant to others, a lovable person who loves scholars).
10. Quoted by Rabbi Nathan Kamenetsky, in an interview with E. Schochet, Mar. 16, 1997.
11. Jacob Neusner, letter dated Dec. 10, 1981. See Saul Lieberman Archives, box 6, "N–O" file. Cited by David Golinkin, "The Influence of Seminary Professors on Halakha in the Conservative Movement: 1902–1968," in *Tradition Renewed,* ed. Jack Wertheimer (New York, 1997), 2:473 n. 36. This accolade does not reflect Neusner's more recent views on Lieberman's scholarship. See, e.g., J. Neusner, "When Intellectual Paradigms Shift: Does the End of the Old Mark the Beginning of the New?" *History and Theory: Studies in the Philosophy of History* 27, no. 3 (1988): 241–60; *Wrong Ways and Right Ways in the Study of Formative Judaism: Critical Method and Literature, History, and the History of Religion* (Atlanta, 1988), pp. 3–27; *Studying Classical Judaism: A Primer* (Louisville, 1991), pp. 39–52; and *Why There Never Was a "Talmud of Caesarea": Saul Lieberman's Mistakes* (Atlanta, 1994), pp. 1–35.
12. Spiro, interview with Eli Ginzberg, Jan. 31, 1996.
13. Chaim Herzog, letter to Rabbi William Berkowitz, Aug. 16, 1983, in *In Praise*

of a Master: Tributes to Professor Saul Lieberman, ed. William Berkowitz, American Jewish Heritage Committee (New York, 1987), p. 12 of the 35 unnumbered pages.

14. Yitzhak Raphael, "Point of View: In the Company of the Great," *Jewish Press,* May 22, 1981, p. 50.
15. Yitzhak Raphael, "Professor Rabbi Shaul Lieberman," eulogy, *Sinai* 93 (5743 [Apr./May 1983]): 92.
16. Gilat, "The Life's Work of Professor Saul Lieberman," p. 53.
17. Rosenthal, "Hamoreh," 1–71, from an excerpt trans. Shamma Friedman, "Saul Lieberman and the Study of the Tosefta," p. 1.
18. Yehezkel Kutscher, "Prof. Saul Lieberman and His Linguistic Achievement (Heb.), *Hadoar* 42, no. 23 (Apr. 5, 1963): 377.
19. Shraga Abramson, "Darko shel Harav Shaul Lieberman b'Heker Hasifrut Hatalmudit," in *l'Zikhro shel Shaul Lieberman,* Israel Academy of Sciences and Humanities Annual (Jerusalem, 1984), p. 23.
20. Morton Smith, review of *Hellenism in Jewish Palestine,* by S. Lieberman, *Journal of Biblical Literature* (Mar. 1952): 55.
21. Marc B. Shapiro, ed., *Collected Writings of Rabbi Yehiel Yaakov Weinberg* (Heb.) (Scranton, 1998), 1:137–38. Weinberg letter to Lieberman is dated Nov. 27, 1956. The first three volumes received by R. Weinberg would likely have been *Zera'im,* published in 1955.
22. Abraham Goldberg, review of *Tosefta Kifshutah, Order Nashim,* by S. Lieberman, *Bibliotheca Orientalis* 26, nos. 1–2 (Jan.–Mar. 1969): 108.
23. Jacob Neusner, ed., *The Modern Study of the Mishna* (Leiden, 1973), pp. xvi–xvii.
24. Spiro, interview with Menahem Schmelzer, Dec. 3, 1996.
25. Yehezkel Kutscher, quoted in Aaron Kirschenbaum letter to S. Schochet, Oct. 6, 1997.
26. Daniel A. Greenberg and Daniel E. Gershenson, *Anaxagoras and the Birth of Physics* (New York, 1964), p. xxiv.
27. N. Kamenetsky, interview with Chaya Miriam Schulman, May 1997; Kamenetsky, *Making of a Godol: A Study of Episodes in the Lives of Great Torah Personalities* (Jerusalem, 2002).
28. See Saul Lieberman, "Bimhitzat Rabbanim," in *Mehkarim b'Torat Eretz Yisrael* (*Studies in Palestinian Talmudic Literature*), ed. David Rosenthal (Jerusalem, 1991), p. 517: Lieberman found the sum extravagant, feeling that he could not possibly spend the entire amount.
29. Rabbi Yaakov Kamenetsky related the episode to Schochet, July 1979. See Meir Halperin, *Hagadol Miminsk: R. Yerucham Yehuda Leib Perelmann* (Jerusalem, 1991). This book relates that R. Rabinowitz was chosen to be the husband of R. Perelmann's daughter, Feige, only after he passed rigorous written and oral examinations in Talmud. R. Rabinowitz, adopting the same criteria that his father-in-law had employed in choosing him, sought the most outstanding student of Slobodka as the husband for his daughter, Rachel.
30. Spiro, interview with Dr. Tibor Juda, Oct. 28, 1999.
31. Mark Jay Mirsky, interview with Lieberman in Jerusalem, 1982.
32. Spiro, interview with Haym Soloveitchik, Feb. 4, 1996.

33. Spiro, interview with Meir Lieberman, Aug. 10, 1999.
34. Spiro, interview with Haym Soloveitchik, Feb. 4, 1996.
35. Mirsky, interview with Lieberman, 1982.
36. Nissin Wachsman, "Lidmuto shel Hagaon Rav Shlomo Polachek z'l," *Talpiot* 1–2 (1953): 3–35.
37. *Beit Habehirah,* commentary on *Sanhedrin,* chap. 7, ed. Abraham Sofer, p. 210.
38. *Tosefta Bikkurim* 2:3; see *Tosefta Kifshutah Zera'im,* pt. 2, pp. 840–41.
39. Related to Nathan Kamenetsky by R. Samuel Hayyim Domb.
40. Abramson, "Darko shel Harav," p. 29.
41. Spiro, interview with David Rosenthal, Aug. 8, 1999.
42. Abraham Halkin to Schochet, July 1964.
43. The letters are dated Feb. 6, 1935, and May 23, 1940.
44. E.g., letters sent by Lieberman on May 31, 1937, Apr. 26, 1938, and Dec. 17, 1939.
45. E.g., letters sent on Jan. 11, 1930, and June 9, 1939.
46. "Did Saul Lieberman Know Latin or Greek?" in Jacob Neusner, *Why There Never Was a "Talmud of Caesarea,"* appendix 1, p. 137.
47. The Howard Jacobson paper, "Did Saul Lieberman Know Greek and Latin?" was delivered at a NAPH (National Association of Professors of Hebrew) panel, Nov. 20, 1995; repr. in *Saul Lieberman, 1898–1983: Talmudic Scholar,* ed. Meir Lubetski (Lewiston, N.Y., 2002), p. 19. Sara Mandell's response may be found in *Approaches to Ancient Judaism* 10, ed. Jacob Neusner (Atlanta, 1997), pp. 1–16.
48. Dec. 18, 1995, letter to Sara Mandell, p. 9. This letter was circulated among nineteen professors. See Howard Marblestone, "Lieberman **ΦΙΛΟΛΟΓΟΣ**: Professor Saul Lieberman as Lexicographer: Hebrew, Greek, Latin," in *Saul Lieberman, 1898–1983: Talmudic Scholar,* ed. Lubetski, p. 27.
49. Howard Marblestone, "Professor Saul Lieberman as Lexicologist and Philologist: Hebrew, Greek, Latin," paper delivered at NAPH panel (Nov. 20, 1995), p. 17; repr. as "Professor Saul Lieberman as Lexicographer: Hebrew, Greek, Latin," in *Saul Lieberman, 1898–1983: Talmudic Scholar,* ed. Lubetski, p. 25.
50. Marblestone, "Professor Saul Lieberman as Lexicologist," p. 1.
51. E. E. Urbach, "Shaul Lieberman Uterumato Lehlal Mada'ei Hayehudit," in *l'Zikhro,* pp. 14–15.
52. Florence Bar-Ilan, letter to Schochet, Apr. 1, 1996.
53. Spiro, interview with Abraham Goldberg, Aug. 2, 1999.
54. Histadrut Ivrit–*Hadoar* banquet on the (belated) occasion of Lieberman's seventy-fifth birthday, Feb. 13, 1977, New York. See Elie Wiesel, "Mori, Verabi" (My teacher, my rabbi), *Hadoar* 56, no. 17 (Feb. 25, 1977): 258–59 for a Hebrew text of the speech.
55. Elijah and Penina Schochet were with the Liebermans at Edgartown harbor on Martha's Vineyard during the first week of Aug. 1965.
56. Spiro, interview with Itamar Aviad, Aug. 12, 1999.
57. Lieberman solicited support for the publication of Grade's magnum opus, *Zemach Atlas,* from the Lucius N. Littauer Foundation and, on Sept. 18, 1968, received from Harry Starr, president of the foundation, a check for $2,000 for

Grade's publication. Lieberman, as president of the American Academy for Jewish Research, wrote to Grade, "On the Occasion of the Presentation of the Morris Adler Prize," Mar. 1967, commending the writer for offering an understanding of the life of Eastern European Jews and shedding light on the *musar* (ethics) movement. In Lieberman's words, "The work *Zemach Atlas* . . . possesses general human value as it illuminates the passions of youth in conflict and struggle with the higher dictates of ethics and morality." When Lieberman believed in the value of a person's work, and the honesty and integrity of the scholar or writer, he went to great lengths to assist him or her.

58. Spiro, interview with Dov Zlotnick, Sept. 21, 1995.
59. Lieberman, "A Testimonial" (Yiddish), *Di Goldene Kayt* 102 (1980): 8–11.
60. Many of those familiar with Finkelstein's desire to import elements of the Lithuanian yeshiva into the JTS atmosphere are surprised to learn that he was born in the United States and did not study in a Lithuanian yeshiva.
61. Lieberman, letter to Hayim Leaf, Feb. 19, 1981.
62. Ibid. The Leaf translation into Hebrew of Lieberman's Yiddish essay "An Eyduss" ("Al Chaim Grade Hamesapeir: Rishmei-Korei") appears in *Bitzaron* 3 (1981): 28–30.
63. Lieberman's letter to Anita Shapira, May 11, 1982, is a fine example of his literary power of expression. See below, section entitled "Integrity," for more on this letter.
64. Gilat, "The Life's Work of Professor Saul Lieberman," p. 52.
65. Seymour Siegel, in *In Praise of a Master,* ed. Berkowitz, pp. 22–23 of unnumbered pages.
66. Spiro, interview with Yehuda Shapira, Aug. 12, 1999.
67. Judith Lieberman, letter to Jessica Feingold, Apr. 29, 1955.
68. Spiro, interview with Burton Visotzky, Sept. 8, 1998.
69. Spiro, interview with Yitzhak Herzog, Aug. 9, 1999.
70. Spiro, interview with D. Rosenthal, Aug. 8, 1999.
71. Lieberman, letter to Jacob David Abramsky, June 28, 1968.
72. Spiro, interview with D. Zlotnick, Sept. 2, 1996.
73. Spiro, interview with Rabbi Haskel Lookstein, Nov. 13, 2000. This was Lookstein's recollection of his mother's account of Lieberman's response to her husband's question.
74. Spiro, interview with Y. Herzog, Aug. 9, 1999.
75. Lieberman, letter to Scholem, Feb. 5, 1956.
76. Lieberman, letter to Yalon, Nov. 1, 1965. Yalon had asked for permission to publish the comments, assuring Lieberman that he would make no changes. Lieberman explained that he had written the comments late at night without attention to style, since they were not written for publication. Lieberman said that he would accept any stylistic changes, provided they did not change the substance of his comments. In fact, the changes were minor and insignificant.
77. N. Kamenetsky, interview with Moshe Greenberg, Feb. 1999.
78. Spiro, interview with Itamar Aviad, Aug. 12, 1999.
79. Florence Bar-Ilan, letter to Schochet, Apr. 1, 1996; Lieberman, letter to Anita Shapira, May 31, 1982.

80. Lieberman, letter to Scholem, Dec. 22, 1974.
81. As a trustee for various funds and foundations, Lieberman was responsible for supervising the investment of funds. For example, a letter to Lieberman from Joseph Feuchtwinger of Loeb, Rhodes and Co. with regard to the AAJR (American Academy for Jewish Research) portfolio recommends to Lieberman a number of dispositions and acquisitions of securities.
82. Schochet, interview with Chaim Rogoff, Aug. 1997.
83. Formerly, Esso Corporation. Spiro, interview with D. Zlotnick, June 21, 1998. Zlotnick, Lieberman's student and intimate, served as the executor of Lieberman's estate.
84. Florence Bar-Ilan, letter to Schochet, Apr. 1, 1996.
85. Spiro, interview with Reuben Fink, Aug. 15, 1999.
86. Spiro, interview with Yaacov Sussmann, Aug. 5, 1999.
87. Haim Zalman Dimitrovsky, "Miparshanut l'Mehkar," in *l'Zikhro,* p. 38.
88. Lieberman, "A Talmud Written by the People in Their Own Land," an address on the dedication of a chair in the Jerusalem Talmud in Professor Lieberman's honor at Bar-Ilan University in Israel. The address was given in New York on June 4, 1980.
89. Tuvia Preschel, "Mahalakh Hayav Udmuto Haruhanit shel Rav Shaul Lieberman," *Hadoar* 42, no. 23 (Apr. 5, 1963): 370.
90. Urbach, "Shaul Lieberman Uterumato," p. 9; *Hayerushalmi Kifshuto* (Jerusalem, 1934).
91. Pinchas Peli, "Prof. Lieberman 'Kifshutah,'" *Hadoar* 65, no. 25 (May 9, 1986): 15–16.
92. Lieberman, letter to Scholem, Feb. 9, 1957; Lieberman, letter to Simha Assaf, Mar. 20, 1941.
93. N. Kamenetsky, interview with Aaron Kirschenbaum, July 10, 1997. Ta-Shma tells of a similar instance in which Lieberman reviewed by memory the entire Jerusalem Talmud in three minutes to find the discussion of a particular law. See Israel M. Ta-Shma, "Professor Saul Lieberman: In His Memory" (Heb.), in *Saul Lieberman, 1898–1983: Talmudic Scholar,* ed. Lubetski, p. 88.
94. Spiro, interview with Visotzky, Sept. 8, 1998.
95. David Weiss Halivni, eulogy for Lieberman, *Hadoar* 62, no. 25 (May 27, 1983): 404.
96. Urbach, "Shaul Lieberman Uterumato," p. 10.
97. Peli, "Prof. Lieberman 'Kifshutah,'" p. 16. See also P. Ben-Yair, a pseudonym for Pinchas Peli, "Hagaon Kifshuto," *Panim el Panim,* no. 517 (Apr. 18, 1969): 10.
98. Lieberman, letter to Eliezer Rosenthal, June 9, 1954.
99. D. Zlotnick, eulogy for Lieberman, "Professor Saul Lieberman z'l," *Proceedings of the Rabbinical Assembly* (1983), p. 204. This eulogy, "Professor Saul Lieberman, of Blessed Memory," appears as appendix IV to this volume.
100. Lieberman, "How Much Greek in Jewish Palestine?" in *Biblical and Other Studies,* ed. Alexander Altmann (Cambridge, Mass., 1963), p. 130; repr. in S. Lieberman, *Texts and Studies* (New York, 1974), p. 223.
101. Ibid., *Biblical and Other Studies,* p. 141; *Texts and Studies,* p. 234.
102. Lieberman, *Hellenism in Jewish Palestine* (New York, 1950, 1962), p. 120.

103. Lieberman, "Jewish Life in *Eretz Yisrael* as Reflected in the Palestinian Talmud," in *Israel: Its Role in Civilization,* ed. M. Davis (New York, 1956), p. 83, and in *Texts and Studies,* p. 181. Quotations from Lieberman texts referenced in nn. 100–103 above may be found in Shamma Friedman, "Kavim Lidmuto Hamada'it shel Profesor Shaul Lieberman z'l," *Newsletter of the World Union of Jewish Studies,* no. 23 (winter 1984): 25, second part of n. 6.
104. Elie Wiesel, *All Rivers Run to the Sea* (New York, 1995), p. 379.
105. Seymour Siegel said, "Above all he had amazing intellectual ability. His late wife, Judith Berlin Lieberman, once told me that he avoided reading newspapers. He had a photographic memory and therefore everything he read he retained. He did not want to clutter up his mind with ephemeral matters." *Sh'ma* 13, no. 253 (Apr. 29, 1983): 102–3, and in *In Praise of a Master,* ed. Berkowitz.
106. Tuvia Preschel, "R. Saul Lieberman: On Receiving the Israel Prize for Studies in Judaica," *Hadoar* 50, no. 25 (Apr. 30, 1971): 423.
107. Lieberman, *Hilkhot Hayerushalmi of Rabbi Moses ben Maimon* (New York, 1947).
108. Ibid., p. 3. L. Ginzberg, *Yerushalmi Fragments from the Geniza,* Jewish Theological Seminary (New York, 1909).
109. J. N. Epstein, "Lisredei Hayerushalmi" (Epstein's additions to the *Yerushalmi Fragments* of Louis Ginzberg), *Tarbiz* 3 (Oct. 1931): 21.
110. R. Isaac ben Jacob Alfasi (the Rif) was the author of *Sefer Hahalakhot,* the most important code prior to Maimonides' *Mishne Torah.*
111. See Y. K. Miklishansky, "Hibbur Hadash Larambam: A Newly Identified Work of Rambam," *Hadoar* 28, no. 7 (Dec. 17, 1948): 165–66. Although Miklishansky agrees that these fragments may be attributed to Maimonides, he suggests that they were not intended to serve as a code, but rather to assist him in the preparation of his code. He contends that Maimonides' normal practice was not simply to quote a source without in some way varying the style, adding and elaborating upon it; whereas this manuscript appears to be a plain and simple recitation of the law as stated in the *Yerushalmi* without variation or annotation. At the very least, contends Miklishansky, Lieberman has not proven his case. Miklishansky notes that Lieberman, at the conclusion of his analysis, is careful to leave open the possibility that this text may not be a code. Despite his dissent from Lieberman's hypothesis, Miklishansky expresses the highest praise for Lieberman's scholarship, noting the introduction to Lieberman's *Hilkhot Hayerushalmi,* a most erudite discussion of the different manuscripts of Maimonides' *Perush Hamishnayot* (commentary on the Mishnah), along with an analysis of apparent contradictions between the latter and the *Mishne Torah* (the Code) in the light of variant readings between the manuscripts and the printed edition. This lengthy introduction constitutes a successful blending of the "old" (yeshiva) style of talmudic learning with the modern scientific approach. Furthermore, Lieberman's great strength is reflected in his restoration of the text of the *Ketubot* portion, where he faced an especially deficient text. Miklishansky asserts that Lieberman prepared this introduction, text, and extensive explanatory notes with careful attention to every detail, bringing his "abundant wisdom and knowl-

edge that comes from intense diligence, scientific precision, and love of the subject matter all together." In "Mifa'alo shel Gaon" (The gaon's work), which appeared in the special edition of *Hadoar* honoring Lieberman, 11 Nissan 5723 (Apr. 5, 1963): 374–75, Miklishansky summarizes his earlier views, which are unchanged from those set out in his 1948 essay.

See also "Manuscript Discovered in Cairo 50 Years Ago Found to Have Been Written by Maimonides," *New York Times,* Dec. 11, 1947, and "Seminary Progress," Jan. 1948, pp. 6, 11, reporting on a Seminary luncheon to mark the publication of the Maimonides text, in which Rabbi Meir Berlin, president of the World Mizrachi Organization and Lieberman's father-in-law, was a guest speaker.

112. E. S. Rosenthal, in "Hamoreh," pp. 32–34, cites a number of instances where Lieberman's textual revisions, arrived at by logical reasoning, were subsequently confirmed by the appearance of new manuscripts. For example, Lieberman's "Tikkunei Yerushalmi," *Tarbiz* 2, no. 2 (1931): 235, 239 (*Mehkarim b'Torat Eretz Yisrael,* pp. 174, 178), discusses a reference in the Palestinian Talmud (*Kiddushin* 1:5; 58:3) to "R. Yochanan D'Tzipori." This reference is puzzling because R. Yochanan was not identified with Sephorus, having studied instead in the yeshiva in Caesarea. Bacher dealt with the difficulty by simply changing the name of the amora to R. Chanen (R. Chanina). Lieberman, however, sensed that this text was faulty because the Palestinian Talmud never spells the term Tziporin "Chasear" (i.e., with the *vav* missing) and concluded, on the basis of *Bereshit Rabbah* 18:5 (Theodor Albeck, p. 167), that the passage should read: "R. Yochanan Amar Diyuparin." (In the event of divorce, a gentile woman gives her husband a double payment.) Lieberman suggested that the copyist had deleted the word *amar* and joined the letters *yod* and *vav* to read *tsadi.* This reading allows Lieberman to restore a portion of the text that had been omitted by the copyist. Four years later, in his *Hayerushalmi Kifshuto* (Jerusalem, 1934), introduction, p. 18, Lieberman reported that his reading found support in the Leiden manuscript of the Palestinian Talmud.

See also Rosenthal above, and Lieberman, "Tikkunei Yerushalmi," *vav* (sixth essay in series), *Tarbiz* 5, no. 1 (Oct. 1933): 97, 107–10; *Mehkarim b'-Torat Eretz Yisrael* (*Studies in Palestinian Talmudic Literature*), pp. 201–13, for explanations of terminology; for example, *garash, garas,* which means "etc." and refers to a phrase that is found elsewhere in the rabbinic literature. Lieberman explains that where certain phrases appeared elsewhere in rabbinic literature and were thought to be well known, there was no need to reproduce them in the instant text. However, scribes were often unaware of this, and emended or misinterpreted the word *garash,* with the result that its meaning was obscured, with Lieberman even citing a text where it was thought to be an acrostic.

Thus, where a particular statement or sequence of statements was familiar to the scribe because it appeared elsewhere in rabbinic literature, it was either condensed or was not referred to at all in the text. (See above, "Tikkunei Yerushalmi"; *Mehkarim b'Torat Eretz Yisrael,* pp. 200, 210–13). When the Palestinian Talmud frequently repeated statements in a number of different contexts, subsequent scribes or copyists were accustomed to delete the text that was the same as that found in other sections of the *Talmud Yerushalmi* (Lieberman, *Hilkhot Hayerushalmi,* introduction, p. 15). However, when a copyist chose not to include para. 1 in section A because it was repeated in section B, and section B itself was missing in subsequent editions of the *Yerushalmi,* the result would be the loss of para. 1, which could not be reconstituted by reference to the other section of the *Yerushalmi* itself! Lieberman would attempt to fill such gaps by reference to the works of the rishonim (early authorities, from about the mid-eleventh to the mid-fifteenth century). For example, Lieberman located a section in our literature, *Yalkut Hamakiri,* which, by noting the similarity in the pattern of the phrasing, he identified as belonging to the second chapter of *Yerushalmi Makkot,* where the term *gorash* indicated a missing section. "Tikkunei Yerushalmi" (1933): 109.

Twelve years later, Shlomo Wiedder published "A Fragment of Yerushalmi from Geniza Fragments in Budapest," *Tarbiz* 17, nos. 3–4 (Apr.–July 1946): 129 (cited in Rosenthal, "Hamoreh," pp. 32–33), which included the text that Lieberman had restored. Wiedder wrote (p. 130), "Everything that was missing and abbreviated in our text is found in its entirety in a section of this manuscript [and] everything was found in the manuscript just as Lieberman had explained in *Tarbiz.*"

Lieberman had also reconstructed an entire missing section at the end of Yerushalmi *Makkot* chap. 3, by referencing a number of texts (*Sefer Ha'emunah v'Habitahon Hameyuhas Laramban; Matnot Kehuna* on *Bereshit Rabbah;* midrash *Tehillim;* R. Shimon ben Zemach Duran's *Magen Avot; Devarim Rabbah*), on the basis of which he was able to reconstruct his version of the missing text (Wiedder, p. 130; Rosenthal, pp. 32–33; *Hilkhot Hayerushalmi,* supplement 1, pp. 67–68). Wiedder's manuscript confirmed Lieberman's reconstruction in every detail, including the order of the passages.

In *Hilkhot Hayerushalmi,* supplement 1, pp. 67–68, Lieberman reproduces *Yerushalmi Makkot,* chap. 3, and refers to Wiedder's manuscript confirming the text he had reconstructed *al pi hasvara* (by logical deduction). He adds, "*uvarukh megaleh ha'emet* [blessed is he who reveals the truth]," p. 67. Lieberman thus congratulates Wiedder for disclosing a text that confirms what was previously only a hypothesis on Lieberman's part. Of course, the reference may be to Lieberman himself. This is indeed Lieberman's objective: to find the truth, the true text, the *peshat,* the true interpretation.

113. Kutscher, "Prof. Saul Lieberman and His Linguistic Achievement," pp. 377–78. Kutscher cites examples where Lieberman explains difficult words. In addition, he recounts Lieberman's formulation of the two views dealing with the publication of the Mishnah, namely, that "every scholar wrote the Mishnah for his private use, whereas others maintain that the Mishnah and the Talmud were not reduced to writing until the post-talmudic period." Lieberman, "The Publication of the Mishnah," in *Hellenism in Jewish Palestine,* pp. 83–84. Kutscher is impressed with how Lieberman marshals the evidence in favor of the first view, supporting it with references to the talmudic sources, along with the recounting of the reality of the way books were published in the ancient world.

114. A. Goldberg, review of *Tosefta Kifshutah, Nashim,* p. 108.
115. Solomon Spiro, "The Moral Vision of Saul Lieberman: A Historiographic Approach to Normative Jewish Ethics," *Conservative Judaism* 46, no. 4 (summer 1994): 64, 71–72.
116. Lieberman, "The Martyrs of Caesarea," *Annuaire de l'institut de philologie et d'histoire orientales et slaves* 7 (1939–44): 395, emphasis added.
117. *Ha'azinu,* para. 307, Finkelstein, ed., p. 346; cited in S. Lieberman, "The Persecution of the Jewish Religion," in *Jubilee Volume in Honor of Salo W. Baron,* ed. Lieberman (Jerusalem and New York, 1974), p. 213, and in *Studies in Palestinian Talmudic Literature,* ed. D. Rosenthal, p. 348. Lieberman analyzes the rabbinic sources concerning the Hadrianic persecutions from a historiographic perspective. See also Spiro, "The Moral Vision of Saul Lieberman," pp. 69–75, for a discussion of Lieberman's treatment of the Hadrianic persecution.
118. Lieberman, "The Persecution of the Jewish Religion," p. 218, and *Studies in Palestinian Talmudic Literature,* p. 353.
119. Lieberman, "The Persecution of the Jewish Religion," p. 232, and *Studies in Palestinian Talmudic Literature,* p. 367. See also Spiro, "The Moral Vision of Saul Lieberman," p. 73.
120. Lieberman, "The Persecution of the Jewish Religion," pp. 218–19, and *Studies in Palestinian Talmudic Literature,* pp. 353–54.
121. S. Lieberman, *Tosefta Kifshutah* (New York, 1973), 8:904; *Studies in Palestinian Talmudic Literature,* p. 13. Lieberman refers to the interpretation he described with the words *karov b'einai* as a *hashara* (a conjecture).
122. Lieberman, *Hilkhot Hayerushalmi of Rabbi Moses ben Maimon,* preface, p. 3: "Whether the manuscript was from the hand of the Rambam or from a scribe who copied it, *hasefer atsmo hu bivadai shel haram.*"
123. N. Kamenetsky, interview with Meir Lieberman, Sept. 18, 1996.
124. Bernard Mandelbaum, *Tales of the Fathers of the Conservative Movement* (New York, 1989), p. 22.
125. Cited in Louis Finkelstein, "Doctor Saul Lieberman: An Appreciation," *United Synagogue Review* (fall 1983): 3.
126. Spiro, interview with David Novak, Oct. 26, 1999.
127. Moshe Zucker to Elijah Schochet at a national convention of the Rabbinical Assembly of America.
128. E. S. Rosenthal, "Hamoreh," pp. 70–71.
129. Spiro, interview with H. Soloveitchik, Nov. 9, 1998.
130. Halivni, eulogy for Lieberman, p. 404.
131. N. Kamenetsky, interview with Shamma Friedman, Feb. 1999.
132. David Weiss Halivni, *The Book and the Sword* (New York, 1996), pp. 80–81.
133. Lieberman, letter to Finkelstein, Apr. 28, 1969. Obviously, he means "bother" in the sense of "pester."
134. Spiro, interview with Eli Ginzberg, Jan. 31, 1996.
135. Lieberman, letter to H. Oberman, Mar. 21, 1966.
136. Lieberman, letter to G. D. Kilpatrick, Dec. 19, 1952.
137. Lieberman, letter to William Henderson, editorial director of the Standard Reference Library, Feb. 16, 1970.

138. A. D. Nock, letter to Lieberman, Feb. 9, 1948. Dimitrovsky reports that Lieberman had great respect and high regard for Nock. Dimitrovsky, "Miparshanut l'Mehkar," p. 39 ("From Commentary to Scholarship," appendix III, p. 284).
139. Lieberman, letter to Israel Elfenbein, Mar. 21, 1960. Elfenbein listed the names of the scholars who were scheduled to participate, in order to impress and entice Lieberman. But among them were names of some scholars whom Lieberman did not particularly respect. This explains his somewhat caustic response.
140. Lieberman, letter to Kilpatrick, Dec. 19, 1952.
141. N. Kamenetsky, interview with Kirschenbaum, Mar. 10, 1977.
142. Mandelbaum, *Tales of the Fathers,* pp. 30–31; another reference to this incident is in Finkelstein, "Doctor Saul Lieberman: An Appreciation," p. 3.
143. Moshe Zevi Neriah, ed., *Likkutei Hare'ayah* (Bene Berak, 1990), 2:92.
144. Lieberman, letters to Finkelstein, July 9, 1945, and July 30, 1946.
145. Lieberman, letter to Finkelstein, July 21, 1947. Translation in brackets added. See Harvey E. Goldberg, "Becoming History," in *Tradition Renewed,* ed. Wertheimer, 1:355, 372 n. 62, and 428, for a discussion of Lieberman's humor and use of the double entendre in the letter to Finkelstein.
146. Judith Lieberman, letter to Jessica Feingold, Aug. 8, 1971.
147. Lieberman, "Bimhitzat Rabbanim," p. 609 n. 27.
148. Spiro, "The Moral Vision of Saul Lieberman," pp. 66–67.
149. Spiro, interview with Novak, Oct. 26, 1999. Novak describes how Lieberman stood secluded behind a curtain with a Talmud text on his *shtender,* his face luminous with the *ziwha shekhina* (divine splendor) reflecting the joy he found in the study of Torah. Novak recalls that when a student in his class offered a correct interpretation of a difficult section of the Talmud, Lieberman's face would reveal that same expression of joy.
150. Lieberman, "A Talmud Written by the People in Their Own Land."
151. In reality, Lieberman's brother, Meir, was a younger brother, having been born in 1908.
152. Wiesel, *All Rivers Run to the Sea,* p. 401.
153. Spiro, interview with Judith Hauptman, Oct. 20, 1999.
154. Siegel, *In Praise of a Master,* ed. Berkowitz, p. 23.
155. David Golinkin, *The Responsa of Professor Louis Ginzberg* (New York, 1996), pp. 4–6.
156. Eli Ginzberg, *Keeper of the Law: Louis Ginzberg* (Philadelphia, 1966), p. 330.
157. Louis Finkelstein, in his tribute to Ginzberg and Marx, observed that the Gaon's "method and urge were the source of Professor Ginzberg's approach." Finkelstein, "Our Teachers," *Proceedings of the Rabbinical Assembly of America* 18 (1955): 171.
158. Lieberman wrote "Mishnat Shir Hashirim," in *Jewish Gnosticism, Merkabah Mysticism, and Talmudic Tradition,* ed. G. Scholem (New York, 1965), pp. 118–26, as well as an essay in the appendix for *Apocalyptic and Merkabah Mysticism,* ed. Ithamar Gruenwald (Leiden, 1980), pp. 235–44, in addition to supplying Scholem with much research on Gnosticism.
159. Wiesel, *All Rivers Run to the Sea,* p. 398. Some among the Orthodox, suspi-

cious of Lieberman because of his affiliation with JTS, have used this statement to condemn him as an *apikores* (nonbeliever). One should not, however, draw such conclusions from a mere desire to be clever and joke with a dear friend. Lee Levine recalls Lieberman using the identical "nonsense" phrase when introducing Yigal Yadin, although he clearly had no lack of respect for the findings of archaeology. Cynthia Ozick, in "The Heretic: The Mythic Passions of Gershom Scholem" (*The New Yorker,* Sept. 2, 2002, pp. 143–48), portrays young Gershom emerging from an assimilated family to assert his commitment as a Zionist. It is unfortunate that Ozick repeats the "now legendary maxim" about nonsense (p. 145), thereby leaving the reader with the impression that this quip accurately reflected the relationship between Lieberman and Scholem. The extent to which Lieberman's extensive correspondence with Scholem reveals Lieberman's feelings about various issues (e.g., his relationship with JTS, his views on other scholars, and even his regret about not being in Israel at critical times) attests to the close relationship between these two intellectual giants. Ozick's illuminating portrait of Scholem reveals his great courage in breaking away from an environment characterized by intense loyalty to "the fatherland" to assert his commitment to Zionism and Jewish scholarship. Lieberman would likely not have regarded his friend and colleague as a purveyor of "nonsense" in the way that this account might suggest.

160. Spiro, interview with Schmelzer, Mar. 22, 1996. We thank Prof. Schmelzer for making a copy of the letter available to us. See Aviad Hacohen, "Litoldot Mada'ei Hayahadut: Igrot Chachamim" (The history of Jewish studies: Letters of scholars), *Mada'ei Hayahadut* 33 (1993): 33, for discussion of Immanuel Loew, his correspondence, and two letters to Saul Lieberman.
161. Lieberman, "The Role of Professor Louis Ginzberg in Jewish Scholarship," address delivered on Nov. 28, 1943, at JTS.
162. Halivni, *The Book and the Sword,* p. 89.
163. Introduction to *Beurai Hagra al Shulhan Arukh, Orah Hayyim* (Vilna, 1874/75); Joshua Heschel Lewin, *Aliyot Eliahu* (Vilna, 1855), p. 38a n. 77.
164. Elijah Judah Schochet, *The Hasidic Movement and the Gaon of Vilna* (Northvale, N.J., 1994), pp. 188–89.
165. Solomon Schechter, "The Beginnings of Jewish *Wissenschaft,*" in idem, *Seminary Addresses and Other Papers* (New York, 1969), p. 183.
166. Lieberman likewise criticized those who neglected to consult these texts, very often in a subtle, but no less forthright, manner.
167. Schochet, *The Hasidic Movement,* p. 195 n. 191.
168. Lawrence Kaplan, "The Hazon Ish: Haredi Critic of Traditional Orthodoxy," in *The Uses of Tradition: Jewish Continuity in the Modern Era,* ed. Jack Wertheimer (New York, 1992), p. 155 n. 33. Kaplan notes, with respect to the comparison: "This, of course, is not to deny the many important differences between their approaches."
169. Baruch of Shklov, "Introduction and Translation of Euclid's Geometry," in *Sefer Euclides* (The Hague, 1780). Baruch was a paternal ancestor of Lieberman. Lieberman, letter to Scholem, Oct. 26, 1971.
170. Hillel of Shklov, *Kol Hator* (Jerusalem, 1969), 2:5. Cited in Joshua Levi, *Torah*

Study (New York, 1990), p. 248. See Schochet, *The Hasidic Movement,* pp. 149–51.

171. Schochet, *The Hasidic Movement,* p. 150.
172. Ibid., p. 233 n. 23. See approbation of Avraham Simcha of Amtishyislov to Kalman Shulman's translation of Josephus's *War of the Jews* (1883).
173. Cited in Shamma Friedman, "Shaul Lieberman: Hora'ato Be'al Peh Uviktav," in *l'Zikhro,* p. 55.
174. Saul Lieberman, *Hellenism in Jewish Palestine* (New York, 1950), p. 19; also, Lieberman, *Greek in Jewish Palestine / Hellenism in Jewish Palestine,* with a new introduction by Dov Zlotnick (New York, 1994).
175. Introduction of Hayyim of Volozhin to Gaon's commentary on *Sifrei Dizeniuta* (Vilna, 1882).
176. Lieberman, letter to Yaakov Kenaani, July 29, 1963. Kenaani was the main author (assisted by other scholars) of an eighteen-volume work entitled *Otsar Halashon Ha'ivrit* (Tel Aviv, 1960). He sent Lieberman four volumes (probably the first four), whose receipt he acknowledged in the above letter. Kenaani continued to send him single volumes as they were published. When Lieberman suggested that he incorporate the work of the ancient liturgical poets, Kenaani concluded that Lieberman was critical of his books. Lieberman wrote Kenaani that it pained him that he had made such an inference and reassured him of his regard for his work and reminded him that he had secured funding for the publication of his book from a fund that Rabbi Morris Adler had placed at Lieberman's disposal (letter from Lieberman to Kenaani, June 9, 1974).
177. Dimitrovsky, "Miparshanut l'Mehkar," p. 42 ("From Commentary to Scholarship," appendix III, p. 287); introduction to *Pe'at Hashulhan of Israel b. Samuel Ashkenazi of Shklov* (Safed, 1836; repr. Jerusalem, 1958). See Schochet, *The Hasidic Movement,* pp. 190–91.
178. Albeck letters are dated Dec. 27, 1955, and Sept. 18, 1957; Aptowitzer letters from Lieberman are dated Nov. 17, 1938, and Dec. 21, 1938; Assaf letters from Lieberman are dated Sept. 13, 1941, and June 26, 1953; Nock letters are dated Jan. 12, 1951, and Feb. 9, 1948; Urbach letters are dated Mar. 2, 1982, and Nov. 1, 1982; Smith letter, July 15, 1979; Braude letter, Sept. 23, 1962; Baer letter, Apr. 17, 1953; and Bickerman letter, undated.
179. Lieberman, letter to Scholem, Jan. 6, 1972.
180. Letters, Apr. 30, 1956, and Feb. 27, 1970, respectively.
181. Letter, Feb. 1, 1972.
182. Letter, undated.
183. Shapiro, ed., *Collected Writings of Rabbi Yehiel Yaakov Weinberg,* pp. 73–74 n. 20. Letter from Rabbi Weinberg to Lieberman, Sept. 27, 1954. The ceremony releasing the widow from the biblical ordinance of levirate marriage includes the requirement concerning a special *halitsah* shoe to be worn on the right foot.
184. Lieberman explains in his letter intended for Levi Eshkol, the prime minister of Israel, that despite the pressure to do so, he does not wish to offer an opinion on the issue of the performance of autopsies in Israel. Israel, he says, has enough problems on this issue from its own people, and for his

part he is not prepared to add "confusion upon confusion." However, Lieberman continues, he is obligated to warn that the problem is not merely a religious one. He noted that we have here an issue arousing deep feelings on a universal basis. The practice in Israel of performing autopsies without the permission of the family is liable to bring about damage to the country whose serious consequences are difficult to estimate. While professing not to offer an opinion on the issue, Lieberman's sensitive and humane proposal goes a long way to solving the problem in Israel. Once the permission of the family is required to perform an autopsy, it would be open to a religious family to forbid it.

185. Lieberman, letter to Ben-Gurion, Dec. 16, 1949, reproduced in *Jewish Identity, Modern Responsa and Opinions on the Registration of Children of Mixed Marriages: David Ben-Gurion's Query to Leaders of World Jewry,* a documentary compilation by Baruch Litwin, ed. Sidney B. Hoenig (New York, 1965), pp. 236–39.
186. Lieberman, letter to Chaim Levanon, mayor of Tel Aviv, Oct. 2, 1957.
187. Mordecai Margulies, in a letter to Lieberman, Dec. 26, 1958, wrote that the Bialik Prize was far more prestigious than the Kook Prize.
188. The prize was awarded to Lieberman by the Haifa Technion "in recognition of his investigations into the civilizations of the peoples of the Middle East in the Hellenistic and Roman periods and of his great and profound commentaries of the sources of talmudic literature. His erudition in Hebrew literature over the ages, his mastery of Greco-Roman literature and its offshoots, joined with his brilliant exegetic insight, unearthed a wealth of information highly significant for understanding the history of religions, popular beliefs, law, legal institutions, medicine, and mores of daily life." At the award ceremony, Lieberman delivered a lecture, "Kashe Hi Haleitsut," which appears in *Hadoar* 56, no. 15 (Feb. 11, 1977): pp. 226–27, and in *Studies in Palestinian Talmudic Literature,* p. 618.
189. J. Lookstein, letter to Professor O. Schachter, June 1, 1966.
190. J. Lookstein, letter to Lieberman, Mar. 18, 1970.
191. Jan. 5, 1966. This was a two-page, single-spaced Hebrew typewritten letter, wherein Lieberman presented a discourse on university administration, suggesting that faculty members should not be involved in administration and should concentrate their efforts on their studies. We are grateful to Rabbi Haskel Lookstein for granting us access to the archives of his father, Rabbi Joseph Lookstein.
192. Shapira letter dated May 14, 1968; Warhaftig letters dated Jan. 28, 1972, and Mar. 21, 1972.
193. Letter dated Jan. 5, 1966, p. 2.
194. Lieberman, letter to Samuel Rothberg, Sept. 24, 1971.
195. Frank Moore Cross, letter to Schochet, Mar. 3, 1997. These events took place in 1964. Cross says, "A few years later I nominated [Lieberman] for an honorary doctorate," and Lieberman was awarded the degree by Harvard University, June 16, 1966.
196. E. Ginzberg, letter to Schochet, Aug. 8, 1997.
197. Zlotnick, introduction to *Greek in Jewish Palestine / Hellenism in Jewish Pales-*

tine, p. xiii; "Professor Saul Lieberman, of Blessed Memory," appendix IV to this volume.

198. Cited in Dimitrovsky, "Devarim al Gedol Hakhmei Doreinu," *Hadoar* 56, no. 15 (Feb. 11, 1977): 227.
199. Raymond Martini, a Spanish Dominican friar of the thirteenth century, wrote *Pugio Fidei,* in order to derive proofs of the Christian faith from rabbinic texts. Lieberman, interested in the versions of the texts cited, had an extensive discussion of the text and the author in *Shkiin,* cited below, next note.
200. *Shkiin*/Yemenite midrashim, 2d ed. (Jerusalem, 1970), pp. iii–vi (Eng.); pp. 43–102 (Heb.). It should be noted that Yitzhak Baer took issue with Lieberman, contending that Martini's work was a fabrication: "The Forged Midrashim of Raymond Martini and Their Place in the Religious Controversy of the Middle Ages," in *Studies in Memory of Asher Gulak and Samuel Klein* (Heb.) (Jerusalem, 1942), pp. 28–48. See also Lieberman's response to Baer's argument: "Raymond Martini and His Alleged Forgeries," in *Historia Judaica* 5 (1943): 87–102, reprinted in Lieberman, *Texts and Studies,* pp. 285–300. Robert Chazan, commenting on this difference between the two scholars, concludes, "It is striking that in this matter the historical judgment of the talmudist Lieberman was superior to that of the historian of medieval Spanish Jewry, Baer." Chazan, *Daggers of Faith: Thirteenth-Century Christian Missionizing and Jewish Response* (Berkeley, 1989), p. 202 n. 9.
201. Jacob Neusner, *Symbol and Theology in Early Judaism* (Minneapolis, 1991), pp. 172–73.
202. Lieberman, "The Alleged Ban on Greek Wisdom," in *Hellenism in Jewish Palestine,* p. 100; "The Persecution of the Jewish Religion," p. 213; "The Phenomenon of the *Bat Kol,*" in *Hellenism in Jewish Palestine,* appendix 1, p. 194.
203. E. S. Rosenthal, "Hamoreh," pp. 10–11.
204. A phrase employed by Haym Soloveitchik to indicate that Lieberman had concentrated on and illuminated neglected texts. Similarly, Abraham Goldberg, in his review in the *Jerusalem Post* of Lieberman's *Sifrei Zuta* and the Talmud of Caesarea states: "Yet [Lieberman] has made his mission in particular the restoration to their proper place of importance of those classic works of the mishnaic and talmudic eras that have been unjustly eclipsed and neglected because of the dominating place of the Babylonian Talmud."
205. E. S. Rosenthal, "Hamoreh," pp. 59–60.
206. Schochet, interview with Rogoff, a distant cousin of Lieberman, Aug. 1997.
207. Preschel, "Mahalakh Hayav," p. 370.
208. Meir Lieberman explained that Rabbi Gershonowitz, while living with his father-in-law in Motol, perceived Lieberman's great genius and not only advised him to go to Malch, but physically brought him to the yeshiva there. Rabbi Gershonowitz eventually took a position in B'nai Brak. Spiro, interview with Meir Lieberman, Aug. 4, 1999.
209. Preschel, "Mahalakh Hayav." Also, Abramson, "Darko shel Harav," p. 25. Meir Lieberman told Zlotnick that the laudatory letter was sent by Lieberman's grandfather.
210. Spiro, interview with D. Zlotnick, Nov. 6, 1997.
211. Richard L. Rubenstein, *Power Struggle* (New York, 1974), p. 127.

212. Yonason Rosenblum, *Reb Yaakov: The Life and Times of HaGaon Rabbi Yaakov Kamenetsky* (Brooklyn, N.Y., 1993), p. 20.
213. Abramson, "Darko shel Harav," p. 25.
214. Lieberman, letter to Scholem, Mar. 8, 1960.
215. Lieberman, *Sifrei Zuta* (Heb.) (New York, 1968), introduction, p. viii. Part 2 of the book is "The Talmud of Caesarea," a response to Epstein's criticism of Lieberman's thesis concerning the origins of the Palestinian Talmud, *Nezikin.*
216. Ibid. Lieberman describes it as *k'tavlin bin'ima* (spice in a melody). The reference is to *Arakhin* 2:6, which refers to *tevel bin'ima,* designating children who join in the singing in the Temple service, thereby adding spice and sweetness to the melody of the adults.
217. "Lahpor Pairot Vela'ataleifim," in *Studies in Palestinian Talmudic Literature,* pp. 466–69.
218. Ibid., p. 468.
219. *Bava Metzia* 84b. See Lieberman, *Greek in Jewish Palestine,* pp. 146–47, for a discussion of the statement by R. Mathia b. Heresh, "Be a tail to lions and not a head to foxes."
220. Spiro, interview with Emanuel Gettinger, Mar. 21, 1996.
221. N. Kamenetsky, interview with Abramson, Oct. 4, 1997.
222. Lieberman to Rabbi Jacob Schochet, "*Er iz geven a kluger—der alter.*"
223. Cf. *Levush Mordechai* of R. Moshe Mordechai Epstein.
224. Spiro, interview with Emunah Katzenstein, Aug. 3, 1999.
225. Abramson, "Darko shel Harav," p. 26.
226. For more on the *musar* movement, see Immanuel Etkes, *Rabbi Israel Salanter and the Musar Movement* (Philadelphia, 1993); and Dov Katz, *Tenuat Hamusar,* 5 vols. (Heb.) (Tel Aviv, 1956–65).
227. Lieberman, letter (Heb.) to Anita Shapira, May 31, 1982. The Hebrew *sin'ah tiv'it* means "ingrained antipathy" to mendacity and hypocrisy.
228. Lieberman, letters to Scholem, Jan. 5, 1959, and Nov. 10, 1958.
229. Gershom Scholem, "New Contributions to the Biography of Rabbi Joseph Ashkenazi of Safed," *Tarbiz* 28, no. 1 (Oct. 1958): 59–89. Upon receipt of the article, Lieberman wrote Scholem (Nov. 10, 1958) of his earlier displeasure when first informed that Scholem had planned to dedicate an article to him, because he wished on principle to discourage such tributes. However, after reading the article and the dedication, Lieberman felt better about it—presumably because of the stellar character and honest scholarship of Ashkenazi, and the dedication to "R. Saul Lieberman, the Tanna of New York, on His Jubilee [sixtieth birthday]."
230. Lieberman, foreword to *Hasdei David* (Jerusalem, 1970).
231. Lieberman, *Sifrei Zuta* (New York, 1968), p. 136. See also Urbach, "Shaul Lieberman Uterumato," p. 20.
232. Spiro, "The Moral Vision of Saul Lieberman," pp. 77–78.
233. D. Rosenthal, *Studies in Palestinian Talmudic Literature* (Heb.), p. 12; see Spiro, "The Moral Vision of Saul Lieberman," pp. 67–68.
234. Lieberman, "Palestine in the Third and Fourth Centuries," *Jewish Quarterly Review* 36, no. 4 (Apr. 1946): 353; repr. in Lieberman, *Texts and Studies,* p. 136.

235. Lieberman, "How Much Greek in Jewish Palestine?" in *Biblical and Other Studies,* p. 134; in *Texts and Studies,* p. 227. See Spiro, "The Moral Vision of Saul Lieberman," p. 76.
236. Lieberman, "This Is the Way It Was" (Heb.), in D. Rosenthal, *Studies in Palestinian Talmudic Literature,* p. 331. See Spiro, "The Moral Vision of Saul Lieberman," p. 79.
237. See Spiro, "The Moral Vision of Saul Lieberman," pp. 79–80 n. 89, referring to Lieberman's supplementary note to *Vayikra Rabbah,* ed. Margulies.
238. Ibid., pp. 80–81.
239. Lieberman, *Greek in Jewish Palestine,* p. 84.
240. Gedalyahu Alon, review of *Greek in Jewish Palestine,* by S. Lieberman (Heb.), *Kiryat Sefer* 20 (1943/44): 76, repr. in G. Alon, *Studies in Jewish History in the Times of the Second Temple, the Mishnah, and the Talmud* (Jerusalem, 1958), 2:248. See Spiro, "The Moral Vision of Saul Lieberman," p. 80 n. 92, for a discussion of Alon's contention.
241. See Spiro, "The Moral Vision of Saul Lieberman," pp. 83–84.
242. Lieberman respected Urbach's achievements at the same time as he enjoyed his friendship. In 1950, Lieberman invited Urbach to join the JTS faculty. Urbach declined the invitation, not wanting to leave Israel (Spiro, interview with Hannah Urbach, Aug. 10, 1999). In 1956, Lieberman recommended Urbach for a promotion from lecturer to associate professor at the Hebrew University. In 1960, Lieberman, protective of Urbach's reputation, was incensed when Albeck severely criticized Urbach for a review of Albeck's work. See below, n. 480.
243. Spiro, interviews with H. Soloveitchik, Feb. 4, 1996, and Nov. 9, 1998.
244. Of course, this may have been something of a rationalization. The real reason may have been that he wanted to enlist the prestige of Ginzberg on behalf of his position.
245. Lieberman, *Hellenism in Jewish Palestine.* Cf. the chapter "Rabbinic Interpretation of Scripture," pp. 47 ff. The point referring to Lieberman's reluctance to draw conclusions from the sources he has gathered was suggested to us by Burton Visotzky.
246. A. Shapira, *Berl Katznelson: A Biography* (Tel Aviv, 1980). Lieberman, letter to Anita Shapira, May 31, 1982.
247. Lieberman, letter to Shapira. Berl Katznelson, too, was a descendant of a prominent Lithuanian rabbinical family. His father, R. Moses Katznelson, was a son-in-law of R. Moshe Feinstein's maternal grandfather, R. Yitzhak Yehiel Davidowitz. See Moshe David Tendler, *Responsa of Rav Moshe Feinstein, Translation and Commentary* (Hoboken, N.J., 1996), vol. 1.
248. JTS rabbinical students in their senior year were required to deliver the sermon during a Sabbath morning service in the JTS synagogue.
249. Baruch A. Levine, Skirball Professor Emeritus of Bible and Near Eastern Studies, New York University. Spiro's interviews with Levine, Mar. 21–22, 2000, and May 13–14, 2003, provided information for the account of Lieberman's response to Levine's sermon.
250. Lieberman, "Perurim Yerushalmiyim," *Tarbiz* 6 (1935): 235; *Studies in Palestinian Talmudic Literature,* p. 215. Meir Bar-Ilan discusses Lieberman's self-

criticism extensively in "Saul Lieberman: The Greatest Sage in Israel," in *Saul Lieberman, 1898–1983: Talmudic Scholar,* ed. Lubetski, p. 79, under the headings "A Great Man Who Erred," pp. 82 ff., and "Admits Error," pp. 85 ff.

251. Cited by Preschel, "Mahalakh Hayav," p. 370. See also Lieberman's "Mishnat Shir Hashirim," appendix D, in *Jewish Gnosticism, Merkabah Mysticism, and Talmudic Tradition,* ed. Scholem, 2d ed. (New York, 1965), pp. 118, 125 n. 42, where Lieberman explicitly rejects an interpretation he offered in his *Tosefet Rishonim,* pt. 3 (1939).

252. *Zera'im Bikkurim,* p. 851. Cited by Preschel, "Mahalakh Hayav," p. 371.

253. Lieberman, *Devarim Rabbah,* 1st ed. (Jerusalem, 1940), introduction, p. xix n. 3. Lieberman, *Shkiin* (Jerusalem, 1939, 1970).

254. Lieberman, *Devarim Rabbah,* 2d ed. (Jerusalem, 1965), "Hosafot Vehashlamot," p. 135 n. 15 (pp. 30–31 of the 1st and 2d ed.).

255. *Nashim,* vol. 8, introduction, p. 13.

256. Cited by Norman Solomon, "Saul Lieberman (1898–1983): A Revolutionary in Rabbinic Scholarship," in *Survey of Jewish Affairs,* ed. William Frankel (London, 1983), p. 249.

257. Cited in Preschel, "Mahalakh Hayav," p. 370.

258. See Halperin, *Hagadol Miminsk,* pp. 15–16.

259. The JTS Ratner Center Archives contain Finkelstein's letter to Lieberman (July 28, 1942), inviting him to deliver the lecture, and Lieberman's positive letter of response (July 31, 1942).

260. Lieberman, "The Martyrs of Caesarea," *Annuaire de l'institut de philologie et d'histoire orientales et slaves* 7 (1939–44): 395–446.

261. See Spiro, "The Moral Vision of Saul Lieberman," pp. 69–75, for a discussion and comparison of the two essays.

262. Lieberman, *Texts and Studies,* preface, p. vii.

263. For a brief description of the Leiden manuscript, see Michael Krupp, "Manuscript of the Palestinian Talmud," an appendix to Abraham Goldberg, "The Palestine Talmud," in *The Literature of the Sages,* pt. 1, ed. Shmuel Safrai (Philadelphia, 1987), p. 318.

264. Yaacov Sussmann, *Introduction to Talmud Yerushalmi, According to Ms. Or. 4720* (Scal. 3) of the Leiden University Library with Restorations and Corrections (Heb.) (Jerusalem, 2001), pp. 13–14 n. 46.

265. The statement appears in Lieberman, introduction to *Hayerushalmi Kifshuto,* p. 16. It is cited in Sussmann, *Introduction to Talmud Yerushalmi,* p. 13 n. 46.

266. Lieberman, *Introduction to Ms. Leiden* (Jerusalem, 1971), p. 5.

267. *Researches in Talmudic Literature: A Study Conference in Honour of the Eightieth Birthday of Shaul Lieberman,* Israel Academy of Sciences and Humanities (Jerusalem, 1983).

268. Often, even the first edition included such a section. See the first edition of Lieberman's *Devarim Rabbah* (Jerusalem, 1940), "Tikkunim Vehosafot," p. 133. The second edition, 1965, includes *hosafot vehashlamot* (additions and supplements), pp. 133–39, as well as additional footnotes in the body of the text. The third edition, 1974, includes additional footnotes in the body of the text. *Sifrei Zuta: The Talmud of Caesarea* (New York, 1968) includes *tikkunim vehash-*

lamot (corrections and supplements), pp. 141–48. *Tosefta Kifshutah, Mo'ed* was published in 1962, and in the same year Lieberman published a fourteen-page booklet, *kuntres tikkunim v'hashlamot l'tosefta kifshutah seder mo'ed* (corrections and supplements), including a brief explanation of the circumstances that impelled him to publish a separate booklet of revisions. The *Tosefta Kifshutah, Nashim,* pt. 7, includes *hosafot* (additions), p. 588, referring to the immediately preceding volume, *Nashim,* pt. 6, and *tikkunim vehosafot,* pp. 589–98, referring to the three volumes of commentary of *Mo'ed.* Lieberman explained that these revisions were not included in the *kuntres* (booklet). The pattern he established in *Tosefta Kifshutah* is that subsequent volumes included corrections and additions applicable to earlier volumes. For Lieberman, striving to achieve the true interpretation was an ongoing process that is never completed.

269. Lieberman, *Greek in Jewish Palestine* (New York, 1942), "Additions and Corrections to the Second Edition," pp. 194–201.
270. D. Rosenthal, ed., introduction to *Mehkarim b'Torat Eretz Yisrael.*
271. Lieberman, *Sifrei Zuta,* p. 136.
272. Ibid., n. 40. This is a play on the words *ro'ote* and *rotsot. Ein lo ladayan elah mah she'einav rotsot.*
273. Undated letter to Vienna, likely sent in the late 1930s.
274. Lieberman, letters to his close friend Abraham Meir Habermann, May 18, 1952, and June 27, 1952.
275. Lieberman, in a letter to Scholem, Nov. 18, 1951, does not name his critic. Lieberman is apparently reacting to Binyamin Zev Benedikt's criticism of his *Hilkhot Hayerushalmi* in *Kiryat Sefer* (Sept. 1951): 329–49: and to Benedikt, p. 389, the same issue of *Kiryat Sefer,* "Variations in Old Texts," where he purports to correct Lieberman's methodology.
276. Luitpold Wallach, review of *Greek in Jewish Palestine,* by S. Lieberman, *Review of Religion* 8, no. 1 (Nov. 1943): 61–66; and Lieberman, "Critical Comments: A Reply to Dr. Wallach," *The Review of Religion* 8, no. 3 (Mar. 1944): 320–23.
277. Isaiah Sonne, "The Use of Rabbinic Literature as Historical Sources," *Jewish Quarterly Review* 36 (1945): 147 ff.; Lieberman, "The Martyrs of Caesarea" (response), *Jewish Quarterly Review* 36, no. 3 (1946): 239 ff.; I. Sonne, "Word and Meaning: Text and Context," *Jewish Quarterly Review* 37, no. 3 (Jan. 1947): 307 ff.; this is followed, on p. 329, with Lieberman's "Rejoinder," which ends with: "With this I close the argument."
278. Sonne raises questions concerning the historical value of the talmudic sources that Lieberman uses to effect historical constructions in "The Martyrs of Caesarea." However, Sonne speaks glowingly of Lieberman's scholarship: "His undisputed mastery of the talmudic writings combined with profound erudition in the late Hellenistic literature . . . makes his essays an inexhaustible mine of information for historians." Sonne, "The Use of Rabbinic Literature as Historical Sources," p. 147.
279. Lieberman, handwritten letter to Baron, Jan. 22, 1951; a second Lieberman letter to Baron, typewritten and also dated Jan. 22, 1951, includes a painstaking account of the failure to send a copy of the minutes to Sonne, together with a profuse apology to Sonne, whom Lieberman compliments

for his interest in the affairs of the academy. This letter, while addressed to Baron, was intended to be forwarded to Sonne. Lieberman explained in his letter to Baron: "In order to save you work, I enclose . . . a typewritten letter to you which you may forward to Dr. Sonne if you choose to do so."

280. Salo W. Baron, *A Social and Religious History of the Jews,* 2d ed. (New York, 1952), 2:398 n. 11, where he claimed, "S. Lieberman seems to have gone too far in underestimating the extent of the Jewish 'sedition' under Gallus." Lieberman, letter to Baron, Mar. 7, 1952.
281. Baron, letter to Lieberman, Mar. 16, 1952; Lieberman, letter to Baron, Mar. 20, 1952.
282. Michael Higger, "The Identification and Classification of the Baraitot," *Proceedings of the American Academy for Jewish Research* 9 (1938–39): 54, where Higger writes, "Incidentally, this tendency to generalize on the basis of one baraita is also to be found, unfortunately, among modern students of the Talmud. Rabbi Lieberman of Jerusalem builds up a theory on the grounds that there is only one baraita of Levi recorded in the *Yerushalmi.* A glance, however, at the chapter on the baraitot of Levi in the first volume of the *Otsar Habaraitot* should convince anyone that there are a number of baraitot of Levi in the *Yerushalmi.*"
283. Lieberman, letter to Finkelstein, Jan. 21, 1940, where he says that Higger's words are "false from beginning to end," and notes that Higger failed to provide a citation for Lieberman's alleged statement. Lieberman explained that the only place where he had written about Levi's baraitot was *Talmudah shel Kisrin,* p. 6, where he says that in the *Yerushalmi Bavot* (*Bava Kamma, Bava Metzia, Bava Batra*), there are four baraitot of Levi, and in the rest of the *Yerushalmi* (apart from the *Bavot*), there is one. Lieberman wrote also to Ginzberg, Jan. 21, 1940, with a brief statement of Higger's allegation, referring him to the more detailed account in the Finkelstein letter. He asked Ginzberg to rectify the matter by writing a purely factual piece for publication, which would not be hurtful to Higger, and to sign Lieberman's name to it. We suggest that he wanted Ginzberg to sign the piece, but felt he could not ask him to do so. He explained that it was best for Ginzberg to write it because he understood Higger's situation and would not overstate the matter. He asked him to consult with Finkelstein and not to proceed unless Finkelstein said there was no alternative. Lieberman implored Ginzberg to set the matter straight with a mere recital of the facts, saying that he turned to him because he would do the same thing for him. Perhaps Ginzberg's failure to appreciate the depth of Lieberman's hurt left resentment that chilled the relationship when Lieberman assumed his position at JTS.
284. Lieberman published a critical review of Higger's edition of *Masekhet Semahot* in *Kiryat Sefer* 9 (1932–33): 53–56. Higger wrote a review of Lieberman's *Tosefet Rishonim* and *Tashlum Tosefta* (*Jewish Quarterly Review* 28 [1937–38]: 351–54), with Lieberman's reply appearing in *Jewish Quarterly Review* 29 (1938–39): 81–82. Lieberman wrote a highly critical review of Higger's *Masekhet Sofrim* in *Kiryat Sefer* 15 (1938–39): 56–60.
285. Gedalyahu Alon, review of *Greek in Jewish Palestine,* by S. Lieberman, *Kiryat Sefer* 20 (1943–44): 76–95.

286. Lieberman, letter to Scholem, Nov. 6, 1944. The letter makes it clear that Lieberman was aware of the policy, first published in *Kiryat Sefer* 15, no. 3 (Oct. 1938): "*Kiryat Sefer* does not publish polemical responses to critiques." Nevertheless, the letter included a detailed response to Alon's review in the hope that Scholem might persuade the editor to waive the long-standing policy and permit the publication of Lieberman's response. Lieberman suggested that his own essay was not a response to criticism, but was simply setting the record straight, since Alon must have reviewed a book other than Lieberman's *Greek in Jewish Palestine!* Lieberman's reply was never published. Either Scholem approached the editor unsuccessfully, or, more likely, he simply advised Lieberman that it would be best to remain silent on the matter.
287. Lieberman, *Greek in Jewish Palestine,* 2d ed. (New York, 1944), pp. 194–95.
288. Lieberman, "Six Words from Koheleth Rabbah," in *Studies in Jewish History and the Hebrew Language,* ed. Menahem Dorman, Shmuel Safrai, and Menahem Stern (Tel Aviv, 1970), pp. 227–35.
289. Lieberman, "Hazanut Yannai," *Sinai* 4 (Jan./Feb. 1939): 221–50. Like many of Lieberman's essays, it would have been publishable in book form. Menahem Zulay, *Piyyutai Yannai* (Berlin, 1938). Zulay (1901–54) was a scholar of Hebrew poetry and liturgy.
290. Undated letter from Lieberman to Zulay—most likely sent in early 1940, not long after the publication of Lieberman's essay.
291. Apparently, Lieberman's effort at reconciliation was successful. Some years later, in an introduction to an essay analyzing the language of Yannai's liturgical compositions, Zulay wrote: "I owe thanks to Professor Saul Lieberman for a number of important comments, which are cited below in his name, and for the love and diligence with which he answered my questions." From "Studies in the Language of Yannai's Liturgical Poetry" (Heb.), in Zulay, *Eretz Israel and Its Poetry,* ed. Ephraim Hazan (Jerusalem, 1995), p. 452.
292. Spiro, interview with Sussmann, Aug. 5, 1999.
293. Lieberman, "Bimhitzat Rabbanim," p. 608. See Spiro, "The Moral Vision of Saul Lieberman," pp. 66–67.
294. Spiro, interview with Soloveitchik, Feb. 4, 1996.
295. In *Tosefta Kifshutah* and *Sifrei Zuta,* Lieberman insisted that his father's name appear in larger type than his own. At first, the printer resisted, saying that it would be inappropriate to have different-size letters on one line. Lieberman maintained his position, which, to him, was ethically and aesthetically correct. Lieberman cited *Sheyare Kenesset Hagedolah* (a commentary on the *Shulhan Arukh, Yoreh De'ah,* the code of Jewish law dealing with, among other things, the commandment to honor one's parents), where the author (Hayyim Benveniste) referred to the practice of printing a father's name in larger print than one's own. Tuvia Preschel, "R. Saul Lieberman: On Receiving the Israel Prize for Studies in Judaica," *Hadoar* 50, no. 25 (Apr. 30, 1971): 423. The *Tosefta Kifshutah* is dedicated to Lieberman's parents, "who were taken in their youth" with his mother's ("Liba Badena's") father identified as "the Gaon Rav Saul Katzenellenbogen."
296. Florence Bar-Ilan, letter to Schochet, Apr. 29, 1996.

297. Lieberman, letter to Abramsky, Dec. 26, 1963.
298. *The Responsa of Rav Moshe Feinstein,* translation and commentary by Moshe David Tendler (1996), 1:8.
299. Lieberman, letters to Kenaani, July 11, 1963, and July 29, 1963. It is clear from Lieberman's letters that Kenaani complained that Lieberman did not give him proper credit for his achievement.
300. Lieberman, *Tosefta Kifshutah, Zera'im* (New York, 1955), "Mavo Labi'ur Ha'arokh" (introduction), p. 17.
301. M. S. Zuckermandel, edition of Tosefta based on the Erfurt and Vienna codices, 1st ed., 1881; 2d ed., 1937; new ed., Jerusalem, 1970. Lieberman discusses Zuckermandel's work, *Tosefta Berakhot* (text), 1955, introduction, pp. 7–8. Note that the Lieberman *Tosefta* volumes with the extensive commentary are titled *Tosefta Kifshutah,* while the volumes with the text and the brief commentary are titled *Tosefta.*
302. Lieberman, introduction to *Hayerushalmi Kifshuto* (Jerusalem, 1934), p. 8.
303. Ibid., esp. pp. 16–30, where he cites in great detail the various categories of circumstances that led to errors in the Leiden manuscript of the *Talmud Yerushalmi.* Lieberman refers to the two "important" Epstein articles on the Leiden manuscript, explaining that he used the first article for purposes of this text (*Hayerushalmi Kifshuto*) and credits Epstein with the points he cites from Epstein's work. The second Epstein article on the Leiden manuscript was published after Lieberman completed his text. Lieberman introduces a list of examples of errors to be found in the texts, with, "I list examples upon which Epstein has not yet managed to comment." The last comment in particular, coming from the thirty-five-year-old scholar who was his student not so long ago, could hardly have pleased Epstein.
304. Finkelstein, "Doctor Saul Lieberman: An Appreciation," p. 3.
305. Lieberman to S. Assaf, Dec. 28, 1942. This was presumably a box of books from his personal library, shipped from Jerusalem to New York. He told Assaf about the loss because the box contained all the books by Assaf, which Lieberman now wanted to purchase from him.
306. Lieberman, letter to Scholem, Nov. 1944. Lieberman's practice was to give his letters addressed to the Scholems to Judith in order for her to add her own words. In this instance, Lieberman explained that he hadn't yet told Judith about the Alon review, wishing to spare her the pain; thus, there was no added note from Judith.
307. Spiro, interview with Halivni, Jan. 28, 1996.
308. Mandelbaum, *Tales of the Fathers,* p. 24.
309. Spiro, interview with E. Katzenstein, Aug. 3, 1999. The story was related to Emunah by her father, Louis Finkelstein.
310. Finkelstein, "Doctor Saul Lieberman: An Appreciation," p. 3.
311. Lieberman, letter to Assaf, Sept. 15, 1952.
312. Lieberman, letter to Assaf, June 26, 1953. Lieberman's perceptive assessment of young Dudi was substantiated when Dudi went on, some time later, to obtain an M.Sc. in mathematics and a Ph.D. in statistics. He later became a professor in the statistics department at the Hebrew University as well as department chairman.

313. Jonathan Sarna, in *In Praise of a Master*, ed. Berkowitz, p. 19 of unnumbered pages.
314. Spiro, interview with Penina Herzog and her son Yitzhak, Aug. 11, 1999.
315. Judith Lieberman, letter to Sonja Aviad, Mar. 1, 1964, with a note from Saul Lieberman.
316. Spiro, interview with Meir Lieberman, Aug. 4, 1999. Meir had one daughter, who had eight children, all of whom were very close to Saul Lieberman. Indeed, Saul Lieberman's last trip to Israel was made for two purposes: to spend Passover in Jerusalem with his brother's family; and to attend the wedding of Meir's granddaughter Liba (named after Meir and Saul's mother), following Shavuot.
317. Spiro, interview with Susannah Heschel, Mar. 23, 1998; and with Sylvia Heschel, Mar. 26, 1998.
318. July 26, 1951, RG I–G 97/45, cited in H. Goldberg, "Becoming History," 1:377.
319. Spiro, interview with Visotzky, Sept. 8, 1998.
320. Of J. Neusner's translation of three tractates of the Palestinian Talmud, Lieberman wrote a severely critical review: "A Tragedy or a Comedy?" *Journal of the American Oriental Society* 104 (1984): 315–19. In this instance, the exception proves the rule.
321. Spiro, interview with Visotzky, Sept. 8, 1998. Halivni was noted for his considerable work in source criticism. Visotzky explained that Lieberman would not generally openly attack a scholar by name but would rather differ with theories, interpretations, or approaches of other scholars without identifying them. Visotzky attended Lieberman's class for seven years, continuing for a number of years following his ordination.
322. Mandelbaum, *Tales of the Fathers,* p. 21.
323. Lieberman, letters to Jacob David Abramsky (son of R. Yehezkel Abramsky, an alumnus of the Slobodka yeshiva), May 26, 1963; Dec. 2, 1961; Dec. 29, 1962; Dec. 21, 1963; Nov. 9, 1962; Sept. 21, 1967; and Sept. 1964.
324. The correspondent was not identified in Lieberman's letter, dated 1963 or 1964.
325. Letter of June 13, 1938. Moshe Davis was ordained by JTS in 1942 and went on to achieve prominence in the field of education and American Jewish history. He served as dean of JTS's Teachers' Institute and as provost of JTS.
326. Lieberman wrote letters of recommendation for Stanley Kazan to Yale University (June 20, 1956), and for David Blumenfeld to Hebrew University (Oct. 4, 1960). Lieberman recommended David Halivni for a Bar-Ilan professorship (Apr. 10, 1996); Shmuel Safrai for an appointment to Tel Aviv University (Feb. 27, 1970); and Zvi Ankori to teach at the Haifa Technion (Apr. 1, 1968).
327. Margulies, letters to Lieberman, Jan. 4, 1950, and Dec. 21, 1955. Zimmerman letter to Lieberman is undated.
328. Halivni, *The Book and the Sword,* p. 140.
329. Finkelstein, letter to Yehuda Shapira, Apr. 1, 1955. Edward Gershfield suggests that more important to Lieberman than the completion of the translation was the objective of providing Berger with a livelihood. Spiro, interview with Gershfield, Jan. 30, 1996.

330. Lieberman, letter to Yehuda Shapira, Mar. 31, 1955; Harry Starr, of the Lucius Littauer Foundation, letter to Lieberman, Sept. 18, 1968.
331. N. Kamenetsky, interview with Kirschenbaum, Mar. 10, 1997.
332. Letters, Mar. 30, 1963; Aug. 2, 1962; Mar. 18, 1964; etc.
333. "To Dr. Chaim Grade on the Occasion of the Presentation of the Morris Adler Prize," signed by Saul Lieberman and Abraham Halkin, Mar. 6, 1967; letter from Starr to Lieberman, Sept. 18, 1968.
334. Herman Kieval, letter to Lieberman, 1971.
335. Margulies, letter to Lieberman, Jan. 22, 1959.
336. Schreiber, letter to Lieberman from Budapest, undated.
337. Letter, Apr. 18, 1955.
338. Letter, Oct. 17, 1955.
339. Spiro, interview with Robert Chazan, Apr. 4, 2000. Chazan, who served several terms as president of the AAJR, credited Baron and Lieberman with leaving the AAJR in excellent financial condition. In fact, it was their prudent investment policy that enabled the AAJR of the nineties to finance new programs.
340. Letter from the American Friends of the Hebrew University to Lieberman, Jan. 7, 1969.
341. Morris Adler, letter to Lieberman, Jan. 12, 1966. In a letter, Mar. 10, 1971, acknowledging the response of one of the authors to a request for a charitable donation, Lieberman wrote, "It is sometimes worthwhile asking for money in order to get letters from my beloved pupils."
342. Letter from Alan Stroock, of the Alan and Katherine Stroock Fund, to Lieberman, Jan. 20, 1975, sending Lieberman two checks to be forwarded: one to Bar-Ilan University, and the other to the AAJR. Letter from Starr to Lieberman, Sept. 18, 1968, sending a check toward the publication of the second volume of *Zemach Atlas* by Chaim Grade—"To Dr. Chaim Grade on the Occasion of the Presentation of the Morris Adler Prize."
343. Spiro, interview with Yosef Ciechanover, Sept. 23, 1999.
344. Mandelbaum, *Tales of the Fathers*, p. 26.
345. Mrs. Mandelbaum said that Lieberman had purchased an apartment in Israel for his brother Meir's daughter. Spiro, interview with the Mandelbaums, June 7, 1997.
346. Lieberman, letter to A. Z. Ben-Yishai in Tel Aviv, Dec. 26, 1957. These funds were provided in the form of a scholarship to the student, Yaacov Sussmann (later Professor Sussmann), with Lieberman informing Scholem that he was extremely pleased that Sussmann was awarded the funds. Letter dated Feb. 1, 1959. Sussmann confirmed that the prize he received was financed by Lieberman's Bialik Prize money. Spiro, interview with Sussmann, Aug. 5, 1999.
347. Lieberman responded to the school's letter of Nov. 14, 1955, with instructions that his contribution be for scholarships and not for the building fund. In his later years, he donated $50,000 to the Shulamith School in honor of his wife. See Mandelbaum, *Tales of the Fathers*, p. 23.
348. R. Nochum Stilerman, letter to Lieberman (Mar. 10, 1981), thanking him for attending the school's anniversary dinner.
349. Schmelzer, letter to Lieberman, Nov. 23, 1971.

350. Gerson Cohen, letter to Lieberman, Mar. 6, 1981.
351. Jacob Flug, letter to Lieberman, Sept. 15, 1971, endorsed by Lieberman with a note and a check enclosed; Benjamin Hershman, thank-you letter to Lieberman, Jan. 1, 1970.
352. Lieberman, letter to S. Greineman, Dec. 18, 1952.
353. Sperber, letter to Schochet, Sept. 1, 1999.
354. Spiro, interview with Yerushalmi, June 6, 1996. Yerushalmi was so touched and impressed by Lieberman's act of kindness to him and the manner in which it was performed that he implored us to tell this story: "I want it known."
355. Spiro, interview with David Kogen, Sept. 8, 1998.
356. Lieberman's will, dated Nov. 6, 1979, included a gift of $10,000 to the Lubavitch Merkas l'Inyonei Hinukh.
357. Spiro, interview with D. Zlotnick, Sept. 21, 1996. Zlotnick recalls that Lieberman had attended Selichot services at the late rebbe's synagogue, and later recognized among the worshipers a fellow Slobodka alumnus. The two Litvaks looked at each other with the question, What are you doing here? Zlotnick reports that the rebbe respected Lieberman and had acquired his major works, including the *Tosefta Kifshutah*.
358. Schochet, interview with Rogoff, Aug. 1997.
359. Letter from Max Schreiber, Nov. 6, 1968. Schreiber was one of several brothers, each of whom concentrated on a particular category of *tzedakah,* Max's being *mikvaot*. In his thank-you letter to Lieberman (Nov. 11, 1968), Schreiber refers to his very personal relationship with Rabbi N. Riff, Judith's cousin, mentioning that he built a *mikveh* in memory of Lieberman's father-in-law, R. Meir Bar-Ilan. Lieberman's great respect for and closeness to the Bar-Ilan family were well known.
360. Rabbi M. Levine, letter to Lieberman, Jan. 25, 1954.
361. Spiro, interview with Emanuel Gettinger and his wife, Racheil (daughter of Rabbi Riff), Mar. 28, 1996.
362. Florence Bar-Ilan, letter to Schochet, Apr. 29, 1996.
363. N. Kamenetsky, interview with Kirschenbaum, Mar. 10, 1997.
364. Spiro, interview with Harold (Zvi) Kraushar, Oct. 7, 1995.
365. David Novak relates that whenever he knocked on Lieberman's office door to ask a question about the Talmud, Lieberman was invariably welcoming and responsive. Some years later, following his ordination, Novak attended a Lieberman Talmud session at a Rabbinical Assembly convention. Following the session, Lieberman approached Novak and asked him why he did not have any questions for him! (Spiro, interview with Novak, Oct. 26, 1999).
366. E. Ginzberg, *Keeper of the Law: Louis Ginzberg*. In the acknowledgments, p. 333, E. Ginzberg says, "Professor Saul Lieberman read aloud to me the biographical pieces on my father which David Druck had written in Yiddish. (As he read, he illuminated many obscure points with his own comments.) He also reviewed the draft manuscript." Druck had written an extensive series of articles in Yiddish on Louis Ginzberg, which had appeared in the *Jewish Morning Journal* and the *Jewish Daily News* weekly from Dec. 4, 1933, to Mar. 5, 1934. See "Sources and Bibliography," in *Keeper of the Law,* p. 335.

Simply reading aloud each of these articles, even without translating and explaining, would entail a considerable investment of time. Eli Ginzberg told Spiro (Jan. 31, 1996) that he visited Lieberman at his summer home on Martha's Vineyard and received much assistance in preparing the biography.

367. Eli Ginzberg, letter to Schochet, Aug. 8, 1997.
368. Mandelbaum, *Tales of the Fathers,* p. 27.
369. Spiro, interview with Ciechanover, Sept. 23, 1999. Ciechanover's work was for his doctoral dissertation, "Suicide in the Jewish Tradition," submitted to Boston University, 1991.
370. Lieberman, attending a lecture given by S. D. Goitein, made a suggestion that led to Goitein's apparent discovery of a letter to Maimonides from his brother, David. In the words of Goitein, "The discovery of [David's] letter is a fantastic story in itself. In 1954 I gave a lecture in New York on my *India Book.* . . . Professor Saul Lieberman, who was present, remarked that it would be a fine thing if the Geniza could produce a letter from David, Moses Maimonides' beloved brother, who drowned in the Indian Ocean." *Letters of Medieval Jewish Traders,* trans. from Arabic with introduction and notes (Princeton, N.J., 1973), p. 208 n. 3. We are grateful to Harold Kraushar, bookseller to JTS faculty and students for many decades, who brought this text to our attention.
371. Baron, letter to Lieberman, May 2, 1975.
372. Soloveitchik acknowledged that Lieberman was "kind enough to comment on the manuscript" of the essay, which is a part of his doctoral dissertation, "Pawnbroking: A Study in Usury and of the Halakah in Exile," *Proceedings of the American Academy for Jewish Research* 38–39 (1972): 203.
373. "I am profoundly grateful to Professor Saul Lieberman for the sustained cordial interest which he has shown in my work and for letting me benefit so liberally from his vast knowledge. His careful reading of my manuscript led to some important additions and necessary modifications and enriched me greatly." Twersky, *Rabad of Posquieres: A Twelfth-Century Talmudist* (Philadelphia, 1962, 1980), p. viii.
374. Lieberman, letter to Yalon, Sept. 4, 1964. In his preface to *Yerushalmi Kifshuto,* 1934, Lieberman thanks Yalon for his generosity in allowing him to use his excellent library. Thus, the friendship goes back a long time; one of Lieberman's cardinal principles was everlasting loyalty to his friends.
375. Lieberman, letter to Yalon, Oct. 11, 1964. Yalon's response to Lieberman's Sept. 4, 1964, letter is apparent from Lieberman's comments.
376. See above, section entitled "Breadth of Knowledge," with regard to Lieberman's response to Yalon's assurance that he would make no changes in Lieberman's comments.
377. *Leshoneinu* 29 (1965): 59–61. Lieberman's notes appear under "Comments and Corrections to *Introduction to the Vocalization of the Mishnah.*" Repr., *Mehkarim b'Torat Eretz Yisrael,* pp. 463–65.
378. Lieberman's appendix D to the Scholem text *Jewish Gnosticism, Merkabah Mysticism, and Talmudic Tradition* (New York, 1965). "Mishnat Shir Hashirim" was published in Hebrew.
379. Mandelbaum, *Tales of the Fathers,* p. 31.

380. *Yerushalmi, Nezikin,* edited from the Escorial manuscript with an introduction by E. S. Rosenthal, and introduction and commentary by S. Lieberman (Jerusalem, 1983), p. vi.
381. Raphael, "Professor Rabbi Shaul Lieberman," pp. 91–92.
382. Lieberman, "A Talmud Written by the People in Their Own Land," pp. 3–4.
383. Spiro, interview with Penina and Yitzhak Herzog, Aug. 9, 1999.
384. Spiro, interviews with Itamar Aviad, Aug. 12, 1999; Yakov Aviad, Aug. 14, 1999; and Yehuda Shapira, son of Moshe Hayyim and Leah Shapira, Aug. 12, 1999.
385. J. Lieberman, letter to the Scholems, Aug. 26, 1941; Saul Lieberman, letter to Scholem, Feb. 2, 1941.
386. Wiesel, *All Rivers Run to the Sea,* pp. 399–400. For more on Heschel, see Edward K. Kaplan and Samuel H. Dresner, *Abraham Joshua Heschel: Prophetic Witness* (New Haven, 1998), vol. 1.
387. Spiro, interview with A. Goldberg, Aug. 2, 1999.
388. See above, section entitled "Support for Scholars," with regard to Lieberman's response to Yalon's *Mavo Linikud Hamishnah*.
389. Heschel, letter to Lieberman, Dec. 5, 1962.
390. N. Kamenetsky, interview with M. Greenberg, Jan. 1999. Lieberman's commitment to the study of aggadah was such that he did not have to be convinced of its importance. However, he drew a distinction between the study of aggadah and philosophical speculation, deeming the latter to be among the least productive subjects in Jewish studies.
391. Lieberman, letter to Scholem, Nov. 12, 1962. In all of Lieberman's correspondence and papers that we have examined, we found no negative or derogatory references to Heschel. If Lieberman had ever made comments critical of Heschel, they would have been reflected in his correspondence with Scholem, with whom he was very open. We could find only positive comments about Heschel on the part of Lieberman and Judith in their correspondence with Scholem.
392. Lieberman, letter to Scholem, Dec. 12, 1974. The book that he sent is most likely Heschel's book on the Kotzker called *A Passion for Truth* (New York, 1973), and not the two-volume work in Yiddish, *Kotzk,* which was published in Israel in 1973.
393. Spiro, interview with Sylvia Heschel, Mar. 26, 1998. A. Heschel, *The Sabbath: Its Meaning for Modern Man* (New York, 1951). One might have expected Lieberman to consider *Torah min Hashamayim* Heschel's best book, but Lieberman was most likely choosing from among those written in English and addressed to a wider audience.
394. Lieberman letter, June 20, 1942.
395. Letter from Maxwell Abbell, major financial supporter of JTS, to Lieberman, Oct. 31, 1956, on the eve of the presidential election.
396. Probably *Look at America,* a book compiled by *Look* magazine editors. J. Lieberman, letter (from Martha's Vineyard) to Jessica Feingold, Aug. 24, 1955.
397. Spiro, interview with Gershfield, Jan. 29, 1996. Gershfield conjectured that Lieberman might have viewed Heschel's activities as "grandstanding."
398. Spiro, interview with A. Goldberg, Aug. 2, 1999.

399. Spiro, interview with Sylvia Heschel, Mar. 26, 1998.
400. Schochet, telephone conversation with Susannah Heschel, July 13, 1998.
401. Spiro, interview with Susannah Heschel, Mar. 23, 1998.
402. J. Lieberman, letter to the Scholems, Aug. 1947. Heschel married Sylvia Straus in Dec. 1946, not long after he assumed his position at JTS. See introduction to *Moral Grandeur and Spiritual Audacity: Essays,* ed. Susannah Heschel (New York, 1996), p. xx.
403. Spiro, interview with Y. Aviad, Sept. 25, 1999. Aviad, a member of Israel's diplomatic mission in New York, was frequently invited to join the Liebermans to dine in the Seminary sukkah.
404. A. Heschel, "Did Maimonides Strive for Prophetic Inspiration?" (Heb.), in *Louis Ginzberg Jubilee Volume on the Occasion of His Seventieth Birthday,* American Academy for Jewish Research (New York, 1945), p. 159.
405. A. Heschel, "The Holy Spirit in the Middle Ages," in *Jubilee Volume in Honor of Alexander Marx,* ed. S. Lieberman (New York, 1950), p. 175.
406. Mandelbaum, *Tales of the Fathers,* pp. 25–26.
407. J. Lieberman, letter to S. Aviad, Mar. 1, 1964.
408. Spiro, interview with Michael Shashar, Aug. 11, 1999.
409. Observed by Schochet when he visited Lieberman on Martha's Vineyard in Aug. 1965. David Rosenthal relates that when he and his parents approached the harbor on their visit to the Liebermans on Martha's Vineyard, they could not identify Lieberman because he was near the anchor point, showing the sailors how to tie the rope (Spiro, interview with D. Rosenthal, Aug. 9, 1999).
410. Spiro, interview with Yehuda Shapira, Aug. 12, 1999. Shapira related Lieberman's interest in people from all walks of life with the way his writings reflect an interest in "how people lived in the ancient world, how they celebrated holidays, carried on business—how they taught, bought, and acquired. Even complex legal matters are described with great clarity."
411. Spiro, interview with Haym Soloveitchik, Feb. 4, 1996.
412. Cross, letter to Schochet, Mar. 3, 1997.
413. Spiro, interview with Visotzky, Sept. 8, 1998.
414. Mirsky, interview with Lieberman.
415. *Trial and Error: The Autobiography of Chaim Weizmann* (New York, 1949), pp. 7–9.
416. Lieberman, letter to Finkelstein, Aug. 14, 1955. For the proposition that a learned person must adhere to a higher standard of ethical behavior than that to which the "ordinary" individual is subject, see TB *Yoma* 80a, and Maimonides, *Mishne Torah, Sefer Hamada, Hilkhot Yesodai Hatorah,* 5:11. Lieberman was aware that he was subject to a very high standard of ethical conduct.
417. Finkelstein, "The Tosefta: Text and Commentary," p. 16 of the convocation program "The Law as a Moral Force," Sept. 15, 1957, JTS.
418. See Spiro, "The Moral Vision of Saul Lieberman," pp. 77–78.
419. Notes of a meeting held by Lieberman with the Ph.D. students of the Herbert Lehman Institute of Ethics, Nov. 2, 1961, submitted by Eugene Wiener.
420. July 31, 1942. See above, section entitled "Self-Criticism," regarding the lecture.

421. Lieberman, *Greek in Jewish Palestine,* p. 85; *Bava Batra* 2 (end), 13c.
422. Zlotnick, introduction to *Greek in Jewish Palestine / Hellenism in Jewish Palestine,* p. xxi.
423. Epstein, letter to Ginzberg, May 9, 1933.
424. Lieberman, letter to Scholem, Jan. 2, 1960.
425. J. N. Epstein, *Mevo'ot Lesifrut Ha'amoraim* (Jerusalem, 1962), pp. 282 ff.
426. See *Sifrei Zuta,* pp. 135–36. See above, section entitled "Criticism from Others."
427. Lieberman, letter to Ginzberg, June 19, 1939. Lieberman had been dismissed from his teaching position at the Hebrew University on Mar. 17, 1937.
428. Epstein assigned Lieberman to prepare an index of references to the Tosefta in the writings of the rishonim. This led eventually to the publication of *Tosefet Rishonim* and a lifetime commitment to the study of the Tosefta (Spiro, interview with A. Goldberg, Aug. 2, 1999).
429. Spiro, interview with I. Aviad, Aug. 12, 1999.
430. A friend of Lieberman's reported that about eight months before Lieberman died, he pulled from his pocket a paper, yellowed by time, which was a dismissal letter signed by Epstein. This is likely a different letter from the dismissal letter dated Mar. 17, 1937, and signed by a Hebrew University administrator. The friend said it was out of character for Lieberman to share such personal matters with him; however, the Hebrew University wound never healed completely.
431. Spiro, interview with Dimitrovsky, Aug. 2, 1999; with A. Goldberg Aug. 2, 1999; and with D. Rosenthal, Aug. 9, 1999.
432. Letters to Lieberman from J. N. Epstein; his wife, Tzipora; and from their son, Hayyim, Mar. 7, 1947.
433. J. N. Epstein, "An Arabic Translation of the Mishnah" (Heb.), in *Jubilee Volume in Honor of Alexander Marx* (New York, 1950), pp. 23 ff.; Epstein, letters to Lieberman, Jan.–Feb. 1948, and June 28, 1949.
434. Spiro, interview with A. Goldberg, Aug. 2, 1999. Lieberman describes his great anger when, during a visit to Ginzberg's home, a scholar removed Epstein's *Mavo l'Nusah Hamishnah* from the bookshelf, turned a few pages, and proclaimed "nothing," i.e., "it's worthless." Lieberman, letter to Scholem, Jan. 2, 1960. Meir Bar-Ilan, Lieberman's nephew, recalls that Lieberman had told him that he was Epstein's choice to succeed him as head of the Talmud department at the Hebrew University. Meir Bar-Ilan, "Saul Lieberman: The Greatest Sage in Israel," in *Saul Lieberman, 1898–1983: Talmudic Scholar,* ed. Lubetski, p. 81 n. 7. This observation is consistent with the idea of reconciliation between the two scholars after their earlier misunderstandings and jealousies. See above, section entitled "Honors, Affiliations, and Invitations," regarding the invitation extended by the Hebrew University to Lieberman in 1950 to succeed Epstein as professor of Talmud.
435. N. Kamenetsky, interview with Friedman, Feb. 1999; Spiro, interview with Novak, Oct. 26, 1999.
436. Finkelstein, "Doctor Saul Lieberman: An Appreciation."
437. Lieberman, letters to Scholem: June 17, 1942; May 17, 1942; Mar. 9, 1942; Sept. 12, 1948; July 9, 1967; Dec. 22, 1974; and Feb. 6, 1969.

438. Cited in H. Goldberg, "Becoming History," p. 367.
439. Spiro, interview with Sussmann, Aug. 5, 1999. Sussmann describes a frantic Finkelstein desperately seeking a way to bring Lieberman back to New York so that he might consult with him on an urgent matter, and asking Judah Goldin to inquire as to the cost of a private plane.
440. N. Kamenetsky, interview with Beverly Gribetz, Dec. 1998.
441. Lieberman, letter to Scholem, Apr. 2, 1941.
442. One need only read Moshe Greenberg's *Studies in the Bible and Jewish Thought* (Philadelphia, 1995) and Yochanan Muffs's *Love and Joy: Law, Language and Religion in Ancient Israel* (New York, 1992) to appreciate the knowledge of rabbinic literature enjoyed by both scholars.
443. Spiro, "The Moral Vision of Saul Lieberman," pp. 67–68.
444. Gedalyahu Alon, "The Lithuanian Yeshivas," in *The Jewish Expression,* ed. Judah Goldin (New York, 1970), p. 452.
445. Moshe Greenberg, who studied *Avodah Zarah* with Lieberman, was amazed at Lieberman's ability to make the aggadot come alive, especially when he would analyze the discussions that the Rabbis envisioned to have transpired between various biblical figures. N. Kamenetsky, interview with M. Greenberg, Jan. 1999.
446. See Hyman E. Goldin, *Hebrew Criminal Law and Procedure* (New York, 1951), pp. 11–14; pp. 55–57 contains a discussion of the fines imposed for financial offenses in Jewish law.
447. *Mo'ed Katan* 17a.
448. *Talmud Yerushalmi, Hagigah* 1:7.
449. *Sanhedrin* 9b.
450. See Norman Lamm, "The Fifth Amendment and Its Equivalent in the Halakhah," *Judaism* 5, no. 1 (winter 1956): 53–59, esp. p. 54, where the difference between the Fifth Amendment to the U. S. Constitution and the halakhah is discussed.
451. *Sifrei, Shoftim* chap. 188, para. 15, Finkelstein, ed., p. 228.
452. Lieberman explained the parallel passage in the Tosefta Shevu'ot, *Tosefet Rishonim,* 2d sec., chap. 5, p. 177. Consistent with his conservative approach toward emending texts, Lieberman rejected the emendation of *mimonot* for *mitah*. See also *Sifrei: A Tannaitic Commentary on the Book of Deuteronomy,* trans. Reuven Hammer (New Haven, 1986), pp. 208–9 and 459 n. 5.
453. Lieberman describes in vivid detail some of the horrors of Roman justice, i.e., the use of torture to extract a confession, in "Roman Legal Institutions," *Jewish Quarterly Review* 35, no. 1 (July 1944), repr. in *Texts and Studies,* p. 57.
454. *Sanhedrin* 37b; *Mekhilta,* Lauterbach ed. (Philadelphia, 1949); *Mishpatim* 23:7, pp. 169–71.
455. See *Sefer Hamitzvot, Lo Ta'aseh* 190, Heller ed., p. 172, where Maimonides quotes from *Sanhedrin* 37b, the classic case in which the Talmud rejects circumstantial evidence in a capital case.
456. Maimonides, *Hilkhot Melahim* 3:10.
457. *Sanhedrin* 9:5.
458. Lieberman, "Perushim b'Mishnayot," in *Mehkarim b'Torat Eretz Yisrael,* pp. 3–7.

459. Lieberman, *Tosefet Rishonim,* vol. 2, *Nezikin, Sanhedrin,* chap. 9, p. 160.
460. *Sanhedrin* 6:5, Blackman trans.
461. Muffs, *Love and Joy,* p. 160. The bracketed reference is to a letter from Lieberman to Muffs. Maimonides, commentary on the Mishnah, *Masekhet Sanhedrin* (Heb.), ed. Manuel Gottlieb (Hannover, 1906), p. 22. See also Lieberman's comment on Yalon's discussion of R. Meir's aggadah, *Hahed* 7, no. 7 (1932): p. 21; appendix A, no. 10.
462. Deut. 17:5–13; *Sanhedrin* 87a.
463. *Talmud Yerushalmi, Kiddushin,* chap. 1, halakhah 9.
464. *The Mishnah of Rabbi Eliezer or the Midrash of Thirty-Two Hermeneutic Rules,* ed. Enelow (New York, 1933; repr. 1970), chap. 6, p. 121.
465. *Mishne Torah, Hilkhot Melahim,* chap. 8, halakhah 11.
466. *Sifra, Kedoshim,* ed. with traditional commentaries (Jerusalem, 1959), sec. 1, p. 86a.
467. *Bava Metzia* 61b.
468. Ibid.
469. *Bava Metzia* 62a.
470. Lieberman, "How Much Greek in Jewish Palestine?" in *Texts and Studies,* pp. 216–20.
471. Spiro, interview with D. Rosenthal, Aug. 8, 1999.
472. This was usually when a student was reading the commentary of Rashi or Tosafot (Spiro, interview with D. Zlotnick, Jan. 9, 2000).
473. N. Kamenetsky, interview with M. Greenberg, Jan. 1999.
474. Spiro, interview with Joel Roth, Sept. 23, 1999.
475. N. Kamenetsky, interview with M. Greenberg, Jan. 1999.
476. Spiro, interview with Aaron Singer, Aug. 5, 1999.
477. Spiro, interview with Hauptman, Oct. 20, 1999.
478. Spiro, interview with Ezra Finkelstein, Dec. 15, 1998.
479. Spiro, interview with H. Soloveitchik, Nov. 11, 1998.
480. Lieberman, letter to Scholem, Feb. 2, 1960. Urbach had written a critique of Hanoch Albeck's *Mavo l'Mishnah* in *Molad* 17, nos. 133–34 (Sept.–Oct. 1959): 422–40. Albeck wrote a reply, severely criticizing Urbach and Epstein, *Sinai* 46, no. 4 (Jan. 1960): 235–55. Albeck's criticism of two scholars whom Lieberman admired and respected caused him consternation.
481. Spiro, interview with D. Rosenthal, Aug. 8, 1999, and with Y. Herzog, Aug. 9, 1999.
482. Spiro, interview with Y. Herzog, Aug. 9, 1999.
483. Lieberman related the story to Rabbi F. E. Rottenberg while visiting him in Los Angeles in the late 1970s.
484. Mirsky, interview with Lieberman.
485. *Tosefta Kifshutah,* 1:20 n. 35.
486. Spiro, interview with Sussmann, Aug. 5, 1999, and with D. Rosenthal, Aug. 9, 1999.
487. Lieberman refers to *Bava Batra* 16a. Lieberman, "Masoret Kabbalah Bidivrai Hageonim," in *Mehkarim b'Torat Eretz Yisrael,* pp. 153, 156.
488. Spiro, interview with D. Rosenthal, Aug. 9, 1999.

489. "Haghoteihem shel Rabi Betsal'el Ashkenazi Verabi Yehosef Ashkenazi," in *Asufot,* ed. Meir Benayahu (Jerusalem, 1987), 1:67.
490. N. Kamenetsky, interview with Gribetz, Dec. 1998.
491. Quoted by Mark Jay Mirsky in an unpublished essay.
492. Halivni, "Professor Saul Lieberman," 6–7.
493. Address given by Elie Wiesel, in English translation, as he presented the guest of honor, Prof. Saul Lieberman, at the luncheon of the Histadrut Ivrit–*Hadoar,* Feb. 13, 1977.
494. Dec. 21, 1963. The addressee is not identified. See above, section entitled "Kindness and Generosity."
495. Lieberman, *Greek in Jewish Palestine,* p. 66.
496. Spiro, interview with Halivni, Jan. 28, 1996.
497. Urbach, "Shaul Lieberman Uterumato," p. 21.
498. Wiesel, *All Rivers Run to the Sea,* p. 396. Emphasis our own.
499. Spiro, interview with I. Aviad, Aug. 12, 1999.
500. *Berakhot* 8a, 8b, 17a.
501. Dimitrovsky, letter to Spiro, June 29, 2002.
502. Solomon, "Saul Lieberman," p. 252.
503. The Christian philosopher-theologian Bernard Chartres (d. 1126) first used this aphorism, which was later employed by R. Isaiah di Trani (ca. 1200–60) in his *Teshuvot ha-Rid,* no. 62. See David Golinkin, "President's Message," in Thirteenth Ordination and Commencement Exercises: Schechter Institute of Jewish Studies (Jerusalem, Nov. 21, 2000).
504. Spiro, interview with Morton Leifman, 1997; and with Novak, Oct. 26, 1999.
505. Lookstein, letter to Spiro, Nov. 27, 2000.
506. Spiro, interview with Novak, Oct. 26, 1999. Novak was present as Haskel Lookstein related this incident in a speech delivered on a Lieberman Yahrzeit. A similar episode transpired almost ninety years earlier in the life of Soloveitchik's great-grandfather, R. Yosef Dov Baer Soloveitchik (1820–92). While R. Dov Baer's mentor, R. Yehudah Leib Diskin, was imprisoned on false charges by the Russian authorities, R. Dov Baer sank into a deep depression, remaining isolated in his room, unable to perform any of his rabbinical functions. His student R. Meir Simha Hakohen paid him a visit and succeeded in arousing him from his depression by citing and then disputing a number of R. Diskin's novellae before R. Dov Baer. This strategy proved to be most effective because a newly energized R. Soloveitchik rose to vigorously defend his teacher, regaining in the process his emotional equilibrium and emerging from his depression. Hayyim Karlinsky, *Harishon l'Shalshelet Brisk* (Jerusalem, 1984), pp. 276–79.

APPENDICES

Appendix I
Selected Works Cited

Abramson, Shraga. "Darko shel Harav Shaul Lieberman b'Heker Hasifrut Hatalmudit," in *l'Zikhro shel Shaul Lieberman,* Israel Academy of Sciences and Humanities Annual (Jerusalem, 1984).

Allen, R. Wayne, ed. *Tomeikh Kehalakhah,* responsa of the panel of halakhic inquiry, Union for Traditional Conservative Judaism (New York, 1986).

Alon, Gedalyahu. "The Lithuanian Yeshivas," in *The Jewish Expression,* ed. Judah Goldin (New York, 1970); originally from *Mehkarim Betoledot Yisrael* (*Studies in the History of Israel*), vol. 1 (Jerusalem, 1957).

———. Review of *Greek in Jewish Palestine,* by S. Lieberman, *Kiryat Sefer* 20 (1943/44): 76–95.

Baer, Yitzhak. "The Forged Midrashim of Raymond Martini and Their Place in the Religious Controversy of the Middle Ages," in *Studies in Memory of Asher Gulak and Samuel Klein* (Heb.) (Jerusalem, 1942), pp. 28–48.

Bar-Ilan, Meir. "Saul Lieberman: The Greatest Sage in Israel," in *Saul Lieberman, 1898–1983: Talmudic Scholar,* ed. Meir Lubetski (Lewiston, N.Y., 2002), pp. 79–87.

Berkowitz, William, ed. *In Praise of a Master: Tributes to Professor Saul Lieberman,* American Jewish Heritage Committee (New York, 1987).

Bernstein, Louis. *Challenge and Mission: The Emergence of the English-Speaking Rabbinate* (New York, 1982).

Chazan, Robert. *Daggers of Faith: Thirteenth-Century Christian Missionizing and Jewish Response* (Berkeley, 1989).

Dimitrovsky, Haim Zalman. "Devarim al Gedol Hakhmei Doreinu," *Hadoar* 56, no. 15 (Feb. 11, 1977).

———. "Miparshanut l'Mehkar," in *l'Zikhro shel Shaul Lieberman,* Israel Academy of Sciences and Humanities (Jerusalem, 1984), pp. 34–49; trans. Baruch Feldstern, "From Commentary to Scholarship," as appendix III.

Dresner, Samuel H. *Heschel, Hasidism, and Halakha* (New York, 2002).

Epstein, J. N. (Jacob Nahum). *Mavo Lenusah Hamishnah* (Jerusalem, 1948, 1964, 2000).

———. *Mevo'ot Lesifrut Ha'amoraim: Bavli v'Yerushalmi* (Jerusalem, 1962).

Finkelstein, Louis. *Akiba: Scholar, Saint, and Martyr* (New York, 1936; Northvale, N.J., 1990).

———. "Doctor Saul Lieberman: An Appreciation," *United Synagogue Review* (fall 1983): 3.

———. "Emendations of the Sifrei," *Tarbiz* 3, no. 2 (Jan. 1932): 198–204.

———. "Our Teachers," eulogy for Ginzberg and Marx, *Proceedings of the Rabbinical Assembly of America* 18 (1955): 174.

———. "The Pharisees: Their Origin and Their Philosophy," *Harvard Theological Review* 22 (1929): 185–261.

———. *The Pharisees: The Sociological Background of Their Faith,* 2 vols. (Philadelphia, 1938, 1940, 1962).

Friedman, Shamma. "Kavim Lidmuto Hamada'it shel Profesor Shaul Lieberman z'l," *Newsletter of the World Union of Jewish Studies,* no. 23 (winter 1984).

———. "Saul Lieberman and the Study of the Tosefta," *Proceedings of the American Academy for Jewish Research* 31 (1963): 4.

———. "Shaul Lieberman: Hora'ato Be'al Peh Uviktav," in *l'Zikhro shel Shaul Lieberman,* Israel Academy of Sciences and Humanities Annual (Jerusalem, 1984).

———, trans. "From Prodigy to Master: An Introduction to the Scholarship of Saul Lieberman," Saul Lieberman Institute of Talmudic Research (lecture delivered by Shamma Friedman at the Jewish Theological Seminary, Feb. 1987).

Gilat, Yitzhak. "The Life's Work of Professor Saul Lieberman" (Heb.), *Bitzaron,* n.s., 9, nos. 35–36 (Sept. 1987): 49–54.

Ginzberg, Eli. *Keeper of the Law: Louis Ginzberg* (Philadelphia, 1966).

Ginzberg, Louis. *A Commentary to the Palestinian Talmud* (New York, 1941).

———. *On Jewish Law and Lore* (Philadelphia, 1955).

Goldberg, Abraham. "Professor Lieberman's 'Uncompleted' Literary Legacy," in *Saul Lieberman, 1898–1983: Talmudic Scholar,* ed. Meir Lubetski (Lewiston, N.Y., 2002), pp. 46–53.

———. Review of *Tosefta Kifshutah, Order Nashim,* by S. Lieberman, *Bibliotheca Orientalis* 26, nos. 1–2 (Jan.–Mar. 1969).

Goldberg, Harvey. "Becoming History: Perspectives on the Seminary Faculty at Mid-Century," in *Tradition Renewed: A History of the Jewish Theological Seminary of America,* ed. Jack Wertheimer (New York, 1997), vol. 1.

Golinkin, David. "The Influence of Seminary Professors on Halakha in the Conservative Movement: 1902–1968," in *Tradition Renewed: A History of the Jewish Theological Seminary of America,* ed. Jack Wertheimer (New York, 1997), vol. 2.

———. *The Responsa of Professor Louis Ginzberg* (New York, 1996).

Greenbaum, Michael B. "Finkelstein and His Critics," *Conservative Judaism* 47, no. 4 (Sept. 1995): 29.

———. *Louis Finkelstein and the Conservative Movement: Conflict and Growth* (Binghamton, N.Y., 2001).

Gurock, Jeffrey S. "Yeshiva Students at JTS," in *Tradition Renewed: A History of the Jewish Theological Seminary of America,* ed. Jack Wertheimer (New York, 1997), 1:471–514.

Hadoar 42, no. 23 (April 5, 1963) (special issue dedicated to Saul Lieberman).

Hadoar 56, no. 15 (February 11, 1977) (special issue dedicated to Saul Lieberman).

Halivni, David Weiss. *The Book and the Sword: A Life of Learning in the Shadow of Destruction* (New York, 1996).

———. Eulogy for Lieberman, *Hadoar* 62, no. 25 (May 27, 1983): 404.

———. "Professor Saul Lieberman," *Conservative Judaism* 38, no. 3 (spring 1986): 5–9.

Halperin, Meir. *Hagadol Miminsk: R. Yerucham Yehuda Leib Perelmann,* ed. Shlomo Slonim (Jerusalem, 1991) (ms., ca. 1915).

Harris, Jay Michael. *How Do We Know This? Midrash and the Fragmentation of Modern Judaism* (Albany, 1995).

Heschel, Abraham. "Did Maimonides Strive for Prophetic Inspiration?" (Heb.), in *Louis Ginzberg Jubilee Volume on the Occasion of His Seventieth Birthday,* American Academy for Jewish Research (New York, 1945).

———. "The Holy Spirit in the Middle Ages," in *Jubilee Volume in Honor of Alexander Marx,* ed. S. Lieberman (New York, 1950).

Jacobson, Howard. "Did Saul Lieberman Know Greek and Latin?" in *Saul Lieberman, 1898–1983: Talmudic Scholar,* ed. Meir Lubetski (Lewiston, N.Y., 2002), pp. 12–23.

Kamenetsky, Nathan. *Making of a Godol: A Study of Episodes in the Lives of Great Torah Personalities* (Jerusalem, 2002).

Kaplan, Lawrence. "The Hazon Ish: Haredi Critic of Traditional Orthodoxy," in *The Uses of Tradition: Jewish Continuity in the Modern Era,* ed. Jack Wertheimer (New York, 1992).

Kutscher, Yehezkel. "Prof. Saul Lieberman and His Linguistic Achievement" (Heb.), *Hadoar* 42, no. 23 (Apr. 5, 1963).

L'Zikhro shel Shaul Lieberman, Israel Academy of Sciences and Humanities Annual (Jerusalem, 1984).

Landau, David. "The Talmud's Rising Prestige," *Jerusalem Post* interview with Saul Lieberman, Aug. 25, 1970.

Lederhendler, Eli. "The Ongoing Dialogue: The Seminary and the Challenge of Israel," in *Tradition Renewed: A History of the Jewish Theological Seminary of America,* ed. Jack Wertheimer (New York, 1997), vol. 2.

Liberles, Robert. *Salo Wittmayer Baron: Architect of Jewish History* (New York, 1995).

———. "Wissenschaft des Judentum Comes to America," in *Tradition Renewed: A History of the Jewish Theological Seminary of America,* ed. Jack Wertheimer (New York, 1997), vol. 1.

Lieberman, Saul. Works are cited in the section entitled "Works" in Part I of this volume. A comprehensive bibliography of Rabbi Lieberman's work, compiled by Tuvia Preschel, appears in *Sefer Hazikaron L'Rabee Shaul Lieberman* (Saul Lieberman Memorial Volume), ed. Shamma Friedman (New York and Jerusalem, 1993), pp. 1–28.

Lubetski, Meir, ed. *Saul Lieberman, 1898–1983: Talmudic Scholar* (Lewiston, N.Y., 2002).

Mandelbaum, Bernard. *Tales of the Fathers of the Conservative Movement* (New York, 1989).

Marblestone, Howard. "Professor Saul Lieberman as Lexicographer: Hebrew, Greek,

Latin," in *Saul Lieberman, 1898–1983: Talmudic Scholar,* ed. Meir Lubetski (Lewiston, N.Y., 2002), pp. 24–45.

Marx, Alexander. "Dr. Lieberman's Contribution to Jewish Scholarship," *Proceedings of the Rabbinical Assembly of America* 12 (1948): 259–71.

Muffs, Yochanan. *Love and Joy: Law, Language and Religion in Ancient Israel* (New York, 1992).

Neriah, Moshe Zevi, ed. *Likkutei Hare'ayah* (Bene Berak, 1990).

Neusner, Jacob. *Why There Never Was a "Talmud of Caesarea": Saul Lieberman's Mistakes* (Atlanta, 1994).

———. *Wrong Ways and Right Ways in the Study of Formative Judaism: Critical Method and Literature, History, and the History of Religion* (Atlanta, 1988).

Peli, Pinchas (P. Ben-Yair). "Hagaon Kifshuto," *Panim el Panim,* no. 517 (Apr. 18, 1969): 10.

———. "Prof. Lieberman 'Kifshutah,'" *Hadoar* 65, no. 25 (May 9, 1986): 15–16.

Pizenic, Aaron Halevi. "Ishim Degulim Shehekarti," in *Shana b'Shana: L'Halakhah, l'Mahshava Ulba'ayot Hayahadut,* ed. A. H. Pizenic (Jerusalem, 1986).

Preschel, Tuvia. "Mahalakh Hayav Udmuto Haruhanit shel Rav Shaul Lieberman," *Hadoar* 42, no. 23 (Apr. 5, 1963).

———. "R. Saul Lieberman: On Receiving the Israel Prize for Studies in Judaica," *Hadoar* 50, no. 25 (Apr. 30, 1971): 423.

———. "Something about the Shulamith School," *Hadoar* 48, no. 28 (May 30, 1969): 472–73.

Rackman, Emanuel, "Don't Repeat This Attack on Jewish Unity," *Jewish Week,* May 8, 1987.

———. "Political Conflict and Cooperation: Political Considerations in Jewish Interdenominational Relations 1955–56," Bar-Ilan University Political Science Series.

Raphael, Yitzhak. "Point of View: In the Company of the Great," *Jewish Press,* May 22, 1981, p. 4.

———. "Professor Rabbi Shaul Lieberman," eulogy, *Sinai* 93, nos. 1–2 (Apr./May 1983): 91–92.

———, ed. *Yovel Sinai* (Jerusalem, 1987).

Ravid, Zvulun. "Dov Yarden and His Contribution to the Study of Hebrew Poetry of the Middle Ages," *Hadoar* 49, no. 3 (Nov. 21, 1969).

———. "Motele: The City Where Weizmann Was Born," *Hadoar* 42, no. 27 (May 17, 1963): 502–3.

———. "Professor Azriel Shohat," *Hadoar* 56, no. 36 (Sept. 2, 1977): 622–23.

Robinson, Ira. "Cyrus Adler: President of JTS, 1915–1940," in *Tradition Renewed: A History of the Jewish Theological Seminary of America,* ed. Jack Wertheimer (New York, 1997), vol. 1.

Rosenstein, N. "Scion of Sagely Stock: Saul Lieberman in Memoriam," *Jewish Press,* Apr. 29, 1983.

Rosenthal, David, ed. *Mehkarim b'Torat Eretz Yisrael* (*Studies in Palestinian Talmudic Literature*) (Jerusalem, 1991).

Rosenthal, Eliezer Shimshon. "Hamoreh," *Proceedings of the American Academy for Jewish Research* 31 (1963): 1–71.

Rubenstein, Richard L. *Power Struggle* (New York, 1974).

Sarna, Jonathan D. "Two Traditions of Seminary Scholarship," in *Tradition Re-*

newed: A History of the Jewish Theological Seminary of America, ed. Jack Wertheimer (New York, 1997), vol. 2.

Schiffman, Lawrence. "The Pharisees Revisited: Louis Finkelstein on the Second Temple Period," in *Yakar Le'Mordecai: Jubilee Volume in Honor of Rabbi Mordecai Waxman,* ed. Zvia Ginor (New York, 1998), pp. 85–101.

Schochet, Elijah Judah. *The Hasidic Movement and the Gaon of Vilna* (Northvale, N.J., 1994).

Scholem, Gershom. *Jewish Gnosticism, Merkabah Mysticism, and Talmudic Tradition,* 2d ed. (New York, 1965).

Schorsch, Ismar. "Centenary Thoughts: Conservatism Revisited," *Proceedings of the Rabbinical Assembly of America* 48 (1986): 83.

———. *From Text to Context: The Turn to History in Modern Judaism* (Hanover, N.H., 1994).

Scult, Mel. "Kaplan's Heschel: A View from the Kaplan Diary," *Conservative Judaism* 54, no. 4 (summer 2002): 3, 9.

———. "Schechter's Seminary," in *Tradition Renewed: A History of the Jewish Theological Seminary of America,* ed. Jack Wertheimer (New York, 1997), vol. 1.

Shapira, Anita. *Berl Katznelson: A Biography* (Hebrew) (Tel Aviv, 1980).

Shapiro, Marc B. "Scholars and Friends: Rabbi Yehiel Yaakov Weinberg and Professor Samuel Atlas," *The Torah U-Madda Journal* 7 (1997): 105.

———, ed. *Collected Writings of Rabbi Yehiel Yaakov Weinberg,* vol. 1 (Heb.) (Scranton, 1998); vol. 2 (Heb.) (2003).

Shargel, Baila R. "Texture of Seminary Life," in *Tradition Renewed: A History of the Jewish Theological Seminary of America,* ed. Jack Wertheimer (New York, 1997), vol. 1.

Shashar, Michael. "Fanaticism, a Difficult Opponent and a Cheap Substitute for Torah: A Conversation with Professor Saul Lieberman" (Heb.), *Ha'aretz* interview, May 7, 1965.

———. "Keter Torah, Veketer Hokhma," *Hadoar* 56, no. 15 (Feb. 11, 1977): 228–29.

———. "Oseh Torah Kol Yamav," *Hatzofeh,* Mar. 26, 1993, p. 7.

Siegel, Seymour. *Sh'ma* 13, no. 253 (Apr. 29, 1983): 102–3; and in *In Praise of a Master,* ed. Berkowitz.

Solomon, Norman. "Saul Lieberman (1898–1983): A Revolutionary in Rabbinic Scholarship," in *Survey of Jewish Affairs,* ed. William Frankel (London, 1983), pp. 244–53.

Sonne, Isaiah. "The Use of Rabbinic Literature as Historical Sources," *Jewish Quarterly Review* 36 (1945): 147 ff.

Spiro, Solomon. "The Moral Vision of Saul Lieberman: A Historiographic Approach to Normative Jewish Ethics," *Conservative Judaism* 46, no. 4 (summer 1994): 64–84.

Sussmann, Yaacov. *Introduction to Talmud Yerushalmi, According to Ms. Or. 4720* (Scal. 3) of the Leiden University Library with Restorations and Corrections (Heb.) (Jerusalem, 2001).

———. "Mesoret Limud Umesoret Nusah shel Hatalmud Hayerushalmi," in *Mehkarim Basifrut Hatalmudit: Yom Iyun l'Regel m'Lot Shmonim Shana l'Shaul Lieberman* (Jerusalem, 1983), p. 12.

———. "Schechter Hahoker," in *Mada'ei Hayahadut* (Jerusalem, 1998), 38:213–29.

Ta-Shma, Israel M. "Professor Saul Lieberman: In His Memory" (Heb.), in *Saul Lieberman, 1898–1983: Talmudic Scholar,* ed. Meir Lubetski (Lewiston, N.Y., 2002), pp. 88–90.

Tendler, Moshe David. *Responsa of Rav Moshe Feinstein, Translation and Commentary* (Hoboken, N.J., 1996).

Tzinovitz, M. "Litoldot Harabbanut Bikobrin Bimaot Hakodmot," in *Sefer Kobrin,* ed. Bezalel Schwartz and Israel Haim Biltzki (Tel Aviv, 1951), pp. 36–40.

Urbach, Ephraim E. "Shaul Lieberman Uterumato Lehlal Mada'ei Hayehudit," in *l'Zikhro shel Shaul Lieberman,* Israel Academy of Sciences and Humanities Annual (Jerusalem, 1984), pp. 14–15.

Wachsman, Nissin. "Lidmuto shel Hagaon Rav Shlomo Polachek z'l," *Talpiot* 1–2 (1953): 3–35.

Wallach, Luitpold. Review of *Greek in Jewish Palestine,* by S. Lieberman, *Review of Religion* 8, no. 1 (Nov. 1943): 61–66.

Weizmann, Chaim. *Trial and Error: The Autobiography of Chaim Weizmann* (New York, 1949).

Wertheimer, Jack. "JTS and the Conservative Movement," in *Tradition Renewed: A History of the Jewish Theological Seminary of America,* ed. Jack Wertheimer (New York, 1997), vol. 2.

———, ed. *Tradition Renewed: A History of the Jewish Theological Seminary of America,* 2 vols. (New York, 1997).

———, ed. *The Uses of Tradition: Jewish Continuity in the Modern* Era (New York and Jerusalem, 1992).

Wiesel, Elie. *All Rivers Run to the Sea* (New York, 1995).

———. "Mori, Verabi," *Hadoar* 56, no. 17 (Feb. 25, 1977): 258–59.

Zlotnick, Dov. "Hametadologia shel Shaul Lieberman b'Yevanut v'Yevanit b'Eretz Yisrael," in *Divrei Hakongres Hale'umi Ha'ahad Asar l'Mada'ei Hayahadut* (Jerusalem, 1984).

———. Introduction, translation, and notes to *The Tractate Mourning: Regulations Relating to Death, Burial, and Mourning* (New Haven and London, 1966).

———. Introduction to Saul Lieberman's *Greek in Jewish Palestine / Hellenism in Jewish Palestine* (New York and Jerusalem, 1994).

———. "The Methodology of Professor Saul Lieberman in Determining the Correct Reading of a Text," in *Saul Lieberman, 1898–1983: Talmudic Scholar,* ed. Meir Lubetski (Lewiston, N.Y., 2002), pp. 4–11.

———. "Today's Met Mitzvah," in *Best Jewish Sermons of 5727–28,* ed. Saul Teplitz (New York, 1968), pp. 225–32.

Appendix II

Interviews

Material in this volume that is derived from interviews pertains to the following:

Rabbi Nathan Kamenetsky held interviews with:

Rabbi Shraga Abramson, Oct. 4, 1991
Rabbi Shamma Friedman, Oct. 4, 1997, and Feb. 1999
Rabbi Moshe Greenberg, Jan. and Feb. 1999
Beverly Gribetz, Dec. 1998
Rabbi Aaron Kirschenbaum, July 10, 1997
Meir Lieberman, Sept. 18, 1996
Chaya Miriam Schulman, May 1997

Mark Jay Mirsky held interviews with Rabbi Saul Lieberman, spring 1982.

Rabbi Elijah J. Schochet held interviews with:

Arnold Band, May 1997
Amos Funkenstein, Apr. 1985
Eli Ginzberg, Aug. 5, 1997
Rabbi Hillel Goldberg, Mar. 20, 1998
Rabbi Jordan Hoffman, June 6, 1998
Rabbi Nathan Kamenetsky, Mar. 16, 1997, and May 1997
Rabbi Yaakov Kamenetsky, July 1979
Rabbi Chaim Rogoff, Aug. 1997
Rabbi F. E. Rottenberg, Sept. 1994

Rabbi Moshe Tendler, Mar. 1990

Rabbi Solomon Spiro held interviews with:

Dr. Itamar Aviad, Aug. 12, 1999
Yakov Aviad, Aug. 14, 1999
Meir Benayahu, Aug. 13, 1999
Rabbi Robert Chazan, Apr. 4, 2000
Yosef Ciechanover, Sept. 23, 1999
Rabbi Haim Zalman Dimitrovsky, Aug. 2, 1999
Dr. Reuben Fink, Aug. 15, 1999
Rabbi Ezra Finkelstein, May 11, 1998, and Dec. 15, 1998
Rabbi Edward Gershfield, Nov. 7, 1995, and Jan. 30, 1996
Rabbi Emanuel Gettinger, Feb. 2, 1996, and his wife, Racheil, Mar. 28, 1996
Eli Ginzberg, Jan. 31, 1996
Rabbi Abraham Goldberg, Aug. 1999
Rabbi David Weiss Halivni, Jan. 1996
Judith Hauptman, Oct. 20, 1999
Penina Herzog, Aug. 1999
Yitzhak Herzog, Aug. 9, 1999
Susannah Heschel, Mar. 23, 1998
Sylvia Heschel, Mar. 26, 1998
Chaya Hirschprung, Aug. 25, 2001
Rabbi Arthur Hyman, Mar. 1997
Erica Jesselson, June 6, 1996
Dr. Tibor Juda, Oct. 28, 1999
Emunah Katzenstein, Aug. 3, 1999
Rabbi David Kogen, Sept. 8, 1998
Harold (Zvi) Kraushar, Oct. 7, 1995
Rabbi Morton Leifman, 1997
Rabbi Baruch A. Levine, Mar. 21–22, 2000, and May 13–14, 2003
Meir Lieberman, Aug. 4 and 10, 1999
Ruth Link-Salinger, Mar. 1997
Rabbi Haskel Lookstein, Nov. 13, 2000
Rabbi Bernard Mandelbaum, June 7, 1996
Rabbi David Novak, Oct. 26, 1999

Aaron M. Nussbaum, Sept. 9, 1996

Rabbi Emanuel Rackman, June 6, 1996

David Rosenthal, Aug. 8, 1999

Rabbi Joel Roth, Sept. 23, 1999

Rabbi Raymond P. Scheindlin, Jan. 10, 1999

Menahem Schmelzer, Dec. 3, 1996

Yehuda Shapira, Aug. 12, 1999

Michael Shashar, Aug. 11, 1999

Rabbi Aaron Singer, Aug. 5, 1999

Rabbi Haym Soloveitchik, Feb. 4, 1996, and Nov. 9, 1998

Yaakov Sussmann, Aug. 5, 1999

Hannah Urbach, Aug. 10, 1999

Rabbi Burton Visotzky, Sept. 8, 1998

Rabbi Yosef Hayim Yerushalmi, June 6, 1996

Alice Zlotnick, May 15, 2001

Rabbi Dov Zlotnick, Sept. 21, 1995, Sept. 2, 1996, June 21, 1998, Jan. 9, 2000, and October 1, 2003

Rabbi Moshe Zwick, May 1, 2002

APPENDIX III

From Commentary to Scholarship[1]

Haim Zalman Dimitrovsky

Much has already been said, and surely much more will be said, about the awe-inspiring scholarly enterprise of our teacher, R. Saul Lieberman, of blessed memory. This enterprise is rooted, as is well known, in the soil of the Torah of Eretz Yisrael, but its vistas and branches extend and expand to encompass the entire breadth of Jewish scholarship. Quantitatively, it sprawls over tens of substantial volumes, while in quality, though it be one thousand measures, it is choice flour. There is no area in Jewish studies, large or small, to which Professor Lieberman did not make substantial contributions or on which he did not leave his imprint.

It would be appropriate to expound on Lieberman's contribution to Hebrew philology, which greatly enriched the rabbinic lexicon and solved many of its mysteries; on his contribution to our understanding of the ways of the Sages and the culture of the Jewish community in the talmudic period, at a time when it was hemmed in by a gentile environment and surrounded by alien civilizations; on the tendencies and concealed meanings that he illuminated in passages of law and lore that had been consigned to oblivion or banished by exclusion from the traditional canon; and, above all, on the great light that he shed on the learning of tannaitic and amoraic literature in Palestine. And still, we would have enumerated only the major chapter headings of his work.

Even if I attempted to address only a portion of the above-mentioned

[1]This essay originally appeared in Hebrew as "Miparshanut l'Mehkar," in *l'Zikhro shel Shaul Lieberman*, Israel Academy of Sciences and Humanities (Jerusalem, 1984), pp. 34–49.

topics, I would fall short. Moreover, all of the areas listed above are subjects that are normally relegated to specialists, whereas Lieberman was not a specialist. Linguistics served him as a tool, but he was not a linguist; likewise, he employed the tools of the historian, but neither was he a historian; and I daresay that he was not even a Talmud scholar in the usual sense. What was he, then? To answer that question, even tentatively, we must examine one phenomenon that runs like a scarlet thread throughout his prodigious work and accompanies virtually all of his research, namely, a single-minded focus on the text itself and its meaning.

Although all of talmudic literature's hidden treasures—legal and legendary, tannaitic and amoraic, Palestinian and Babylonian—were in Lieberman's possession, he largely avoided and never directly confronted the problems of chronology in this literature, despite the fact that such problems were at the center of talmudic research from its inception, precisely when Lieberman moved from the yeshiva to academia. Moreover, he touched only parenthetically on problems of editing, source criticism, and the identification of authors and redactors—problems that are the point of departure for critical exegesis of the Talmud; these never constituted his primary path or his starting point. Even in his monumental commentary to the Tosefta, these issues are submerged, addressed only obliquely. It is instructive that what Lieberman did in the introduction to his *Hilkhot Hayerushalmi* he did not do for the Tosefta, not relating even to the questions of where or when the Tosefta was edited or by whom. (From the introduction to *Tosefta Kifshutah, Zera'im,* we learn that he intended to compose a general introduction as an appendix to the commentary, but on the basis of the content of the wide-ranging and detailed commentary, we may conclude that even in that introduction these matters would assume only a marginal place. And from the order of the opus as conceived by the author, we learn that the introduction was intended to flow from the commentary, not vice versa. Under any circumstances, we can now only regret that we will not see the introduction, and not even the completion of the commentary.) An explanation of this absolute concentration on the text could shed light on the nature and characteristics of his creativity and on the texture of his enormous output, which, despite its prodigious richness, manifold facets, and variegated hues, possesses marvelous unity and undisputed consistency.

As noted above, this phenomenon marks nearly all his work, but not absolutely all. His early work, including his first two monographs, *Al Hayerushalmi* (1929) and *Talmudah shel Kisrin* (1931), is different in character.

The first of these monographs remains to this day, more than half a century after its appearance, the most complete guide to the critical editing of the *Talmud Yerushalmi.* The second constitutes a singular, perfect example of the application of the methodology—accepted since the beginning of *Wissenschaft des Judentums*—for assigning an identity, time, and location of the redaction of an anonymous literary unit, a methodology rooted in comparative examination, identification of unattributed passages, and deciphering of stylistic and linguistic clues. The latter work is unique, therefore, not in methodological or technical originality, but in the piercing vision and sweeping mastery that expose every mystery and obscurity of the *Yerushalmi.*

The first work, *Al Hayerushalmi,* addresses textual difficulties of the *Yerushalmi,* but not in the narrow sense. Here, too, the routine problems of the talmudic scholars' study hall emerge. This apologia is offered in the introduction:

> For reasons beyond my control, I have not touched here on all the questions that confront the student of the *Yerushalmi* (the Mishnah underlying the *Yerushalmi,* its manner of introducing Mishnah and baraita, the redaction of chapters, and so forth). With God's help, I will speak of all these elsewhere.

It is quite certain that *Talmudah shel Kisrin* is but a partial realization of the author's desire to address all these problems elsewhere, and it is to be regretted that this hope did not fully materialize.

What is the explanation for this sudden shift in Lieberman's scholarly agenda following the composition of these two works? It would seem, considering the time and circumstances, that these two works reflected a passing necessity. These works emerged from his studies at the nascent Hebrew University, under the tutelage of his teacher, our teacher, J. N. Epstein. Since all the problems addressed in these two works were central to the teacher's research, the student undertook to follow suit. Indeed, all the topics (the

Mishnah underlying the *Yerushalmi* and so on) that he did not address, as noted above, constitute central chapters in J. N. Epstein's book *Mavo l'Nusah Hamishnah*. In his later years, Lieberman spoke almost nostalgically of those first years at the university:

> About fifty years ago, the Hebrew University of Jerusalem was founded. . . . The core of the university at that time was the Institute for Jewish Studies. This institute was intended to be a research center that would neither grant degrees nor require secular academic credentials. Students were admitted on the basis of their expertise in rabbinic literature. This was an excellent idea that held much promise. Most of the students were extremely proficient in Jewish sources and received guidance and instruction in research methods from the most outstanding teachers in each field.[2]

Fifty years could not dispel the taste of the encounter between the mastery that Lieberman brought with him from the Lithuanian yeshiva and the research methods that were revealed to him within the walls of the university. On the one hand, he still stands fully within the world of Torah. In the introduction to *Al Hayerushalmi,* he writes about the most difficult passages in the *Yerushalmi,* even those few cases that were spared having been "corrected" by the copyists: "Who is wise enough to decipher the meaning for us when we have neither Rabbenu Hananel nor Rashi, neither Ramban nor Rashba to clarify for us . . . and solve the riddles?" Here we see who, in his opinion, possessed the keys to the Talmud. On the other hand, he had already been exposed to the beauty of secular disciplines, and, as a disciple who sits before his master, he quotes in *Al Hayerushalmi* the master's words:

> My teacher, Professor J. N. Epstein, alerted me to the fact that occasionally the commentators reorder the talmudic (*Yerushalmi*) de-

[2]Saul Lieberman, from a lecture at the opening of the Institute for Jewish Studies at Harvard University in 1978.

> bate because they did not realize that the *Yerushalmi* had a different order in the Mishnah.

This secret, which every beginning student today knows, was communicated privately to the disciple by his master, and the disciple cites it in the master's name as a great discovery.

Another work by Lieberman, similar in style and aim to *Talmudah shel Kisrin,* is *Sifrei Zuta,* to which the author appended a subtitle, *Midrashah shel Lod,* reflecting the nature of the book. It shows that this halakhic midrash to Numbers came from the Sages of the south, and establishes when and by whom it was composed—all of which accords with what could be inferred from the name of his previous work, *Talmudah shel Kisrin*. Note that although this book appeared only fifteen years ago, it, too, was produced as an outgrowth of Lieberman's time spent studying under J. N. Epstein and subsequent exchanges between them. *Sifrei Zuta* has an appendix entitled "Talmudah shel Kisrin," which is a reiteration and completion of the article by the same name; this appendix also was written in reaction to what J. N. Epstein had written about tractate *Nezikin* of the *Yerushalmi* in his *Mavo Hayerushalmi*. Although *Sifrei Zuta* and its appendix deal with problems similar to those of *Talmudah shel Kisrin,* its style is different, and it reveals less than it conceals, to the point where its chronological findings are peripheral and the substantive analysis is central—even though the object is primarily historical.

Regarding this period, permit me to recall a casual remark that I heard from Lieberman many years ago, which reflects the great impact of his encounter with the world of scientific research. Although I cannot guarantee that the quotation is exact, his words remain fresh in my mind:

> Until I came to the Hebrew University, I had not even heard the name of Zacharias Frankel. And when I heard his name for the first time from Professor Epstein, and that he had written a book entitled *Mavo Hayerushalmi,* I wondered out loud and asked him, what is the need for an introduction to the *Yerushalmi,* and how can it facilitate learning the *Yerushalmi?*

I do not know what Epstein's reply was, but the question is enough to show

Lieberman's view regarding the nature and substance of talmudic research: the introduction is not important; the content is what is important. To conduct research on the *Yerushalmi,* one must learn *Yerushalmi.* Indeed, from Lieberman's brother, Meir, I heard that in Europe Lieberman had not learned the *Talmud Yerushalmi* at all, and that he began learning *Yerushalmi* only after immigrating to Palestine. One may assume that he began to think about the *Yerushalmi* only as a result of the scientific challenge that he confronted in that very Institute for Jewish Studies that he recalled in idyllic terms as having been created only for research, not to grant diplomas or degrees. In that atmosphere of pure research, Lieberman reflected the qualities of the perfect scholar: far-reaching expertise and absolute control of the subject matter, as well as perfect command of research methodology and intimate knowledge of all ancillary resources required for the relevant specialization. Indeed, after Lieberman had assumed academic positions, moving from one place to another and acquiring a reputation, he would depict for students who sought his academic guidance the image of the true scholar according to the same qualities and standards that he had adopted for himself. But the essence of his response, which he would repeat 101 times, always conveyed that there is a fundamental difference between learning and research: whereas through learning one immerses himself in the world of Torah and acquires a great deal, research provides the scholar, even in the best of circumstances, with only a limited understanding. Typically, he would add pointedly: Scholar X is truly learned, and his Torah proclaims his scholarship; whereas Scholar Y manages through encyclopedias and concordances, but he does not even know how to search those works properly.

Lieberman always placed scholars into two categories: average scholars and learned scholars. For the latter, he showed respect even when he disagreed with them. Regarding the works of some early medieval authorities, he would say that they had no place except in a bibliography. He would even categorize non-Jewish scholars and academicians in other fields in this way; one need only recall the esteem in which he held the Anglo-Catholic Arthur Nock and Immanuel Loew, the Jewish scholar and botanist.

The emergence of this unique scholar was the result of a combination of factors: on the one hand, a sense of belonging to the glorious tradition of classical learning, including a deep regard for the outstanding scholars who carried on that tradition, from the early geonim through the giants of the nineteenth century (Lieberman's admiration for Rabbi David Pardo, Rabbi Meir Simha of Dvinsk, the author of *Or Same'ah*, and others knew no bounds), and a belief that the purity of their methods of learning and research assured the accuracy of their conclusions; and on the other hand, the encounter with the world of science, which was bound up with mastering a great new work—the *Talmud Yerushalmi*—in a methodical and consummate manner. This combination of factors gave rise to a unique type of scholar, one who could not be an imitation or duplication of his new teachers.

The first factor—the classical tradition of learning—is exegetical in its essence. In this tradition, the talmudic material is conceived of as one piece and monolithic, evincing a consistent methodology as well as a coherent and flowing organization. This is not to say that the bearers of this tradition failed to see that the Talmud comprises materials from a variety of sources and academies; however, they assumed that the process of redaction rendered the material smooth and integrated, newly fitted into a uniform pattern and a precise regimen. No traces of the sources remained, other than where the editor left them, intentionally and in accordance with preestablished rules. The highest goal of this tradition is, therefore, to show that perfect harmony reigns among all parts of the Talmud—between the links of the *sugya* itself as well as between the various tractates. By its very nature, this tradition relates to the text with true reverence, and where the text does not lend itself to interpretation in accordance with these principles, the explanation is sought in deficiencies in the chain of transmission. Traces of this exegetical approach are embedded in the gaonic commentaries, and the approach reaches its culmination among the Sages of Franco-Germany, for whom correcting the talmudic text to achieve the desired harmony became an underlying exegetical principle.

The second factor—critical talmudic research—consists of two components. One is diametrically opposed to the underlying premise of the first factor, the classical tradition. According to this component, not only did the editing of the Talmud fail to weld together and reconstitute its various sources—sometimes in consequence of a faulty understanding of the individual sources—but the editors even combined, consciously and unconsciously, different and even contradictory sources. An exegesis that is based on this conception ends where classical exegesis begins. According to this first component, once the difficulties or contradictions in the final text of the Talmud as we have it are exposed and the sources are uncovered, we have arrived at the pristine condition of the text: a mosaic of different fragments. Moreover, it emerges that the meaning of this text is not as it appears to the untrained eye (i.e., classical exegesis), but that it has several discrete messages, commensurate with the number of sources, which may or may not coalesce. In contrast, classical exegesis commences from the final—present—state of the text. The assumption is that the text as it is before us conveys one single message, which the exegesis aims to reveal.

The second component of critical Talmud study, as formulated by Professor Epstein in his well-known lecture "Critical Talmud Study and Its Requirements"[3] and as actualized in his university instruction, was philology in its broadest sense: mastery of the various branches of Semitic and classical languages and grammar; knowledge of the realia and cultural and social background underlying talmudic literature; and, above all, resort to the range of substantive witnesses: manuscripts, archaeological finds, papyri, and contemporaneous literature, to restore the authentic wording of the talmudic text. Not only does this component not clash with classical exegesis, but elements of it already make an appearance among the great classical commentators. To his great credit, Epstein gave equal weight to these two components, and though he never ceased to engage in higher criticism, he remained fully immersed in lower criticism, attentive to every jot and tittle in the text.

Of these components of the scientific approach, the latter coincides with Lieberman's history of classical learning, and he adopted it and made it his own, with its full range and richness. As for the first component, which stood in contradiction to the great spiritual cargo that he brought with him from the Torah world, where he matured before coming to Eretz Yisrael, he had recourse to it only obliquely.

It was the complete identification with the classical tradition of learning,

[3]"Madda Hatalmud U'tserakhav," in *Mehkarim B'sifrut Hatalmud U'vilshonot Shemiot* (Jerusalem: Magnes, 1984–91), vol. 2, pt. 1, pp. 1–18.

along with the encounter with the philological exegesis of J. N. Epstein, that set Lieberman's future path and determined his scholarly character: a commentator blending the old and the new. This type of scholar, who saw scientific exegesis as his primary mission, did not exist at the beginning of *Wissenschaft,* Rabbi Israel Levy notwithstanding.

In light of the foregoing, the other enigma in Lieberman's development can also be solved: it is certain that when he immigrated to Eretz Yisrael, he did not "sit one hundred fasts" so as to forget his Babylonian Talmud (and if he did, it did not help), so why did he invest all his creative energies in the Torah of Eretz Yisrael, which he acquired only after reaching maturity? (Permit me a brief digression: I recall from my childhood legends in Jerusalem about the extraordinary constancy with which he learned and relearned *Talmud Yerushalmi,* to the point where it was said that he learned *Yerushalmi* every night for three years straight while his feet were immersed in bowls of water—to ward off sleep.) However, for one who saw as his prime scholarly mission textual exposition as uniquely conceived due to the circumstances in which he found himself in the years following his aliyah to Eretz Yisrael, including his university studies, it is not surprising that he saw the *Talmud Yerushalmi* as the field in which he was destined to distinguish himself. As for the Babylonian corpus, which he had studied extensively in Europe, he had achieved a one-sided mastery—the tradition of classical scholarship. But this corpus already had commentators such as Rabbenu Hananel, Rashi, Ramban, and Rashba, and all he could have added was the other side of the coin, philological exegesis. Such restriction was obviously not to his liking. In contrast, the Torah of Eretz Yisrael was confined to a corner—hidden away, waiting for someone to come and unveil her face.

The distinctly interpretive nature stands out in all his scholarly work during his period in Eretz Yisrael, which lasted for more than a decade. After *Al Hayerushalmi,* which strongly echoes the universal academic approach to the *Yerushalmi* that pervaded the walls of the university and the classroom of J. N. Epstein, Lieberman began to publish strings of notes entitled "Tikkunei Yerushalmi," which regularly appeared in the first ten volumes of the journal *Tarbiz.* These "strings," as their name testifies, were interpretive and restricted to textual annotations (and I so designate them because, if my memory does not deceive me, he published barely anything in this entire period that could be characterized as an article in the normal sense; only when he came to the United States did he begin to publish articles, and even those with a unique style, of which more below). Two facts stand out with regard to these annotations. The first is Epstein's methodological, philological influence. The annotations reflect maximal attention to matters of formulation and variant readings; extensive recourse to the Leiden manuscript and to citations of the *Yerushalmi* in works of the rishonim (legal authorities of the late Middle Ages); and comparative scholarship related to classical languages and realia. Second, these annotations show evidence of having taken form in the course of his study of the *Yerushalmi;* they are scattered throughout the *Yerushalmi* from start to finish, and their order reflects sequential study, from halakhah to halakhah. In the later annotations, a kind of maturation becomes increasingly pronounced, a sense of freedom and independence from the teacher's authority; more and more, the expertise and mastery of the vast expanse of the *Talmud Yerushalmi* stands out, and the scope and content of the annotations progressively expand.

Indeed, about midway through this period (in 1934), he published a complete commentary to three large tractates of the *Yerushalmi.* This is neither the time nor place to describe this commentary at length. Suffice it to say that although one can detect in the commentary hesitations and doubts as to the scope that the commentary should take, its nature and aim is clear: "I determined to expound at length regarding every detail so as to clarify the true interpretation of the *Yerushalmi*" (from the introduction). The author did not specify here which details he had in mind, or what the true interpretation meant, but these would be clarified and elucidated in later works. Similarly, it is already clear what is not to be included in a commentary. The closing words of the introduction are instructive: "As for the *Yerushalmi*'s halakhah, its relationship to the Babylonian Talmud, the great academies in Eretz Yisrael, the overall conditions there in the talmudic period—all of this, God willing, [will be addressed] elsewhere." It is almost certain that this alludes to a general introduction to the *Talmud Yerushalmi* that he intended to write but that, to our sorrow, he never accomplished (see below). At any rate, there is no hint here of the issues of higher criticism that were referred to in *Al Hayerushalmi,* and attention is directed entirely to history and realia.

In 1936, approximately two years after the appearance of this volume on the *Yerushalmi,* Lieberman published the first part of *Tosefet Rishonim.* Based on the chronology, we may surmise with near certainty that immediately upon the publication of that part of the commentary on the *Yerushalmi,* he began the work on the Tosefta and retreated from his plan to issue a new edition of the *Yerushalmi.* Several times, I sought his explanation for the shift, but he did not answer. Since we have no other answer, we must make do with a hint that appears in his introductory remarks to the second part of *Tosefet Rishonim:* "In my brief introduction to *Tashlum Tosefta,* I alluded to the history of this book. It was written at the invitation of the publishing house Bamberger and Wahrman." It cannot be established with certainty if this was what turned Lieberman's attention away from the commentary to the *Yerushalmi.* Under any circumstances, from 1936 on, he was constantly preoccupied with a commentary to the Tosefta; yet even if the content changed, the technique of the commentary did not. He consulted and adapted to the Tosefta notebooks and memoranda that were at hand on how to treat the core text of the *Yerushalmi* and its surrounding commentary, using their format for the core text of the Tosefta and writing its commentary. Nearly fifteen years passed from his laying the foundation for elucidating the Tosefta in *Tosefet Rishonim,* where he gathered the building blocks and the blueprints, until he began to erect the splendid edifice of *Tosefta Kifshutah,* with all its halls, chambers, passageways, and ornamentation. During this time, he crystallized the final format in which he would organize the core text and its surrounding apparatus, a format suited to every ancient text, as outlined below.

An ancient text embodies two truths of disparate antiquity: historical truth, which is older; and a subsequent textual truth. The foundation of the text is the historical truth, unique and indivisible, possibly susceptible to disclosure through source criticism. Over time, the historical truth is displaced from its primacy, its place taken by the textual truth. This latter truth, even if no corruption entered the text in the process of transmission, can possess more than a single facet. It is dependent on the early institutions of transmission through which the text passed before it reached our hands.

Undoubtedly, this formulation not only carries forward the conception of classical talmudic exegesis, but also revamps the entire conception: the textual truth is not sealed with the conclusion of the editing and redaction; rather, it continues to take on new aspects in the learning centers of Eretz Yisrael and Babylonia, and even within the academies of each of these centers. The process of transmission is not the mechanical act of a monkey, but contains a creative, exegetical component that imprints its seal and leaves its impression on the transmitted text. This component is subject to the substantive background and living reality of the environment, to the popular and literary language, and to the cultural texture within which the institutions of transmission operate—above all, to the content of the subject matter being transmitted. The first task of exegesis is to disclose this truth as it was understood by its transmitters and as they sought to preserve it for posterity.

The development and application of this exegetical conception are uniquely reflected in the two editions of Lieberman's monumental commentary to the Tosefta. The first edition, as noted above, was *Tosefet Rishonim,* and the second, *Tosefta Kifshutah.* The first edition, which was completed nearly a half century ago, reflects the author's affinity to the approach of the rishonim and his sense that his work constitutes a direct continuation of the classical exegetical tradition. Not only are the textual variants of the rishonim to the Tosefta gathered together in this book, but their implications for an understanding of the Tosefta are clarified and elucidated, as is the importance of taking precise account of the comments of the rishonim in interpreting the Tosefta. In this respect, this work stands apart from earlier compositions that also collected variant readings of the rishonim.

The second edition represents the full-grown fruits of the period in which Lieberman already had accumulated all the raw material for his commentary and consolidated all the components of his methodology. (Lieberman viewed this period as a stage of renewed intellectual maturation, and in the many hours that I sat in his company, reviewing page proofs of the Tosefta text and *Tosefta Kifshutah,* I detected more than once in the interstices of his conversation echoes of that feeling.) Almost certainly, the characterization *Kifshutah* in the title of this work was not intended to draw a contrast with works composed on the Tosefta that shunned a *peshat* approach, adopting, for example, a pilpulistic approach, but rather aimed to make a positive claim—that this commentary comes to determine and disclose the full textual truth of the Tosefta. Consequently, every detail of the

Tosefta text is addressed, narrow and wide-ranging, beginning with household realia such as furniture, kitchenware, and clothing, and extending to artisans' tools; social customs of the Sages and the masses when dining on weekdays or festivals, especially at public gatherings; folk beliefs and the Sages' response to them; the encounter between the wisdom of the enlightened gentile world and the doctrines of the *beit midrash,* and the intellectual challenge posed by pagan thinkers to the Sages of Israel; and local dialects and the language of literature and scholars. In short, there is no aspect, large or small, of Jewish life in the talmudic period on which new light is not shed by this commentary on the Tosefta. There is no doubt that Lieberman was aiming at precisely this comprehensiveness and this kind of faithful commentary when he wrote in his preface to *Yerushalmi Kifshuto,* as cited above, of his intention "to expound at length regarding every detail so as to clarify the true interpretation of the *Yerushalmi.*"

Such comprehensiveness "regarding every detail so as to clarify the true interpretation" is found in *Tosefta Kifshutah* first and foremost with regard to the central focus of the Tosefta—its halakhic content. It is the textual truth—and not the historical truth or even the halakhic truth, that is, the legal pronouncements and practical decisions reached by decisors throughout the generations—that is the sole determinant of the faithful commentary. Each of the variants, numerous lines of which are found in the Tosefta's wording in manuscripts and citations in the works of rishonim, represents, if we are certain that it is not a scribe's or copyist's error, a textual truth, a truth that emerged, crystallized, and took form under the influence of geographic factors such as local customs, halakhic traditions, and opinions of rabbinic authorities. Consequently, the differences within these lines of variants are not limited only to language, realia, and the like, but emerge also in the domains of law and religious practice. The true interpretation must expose the unique background of the text's formulation, and only against that background can it be interpreted.

The single-minded adherence to this conception is reflected in every stage of the commentary to the Tosefta, starting with the detailed classification of the versions by their geographical branches (something to which scholars already were attuned with regard to the Mishnah, and which he established with respect to the Tosefta). Next would be the disclosure of the connection between a reading and its understanding as reflected in the narrow exegesis of that specific text—for example, the approach of the *Yerushalmi* as distinct from the *Bavli* and the approaches of various academies and Sages in each of these talmudic centers. This disclosure evolves from generation to generation and from place to place, starting with the academies of the geonim in Babylonia and Eretz Yisrael and proceeding via Byzantium, Italy, and Franco-Germany, concluding with the later authorities such as the author of *Hasdei David,* and the most recent authorities such as the author of *Or Same'ah,* all of whom sought in their way the true interpretation. It is difficult to find a truth-seeking scholar whose views are not taken into consideration. The degree to which Lieberman succeeded in this approach we can learn from the fact that in a work that extends over thousands of pages, such as *Tosefta Kifshutah,* which is a commentary on a text as recalcitrant as the Tosefta, he barely has recourse, for exegetical purposes, to textual emendations, and a child could count the number of corrections in this massive work.

This emotional tie to the text and the absolute adherence to it left a striking imprint on the structure and style of Lieberman's many articles, which ostensibly are independent pieces dealing with defined topics or specific problems. However, reading carefully and noting the links between the articles, one sees immediately that this is not the case. Neither the topic nor the problem constituted the challenge that stimulated the exposition of sources treated in the articles, their organization or examination, or the drawing of conclusions. On the contrary, nearly all his articles, including the extended monographs, begin with a difficult and obscure text that requires explication. The interpretation of the opening text leads to another text—also difficult and requiring interpretation, and thus from article to article, from explanation to explanation, facets of a problem emerge, building blocks accumulate and are laid one on top of the other, until the entire edifice stands in place. Only at the conclusion does it emerge that the problem and its solution reach their full expression at the same time. This form of expression is a sign of the writer's total identification with the world of the talmudic text; one can detect here the structure of the lessons and the style of the great Lithuanian heads of yeshivot, in whose presence Lieberman was educated in his youth. As is well known, these heads of yeshivot fashioned public lessons, without a plan or a topic set in advance, basing them instead on uncertainties and difficulties that arose in the course of ongoing, sequential learning. On occasion, the initial challenge was not following the complex structure of a long lesson, but the difficulty of predicting in what direction and to what conclusion some severe problem might lead. However, if the heads of the Lithuanian yeshivot did not have the benefit of a plan, they did possess a set style—from difficulty to resolution, from refutation to reconciliation, the lesson took shape, often expanding through improvisation in the course of the lecture.

In Lieberman's case as well, the research grew out of continuous and unceasing study. Consequently, his research was not produced piecemeal but as one comprehensive teaching. Indeed, if I am not mistaken, he wrote virtually no articles that stand alone. A few of his articles were written as responses or annotations to works of others or as commentaries. Most were in honor of scholars in Jubilee volumes and *Festschriften,* and their style and form testify that Lieberman culled them from his commentaries, expanding and adapting them to serve as articles.

This quality is no less striking in his two books that were written originally in English (later translated into Hebrew), *Hellenism in Jewish Palestine* and *Greek in Jewish Palestine.* These two books, which deal with the life of the Jews in Eretz Yisrael in the talmudic period, established Lieberman's reputation among the top rank of scholars of classical literature by dint of the enormous knowledge and total mastery that he demonstrated in every area of research of the classical world—philology, realia, theology, philosophy, and literature. In addition, these books, despite their broad and non-talmudic titles, carry the clear imprint of the author's talmudic world. In every chapter of these books, the undeviating direction of the research—from the talmudic source outward—can be discerned, even to the untrained eye. The style and structure are equally fixed: the point of departure of every chapter is a difficult talmudic text that is elucidated, after which the discussion evolves in a seemingly improvisational manner in different directions through verbal and thematic association. Note, for example, in the chapter "The Publication of the Mishnah" in *Hellenism in Jewish Palestine,* what Lieberman concludes from the seemingly innocent phrase "written and deposited," applied to written texts in rabbinic terminology, and how many major points he learns from this regarding the manner in which the Mishnah and other works were transmitted and made public. There are too many examples to enumerate.

Nevertheless, if we try to affix to Lieberman a professional title, we have no choice but the label of commentator. Talmudic research has taken great strides and reached substantial achievements in various fields. Only in the field of commentary have there been no innovations. There have been great and wise Torah scholars who advocated and planned scientific commentaries to the Babylonian and Palestinian Talmuds, but whose nerve failed before making the attempt; others found the courage to begin but withdrew after beginning the work. It is easy to guess the reasons for this: such a commentary involves a plethora of components, and even a great scholar would have difficulty exercising the requisite control needed to extract their core substance and create an integrated commentary combining old and new, criticism and tradition, intelligence and erudition.

Our teacher, R. Shaul, of blessed memory, took a chest and went out. He found bodies of knowledge and placed them inside; he found languages and placed them inside; he found scientific disciplines and placed them inside. When he returned to the study hall, he did not resolve to learn each one independently, but minted them all into coins and from them all fashioned handles for Torah.

Translated from the Hebrew by Baruch Feldstern

Appendix IV

Professor Saul Lieberman, of Blessed Memory[1]

Dov Zlotnick

And Elijah went up by a whirlwind into heaven.
And Elisha saw it and cried, "My father, my father,
the chariot of Israel and the horsemen thereof."
And he saw him no more.
(2 Kings 2:12; cf. ibid. 13:14)

A thousand years later, we find this term of love, "My father, my father," and the biblical metaphor for power and protection, "the chariot of Israel and the horsemen thereof," repeated in the Talmud. At the conclusion of the Sabbath, Rabbi Akiba met the bier of his teacher Rabbi Eliezer being carried from Caesarea to Lud; he beat his breast until the blood fell to the ground. As mourners gathered, he began the oration: "My father, my father, the chariot of Israel and the horsemen thereof," and then added: "I have many coins but no money changer to set them in order."
As Rashi explains:

> "I have many questions to ask
> but there is no one to ask."

Rabbi Akiba's lament for his teacher must be the lament of every serious Jewish scholar in the world today. We all have many questions, but there is

[1]This tribute was delivered on the conclusion of *shloshim* (thirty-day period of mourning) at the Jewish Theological Seminary. It was originally published in *Proceedings of the Rabbinical Assembly* (1983), pp. 202–7.

no one to answer them, that is, no one who can answer them definitively with the preeminent authority of the Professor, of blessed memory, who was for our generation—and I believe will remain for many, many generations to come—the classic model for the perfect scholar. To telescope his life and work in the confines of this tribute is unrealistic. Even to touch on his vast contributions to the field of rabbinic literature is much more than can be done in an array of such tributes. And for me to stand here and try to evaluate his scholarship—well, that would be an act of sheer presumption.

Twenty years ago, a superb talmudist and classicist, Eliezer Shimshon Rosenthal, published a seventy-one-page Hebrew essay entitled "The Teacher"[2] on the scholarship of the Professor. He began this work with a disclaimer insisting that he was inadequate to the task for, alas, in order to do justice to the scholarship of Professor Lieberman, one would have to know all the Professor knew. Since that time, the *Tosefta Kifshuto, Nashim* was published, as well as the *Sifrei Zuta,* countless articles and important appendices and notes to works of other scholars, and another two volumes of *Seder Nezikin* are now in galleys. Moreover, the Talmud tells us: "A man does not fully understand his teacher until forty years of apprenticeship have gone by" (*Avodah Zarah* 5b). I still lack seven years. My own feeling is that even in forty times forty years I could not fully do justice to the Torah of our teacher and master. What has been said about the study of Torah generally can be applied to the literary output of the Professor: "Go over it, go over it—for it has everything" (*Avot* 5:22).

What I shall, nevertheless, try to do is to answer two questions: 1) What is it that Professor Lieberman brought to a rabbinic text when he set out to work on it? 2) What did he distill from it, and what was the result?

First, he brought to it a prodigious memory. This was a special blessing, a gift from heaven. The tractates of Talmud that he had studied as a child prodigy, an *illui,* in the yeshiva at Slobodka, he never forgot. The Sages tell us: "What one learns as a child is not forgotten." His early learning was formidable. But he continued studying all the days of his life, al-

[2]E. S. Rosenthal, "Hamoreh," *Proceedings of the American Academy for Jewish Research* 31 (1963): 1–71.

ways the *matmid.* The schedule he followed in the Seminary, for example, was to come early in the morning, teach four hours a week, attend to his administrative duties, and then return to his own work for the remainder of the morning. After lunch and a nap, he came to his office around five and worked until 1 A.M. This eight-hour period was undisturbed. He did this every day of the week, including Sunday. His schedule was interrupted only on Shabbat, *yom tov,* and *hol hamo'ed.* Even at the conclusion of the Sabbath, he went to his office and worked until the early morning. He could not have worked that way unless he was fiercely disciplined; but he also enjoyed what he was doing. He loved Torah. His devoted wife, Judith, of blessed memory, a granddaughter of the "Netziv" of Volozhin, understood, fully appreciated, and encouraged him in his commitment to Torah.

In this way, the Professor structured his day until he was able to put to various degrees of memory the Mishnah, the Babylonian and the Jerusalem Talmud, and the halakhic and aggadic midrashim of the tannaim. By the time he was forty, he had published the four volumes of the *Tosefet Rishonim,* demonstrating his full grasp of the commentaries and the novellae of the medieval Jewish scholars: Rabbenu Hananel, Rif, Rambam, Rabad, Rabenu Tam, and the Ramban. He was not only able to place and reconstruct the give-and-take of a legal discussion, but was also able to remember the language of these early authorities, their *girsaot* (readings) word for word. So when he worked on the Tosefta, he never worked from notes. He either worked from the manuscripts or first editions of his magnificent library, or from his own memory. He was a veritable storehouse of *girsaot* and *perushim* (readings and explanations). As a result, when he read a line of Talmud, he would immediately hear echoes of parallel texts; or if not exact parallels, then similar texts; if not similar, then divergent texts. But each had to be understood and explained in terms of the material at hand. When one studied Talmud with him, there were always these reverberations, an association of ideas from a variety of sources. He would then focus on this material and in one case justify a reading that seemed hopelessly corrupt and in another case reject a reading that seemed eminently correct, terming it a gloss. Again and again, as new manuscripts and fragments were published by others, his reading, his insight, and his explication of an obscure passage would be proven correct.

To a text, the Professor also brought skills that he learned when he came to the Hebrew University. He was an *illui* from Slobodka, a former student of Rav Moshe Mordechai Epstein, now learning the method of science from Professor Jacob Nahum Epstein. Here he studied Greek and Syriac. He already knew Latin from his student days in medical school in Russia. And as he read Pliny (*Naturalis Historia*), Petronius (*Coena Trimalchionis*), and others, never relying on secondary sources, he became thoroughly familiar with the political and social institutions of the Hellenistic world. And just as he knew the six orders of Mishnah and the realia they reflected, he now also knew the realia of Greek and Roman agriculture, their festivals, their institutions of marriage and divorce, laws of damages and inheritance, what animals they accepted and disqualified as a sacrifice, and their rules of purity and defilement.

What he studied in the Greek and Roman period, he did for the sake of Talmud, for the light it shed on rabbinic literature. It was not Torah, and he clearly distinguished between *ikar* and *tafel,* between matters of primary and secondary importance. Yet as a scholar, he realized that these were indispensable tools and used them with brilliant effect, in keeping with the rabbinic dictum: "You shall not learn to do—but may learn to understand and to teach" (*Shabbat* 95b). I must also add that he enjoyed working with these tools.

He may have had little interest in art and less in music, but his appreciation for the literary classics of Greece and Rome was enormous. He responded to the written word of the ancients. And his high regard for literature is reflected in the rigor and precision of his own writings and in the fact that some of his closest friends were not only the outstanding rabbinic scholars of this century, not only classicists and jurists, businessmen and statesmen, but also men of letters, such as Agnon, Hayyim Hazaz, Chaim Grade, and Elie Wiesel. He enjoyed talking to these people because he loved literature, not only the classic texts of halakhah and aggadah, of which he was the absolute master, not only the pagan writings that he knew, but also the literature of the shtetl, the world in which he was nurtured, a thousand Motoles, a world reduced to ashes that he never forgot.

What is it that the Professor distilled from a rabbinic text? What was the result? In a word: the *peshat,* the simple meaning of the text. In essence, this is what he strove for, and this is reflected in the titles he gave to his major textual commentaries: *Hayerushalmi Kifshuto,* the Jerusalem Talmud according to its simple meaning; *Tosefta Kifshutah,* the Tosefta according to its simple meaning.

The Talmud tells us that Isi ben Judah recounted the praises of the Sages, that is, he tried to capture in a phrase the greatness and uniqueness of various tannaim:

> Rabbi Meir: scholar and scribe
> Rabbi Judah: scholar whenever he wished
> Rabbi Tarfon: a heap of nuts
> Rabbi Ishmael: a fully stocked shop
> Rabbi Akiba: an overflowing storehouse (*Gittin* 67a)

Many of these designations and the others in this context could apply to the Professor, but if a phrase were to be created today to epitomize his genius and unique contribution, I think it could be: *Rabbi Shaul: bohen umefaresh kifshuto* (Rabbi Saul: he examined the text and explained it according to its simple meaning).

He once said to me: "How do you know that you have the *peshat* [the simple meaning]? How do you test it? Well, after you have explained something that no one else has explained, it must sound so reasonable that someone else who hears it will say: 'So what? What's the *hiddush?* [How have you discovered something new?] It is obviously so!' Then you know you have it!"

I learned from him that the greatest textual discovery is the *peshat,* that every dictum of the Rabbis and the smallest detail of a text are inextricably bound up with the whole; and only by acquiring some understanding of the whole can one hope to hear those rabbinic echoes and to make those textual associations that will shed light on a difficult reading. My gratitude to the Professor I can only acknowledge inadequately. For it was he who urged the study of Talmud upon me, and in a sense all that I have learned and whatever there is of value in my work I owe to him.

"Rabbi Saul: he examined the text and explained it according to its simple meaning." He was the perfect scholar. He studied the halakhah with surpassing diligence and followed it in its every detail. He was scrupulously honest in his scholarship and equally honest in his everyday dealings. To those of us who knew him, he was also an exhilarating human being and a great teacher. Rabbi Yosi bar Hanina, a Palestinian amora of the third century, said: "If, for whoever teaches Torah publicly, it is not as sweet to his listeners as the honey flowing from the comb—it is better for him not to have spoken" (Song of Songs, Midrash Rabbah 4:11).

To me, the Professor's Torah was always *d'vash* (honey)—what he taught orally no less than what he wrote. He enjoyed his teaching, and although he called it *his* relaxation, one did not relax in his class, for as he explained a difficult passage he also communicated his excitement to his students and his abiding love for one he called "his jealous mistress"—Torah. As long as Jews feel that the halakhah has a mandate upon them, as long as our people continue to study Talmud, so long will the legacy of the Professor remain like *d'vash* flowing from the comb.

Please permit me to take a moment to correct an inaccuracy repeated in several obituaries in which it was stated that he had no family. This is not so, because there is a brother, Rabbi Meir, in Jerusalem, and there are many nieces and nephews, grandnieces and grandnephews on both sides of the family to whom he felt very close. As a matter of fact, when he was summoned *l'yeshiva shel ma'ala* (to the heavenly academy) he was flying back to Israel to conduct seder for the family.

In a sense, his family was very much larger because, as the Mishnah tells us, the Rav who raises a disciple in the study of Torah takes precedence over the father, "for his father brings him into this world, but his teacher who teaches him wisdom brings him into the World to Come" (*Bava Metzia* 2:11).

His family is very much larger, for it includes three generations of students who studied with him directly and indirectly, in Israel and in America; and also the many, many generations of students who will continue to study his Torah until the coming of the Messiah. It is entirely fitting, I believe, that the lament of Rabbi Akiba for his teacher be repeated by this extended family:

My father, my father, the chariot of Israel and the horsemen thereof.
I have many coins
but no money changer to set them in order.
And as Rashi explains:

I have many *she'elot* [questions] to ask
but there is no one *lish'ol* [to ask].

Appendix V

Reproduction of Letter from Immanuel Loew

(see pp. 53, 139)

LÖW IMMÁNUEL

www.ingramcontent.com/pod-product-compliance
Ingram Content Group UK Ltd.
Pitfield, Milton Keynes, MK11 3LW, UK
UKHW060611180726
13836UKWH00011B/2501